Mission Statement

Our mission is to help students know and believe in themselves, take advantage of resources and opportunities, set and achieve their goals, learn throughout their lives, discover careers that fulfill and support them, build fruitful and satisfying relationships with others from all backgrounds and walks of life, and experience the challenges and rewards that make life meaningful.

A Great Way to Learn and Instruct Online

The Pearson Education Canada Companion Website is easy to navigate and is organized to correspond to the chapters in this textbook. Whether you are a student in the classroom or a distance learner you will discover helpful resources for in-depth study and research that empower you in your quest for greater knowledge and maximize your potential for success in the course.

Companion
Website

[www.pearsoned.ca/carter]

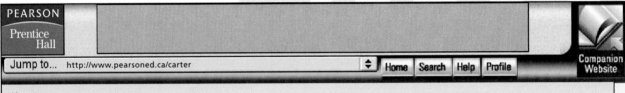

PEARSON
Prentice Hall

Jump to...   http://www.pearsoned.ca/carter   ⇕   Home Search Help Profile

Companion Website

Home >

Companion Website

Keys to Success: Core Concepts, Canadian In-Class Edition, by Carol Carter, Joyce Bishop, Sarah Lyman Kravits, and Sandra Moniz-Lecce

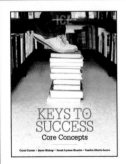

Student Resources

The modules in this section provide students with tools for learning course material. These modules include:

- Objectives
- Multiple Choice
- Essay Questions
- Destinations
- Additional Articles

In the quiz modules students can send answers to the grader and receive instant feedback on their progress through the Results Reporter. Coaching comments and references to the textbook may be available to ensure that students take advantage of all available resources to enhance their learning experience.

Instructor Resources

A link to this book on the Pearson Education Canada online catalogue (vig.pearsoned.ca) provides instructors with additional teaching tools. Downloadable PowerPoint Presentations and an Instructor's Manual are just some of the materials that may be available. The catalogue is password protected. To get a password, simply contact your Pearson Education Canada Representative, or call Faculty Sales and Services at 1-800-850-5813.

KEYS TO SUCCESS

Core Concepts

Carol Carter ✳ Joyce Bishop ✳ Sarah Lyman Kravits ✳ Sandra Moniz-Lecce

CANADIAN IN-CLASS EDITION

Toronto

Library and Archives Canada Cataloguing in Publication

Keys to success : core concepts / Carol Carter ... [et al.]. — Canadian in-class ed.

Includes bibliographical references and index.
ISBN 978-0-13-149277-6

1. College student orientation—Canada—Handbooks, manuals, etc. 2. Study skills—Handbooks, manuals, etc. 3. College students—Canada—Life skills guides. I. Carter, Carol

LB2343.34.C3K482 2007   378.1'98   C2006-906587-X

ISBN-13: 978-0-13-149277-6
ISBN-10: 0-13-149277-2

Editor-in-Chief, Vice-President of Sales: Kelly Shaw
Acquisitions Editor: Chris Helsby
Marketing Manager: Toivo Pajo
Developmental Editor: Charlotte Morrison-Reed
Production Editor: Katie Hearn
Copy Editor: Lenore Latta
Proofreader: Judy Hernandez
Production Coordinator: Janis Raisen
Composition: Hermia Chung, Susan MacGregor
Art Director: Julia Hall
Cover Design: Kerrin Hands
Interior Design: Susan MacGregor
Cover Image: Corbis

Photo credits appear on page p. 317, which constitutes an extension of this copyright page.

1 2 3 4 5   12 11 10 09 08

Printed and bound in the United States of America.

Contents

Preface   ix
About the Authors   xii
Acknowledgments   1

Chapter 1

WELCOME TO POST-SECONDARY EDUCATION: OPENING DOORS TO SUCCESS   2

WHERE ARE YOU NOW—AND WHERE CAN HIGHER LEARNING TAKE YOU?   4

HOW CAN SUCCESSFUL INTELLIGENCE HELP YOU ACHIEVE YOUR GOALS?   6

Successful intelligence focuses on actions • Successful intelligence powers success

HOW WILL *KEYS TO SUCCESS* HELP YOU BUILD SUCCESSFUL INTELLIGENCE?   9

The chapter material • The in-chapter activities • The end-of-chapter exercises

GET CREATIVE! *See Yourself at Your Best*   11

WHAT WILL MOTIVATE YOU TO MAKE THE MOST OF LEARNING?   12

Focus on your self-esteem • Be responsible • Develop positive habits • Face your fears

GET PRACTICAL! *Face Your Fears*   15

HOW CAN WHAT YOU LEARN NOW HELP YOU SUCCEED IN SCHOOL, WORK, AND LIFE?   16

Higher learning helps you value diversity • Higher learning prepares you to learn from failure and celebrate success • Higher learning helps you apply successful intelligence in a changing world

GET ANALYTICAL! *Celebrate Success and Learn from Mistakes*   19

BUILDING SKILLS
for Academic, Career, and Life Success   21

Chapter 2

VALUES, GOALS, TIME, AND STRESS: MANAGING YOURSELF   28

WHY IS IT IMPORTANT TO KNOW WHAT YOU VALUE?   30

Identifying and evaluating personal values • Values affect your educational experience

GET ANALYTICAL! *Explore Your Values   32*

Academic integrity: Ethical values promote success at school • Values and cultural diversity

HOW DO YOU SET AND ACHIEVE GOALS?   35

Set long-term goals • Set short-term goals • Prioritize goals • Work to achieve goals

GET CREATIVE! *Map Out a Personal Goal   38*

HOW CAN YOU EFFECTIVELY MANAGE YOUR TIME?   39

Identify your time-related needs and preferences • Build a schedule • Use scheduling techniques • More suggestions for time management

GET PRACTICAL! *Make a To-Do List   45*

Avoid procrastination • Be flexible

HOW DO YOU COPE WITH THE STRESS OF BEING A STUDENT?   48

Stress management strategies

BUILDING SKILLS
for Academic, Career, and Life Success   52

Chapter 3

LEARNING STYLES, EDUCATION, AND CAREERS: KNOWING YOUR TALENTS AND FINDING YOUR DIRECTION   62

HOW CAN YOU DISCOVER YOUR LEARNING STYLES?   64

The value of learning styles assessments • Putting results of assessments in perspective • Assess your personality with the Personality Spectrum • Assess your Multiple Intelligences

WHAT ARE THE BENEFITS OF KNOWING HOW YOU
   LEARN?   73

   Academic benefits • Career benefits

HOW CAN MULTIPLE INTELLIGENCES HELP YOU
   EXPLORE OCCUPATIONS AND CAREERS?   75

   Use career exploration strategies

BUILDING SKILLS
   for Academic, Career, and Life Success   *80*

Chapter 4

SUCCESSFULLY INTELLIGENT THINKING: ANALYTICAL, CREATIVE, AND PRACTICAL THINKING FOR SOLVING PROBLEMS AND MAKING DECISIONS   86

WHAT IS SUCCESSFULLY INTELLIGENT THINKING   88

   Successfully intelligent thinking is balanced •
   Successfully intelligent thinking means asking and
   answering questions • Successfully intelligent
   thinking requires knowing your purpose •
   Successfully intelligent thinking is yours to build

HOW CAN YOU IMPROVE YOUR ANALYTICAL THINK-
   ING SKILLS?   91

   Gather information • Analyze and clarify information
   • Evaluate information

GET ANALYTICAL! *Assess Analytical Thinking Skills*   *95*

HOW CAN YOU IMPROVE YOUR CREATIVE THINKING
   SKILLS?   97

   Brainstorm • Shift your perspective • Set the stage
   for creativity • Take risks

GET CREATIVE! *Assess Creative Thinking Skills*   *102*

HOW CAN YOU IMPROVE YOUR PRACTICAL THINKING
   SKILLS?   102

   Experience helps develop practical thinking skills •
   Practical thinking means action

GET PRACTICAL! *Assess Practical Thinking Skills*   *105*

HOW CAN YOU USE ANALYTICAL, CREATIVE, AND
   PRACTICAL THINKING TOGETHER TO SOLVE A
   PROBLEM OR MAKE A DECISION?   105

   Solving a problem • Making a decision • Keeping
   your balance

BUILDING SKILLS
   for Academic, Career, and Life Success   *113*

Chapter 5

READING AND LEARNING: FOCUSING ON CONTENT   120

WHAT WILL HELP YOU UNDERSTAND WHAT YOU
   READ?   122

GET CREATIVE! *Be the Author of Your Life*   *123*

HOW CAN YOU SET THE STAGE FOR READING?   124

   Take an active approach to difficult texts • Choose
   the right setting • Define your purpose for reading •
   Use special strategies with math and science texts •
   Develop strategies to manage learning disabilities •
   Build reading speed • Expand your vocabulary

HOW CAN SQ3R HELP YOU OWN WHAT YOU
   READ?   133

   Step 1. Survey • Step 2. Question • Step 3. Read
   • Step 4. Recite • Step 5. Review

GET ANALYTICAL! *Find the Main Idea*   *141*

HOW CAN YOU RESPOND CRITICALLY TO WHAT YOU
   READ?   143

   Use knowledge of fact and opinion to evaluate arguments • Increase media literacy

WHY AND HOW SHOULD YOU STUDY WITH
   OTHERS?   145

GET PRACTICAL! *Form a Study Group*   *146*

   Leaders and participants • Strategies for study
   group success

BUILDING SKILLS
   for Academic, Career, and Life Success   *150*

Chapter 6

RESEARCH AND WRITING: GATHERING AND COMMUNICATING IDEAS   156

HOW CAN YOU MAKE THE MOST OF YOUR
   LIBRARY?   158

   Start with a map • Learn how to conduct an
   information search

GET PRACTICAL! *Discover Your College or University
   Library*   *160*

   Conduct research using a search strategy

HOW CAN YOU USE THE INTERNET TO
   RESEARCH?   164

   Know the basics • Use subject directories and
   search engines • Use analytical thinking to evaluate
   every source

GET CREATIVE! *Google (Yes, It's a Verb)* 167

WHAT IS THE WRITING PROCESS? 168

Planning • Drafting

GET ANALYTICAL! *Avoid Plagiarism* 177

Revising • Editing

BUILDING SKILLS

for Academic, Career, and Life Success 184

Chapter 7

LISTENING, NOTE TAKING, AND MEMORY: RECEIVING, RECORDING, AND REMEMBERING INFORMATION 190

HOW CAN YOU BECOME A BETTER LISTENER? 192

Know the stages of listening • Manage listening challenges • Become an active listener

GET ANALYTICAL! *Discover Yourself as a Listener* 197

HOW CAN YOU MAKE THE MOST OF NOTE TAKING? 197

Prepare to take class notes • Record information effectively during class

GET PRACTICAL! *Face a Note-Taking Challenge* 201

Review and revise your notes

WHICH NOTE-TAKING SYSTEM SHOULD YOU USE? 205

Take notes in outline form • Use the Cornell note-taking system • Create a concept map

HOW DOES MEMORY WORK? 210

Three memory banks • Retaining information in long-term memory

WHAT MEMORY STRATEGIES CAN IMPROVE RECALL? 213

Develop strategies for encoding and recalling • Use mnemonic devices

GET CREATIVE! *Craft Your Own Mnemonic* 220

BUILDING SKILLS

for Academic, Career, and Life Success 221

Chapter 8

TEST TAKING: SHOWING WHAT YOU KNOW 226

HOW CAN PREPARATION IMPROVE TEST PERFORMANCE? 228

Identify test type and material covered • Create a review plan and schedule • Prepare through careful review

GET CREATIVE! *Write Your Own Test* 230

Take a pre-test • Understand the level of learning required • Prepare physically • Make the most of last-minute studying

HOW CAN YOU WORK THROUGH TEST ANXIETY? 235

Prepare thoroughly • Maintain a positive attitude • Use life experiences

WHAT GENERAL STRATEGIES CAN HELP YOU SUCCEED ON TESTS? 238

Write down key facts • Begin with an overview • Read test directions • Mark up the questions • Take special care on machine-scored tests • Work from easy to hard • Watch your time • Master the art of intelligent guessing • Maintain academic integrity

HOW CAN YOU MASTER DIFFERENT TYPES OF TEST QUESTIONS? 240

Multiple-choice questions • True/false questions • Matching questions • Fill-in-the-blank questions • Essay questions

GET ANALYTICAL! *Write to the Verb* 247

HOW CAN YOU LEARN FROM TEST MISTAKES? 249

GET PRACTICAL! *Learn from Your Mistakes* 250

BUILDING SKILLS

for Academic, Career, and Life Success 252

Chapter 9

RELATING TO OTHERS: COMMUNICATING IN A DIVERSE WORLD 258

HOW DO YOU EXPERIENCE DIVERSITY? 260

Diversity affects everyone • Diversity on campus

HOW CAN YOU DEVELOP CULTURAL COMPETENCE? 262

Value diversity • Identify and evaluate personal perceptions and attitudes • Be aware of what happens when cultures interact • Build cultural knowledge

GET CREATIVE! *Expand Your Perception of Diversity* 265

Adapt to diverse cultures

GET PRACTICAL! *Make a Difference* 268

HOW CAN YOU COMMUNICATE EFFECTIVELY? 268

Adjust to communication styles • Make use of constructive feedback • Understand body language

GET ANALYTICAL! *Give Constructive Feedback* 273

Communicate across cultures • Manage conflict • Manage anger

HOW DO YOU MAKE THE MOST OF PERSONAL RELATIONSHIPS?   278

Use positive relationship strategies • Avoid destructive relationships • Choose communities that enhance your life

BUILDING SKILLS
for Academic, Career, and Life Success   283

Chapter 10
CREATING YOUR LIFE: BUILDING A SUCCESSFUL FUTURE   290

HOW CAN YOU MAINTAIN A HEALTHY MIND AND BODY?   292

Eat right • Exercise • Get enough sleep

GET PRACTICAL! *Improve Your Physical Health   294*

Recognize mental health problems

HOW CAN YOU MAKE SUCCESSFULLY INTELLIGENT DECISIONS ABOUT SUBSTANCES AND SEX?   296

Alcohol • Tobacco • Drugs • Identifying and overcoming addiction • Decisions about sex

HOW CAN YOU CONTINUE TO ACTIVATE YOUR SUCCESSFUL INTELLIGENCE?   302

HOW CAN YOU CREATE AND LIVE YOUR PERSONAL MISSION?   304

Live with integrity • Aim for your personal best

GET CREATIVE! *Explore Your Personal Mission   306*

BUILDING SKILLS
for Academic, Career, and Life Success   308

Answer Key   314
Endnotes   315
Credits   317
Index   318

Preface

Keys to Success: Core Concepts, Canadian In-Class Edition is a concise version of the successful Canadian *Keys to Success* text. It is tailored to the needs of professors who have requested a book that can be covered in a class of less than a full semester.

The *Keys to Success* series focuses on the following question: How can students get the most out of higher education and use what they learn to achieve their goals in an ever-changing world? Psychologist Robert Sternberg has developed an important answer in the concept of successful intelligence.[1]

This book builds successful intelligence

Successful people, says Sternberg, are more than their IQ score. Focus on the two most important parts of Sternberg's message and you can change your approach to education in a way that will maximize your learning and *life success*.

One: *Successful intelligence gives you tools to achieve important goals.* Successful intelligence goes beyond doing well on tests (analytical thinking). Only by combining that analytical skill with the ability to come up with innovative ideas (creative thinking) and the ability to put ideas and plans to work (practical thinking) will you get where you want to go.

Two: *Intelligence can grow.* The intelligence you have when you are born does not stay the same for the rest of your life. You can build and develop your intelligence in the same way that you can build and develop physical strength or flexibility.

Every chapter of *Keys to Success* helps you to build successful intelligence. How?

- *Chapter coverage:* The theme is introduced in Chapter 1 and covered in more detail in the thinking chapter (Chapter 4). Successful intelligence concepts are referenced throughout all chapters of the text.
- *In-text exercises:* Three exercises within the chapter text—"Get Analytical!," "Get Creative!," and "Get Practical!"—develop each skill in the context of the chapter material and your personal needs.
- *Synthesis exercise:* At the end of each chapter, the "Putting It All Together" exercise gives you an opportunity to combine all three skills and apply them toward a meaningful task.

This book involves students with the text

As part of Pearson Education Canada's commitment to providing students with value, choice, and the tools for educational success, *Keys to Success: Core Concepts* is a *Canadian In-Class Edition*. This innovative presentation contains the following features:

- Answers to chapter opening *Test Yourself* questions can be found throughout the chapter, as well as on the Companion Website.
- *In-Class Notes* show selected PowerPoint slides covering key concepts, with space provided for students to make notes in class or while reading.
- An *Embedded Study Guide* encourages practice and mastery with chapter-specific multiple choice questions at the end of each chapter.
- The bound-in *Study Chart* highlights the core concepts of each chapter for convenient student reference.

This book connects you with the ideas and experiences of others

To help you excel in a world that is increasingly diverse, this edition of *Keys to Success* introduces the concept of *cultural competence,* using the following features:

- *A focus on cultural competence*, in Chapter 10, shows the value of going beyond tolerance to actively adapt to and learn from people different from you. References to cultural competence and diversity are also woven throughout every chapter, showing how diversity is part of many aspects of school, the workplace, and personal life.
- *Chapter summaries* introduce a word or phrase from a language other than English and suggest how you might apply the concept to your own life.
- *A continuing focus on multiple intelligences* highlights individual diversity and confirms that each individual has a unique way of learning, with no one way being better than another. Chapter 3 introduces and explains this concept, and subsequent chapters include grids with strategies for applying various learning styles to the chapter content.

This book provides strategies and resources that help you do your work

With successful intelligence as the foundation of this edition and cultural competence as an underlying theme, *Keys to Success* presents learning tools and materials that will help you succeed in college and beyond.

The ideas and strategies that help you succeed in higher education also take you where you want to go in your career and personal life. The three parts of this text help you develop a firm foundation for lifelong learning.

- *Defining yourself and your goals:* Chapter 1 provides an overview of today's college experience and an opportunity to evaluate your personal starting point. Chapter 2 gets you on track with ways to manage yourself effectively, focusing on values, goal-setting strategies, time-management skills, and handling stress. Chapter 3 helps you identify complementary aspects of your learning style (your Multiple

Intelligences and your Personality Spectrum), choose strategies that make them work for you, and begin to think about your major.

- *Developing your learning skills:* Chapter 4 puts your learning into action by exploring the concept of successful intelligence in depth, helping you to build analytical, creative, and practical thinking skills and to put them together in order to solve problems, make decisions, and achieve goals. The next few chapters build crucial skills for the classroom and beyond—Reading and Learning (Chapter 5), Research and Writing (Chapter 6), Listening, Note Taking, and Memory (Chapter 7), and Test Taking (Chapter 8).
- *Creating success:* Recognizing that success includes more than academic achievement, Chapter 9 focuses on developing the interpersonal and communication skills you need in a diverse society, and Chapter 10 helps you to manage the stress and wellness issues that so many college and university students face.

Skill-building exercises. Today's graduates need to be effective thinkers, team players, writers, and strategic planners. The set of exercises at the end of each chapter—"Building Skills for Higher Education, Career, and Life Success"—encourages you to develop these valuable skills and to apply thinking processes to any topic or situation:

- *Developing Successful Intelligence: Putting It All Together.* These exercises encourage you to combine your successful intelligence thinking skills and apply them to chapter material.
- *Team Building: Collaborative Solutions.* This exercise gives you a chance to interact, problem solve, and learn in a group setting, building your teamwork and leadership skills in the process.
- *Writing: Discovery Through Journaling.* This journal exercise provides an opportunity to express your thoughts and develop your writing skills.
- *Career Portfolio: Plan for Success.* This exercise helps you gather evidence of your talents, skills, interests, qualifications, and experience. The Career Portfolio exercises build on one another to form, at the end of the semester, a portfolio of information and insights that will help you in your quest for the right career and job.

Supplements

Supplements for students and instructors round out the resources available for *Keys to Success*.

- *Instructor's Manual* For each chapter in the text, this resource provides a detailed outline, list of objectives, discussion questions, and additional activities. There are also key suggestions about how to best utilize the unique integrated features of this in-class edition.
- *PowerPoint Slides* PowerPoint slides highlight the concepts presented in the text. Several key concept PowerPoint slides per chapter from this presentation have been reproduced and integrated within the text itself as In-Class Notes.
- *Companion Website* Tired of reading? Ready for a change of pace? If you like the interactivity of computers, go online to the site www.pearsoned.ca/carter to enrich your learning experience. Visitors will find a range of interactive resources, including
  - articles relating to each text chapter
  - chapter learning objectives that help students organize key concepts
  - online quizzes that include instant scoring and coaching
  - links to recommended websites

The **Instructor's Manual** and **PowerPoint Slides** can be downloaded by instructors from a password-protected location on Pearson Education Canada's online catalogue (vig.pearsoned.ca). Simply search for the text, then click on "Instructor" under "Resources" in the left-hand menu. Contact your local sales representative for further information.

Pearson Canada's *Multiple Pathways to Learning* Assessment Site (www.pearsoned.ca/learningstyles) is an online tool that helps you discover your own personal learning style, including identifying your personal strengths and weaknesses. Not only that, it will map your skills to the features of your textbook, to help you develop productive and effective study practices.

This book is just a start—only you can create the life of your dreams

As you work through this course and move forward toward your goals, keep this in mind: Studies have shown that when students feel that they have a fixed level of intelligence, they improve less, put less effort into their work, and have a harder time in the face of academic challenges. However, students who feel that they can become more intelligent over time are more likely to improve, tend to work harder, and handle academic challenges with more success.[2] *Believe that your intelligence can grow*—and use this book to develop it this semester, throughout your college experience, and afterward as you build the future of your dreams.

Notes

1. Successful intelligence concepts from Robert Sternberg, *Successful Intelligence*. New York: Plume, 1997.
2. David Glenn, "Students' Performance on Tests Is Tied to Their Views of Their Innate Intelligence, Researchers Say," *The Chronicle of Higher Education*, June 1, 2004 [on-line]. Available: http://chronicle.com/daily/ 2004/06/ 2004060103n.htm (June 2004).

About the Authors

Carol Carter is founder of LifeBound, a career coaching company that offers individual coaching sessions and seminars for high school students, college students, and career seekers. She has written *Majoring in the Rest of Your Life: Career Secrets for College Students* and *Majoring in High School*. She has also co-authored *Keys to Preparing for College, Keys to College Studying, The Career Tool Kit, Keys to Career Success, Keys to Study Skills, Keys to Thinking and Learning,* and *Keys to Success*. She has taught welfare-to-work classes, team taught in the La Familia Scholars Program at the Community College of Denver, and conducted numerous workshops for students and faculty around the country. Carol is a national college and career expert and is interviewed regularly in print, on the radio, and for television news programs. In addition to working with students of all ages, Carol thrives on foreign travel and culture; she is fortunate enough to have been a guest in more than 40 foreign countries. Please visit her website and write her at www.lifebound.com.

Joyce Bishop holds a Ph.D. in psychology and has taught for more than 20 years, receiving a number of honours, including Teacher of the Year for 1995 and 2000. For five years she has been voted "favourite teacher" by the student body and Honour Society at Golden West College, Huntington Beach, California, where she has taught since 1987 and is a tenured professor. She worked with a federal grant to establish Learning Communities and Workplace Learning in her district, and she has developed workshops and trained faculty in cooperative learning, active learning, multiple intelligences, workplace relevancy, learning styles, authentic assessment, team building, and the development of learning communities. Joyce is currently teaching on-line and multimedia classes, and she trains other faculty to teach on-line in her district and region of 21 colleges. She co-authored *Keys to College Studying, Keys to Success, Keys to Thinking and Learning,* and *Keys to Study Skills*. Joyce is the lead academic of the Keys to Lifelong Learning Telecourse, distributed by Dallas Telelearning.

Sarah Lyman Kravits comes from a family of educators and has long cultivated an interest in educational development. She co-authored *Keys to College Studying, The Career Tool Kit, Keys to Success, Keys to Thinking and Learning,* and *Keys to Study Skills* and has served as Program Director for LifeSkills, Inc., a nonprofit organization that aims to further the career and personal development of high school students. In that capacity she helped to formulate both curricular and organizational elements of the program, working closely with instructors as well as members of the business community. She has also given faculty workshops in critical thinking. Sarah holds a B.A. in English and drama from the University of Virginia, where she was a Jefferson Scholar, and an M.F.A. from Catholic University.

Sandra Moniz-Lecce holds a Bachelor of Arts degree in psychology from Simon Fraser University and a Master of Arts degree in counselling psychology from the University of British Columbia, Canada. Since 1996, she has held a counselling/teaching faculty position at Kwantlen University College, where she provides personal, academic, and career counselling for students and teaches courses and seminars on strategies for academic success and on career decision making. She has co-authored another book, *The Career Adventure: Your Guide to Personal Assessment, Career Exploration, and Decision Making*. Sandra also home-schools her young daughter, Julia, and has recently returned to school herself. Both personally and through her work as a counsellor and instructor, Sandra has gained insight and experience into the struggles, and fulfillment, of lifelong learning.

Acknowledgments

Many thanks to the reviewers of this text, whose comments and suggestions have helped us in the preparation of this Canadian In-Class Edition:

Darryl Ainsley, Camosun College

Jennifer Auld-Cameron, Nova Scotia Community College

Marc Belanger, Vanier College

Susan Coyne, Fanshawe College

Tracy Fawcett, Southern Alberta Institute of Technology

Phil Jones, Algonquin College

Karen Kotyshyn, Northern Alberta Institute of Technology

Lyne Marie Laroque, Vanier College

Kelly Little, St. Clair College of Applied Arts and Technology

Dana Quenville, Fanshawe College

Thanks to the staff at Pearson Education Canada: acquisitions editors Chris Helsby and Dave Ward; sales rep Carmen Batsford; developmental editors Charlotte Morrison-Reed and John Polanszky; production editors Katie Hearn and Kevin Leung; production coordinator Janis Raisen; and compositor Hermia Chung; and to copy editor Lenore Latta; proofreader Judy Hernandez; and compositor and designer Susan MacGregor.

Also, thank you to Kwantlen University College for its support: the Office of Research and Scholarship; counsellors and colleagues in the Counselling Department, and Dean and Associate Dean of Qualifying Studies and Student Services.

And finally, a great big thank you to Julia and Joey for encouragement, patience, and understanding, and for taking the learning journey with me.

1

Welcome to Post-Secondary Education

OPENING DOORS TO SUCCESS

This chapter is organized as follows:

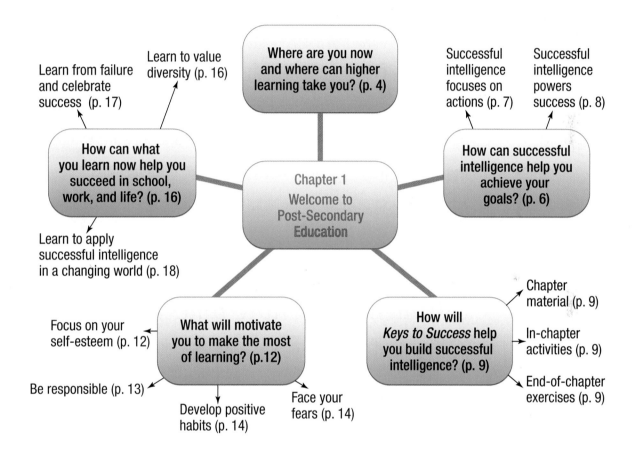

Learn from failure and celebrate success (p. 17)

Learn to value diversity (p. 16)

Where are you now and where can higher learning take you? (p. 4)

Successful intelligence focuses on actions (p. 7)

Successful intelligence powers success (p. 8)

How can what you learn now help you succeed in school, work, and life? (p. 16)

Learn to apply successful intelligence in a changing world (p. 18)

Chapter 1
Welcome to Post-Secondary Education

How can successful intelligence help you achieve your goals? (p. 6)

Focus on your self-esteem (p. 12)

What will motivate you to make the most of learning? (p.12)

Be responsible (p. 13)

Develop positive habits (p. 14)

Face your fears (p. 14)

How will *Keys to Success* help you build successful intelligence? (p. 9)

Chapter material (p. 9)

In-chapter activities (p. 9)

End-of-chapter exercises (p. 9)

TEST YOURSELF

- *What are the benefits of a post-secondary education?*
- *What are the three elements of successful intelligence?*
- *Explain the relationship between successful intelligence and academic success.*
- *What are the two main influences on the motivation to succeed?*
- *How is "self-esteem" defined?*
- *Why is motivation a key element for determining success?*
- *How can a "bad" habit be changed to a "good" habit?*
- *How can what you learn about diversity affect your academic and career success?*
- *When faced with failure, what are the three steps you could take to learn from it?*
- *Explain how successful intelligence helps you adapt to a changing world.*

For the correct answers and additional questions on Chapter 1, visit www.pearsoned.ca/carter.

Welcome—or welcome back—to higher learning. You are embarking on a new phase of life—one that presents challenges, promises hard work, and offers extraordinary rewards. As you contemplate the course of the next few years, you may wonder: How am I going to get from where I am now to a satisfying career? How am I going to make it?

Here's one important part of the answer to that question: *With the help of this book*. Why? Because it will make your life easier. This book, and the course for which you are reading it, has a primary goal: To help you learn successfully, graduate, and reap the personal and professional rewards of a solid education. This chapter gives you an overview of how that will happen—how being a successfully intelligent, motivated, and forward-thinking learner will help you face the challenges of post-secondary education and achieve more than you could have imagined.

Where are you now—*and where can higher learning take you?*

You are standing at the gateway to a new phase of life. Before you think about moving forward, though, take a look at the road that brought you here. You completed high school or its equivalent. You may have built life skills from experience as a partner or parent. You may have been employed in one or more jobs. You have enrolled at a post-secondary institution, signed up for courses, and shown up for class. And, in deciding to pursue further education, you made the choice to believe in your ability to accomplish important goals. You have earned this opportunity to be a student!

If your studying helped you succeed only in the classroom, the benefit of your learning wouldn't last beyond graduation day. However, learning is a tool for life, and education is designed to serve you far beyond the classroom. Here are a few important "life success goals" that higher learning can help you achieve:

Life Success Goal: Increased employability and earning potential. Higher learning greatly increases your chances of finding and keeping a well-paying job. People with education beyond high school usually start with higher earnings and continue to earn more throughout their working lives. Post-secondary (degree) graduates earn, on average, at least $14 000 more per year than those with a high school diploma (see Key 1.1). Furthermore, the unemployment rate for college graduates with a certificate or diploma is less than half that of high school graduates; for university graduates with a degree, less than a third.[1] It is estimated that at least 70 percent of all new job openings in the future will require some form of post-secondary education.

Life Success Goal: Preparation for career success. Your course work will give you the knowledge and hands-on skills you need to achieve your career goals. It will also expose you to a variety of occupations related to your interests, skills, and abilities, many of which you may not have been aware. Higher learning will open doors that may be closed otherwise.

Life Success Goal: Active community involvement and an appreciation of different cultures. Higher learning prepares you to understand complex political, economic, and social forces that affect you and others. This understanding is the basis for good citizenship and encourages community involvement. Your education also exposes you to the ways in which people and cultures are different and how these differences affect world affairs. This not only will benefit you and your understanding of Canada's multicultural society, but also will help you better understand world events and prepare you for the effects of further globalization. Thinking about these more general goals should help you begin to brainstorm, in detail, what you want from your education. What courses do you want to take? What kind of schedule do you want? What credentials, degree, or certificate are you aiming for? Think about academic excellence and whether honours and awards are important goals. If you have a particular occupation in mind, consider the education,

Education affects income.

Median annual income of persons by their highest degree attained, 2000

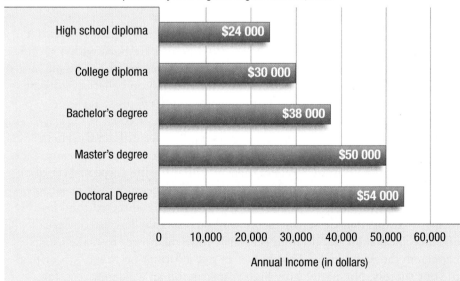

Source: Statistics Canada, "Education in Canada 2000."

training, and/or experience it may require. Finally, consider personal growth, and think about the importance of developing friendships with people who will motivate and inspire you.

> A journey of a thousand miles begins with a single step.

LAO TZU

Now you are beginning to develop a picture of what you want to have gained by the end of your post-secondary experience. The biggest question remains: What gets you from here to there? Not everyone arrives successfully. However, the dedication, hard work, and power that comes from *successful intelligence* will help you make it.

IN-CLASS NOTES

WHERE ARE YOU NOW—AND WHERE CAN HIGHER LEARNING TAKE YOU?

Post-secondary education provides increased potential in:

- Employability
- Earnings
- Awareness

_____
_____
_____
_____
_____

How can *successful intelligence* help you achieve your goals?

Think about how you would define *intelligence*. Chances are that you, like many people, believe that people are born with a specific amount of unchanging intelligence, and that this has a significant effect on their ability to succeed. Another fairly common belief is that standardized assessments, such as IQ (intelligence quotient) tests, accurately measure a person's intelligence and are predictors of success.

Psychologist Robert J. Sternberg views intelligence differently. He believes that traditional intelligence measurements lock people into poor performances and often do not accurately reflect their potential for life success. According to Sternberg, IQ and other standardized assessments measure *inert intelligence*— that is, they require passive repetition rather than goal-directed thinking. He further explains that those who score well on tests may have strong recall and analytical skills but do not necessarily have the power to make things happen in the real world.[2] That power to put information to work is critical to your success. No matter how high you score on an academic test, for example, your knowledge won't serve you unless you can use it successfully.

Successful intelligence focuses on actions

In Sternberg's view, intelligence is not a fixed quantity; people have the capacity to increase intelligence as they learn and grow. In his book *Successful Intelligence: How Practical and Creative Intelligence Determine Success in Life*, Sternberg focuses on what he calls *successful intelligence*—"the kind of intelligence used to achieve important goals."[3] Successful intelligence predicts life success better than any IQ test does because it focuses on actions—what you *do* to achieve your goals—instead of just on recall and analysis.

Everyone knows people who fit the conventional definition of "smart." They score well on tests and get good grades. Instructors expect them to achieve academically, and they do. However, these students may have limited success outside the classroom if they can't translate their "smarts" into real-world actions.

In contrast, other students have a hard time making the grade but are seen as "offbeat," "creative," or "street smart." Some of these students use their practical or creative intelligence to lift themselves above the crowd. Successful people such as Jacques Demers, former NHL coach, or Robert Munsch, children's author, built extraordinary success, despite difficulties in school, by creatively using their strengths and developing practical ways to reach their goals.

Sternberg breaks successful intelligence into three parts, or abilities: *analytical* thinking, *creative* thinking, and *practical* thinking.

- *Analytical thinking*—commonly known as critical thinking—involves analyzing and evaluating information, often in order to work through a problem or decision. Analytical thinking is largely responsible for school success and is recognized and measured through traditional testing methods.

- *Creative thinking* involves generating new and different ideas and approaches to problems, and, often, viewing the world in ways that disregard convention.

- *Practical thinking* means putting what you've learned into action in order to solve a problem or make a decision. Practical thinking enables you to accomplish goals despite real-world obstacles.

These ways of thinking work together to move you toward a goal, as Sternberg describes:

> Analytical thinking is required to analyze and solve problems and to judge the quality of ideas. Creative intelligence is required to formulate good ideas and potential solutions to problems. Practical intelligence is needed to use the ideas and their analysis in an effective way in one's everyday life.[4]

Here are two examples that illustrate how this works.

Successful intelligence in a study group— reaching for the goal of helping each other learn:

- **Analyze** the concepts you must learn, including how they relate to what you already know.

- **Create** humorous memory games to help you remember key concepts.

- **Think practically** about who in the group does what best, and assign tasks according to what you discover.

Successful intelligence in considering an academic path—reaching for a career goal:

- **Analyze** what you do well and what you like to do. Then analyze the course offerings and options until you come up with some that seem to match your strengths and interests.
- **Create** a dream career; then work backward to come up with courses, training, and experience that might support it. For example, if you want to be a science writer, consider studying biology and journalism.
- **Think practically** about your career by talking with students and instructors, looking at course requirements, and interviewing professionals in the fields that interest you.

Successful intelligence powers success

When you understand how learning helps you achieve goals that are important to you, you want to learn. When you want to learn, you work hard to make it happen. When you make the effort to learn, you are most likely to succeed.

Successful intelligence powers this entire process, from understanding to success. By helping you focus on how learning propels you toward specific goals, it boosts your desire to learn. By giving you an action plan with which you can think through problems or pursue goals, it inspires you to work hard and aim high. By helping you make the most of your strengths and compensate for or correct your weaknesses, it helps you capitalize on who you are and what you can do.

More good news for all kinds of learners lies in the fact that successful intelligence has three equally important elements. Students who have had trouble with tests and other traditional analytical skills can take heart, know-

---

IN-CLASS NOTES

HOW CAN SUCCESSFUL INTELLIGENCE HELP YOU ACHIEVE YOUR GOALS?

- Successful intelligence focuses on actions
  - What you do to achieve goals
  - 3 types of thinking:
    - Analytical
    - Creative
    - Practical
- Successful intelligence powers success
  - Clarifies how your learning helps you achieve goals
  - Makes the most of your strengths
  - Helps compensate for weaknesses

ing that creative and practical thinking can help them forge new paths to success. Students who test well can turn their analytical skills into real tools for success through creative thinking and practical action plans.

How will *Keys to Success* help you build *successful intelligence?*

The goal of *Keys to Success* is to help you build the analytical, creative, and practical thinking skills that will get you where you want to go in school and in life. Each element of the book contributes to this goal.

The chapter material

Through your exploration of the various topics in *Keys to Success*, you will work to further develop all three aspects of successful intelligence. The material will often connect a topic to analytical, creative, or practical thinking. Accounts and examples from students, instructors, and professionals show how people use various analytical, creative, and practical skills to accomplish personal goals. In addition, Chapter 4—the chapter on thinking— goes into detail about how you can evaluate and build analytical, creative, and practical skills.

Key 1.2 provides some examples of the practical, analytical, and creative thinking skills that lie within chapter topics.

The in-chapter activities

As you work through the chapters, you will find activities designed to help you turn ideas you read into information you can use.

- *Get Analytical* gives you an opportunity to analyze a chapter topic.
- *Get Creative* prompts you to think creatively about chapter material.
- *Get Practical* provides you with a chance to consider a practical application of a chapter idea.

Working through these activities gives you a double benefit. While building successful intelligence skills, you are also increasing your understanding of chapter material, making it more useful to you in pursuing your goals.

The end-of-chapter exercises

The end-of-chapter exercises give you several opportunities to combine what you have learned and apply it to important tasks.

- *Developing Successful Intelligence: Putting It All Together* unites analytical thinking ("Think it through"), creative thinking ("Think out of the box"), and practical thinking ("Make it happen"). This exercise builds your understanding of successful intelligence as an active process and strengthens your ability to direct its elements toward a goal.

Keys to Success *chapters develop successful intelligence.*

CHAPTER	ANALYTICAL SKILLS	CREATIVE SKILLS	PRACTICAL SKILLS
2	• Thinking about whether your values reflect who you are or want to be • Analyzing how successful a time manager you are	• Coming up with creative ways to manage stress • Thinking about different paths toward a goal	• Planning steps toward a goal • Keeping an effective calendar
3	• Examining how you learn • Matching your learning style to courses, skills, and environments	• When thinking about a major, considering departments or types of majors that are off the beaten path • Opening your mind to new perceptions of you as a learner	• Creating a step-by-step plan toward declaring a major • Linking your learning style to study skills that will help you most
4	• Distinguishing fact from opinion • Evaluating assumptions	• Brainstorming • Using strategies that enhance creative abilities	• Practical problem solving • Making a well-considered decision
5	• Evaluating arguments • Analyzing the hidden perspectives found in all media messages	• Thinking of different ways to review reading material • Finding innovative ways to work with study group members	• Using a practical plan—SQ3R—for maximizing reading comprehension • Expanding your vocabulary
6	• Deciding which information is important enough to record in notes • Examining your particular listening challenges	• Coming up with interesting mnemonic devices • Brainstorming ways to listen more effectively when you don't agree with the speaker	• Memorizing by grouping information • Knowing when and how to use different note-taking systems
7	• Analyzing why you made a particular mistake on a test • Selecting the most important material to study for a test	• Brainstorming a study schedule • Coming up with a variety of review techniques	• Knowing how to handle different types of test questions • Combating test anxiety
8	• Examining how prejudice leads to discrimination • Evaluating the accuracy of your judgments of others	• Finding ways to think expansively about diversity • Brainstorming methods for managing anger	• Making connections with diverse people • Adjusting to different communication styles
9	• Thinking through the consequences of drugs and alcohol • Linking your learning style to related careeer areas	• Brainstorming careers that interest you and suit your talents • Coming up with people with whom you can network	• Keeping credit card use under control • Living your personal mission

- *Team Building: Collaborative Solutions* encourages you to apply various successful intelligence elements to a group setting, building both thinking skills and your ability to work successfully with others.

- *Writing: Discovery Through Journaling* provides an opportunity to put your analysis, creative thoughts, and practical ideas down in words, building writing skills as well as thinking skills.

- *Career Portfolio: Plan for Success* is a chance to see how your own analytical, creative, and practical skills will help you prepare for career success. Through the chapters you will build a tangible and useful portfolio—analyzing workplace opportunities, coming up with creative ideas about careers, and creating practical items that you will use in your job search.

- The *Study Guide* at the end of each chapter provide a series of multiple-choice questions that you can use to review the chapter material and assess your learning. After completing these questions, you can use the Answer Key in the back of the book to check your answers and review the information you found difficult.

With the power of your mind and the tools waiting for you in this book, you possess the keys to success. What remains is to turn the key and get moving toward your goals—and this requires motivation. Here are some ways to find that motivation and put it to work.

SEE YOURSELF AT YOUR BEST

get creative!

Use your creative powers to improve your opinion of yourself and inspire action.

You probably have some idea of where you fit in the post-secondary environment, considering your age, stage of life, and educational background. However, your "student status" is only a minor part of who you are.

Imagine that students gained entry into institutions of higher learning by writing personal ads and posting them on the admissions website. Write a personal ad that you feel would give you the best possible chance of entry. Discuss

- What makes you unique.
- What you will contribute to making the school a better place.
- How your education will bring you personal and professional success.

_____

_____

_____

_____

_____

_____

What will *motivate you* to make the most of learning?

MOTIVATION

A force that moves a person to action; often inspired by an idea, a fact, an event, or a goal.

Success is a process, not a fixed mark—and **motivation** keeps the process in motion. Successfully intelligent people find ways to motivate themselves to learn, grow, and work toward what they want. Everyone has the potential to be motivated. The following strategies will help boost your motivation now, as you are learning, as well as in the future.

Focus on your self-esteem

SELF-ESTEEM

A belief in your value as a person.

When people believe in themselves, their **self-esteem** fuels their motivation to succeed. Belief, though, is only half the game. The other half is the action and effort you put in that help you feel you have earned your self-esteem, as basketball coach Rick Pitino explains: "Self-esteem is directly linked to deserving success. If you have established a great work ethic and have begun the discipline that is inherent with that, you will automatically begin to feel better about yourself."[5]

Think positively

POSITIVE SELF-TALK

Supportive and positive thoughts and ideas that one communicates to oneself.

Your attitudes influence what you will learn from your courses, instructors, and peers. A positive attitude—reinforced by **positive self-talk**—can open your mind to learning and inspire you to action. How can you talk positively to yourself even when times get tough?

- **Stop negative talk in its tracks.** If you catch yourself thinking, "This is too difficult. I'll never be able to do it," replace this negativity with, "I can do this if I take it one step at a time." Then think about specific steps you can take to accomplish the task.

- **Pay yourself a compliment.** Note your successes. Be specific: "I can now create an outline that helps me organize my thoughts for a paper."

- **Replace words of obligation with words of personal intent.**

| I should | *becomes* | I choose to |
| I'll try | *becomes* | I will |

Words of intent give you power and control because they imply a personal decision to act. The following statement from a nursing student illustrates the relationship between positive self-talk and success: "To stay motivated I will always remember that I am doing this to better myself and to learn what I need to in order to be the best nurse that I can be. Making a commitment and staying true to it is not easy, but I know that an uncommitted person will never finish anything."[6]

COMMITMENT

(1) A pledge or promise to do something, or (2) a dedication to a long-term course of action.

Take action

Although thinking positively sets the tone for success, taking action gets you there. Without action, positive thoughts become empty statements.

For example, consider a student in a first year English class. This student thinks positive thoughts: "I write well. I can get at least a B-plus in this class." She even posts her positive thoughts where she can see them. Then, during the semester, she misses about one-third of the class meetings, turns in papers late, and completely forgets to hand in two assignments. *She did not back up her intentions with action.* At the end of the course, when she barely passes the class, she wonders how someone with such a positive attitude could have done so poorly.

Following are some ways to get moving in a positive direction:

- Take responsibility. See yourself as being in charge of your success. Create personal guidelines that support that success—for example, "I pay attention to deadlines."

- Translate general statements into specific actions. Success will come when you make your guidelines real through action. If one of your personal guidelines is "I pay attention to deadlines," one action might be turning in assignments when they are due.

Be responsible

Higher learning requires that you take personal responsibility for your academic success in ways that you may never have had to in high school. Even if you have lived on your own and held a job, helped raise a family, or done both, college or university adds to that responsibility. You, as your own manager, are responsible for making decisions that keep you on track toward achieving what you want.

The theme of responsibility stands out in how these first year university students describe their personal transitions:[7]

- Angie Miller (majoring in Biology): "The hardest part of my first year courses was doing all my work by myself with nobody telling me every day that my homework was due. Also, there was more material covered in a shorter time, so it was more study time than in high school."

- Jason Roach (majoring in Business Computer Systems): "Your classes don't meet as many times a week as they did in high school. As a result, you get more homework. Since you only meet for a minimum of three hours a week, you have a great deal more time to read the book and complete the homework. It is sort of like a 'learn on your own' concept."

Taking responsibility is about living up to obligations. Through action, you prove that you are responsible—think of it as "response-able": able to respond as efficiently as possible and to the best of your ability. Responsible students can be trusted to fulfill obligations like these:

- attending class and participating in activities and discussions
- completing readings and assignments on time
- communicating with instructors and peers

Why are these basic actions the building blocks of school success? First, completing everyday responsibilities promotes good habits. The more you do something, the more it becomes second nature. Second, small accomplishments make a big impression. When you show up to class, pay attention, contribute, and put in the hours necessary to master the material, you show your instructors and others that you are committed to learning.

HABIT

A preference for a particular action that you do a certain way, and often on a regular basis or at certain times.

Develop positive habits

"Bad" habits stall motivation and prevent you from reaching important goals. Some bad habits, such as chronic lateness, cause obvious problems. Other habits, such as surfing the Internet, may not seem bad until you realize that you needed to spend those hours studying.

"Good" habits bring you closer to your goals. You often have to wait longer and work harder to be rewarded for good habits, which makes them harder to maintain. If during one week you reduce your nights out to gain study time, for example, it will take more than one week for your grades to improve.

Define and evaluate your habits to see whether you need to make a change. If a habit is getting in the way of your goals, make a decision to change it. Pick a day to make the change, and then keep it up. To become accustomed to a new habit, be consistent for at least three weeks. Use positive self-talk to encourage your progress, and reward yourself for steps in the right direction.

It's never too late to make an important change in your habits. Returning student Sunny Hobbs is determined and serious, although she had neither trait 30 years ago, when she first enrolled at a post-secondary institution and failed nearly every course. She arrives early for her first class. Sitting in the second row of her Intermediate Algebra course, she works hard to take comprehensive notes. Her positive habits reflect a determination to study elementary education and earn a degree.[8]

Try not to get discouraged if the process seems difficult. Rarely does someone make a change without setbacks. Take it one step at a time; when you lose steam, reflect on what you stand to gain. With persistence and positive thinking, you can reach your goal.

Face your fears

Everyone experiences fear. Anything unknown—new people, experiences, situations—can be frightening because risk is involved. As you begin college or university, for example, you may wonder if you can handle the work, if

FACE YOUR FEARS[9]

get practical!

Use practical skills to conquer a fear you may have that stems from the experience of starting your post-secondary education.

First, describe your fear—and be specific.

_____

_____

Now, list three small activities that may get you closer to working through that fear. If you don't want to start a project because you fear failure, for example, you can begin by reading a book on the subject, brainstorming what you already know about it, or making up a project schedule.

1. _____

2. _____

3. _____

Commit yourself to one step that you will take within the next two days. State it here. Include the time and date you will begin and how much time you will spend.

_____

_____

What reward will you give yourself for taking this step?

_____

_____

Did taking this step help ease your fear? If so, describe how.

_____

_____

Affirm that you have taken that first step and are on the way to success by signing your name here and writing the date.

Name _____   Date _____

you have chosen the right school, or if your education will prepare you for a well-paying job.

> Nobody succeeds beyond his or her wildest expectations unless he or she begins with some wild expectations.

RALPH CHARELL

The challenges you will face in school may require that you face your fears and push your limits. The first step is to acknowledge what you fear. Look for fears that may lurk under symptoms like putting things off and not trying very hard. Then, be specific about what you're afraid of. Focusing on a fear of working in the science lab, for example, helps you brainstorm useful ways of coping.

Once you know what you fear, evaluate what will help you overcome it. For example, if you are concerned about working in the science lab,

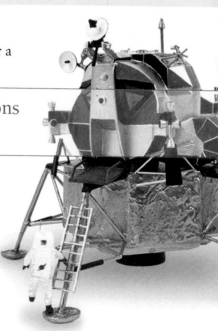

arrange to work with another student who is comfortable there and willing to be a mentor to you.

As you work through your fears, talk about them with people you trust. Everyone has fears, and when people share strategies, everyone benefits.

What should you do if you lose motivation for your studies? Refocus your attention on the practical steps that will lead you toward your goals—for example, attend class, complete your assignments when due, challenge yourself to do your best. Also, remind yourself of the connection between your work in school and your ability to achieve long-term goals in your life.

IN-CLASS NOTES

WHAT WILL MOTIVATE YOU TO MAKE THE MOST OF LEARNING?

- Focus on your self-esteem
  - Think positively
  - Take action
- Be responsible
- Develop positive habits
- Face your fears

_____
_____
_____
_____

How can *what you learn now* help you succeed in school, work, and life?

In his book *Techno Trends—24 Technologies That Will Revolutionize Our Lives*, futurist Daniel Burns describes a tomorrow that is linked to continuing education: "The future belongs to those who are capable of being retrained again and again," he says. "Think of it as periodically upgrading your human assets throughout your career . . . . Humans are infinitely upgradeable, but it does require an investment" in lifelong learning.[10]

In other words, you will need to continue to learn and grow in order to succeed. Here are some ways in which your post-secondary experience will develop your ability to stay open to new information and experiences.

Higher learning helps you value diversity

For most students, college or university provides an opportunity to question the "givens" of life and to open their minds and hearts to people who are different from them. Learning to appreciate the similarities and differences among people and to value diversity in all forms is critical for life success.

Diversity means differences among people. On an interpersonal level, diversity refers to the differences between ourselves and others, between the groups we belong to and the

Students often meet and work with instructors and other students representing a variety of ethnicities, cultural backgrounds, and stages of life.

groups we are not part of. Differences in gender, abilities, ethnicity and national origin, age, physical characteristics, and sexual orientation define this most obvious level of diversity.

Other differences—many of which define people and affect relationships in fundamental ways—lie beneath the surface. Among these are differences in:

- Cultural and religious backgrounds and beliefs, reflected in different values and behaviours.
- Educational background and socioeconomic status.
- Family background (for example, two-parent versus single-parent households).
- Relationship, marital, and/or parental status.

Diversity refers to the differences within people. Another layer of diversity lies within each person. Among the factors that define this layer are:

- Personality traits.
- Preferred learning styles.
- Strengths and weaknesses in analytical, creative, and practical abilities.
- Natural talents and interests.

As you will see in Chapter 9, accepting people for who they are means accepting all aspects of their diversity. In Chapter 3, you will gain a greater understanding of your own and others' learning styles, and in Chapter 4 you will explore differences in analytical, creative, and practical abilities.

Higher learning prepares you to learn from failure and celebrate success

Even the most successful people make mistakes and experience failures. In fact, failure is one of the greatest teachers. Failure provides an opportunity to realize what you don't know so that you can improve. What you learn from a failure will most likely stay with you more intensely and guide you more effectively than will many other things you learn.

Learning from failure

Learning from your failures and mistakes involves successfully intelligent thinking.

Analyze what happened. Consider what caused, or contributed to, the failure. Be specific and assess the situation or causes in terms of your responsibility and control. Avoid pointing the finger at others, but rather look at how you could have affected the situation. For example, imagine that after a long night of studying for a chemistry test, you forgot to complete a paper due for English class the next day. The cause was not that instructors have scheduled tests and assignments too close together, but rather that your focus on the test caused you to overlook other tasks. Now you may face a lower grade on your paper if you turn it in late, plus you may be inclined to rush it and turn in a project that isn't as good as it could be.

Come up with creative ways to change. Consider the causes of this situation and establish ways that you may avoid similar situations in the future. For example, you may make a commitment to note deadlines in a bright colour in your planner and to check due dates more often. You can also try arranging your study schedule so that it is more organized and less last-minute.

Put your plan into action. Do what you have decided to do—and keep an eye on how it is working. Considering the example above, if you rearrange your study schedule, for instance, look carefully at whether it is improving your ability to stay on top of your responsibilities.

Your value as a human being does not diminish when you make a mistake. In fact, one might argue that we really learn more from our mistakes than from the things we do right. That is, usually we do not take notice of the day-to-day things we do right, but we will pay attention to mistakes. People who can manage mistakes and cope with failure demonstrate to themselves and others that they have the courage to take risks and learn. Employers often value risk takers more than they value people who always play it safe.

In order to succeed you must fail, so that you know what not to do the next time.

ANTHONY J. D'ANGELO

Celebrating success

Acknowledging your successes, no matter how small, is as important as learning from your mistakes. Earning a B on an assignment after you had received a C on the previous one, for example, is worth celebrating. Take a moment to acknowledge what you have accomplished, whether it is a good grade, a job offer, or any other personal victory. Let your success help you build your confidence that you can succeed again.

As you would when working to change a habit, reward yourself when you succeed. "Take it seriously and work hard, yes. But don't forget to enjoy yourself every now and then," advises a first year student. "Take a break and see a movie. Read a book that's deliciously trashy, not scholarly. Take a bubble bath as you pat yourself on the back for a job well done. This is a special time. It's costing you time, money, sacrifices to be in school. Enjoy it and embrace it. You're making memories now, so make it count."[11]

Higher learning helps you apply successful intelligence in a changing world

As a post-secondary student, you are making sacrifices to achieve success throughout your life. These changes likely include a significant investment of time and money as well as some lifestyle changes. You are building the analytical, creative, and practical intelligence you need to cope with a changing world:

- Knowledge in nearly every field is doubling every two to three years. That means that if you stop learning, for even a few years, your knowledge base will be inadequate to keep up with the changes in your career.
- Technology is changing how people live and work. The Internet and technology will shape communications and improve knowledge and productivity during the next 20 years and will require continual learning.
- The global economy is moving from a product and service base to a knowledge and talent base. Traditional jobs of the past are being

CELEBRATE SUCCESS AND LEARN FROM MISTAKES

get analytical!

Acknowledge your successes.

Describe a situation, in either your personal, academic, or career life, in which you experienced success. It may be one you consider major, such as being accepted into a particular school or program, or one a bit smaller, such as making it to your class on time. Acknowledge this success by describing it.

_____

_____

_____

How does that success make you feel?

_____

_____

What did you do (or will you do) to celebrate that success?

_____

_____

_____

Analyze what happened when you made a mistake, so that you can avoid the same mistake next time.

Describe an academic situation in which you made a mistake—for example, perhaps you didn't study enough for a test, you didn't complete an assignment on time, or you didn't listen carefully enough in class and missed important information. Describe what happened.

_____

_____

_____

What were the consequences of the mistake?

_____

_____

What, if anything, did you learn from your mistake that you will use in similar situations?

_____

_____

_____

replaced by knowledge-based jobs that ask workers to think critically to come up with solutions.

- Workers are changing jobs and occupations more frequently. Estimates are that the average Canadian now changes occupations three to five times in life. It is becoming more and more common for people to make dramatic career changes such as changing from a firefighter to a florist. Every time you decide to start a new career direction, you need new knowledge and skills.

All of these signs point to the need to become lifelong learners—individuals who continue to build knowledge and intelligence as a mechanism for improving their lives and careers. Through successful intelligence, you will maintain the kind of flexibility that will enable you to adapt to the demands of the twenty-first century.

Facing change means taking risks. When you begin college or university, you accept certain challenges and risks as necessary hurdles on the path toward success. As a successfully intelligent lifelong learner, you will find ways to continue to learn and to strive toward what you want. Welcome to the beginning of the road to your career goals.

IN-CLASS NOTES

HOW CAN WHAT YOU LEARN NOW HELP YOU SUCCEED IN SCHOOL, WORK, AND LIFE?

- Value diversity
- Learn from failure and celebrate success
- Apply successful intelligence in a changing world

In Chinese writing, this character has two meanings: One is "chaos"; the other, "opportunity." The character communicates the belief that every chaotic, challenging situation in life also presents an opportunity. By responding to challenges actively, you can discover the opportunity within the chaos.

Let this concept reassure you as you embark on this phase of your learning. You may feel that you are going through a time of change and chaos. Take heart. No matter how difficult the obstacles, you can choose to persevere. You can build the kind of successful intelligence that helps you learn, grow, and realize your goals.

SUGGESTED READINGS

Evers, Frederick T., James Cameron Rush, and Iris Berdow. *The Bases of Competence: Skills for Lifelong Learning and Employability.* San Francisco, CA: Jossey-Bass, 1998.

Jeffers, Susan. *Feel the Fear... And Beyond: Mastering the Techniques for Doing It Anyway.* New York: Ballantine, 1998.

Lombardo, Alison. *Navigating Your Freshman Year.* New York: Natavi Guides, 2003.

Simon, Linda. *New Beginnings: A Guide for Adult Learners and Returning Students.* 2nd ed. Upper Saddle River, NJ: Prentice Hall, 2001.

Sternberg, Robert. *Successful Intelligence: How Practical and Creative Intelligence Determine Success in Life.* New York: Plume, 1997.

Tyler, Suzette. *Been There, Should've Done That II: More Tips for Making the Most of College.* Lansing, MI: Front Porch Press, 2001.

Weinberg, Carol. *The Complete Handbook for College Women: Making the Most of Your College Experience.* New York: New York University Press, 1994.

INTERNET RESOURCES

Diversity Canada Foundation: www.diversitycanada.org/

Lessons in Successful Intelligence. Psychology Dept., University of Toronto: http://www.psych.utoronto.ca/~reingold/courses/intelligence/cache/sternberg_intelligence.html

Keys to Success Companion Website: www.pearsoned.ca/carter

The Student Center, Student.Com: www.student.com

Prentice Hall Student Success Supersite. Student Union: www.prenhall.com/success/StudentUn/index.html

Success Stories: www.prenhall.com/success/Stories/index.html

BUILDING SKILLS

FOR ACADEMIC, CAREER, AND LIFE SUCCESS

SUCCESSFUL INTELLIGENCE

PRACTICAL CREATIVE

ANALYTICAL

SUCCESSFUL INTELLIGENCE

Developing Successful Intelligence

PUTTING IT ALL TOGETHER

Make your first semester count. Academics is only part of the post-secondary experience. Campus resources, clubs, student activity groups, and other organizations can enrich your experience. Remember that students who make social connections tend to do better in their studies. Put a toe in the water sooner rather than later and you will begin to benefit from what your school has to offer.

Step 1. *Think it through: Analyze yourself as a learner.* Describe who you are as a student—your identity, interests, challenges, and goals. Here are some questions to inspire thought:

- How would you describe your culture, ethnicity, gender, age, lifestyle?

  _____

  _____

- For how long are you planning to attend college or university?

  _____

  _____

- What family and work obligations do you have?

  _____

  _____

- What is your current living situation? How does it support your learning?

  _____

  _____

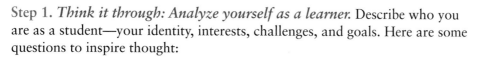

create your future

- What do you think are your biggest challenges?

  _____

  _____

- What do you like to learn about? Why does it interest you?

  _____

  _____

Step 2. *Think out of the box: Brainstorm your ideal extracurricular activities.* How do you want to spend your time outside of your studies? To inspire creative ideas, try using one or more of the following questions as a starting point:

- If you could do anything, what experience or activity would you pursue?

  _____

  _____

- When you were in elementary or high school, what were your favourite activities? What aspects of these activities might transfer into current interests and pursuits?

  _____

  _____

- What kinds of organizations, activities, groups, experiences, or people make you think, "Wow, I want to do that"?

  _____

  _____

- Think about the people that inspire the best in you. What do you like to do with them? What kinds of things are they involved with?

  _____

  _____

- Who are the people with whom you have little in common? How could you benefit from getting to know them?

  _____

  _____

Step 3. *Make it happen: Take practical steps toward the activities you like.* Thinking about how you have described yourself in terms of both academics and extracurricular pursuits, explore your school's calendar or handbook for the resources and organizations your school offers. These may include some or all of those listed in the following grid. Choose at least five services or organizations you most want to check out this semester. Then, using your school calendar or website, or by visiting each of these centres, fill in the information on the grid. Notice that the last column requires action— fill it in when you have made initial contact with each office or organization.

Let this exercise be a jumping-off point for real involvement this semester. If after your initial contact you wish to become more involved, go for it. Remember that the activities that inspire you are often a clue to your career path—and that knowing how to work with others is one of the most important skills you will build.

Service/Organization	Location	Hours/ Meeting Times	What it Offers	Phone or Email	Date of Contact
Academic organizations					
Adult education centre					
Clubs					
Co-op education					
Employment centre					
Fraternities/Sororities					
Financial awards					
International student groups					
Learning centre (for academic support)					
Minority student groups					
On-campus job opportunities					
Services for students with a disability					
Religious organizations					
School publications					
School TV/radio stations					
Sports teams or clubs					
Student associations					
Student government					
Student services					
Volunteer groups					
Other:_____					

Team Building

COLLABORATIVE SOLUTIONS

Motivators. (Small group exercise)

1. Gather in a group of three or four. Together, brainstorm things or situations that might interfere with your motivation to succeed in school.

2. Each person chooses one of the motivation blockers you listed and writes it at the top of a blank sheet of paper.

3. On your own, list three specific actions that you commit to taking in order to keep motivation high when the going gets rough:

   1. _____

   2. _____

   3. _____

Writing

Reasons for higher learning. People attend college or university for technical training, for the sake of learning, for increased earning power, and more. Think about your own reasons. Why are you here, and what do you want out of the experience?

_____

_____

On a scale of 1 (lowest) to 10 (highest), rank your commitment to succeeding in your education. Rank: _____

What sacrifices do you think you might need to make to get what you want and to persevere in your quest for success?

_____

_____

Underline the ones you are willing to make.

Career Portfolio

This is the first of 10 career portfolio assignments you will complete, one for each chapter. By the end, you will have compiled a portfolio that will help you achieve your career goals. Record your portfolio work on a computer and save the documents electronically, on a disk or hard drive, or write your work on paper and keep them together in a file. If you prefer, you can complete the exercises in your book and supplement with additional paper or a computer file.

Setting career goals. Whether you have a current career, have held a few different jobs, or have not yet entered the workplace, now is an ideal time to take stock of your career goals. The earlier in your education that you consider career goals, the more you can take advantage of how post-secondary learning can help prepare you for work, in both job-specific and general ways. Having a strong vision of where you wish to go will also be a powerful motivator as you face some of the inevitable challenges of the next few years.

1. Spend 10 minutes brainstorming everything that you wish you could be, do, have, or experience in your career 10 years from now—the skills you want to have, money you want to earn, benefits, experiences, travel, anything you can think of.

   _____   _____

   _____   _____

   _____   _____

   _____   _____

   _____   _____

   _____   _____

_____   _____

_____   _____

_____   _____

2. Group your wishes in order of priority. This will help you examine how
   your wishes relate to one another.

Priority 1	**Priority 2**	**Priority 3**
_____	_____	_____
_____	_____	_____
_____	_____	_____
_____	_____	_____
_____	_____	_____
_____	_____	_____

3. Circle or highlight the three highest priority wishes.

Chapter Review Questions

Choose the option that BEST completes the statement or answers the question. After completing the questions, check your answers against the Answer Key at the back of this book (p. 314).

1. The benefits of a post-secondary education include increased
   a. ☐ Earning potential.
   b. ☐ Employability.
   c. ☐ Career preparation.
   d. ☐ All of the above.

2. Robert J. Sternberg defines successful intelligence as the kind of intelligence
   a. ☐ Used to achieve important goals.
   b. ☐ Measured by IQ tests.
   c. ☐ Demonstrated by people who score well on tests.
   d. ☐ Used in recall and analysis.

3. Successful intelligence includes thinking
   a. ☐ Creatively, practically, and logically.
   b. ☐ Analytically, practically, and sensibly.
   c. ☐ Analytically, creatively, and practically.
   d. ☐ Creatively, logically, and sensibly.

4. Successful intelligence is your key to success because it
   a. ☐ Means you do *not* have to work so hard to get what you want.
   b. ☐ Inspires you to capitalize on who you are and what you can do.
   c. ☐ Encourages you to use your intelligence to be more successful.
   d. ☐ All of the above.

5. Success is a
   a. ☐ Process.
   b. ☐ Goal.
   c. ☐ Fixed mark.
   d. ☐ Ideal.

6. Motivation is best defined as a force that
   a. ☐ Is inspired by an external reward.
   b. ☐ Is inspired by an internal reward.
   c. ☐ Moves a person to action.
   d. ☐ Is separate from self-esteem.

7. Someone who believes in his or her value as a person is considered to have positive self-_____.
   a. ☐ Worth.
   b. ☐ Value.
   c. ☐ Esteem.
   d. ☐ Arrogance.

8. Self-esteem influences
   a. ☐ Motivation.
   b. ☐ Success.
   c. ☐ Belief in self.
   d. ☐ All of the above.

9. Saying "I will" rather than "I should" is an example of replacing
   a. ☐ Obligation with intent.
   b. ☐ Obligation with choice.
   c. ☐ Choice with action.
   d. ☐ Wishes with action.

10. Developing positive habits and facing fears are two ways that one can
    a. ☐ Get good grades.
    b. ☐ Make positive friendships.
    c. ☐ Think creatively.
    d. ☐ Stay motivated in school.

11. Which of the following statements is NOT an example of positive self-talk?

   a. ☐ I will take it slowly and I will be able to figure this out.

   b. ☐ I will complete this assignment by the deadline.

   c. ☐ I choose to complete half the questions today and the rest tomorrow.

   d. ☐ I should do my homework now.

12. Fill in the blank to create a statement of personal intent:
   I _____ do my homework

   a. ☐ Should.

   b. ☐ Have to.

   c. ☐ Will.

   d. ☐ Must.

13. Completing everyday responsibilities promotes good

   a. ☐ Karma.

   b. ☐ Health.

   c. ☐ Habits.

   d. ☐ Studies.

14. One often has to wait longer and work harder to be rewarded for good habits. This makes rewards

   a. ☐ Harder to attain.

   b. ☐ Not worth attaining.

   c. ☐ Impossible to attain.

   d. ☐ Easier to attain.

15. The first step in overcoming one's fears is to

   a. ☐ Brainstorm what is causing the fear.

   b. ☐ Identify the fear.

   c. ☐ Evaluate ways to overcome the fear.

   d. ☐ Minimize the fear.

16. Taking _____ and translating general statements into _____ are two ways to get moving in a positive direction.

   a. ☐ Chances; Specific statements.

   b. ☐ Risks; Actions.

   c. ☐ Action; Specific statements.

   d. ☐ Responsibility; Actions.

17. Diversity includes differences in

   a. ☐ Race.

   b. ☐ Learning styles.

   c. ☐ Abilities.

   d. ☐ Sexual orientation.

   e. ☐ All of the above.

18. It is useful to view mistakes as

   a. ☐ Things to be avoided.

   b. ☐ Opportunities for learning.

   c. ☐ Common errors in judgment.

   d. ☐ Things to be ignored.

19. Which of the following statements is the most effective way to view failure?

   a. ☐ There is nothing to be gained from failure.

   b. ☐ One should try to ignore failures and pretend they didn't happen.

   c. ☐ There is much to be gained from failure.

   d. ☐ A person's self-worth depends on not failing.

20. People who can manage failure demonstrate to themselves and others that they have the courage to

   a. ☐ Take risks and learn from their experiences.

   b. ☐ Do things over.

   c. ☐ Ignore their mistakes.

   d. ☐ Strive for perfection.

2

Values, Goals, Time, and Stress

MANAGING YOURSELF

This chapter is organized as follows:

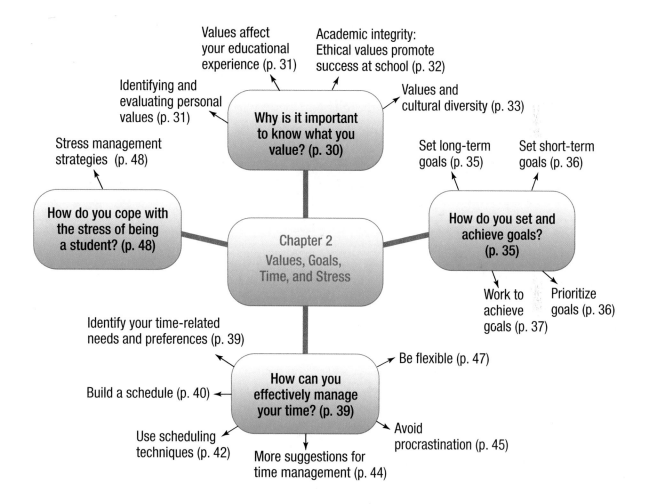

Values affect your educational experience (p. 31)

Academic integrity: Ethical values promote success at school (p. 32)

Identifying and evaluating personal values (p. 31)

Values and cultural diversity (p. 33)

Why is it important to know what you value? (p. 30)

Stress management strategies (p. 48)

Set long-term goals (p. 35)

Set short-term goals (p. 36)

How do you cope with the stress of being a student? (p. 48)

Chapter 2
Values, Goals, Time, and Stress

How do you set and achieve goals? (p. 35)

Work to achieve goals (p. 37)

Prioritize goals (p. 36)

Identify your time-related needs and preferences (p. 39)

Be flexible (p. 47)

Build a schedule (p. 40)

How can you effectively manage your time? (p. 39)

Avoid procrastination (p. 45)

Use scheduling techniques (p. 42)

More suggestions for time management (p. 44)

TEST YOURSELF

- Why is it important to know what you value?
- Describe four positive consequences of choosing to act with academic integrity.
- Define "cultural competence."
- What are three things you should consider when you evaluate your goals?
- Explain how to map out a personal goal.
- Illustrate how you would use a weekly planner to schedule classes and study time.
- List three advantages and three disadvantages of using a monthly calendar for scheduling your time and commitments.
- What are three possible reasons for why people procrastinate?
- Explain one strategy for avoiding procrastination and give an example to illustrate.
- What are four practical strategies for coping with stress?

For the correct answers and additional questions on Chapter 2, visit www.pearsoned.ca/carter.

Achieving your most important goals depends on your ability to manage yourself. As an effective self-manager, you take charge of your life much like a CEO heads up a top-performing business. This chapter divides the indispensable skill of self-management into four parts: using values to guide your goal setting, working through a process to achieve goals, managing time in a way that propels you toward your goals, and, throughout the journey, managing the stress that will often arise.

The realities of school, workplace, and personal life will often bring problems that create obstacles and produce stress. Everyone has problems; what counts is how you handle them. Your ability to manage yourself—accompanied by a generous dose of motivation—will help you cope with what you encounter, achieve your goals, and learn lasting lessons in the process.

Why is it important to know *what you value?*

You make life choices—what to do, what to believe, what to buy, how to act—based on your personal **values.** Your choice to pursue a degree, for example, reflects that you value the personal and professional growth that comes from higher learning. Being on time for your classes shows that you value punctuality. Paying bills regularly and on time shows that you value financial stability.

Values play a key role in your drive to achieve important goals because they help you:

- **Understand what you want out of life.** Your most meaningful goals should reflect what you value most.
- **Build "rules for life."** Your values form the foundation for your decisions. You will return repeatedly to them for guidance, especially when you find yourself in unfamiliar territory.
- **Find people who inspire you.** Spending time with people who share similar values will help you clarify how you want to live and find support as you work toward what's important to you.

Now that you have an idea of how you can use values, focus on how to identify yours.

Identifying and evaluating personal values

Ask yourself questions: What do you focus on in a given day? What do you consider important to be, to do, or to have? What do you wish to accomplish in your life? Answers to questions like these will point you toward your values. The exercise on page 32 will help you think through values in more detail.

After you determine your values, evaluate them to see if they make sense for you. Many forces affect your values—family, friends, culture, media, school, work, neighbourhood, religious beliefs, world events. No matter how powerful these external influences may be, whether a value feels right should be your primary consideration in deciding to adopt it.

Answering the following questions about a value will help you decide if it "feels right."

- Where did the value come from?
- What other different values could I consider?
- What might happen as a result of my adopting this value?
- Have I made a personal commitment to this choice? Have I told others about it?
- Do my life goals and day-to-day actions reflect this value?

If you let your values shift to fit you as you grow, you will always have a base on which to build achievable goals and make wise decisions.

Values affect your educational experience

Well-considered values can lead to smart choices while you are in school. Your values will help you:

Great minds have purposes; others have wishes.

WASHINGTON IRVING

- Keep going when the going gets tough. Translate your value of education into specific actions. Being a student is not always easy. There will be times when you may question what you are doing. Keep your long-term goal in mind, and continue to explore how it fits with your values, what you want, and who you are.
- Choose your career direction. If you've always been an environmentalist, then you might choose to study environmental science. If you feel fulfilled when you help people, then you might consider a career in social work.
- Choose friends and activities that enrich your life. Having friends who share your desire to succeed in school will increase your motivation and reduce your stress. Joining organizations whose activities support your values will broaden your educational experience.

- Choose what you want from education and how much you want to dedicate yourself to it. What kinds of skills and knowledge do you wish to build? How hard are you willing to work to achieve your goals? Going above and beyond will build your drive to succeed and hone your work habits—two items that will be useful in a competitive job market.

Finally, your values affect your success at school and beyond, because the more ethical a student you are, the more likely you are to stay in school and to build lasting knowledge and skills.

Academic integrity: Ethical values promote success at school

ACADEMIC INTEGRITY

Following a code of moral values, prizing honesty and fairness in all aspects of academic life—classes, assignments, tests, papers, projects, and relationships with students and faculty.

Having (academic integrity) promotes learning and ensures a quality education based on ethics and hard work. Read your institution's code of honour, or academic integrity policy, in your student handbook or online. When you enrolled, you agreed to abide by it.

get analytical!

EXPLORE YOUR VALUES

Evaluate what you think is most important to you, and connect educational goals to your top values.

Rate each of the values in the list on a scale from 1 to 5, 1 being least important to you and 5 being most important.

____ Knowing yourself
____ Being liked by others
____ Reading
____ Self-improvement
____ Taking risks
____ Time to yourself
____ Improving physical/ mental health
____ Time for fun/relaxation
____ Lifelong learning

____ Staying fit through exercise
____ Competing and winning
____ Getting a good job
____ Education
____ Spiritual/religious life
____ Making a lot of money
____ Good relationships with family
____ Community involvement

____ Creative/artistic pursuits
____ Helping others
____ Keeping up with the news
____ Other (write below)
____ Being organized
____ Financial stability

_____

Write your top three values here:

1. _____
2. _____
3. _____

Values often affect your educational choices. Choose one top value that is a factor in an educational choice that you have made. Explain the choice and how the value is involved. Example: A student who values mental health makes a choice to pursue a degree in psychology with a plan to work as a school counsellor.

_____
_____
_____

Name an area of study that you think would help you live according to this value.

_____
_____

The Office of Student Conduct at Mount Royal College in Alberta defines academic integrity as a commitment to five fundamental values: honesty, trust, fairness, respect, and responsibility.[1] These values are the positive actions that define academic integrity.

- **Honesty.** Honesty defines the pursuit of knowledge and implies a search for truth in your class work, papers and lab reports, and teamwork with other students.

- **Trust.** Mutual trust—between instructor and student, as well as among students—makes possible the free exchange of ideas that is fundamental to learning. Trust means being true to your word.

- **Fairness.** Instructors must create a fair academic environment where students are judged against clear standards and in which procedures are well defined.

- **Respect.** In a respectful academic environment, both students and instructors accept and honour a wide range of opinions, even if the opinions are contrary to their core beliefs.

- **Responsibility.** You are responsible for making choices that will provide you with the best education—choices that reflect fairness and honesty.

Choosing to act with integrity has the following positive consequences:

- **Increased self-esteem.** Self-esteem is tied to action. The more you act in respectful and honourable ways, the better you feel about yourself, and the more likely you are to succeed.

- **Acquired knowledge.** If you cheat you might pass a test—or perhaps even a course—but chances are you won't retain the knowledge and skills you need for success. Honest work is more likely to result in knowledge that lasts and that can be used to accomplish career and life goals.

- **Effective behavioural patterns.** When you condition yourself to play fair now, you set a pattern for your behaviour at work and with friends and family.

- **Mutual respect.** Respecting the work of others will lead others to respect your work.

The last two points reflect the positive effect that integrity has on your relationships. This is only one way in which values help you successfully relate to, work with, and understand the people around you. Here's another way: Being open to different values, often linked with different cultures, can enhance your understanding of cultural diversity.

Values and cultural diversity

At college or university, you may meet people who seem different in ways that you may not expect. Many of these differences stem from attitudes and behaviours that are unfamiliar to you. These attitudes and behaviours are rooted in the values that people acquire from the influence of their family, community, and culture.

Cultural misunderstandings can interfere with the relationships and friendships you form in school, career, and life. As someone who accepts and

CULTURE

A set of values, behaviours, tastes, knowledge, attitudes, and habits shared by a group of people.

appreciates diversity, you have a goal to develop the cultural competence to understand and appreciate these differences so that they enhance—rather than hinder—communication.[2]

A simple model to help you avoid communication problems with people from other cultures was developed by Edward Hall, an anthropologist and an authority on cross-cultural communication. Hall linked communication styles to what he called high-context and low-context cultures:[3]

- People from *high-context* cultures rely heavily in their communication on context and situation as well as on body language and eye contact. Time (past, present, and future), fate, personal relationships and status, gender roles, trust, gestures, and sense of self and space are just some of the factors that influence communication in these cultures. High-context countries span the world and include China, Japan, Brazil, Saudi Arabia, Italy, and France, for example.

- In contrast, people from *low-context* cultures focus on what is explicitly said or written and pay little attention to context and nonverbal cues. Examples of countries with low-context cultures include Canada, the United States, England, Australia, Germany, and the Scandinavian countries.

As you continue to read *Keys to Success*, look for examples of how cultural diversity impacts everything from teamwork and relationships to listening, questioning, and more. Then think of the wisdom of cultural-diversity consultant Helen Turnbull on turning differences into strengths:

We must suspend our judgment. We should not judge others negatively because they are indirect, or their accents aren't clear, or their tone of voice is tentative, or they avoid eye contact. We must learn patience and suspend judgment long enough to realize these differences don't make one of us right and the other wrong. They simply mean that we approach communication from a different frame of reference and, many times, a different value system.[4]

Although clarifying your values will help you choose your educational path, goal-setting and goal-achievement skills will help you travel that path to the end. Goals turn values into tools and put them to practical use.

IN-CLASS NOTES

WHY IS IT IMPORTANT TO KNOW WHAT YOU VALUE?

Values:

- Influence life choices
- Need to "feel right" for you
- Affect your educational experience
- Promote academic integrity
- Influence cultural competence

_____

_____

_____

_____

_____

_____

How do you *set and achieve* goals?

When you identify something that you want, you set a goal. Actually *getting* what you want—from education, career, or life—demands working to *achieve* your goals. Achieving goals, whether they are short term or long term, involves following a goal-achievement plan. Think of the plan you are about to read as a map; it helps you to establish each segment of the trip, so that you will be able to define your route and follow it successfully.

Set long-term goals

Start by establishing the goals that have the largest scope, the *long-term* goals that you aim to attain over a period of six months, a year, or more. As a student, your long-term goals include attending school and gaining knowledge, training, experience, and, perhaps, a certificate, diploma, or degree. Getting an education is a significant goal that often takes years to reach.

Some long-term goals have an open-ended time frame. For example, if your goal is to become a better musician, you may work at it over a lifetime. These goals also invite more creative thinking; you have more time and freedom to consider all sorts of paths to your goal. Other goals, such as completing all the courses you have registered for, have a shorter scope, a more definite end, and often fewer options for getting from A to Z.

The following long-term goal statement, written by Carol Carter, a *Keys to Success* author, may take years to complete:

> My goal is to build my own business in which I create opportunities for students to maximize their talents. In this business, I will reach thousands of students and teachers through books, the Internet, teacher seminars, and student-oriented programs.

Carol also has long-term goals that she hopes to accomplish in no more than a year:

> Develop and publish one book. Design three seminars for teachers with accompanying PowerPoint slides and other materials. Create Internet-based materials that encourage student success and use them in student seminars.

Just as Carol's goals are tailored to her personality, abilities, and interests, your goals should reflect your uniqueness. To determine your long-term goals, think about what you want to accomplish while you are in school and afterward. Think of ways you can link your personal values and professional aims, as in the following examples:

- Values: Health and fitness, helping others
  Goal: To become a physical therapist
- Values: Independence, financial success
  Goal: To obtain a degree in business and start a company

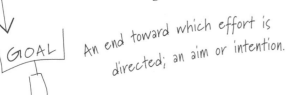

GOAL   An end toward which effort is directed; an aim or intention.

Basing your long-term goals on values increases your motivation. The more your goals focus on what is most important to you, the greater your drive to reach them.

Set short-term goals

Short-term goals are smaller steps that move you toward a long-term goal. Lasting as short as a few hours or as long as a few months, these goals help you manage your broader aspirations as they narrow your focus and encourage progress. For example, a person who has a long-term goal of graduating with a degree in nursing may want to accomplish the following short-term goals in the next six months:

- Learn the names, locations, and functions of every human bone and muscle.
- Work with a study group to understand the muscular-skeletal system.

These same goals can be broken down into even smaller parts, such as the following one-month goals:

- Work with on-screen tutorials of the muscular-skeletal system until I understand and memorize the material.
- Spend three hours a week with a study group.

In addition to monthly goals, you may have short-term goals that extend for a week, a day, or even a couple of hours in a given day. For instance, consider the example above of spending three hours a week with a study partner. To support this month-long goal of regularly meeting with a study partner, one may wish to set the following short-term goals:

- **By the end of today:** Call study partners to ask them about when they might be able to meet
- **One week from now:** Will have scheduled each of our weekly meetings this month
- **Two weeks from now:** Will have attended first meeting
- **Three weeks from now:** Will have typed and sent notes to others from the first meeting; have the second meeting

As you consider your long- and short-term goals, notice how all of your goals are linked to one another. As Key 2.1 shows, your long-term goals establish a context for the short-term goals. In turn, your short-term goals make the long-term goals seem clearer and more attainable.

At any given time, you will be working toward goals of varying importance. Setting priorities helps you decide where and when to focus your energy and time.

Prioritize goals

PRIORITIZE

To arrange or deal with in order of importance.

When you prioritize, you evaluate everything you are working toward, decide which goals are most important, and focus your time and energy on them. What should you consider as you evaluate?

- **Your values.** Thinking about what you value will help you establish the goals that take top priority—for example, completing all your class work on time; developing a strong network of personal contacts.

- **Your personal situation.** Are you going to school and working part-time? Are you a parent with young children who need your attention? Are you an athlete on a sports team? Every individual situation requires unique priorities and scheduling.
- **Your time commitments.** Hours of your day may already be committed to classes, family, team practices, or a job. Your challenge is to make sure these commitments reflect what you value and to establish priorities for the remaining hours.

As you will see later in the chapter, setting clear priorities will help you manage your time and accomplish more.

Goals are dreams with deadlines.

DIANA SCHARF HUNT

Goals reinforce one another.

key
2.1

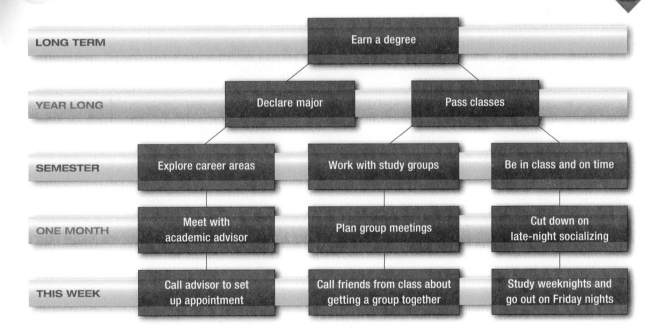

LONG TERM		Earn a degree	
YEAR LONG	Declare major		Pass classes
SEMESTER	Explore career areas	Work with study groups	Be in class and on time
ONE MONTH	Meet with academic advisor	Plan group meetings	Cut down on late-night socializing
THIS WEEK	Call advisor to set up appointment	Call friends from class about getting a group together	Study weeknights and go out on Friday nights

Work to achieve goals

When you've done all the work to think through a goal you want to achieve, these practical steps will help you achieve it. Remember, the more specific your plans, the more likely you are to fulfill them.

- **Define your goal-setting strategy:** *How do you plan to reach your goal?* Brainstorm different paths that might get you there. Choose one; then map out its steps and strategies. Focus on specific behaviours and events that are under your control and that are measurable.
- **Set a timetable:** *When do you want to accomplish your goal?* Set a realistic timeline that includes specific deadlines for each step and strategy you have defined. Charting your progress will help you stay on track.

- Be accountable for your progress: *What safeguards will keep you on track?* Define a personal reporting or buddy system that makes accountability a priority.
- Plan for obstacles: *What will you do if you hit a roadblock?* Define two ways to get help with your efforts if you run into trouble. Be ready to pursue more creative ideas if those don't work.

Through this process, you will continually be thinking about how well you are using your time. In fact, goal achievement is directly linked to effective time management.

Key 2.1 on page 37 is an example of a long-term goal broken down into weekly, monthly, and yearly short-term goals. Accomplishing these short-term goals will support achievement of the long-term goal.

IN-CLASS NOTES

HOW DO YOU SET AND ACHIEVE GOALS?

- Goals are set:
  - long-term
  - short-term
- Goals are achieved by:
  - Working step-by-step
  - Prioritizing

---

get creative!

MAP OUT A PERSONAL GOAL

One way to map out a personal goal plan like the one in Key 2.1 is to work backward to find an interesting path toward an important goal.

Try it here:

Name one important personal goal you have this year.

_____

Now imagine that you have made it to the end—you already achieved your goal—and an impressed friend asks you to describe how you did it. Write your answer here, in a paragraph, as though you were telling this person about the specific steps you took to achieve your goal.

_____

_____

_____

_____

Finally, examine what you've written. You've just created a potential plan! Consider putting it—or a plan similar to it—to work. As you begin, let the image of the success you created in this exercise motivate and inspire you!

How can you effectively *manage your time?*

Time is a universal resource; everyone has the same 24 hours in a day, every day. Depending on what's happening in your life, however, your sense of time may change. On some days you feel like you have hours to spare, while on others the clock becomes your worst enemy.

Your challenge is to turn time into a goal-achievement tool by making smart choices about how to use it. Think of each day as a jigsaw puzzle: You have all of the pieces in a pile, and your task is to form a picture of how you want your day to look. Successful time management starts with identifying your time-related needs and preferences. This self-knowledge sets the stage for building and managing your schedule, avoiding procrastination, and being flexible in the face of change.

Identify your time-related needs and preferences

Body rhythms and habits affect how each person deals with time. Some people are night owls; others are at their best in the morning. Some people are chronically late; others get everything done with time to spare. An awareness of your needs and preferences will help you create a schedule that maximizes your strengths and cuts down on stress. If you are a morning person, for example, look for courses that meet early in the day. If you work best at night, schedule most of your study time then. You will need to find out when your "best" time is and then work around that. It may be late at night when everyone is asleep and the house is quiet or during the day when there is more daylight. However, it is usually best to create a routine schedule whereby you study at approximately the same time every day. Then stick to the routine.

Take the following steps to identify your time-related needs and preferences:

Create a personal time "profile." Ask yourself these questions: At what time of day do I have the most energy? When do I have the least energy? Do I tend to be early, on time, or late? Do I focus well for long stretches or need regular breaks? Your answers will help you find the schedule set-up that works best for you.

Evaluate the effects of your profile. Which of your time-related habits and preferences will have a positive impact on your success at school? Which are likely to cause problems?

Establish what schedule preferences suit your profile best. Make a list of these preferences—or even map out an ideal schedule as a way of illustrating them. For example, one student's preference list might read: "Classes scheduled back to back on Mondays, Wednesdays, and Fridays. Tuesdays, Thursdays, and weekends free for studying and research. Study time primarily during the day and work in the evenings." Another might prefer to distribute classes more evenly throughout the week and study between classes and in the evening. Yet another might take evening classes once or twice a week to allow for work during the day and study on evenings and weekends.

Next, it's time to build the schedule that takes all of this information into account, helping you maximize your strengths and compensate for your weaker time-management areas.

Build a schedule

You've set up your "goal map," with all of the steps that you need to accomplish in order to reach your destination. With a schedule, you place each step in time and, by doing so, commit to making it happen. Schedules help you gain control of your life in two ways: They provide segments of time for tasks related to the fulfillment of your goals, and they remind you of tasks, events, due dates, responsibilities, and deadlines.

Use a planner

A planner is the ideal practical tool for managing your time. With it, you can keep track of events and commitments, schedule goal-related tasks, and rank tasks according to priority. Time-management expert Paul Timm states that "rule number one in a thoughtful planning process is: Use some form of a planner where you can write things down."[5]

There are two major types of planners. One is a book or notebook in which to note commitments. If you write detailed daily plans, look for the kind that devotes a page to each day. Just remember that a week passes very quickly and you must flip the pages to see what is coming up throughout the week. Therefore, if you prefer to see more than one day at a glance, try the planner that shows a week's schedule on a two-page spread. The best planners are often ones that break the day into specific time slots that allow you to plan your time during the day. This way, you can not only schedule what needs to get done, but also when you are going to do it.

The other option is an electronic planner or personal digital assistant (PDA). Basic PDA functions allow you to schedule days and weeks, note due dates, make to-do lists, perform mathematical calculations, and create and store an address book.

Whichever form you choose, the important thing is to have some type of planner that you can carry with you. By far, this is one of the most important strategies for success in post-secondary education.

Keep track of events and commitments

A planner is a necessary tool for success in higher learning because it helps you schedule, commit to, and remember important tasks and events. A quick look at your notations will remind you when due dates and necessary events are approaching. Among the events and commitments worth noting in your planner are

- Test and quiz dates; due dates for papers, projects, and presentations.
- Daily tasks that need to be accomplished for study or assignments.
- Short-term deadlines toward a long-term goal, such as due dates for sections of a large project that has been broken down into a series of smaller tasks.
- Details of your academic schedule, including semester and holiday breaks.
- Club and organizational meetings.
- Personal or family needs—medical appointments, due dates for bills, birthdays, social events.

In addition to the above, in your planner, also include class preparation time including reading and studying, and working on and writing assignments and projects. A formula generally used in post-secondary institutions is to schedule at least 2 to 3 hours of study time each week for every hour you spend in class. That is, if you take a course that requires 3 hours of class time per week, you should study about 6 to 9 hours per week outside of class. This means you must budget approximately 9 to 12 hours total per week for that one course. Using this formula, a full-time college or university student taking 15 credits would require about 15 hours per week of class time plus 30 to 45 hours per week for study outside of class time for a total of 45 to 60 hours per week dedicated to school. However, surveys have shown that many post-secondary students study for fewer than 15 hours per week,[6] which is not enough to learn and master the material.

First year students, in particular, often are not prepared for the workload they encounter in post-secondary courses. As a new student, you must not only budget time to learn the textbook and the material from class, but also plan adequate time to complete assignments and review for tests. *What* you learn in first year may be very different from what you have learned in the past, and more significantly, *how* you learn will also be very different.[7] You will need to become more independent in your learning and to see your instructors as facilitators who are there to help you learn, but you must take charge and be responsible for your own learning. This begins with budgeting enough time to get it all done.

Monday	Tuesday	Wednesday	Thursday	Friday	Saturday	Sunday
9 AM: Economics class Talk with study group members to schedule meeting.	3–5 PM: Study econ chapter 3.	9 AM: Economics class Drop by instructor's office hours to ask question about test	6 PM: Go over chapter 3 7–9 PM: Study group meeting.	9 AM: Economics class—Test 3:30 PM: Meet w/advisor to discuss GMAT and other business school requirements	Sleep in— schedule some down time	5 PM: Go over quiz questions with study partner

Schedule tasks and activities that support your goals

Linking the events in your planner to your goals will give meaning to your efforts and bring order to your schedule. Planning study time for your courses will mean more to you if you link the hours you spend to your short-term and/or long-term goals. For example, when studying for an economics test, keep in mind your goal of being accepted into a business program.

Here is how a student might translate his or her goal of entering a business program into action steps over a year's time:

This year: Complete enough courses to meet entrance requirements for business program and maintain good academic standing

This semester: Complete economics class with a B average or higher

This month: Set up economics study group schedule to coincide with quizzes and tests

This week: Meet with study group; go over material for Friday's test

Today: Review Chapter 3 of economics textbook notes

This student can then arrange time to move in the direction of the long-term goal and schedule activities that support the short-term goal of doing well on the test. These activities are recorded in a planner as shown in the example above. Achieving the overarching long-term goal of doing well in a course needed for a business program is the source of his or her motivation.

Before each week begins, remind yourself of your long-term goals and what you can accomplish over the next seven days to move you closer to them. Key 2.2 (see p. 43) shows parts of a daily schedule and a weekly schedule.

Indicate priority levels

On any given day, the items on your schedule have varying degrees of importance. Prioritizing these items boosts scheduling success in two ways. First, it helps you to identify your most important tasks and to focus the bulk of your energy and time on them. Second, it helps you plan when in your day to get things done. Since many top-priority items (classes, work) occur at designated times, prioritizing helps you lock in these activities and schedule less urgent items around them.

One strategy is to indicate priority levels using three different categories. You can identify these categories by using any code that makes sense to you. Some people use numbers, some use letters (A, B, C), and some use different-coloured pens. The three categories are as follows:

- *Priority 1* items are the most crucial. They may include attending class, completing assignments, working at a job, picking up a child from daycare, and paying bills. Enter Priority 1 items on your planner first, before scheduling anything else.

- *Priority 2* items are important but more flexible parts of your routine. Examples include library study time, completing an assignment for a club, household chores, and exercising. Schedule these around Priority 1 items.

- *Priority 3* items are least important—the "it would be nice if I could get to that" items. Examples include making a social phone call, stocking up on birthday cards, and cleaning out a closet. Many people don't enter Priority 3 tasks in their planners until they know they have time for them. Others keep a separate list of these tasks so that when they have free time they can consult it and choose what they want to accomplish.

Use scheduling techniques

The following strategies will help you turn your scheduling activities into tools that move you closer to your goals:

Plan regularly. Spending time planning your schedule will reduce stress and save you from the hours of work that might result if you forget something important. At the beginning of each week, write down specific time commitments as well as your goals and priorities. Decide where to fit activities like work, studying, exercise, and recreation. For example, if you have a test on Thursday, you can plan review sessions on the preceding days. If you have more free time on Tuesday and Friday, you can plan exercise or recreation activities or other lower priority tasks. Your planner helps you only when you use it—keep it with you and check it and modify it as necessary, throughout the day.

Post monthly and yearly calendars at home. Keeping track of your major commitments on a monthly wall calendar will give you the overview you need to

Note daily and weekly tasks.

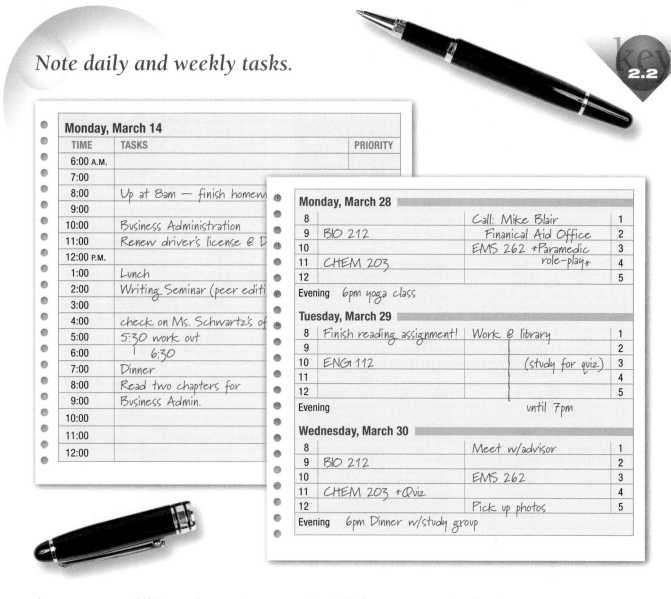

Monday, March 14

TIME	TASKS	PRIORITY
6:00 A.M.		
7:00		
8:00	Up at 8am — finish homew	
9:00		
10:00	Business Administration	
11:00	Renew driver's license @ D	
12:00 P.M.		
1:00	Lunch	
2:00	Writing Seminar (peer editi	
3:00		
4:00	check on Ms. Schwartz's of	
5:00	5:30 work out	
6:00	↓ 6:30	
7:00	Dinner	
8:00	Read two chapters for	
9:00	Business Admin.	
10:00		
11:00		
12:00		

Monday, March 28

8		Call: Mike Blair	1
9	BIO 212	Finanical Aid Office	2
10		EMS 262 *Paramedic	3
11	CHEM 203	role-play*	4
12			5
Evening	6pm yoga class		

Tuesday, March 29

8	Finish reading assignment!	Work @ library	1
9			2
10	ENG 112	(study for quiz)	3
11			4
12			5
Evening		until 7pm	

Wednesday, March 30

8		Meet w/advisor	1
9	BIO 212		2
10		EMS 262	3
11	CHEM 203 *Quiz		4
12		Pick up photos	5
Evening	6pm Dinner w/study group		

focus on responsibilities and upcoming events. Key 2.3 shows an example of a monthly calendar. These calendars are very useful for keeping track of due dates, appointments, or important events. They are useful because, at a glance, you can see how busy you are over a longer period, or how much time you have before a due date or significant event. A helpful thing to do is to post 3 or 4 months side by side on a wall so that you can see a whole season or whole semester at a time. Regularly referring to the calendar can prevent due dates and important commitments from sneaking up on you.

Make and use to-do lists. Use a to-do list to record the things you want to accomplish on a given day or week. Write your to-do items on a separate piece of paper so you can set priorities. Then transfer the items you plan to accomplish each day to open time periods in your planner.

To-do lists are critical time-management tools during exam periods and when major projects are due. They will help you rank your responsibilities so that you get things done in order of importance. Another way to use to-do lists is to prepare one before each study period. Having a clear list of priorities and knowing what needs to be accomplished will help you not only to avoid procrastination but also to stay on task and use your time more efficiently.

Keep track of your time with a monthly calendar.

MARCH

SUNDAY	MONDAY	TUESDAY	WEDNESDAY	THURSDAY	FRIDAY	SATURDAY
	1 WORK	2 Turn in English paper topic	3 Dentist 2pm	4 WORK	5	6
7 Frank's birthday	8 Psych Test 9am WORK	9	10 6:30 pm Meeting @ Student Ctr.	11 WORK	12	13 Dinner @ Ryan's
14	15 English paper due WORK	16 Western Civ paper—Library research	17	18 Library 6 p.m. WORK	19 Western Civ makeup class	20
21	22 WORK	23 2 p.m. meeting, psych group project	20 Start running program: 2 km	25 WORK	26 Run 2 km	27
28 Run 3 km	29 WORK	30 Western Civ paper due	31 Run 2 km			

More suggestions for time management

Avoid time traps. Try to stay away from situations that eat up time unnecessarily. Say "no" graciously if you don't have time for a project; curb excess social time that interferes with academics; delegate chores if you find yourself overloaded; pay special attention to how much time you spend surfing the Internet and chatting online. These activities can waste hours.

Schedule down time. Leisure time is more than just a nice break—it's essential to your health and success. A little down time will refresh you and actually improve your productivity when you get back on task. Even half an hour a day helps. Fill the time with whatever relaxes you—reading, listening to music, watching television, chatting online, playing a game or sport, walking, writing, or just doing nothing.

DOWN TIME

Quiet time set aside for relaxation and low-key activity.

Schedule regular breaks during study time. It is important that you take breaks regularly during your study time. In his time-honoured book, *Make the Most of Your Mind*, Tony Buzan states that recall is highest at the beginning and at the end of a study period. Therefore, you should try to create many beginnings and endings to your study periods. That is, he suggests that it is most effective to organize study time into increments of 10 to 45 minutes, depending on the

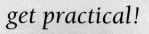

Accomplish practical goals with a to-do list, and reduce stress as a result.

Make a to-do list for what you have to do on your busiest day this week. Include all the tasks and events you know about, including attending class and study time, and the activities you would like to do (exercising at the gym, watching your favourite TV show) if you have extra time. Then prioritize your list using the coding system of your choice.

Date:_____

1. _____   7. _____
2. _____   8. _____
3. _____   9. _____
4. _____   10. _____
5. _____   11. _____
6. _____   12. _____

After examining this list, record your daily schedule in your planner. Include a separate list for Priority 3 items that you can fit into empty time blocks if you finish all your higher priority commitments. At the end of the day, evaluate this system. Did the list make a difference? If you liked it, use this exercise as a guide for using to-do lists regularly.

difficulty of the material, and take short 5- to 10-minute breaks between each. This allows you to process what you have studied and to retain it more effectively than if you study for long periods without breaks. You can still plan two- or three-hour study periods, but take short breaks at least every 30 to 45 minutes.

In addition, try to take a break before your mind begins to wander. This technique not only will make it easier for you to come back to your studies, it will also reward your mind for concentrating. This will reinforce the positive behaviour of concentration rather than the negative mind wandering. Eventually, you will find that you can concentrate for longer and longer periods.

When you come back from your break, take five minutes to review the previous learning before you add new material. You should also review this material again the following day, then weekly and monthly to prevent forgetting. You will find more on this in the chapter on memory.

Avoid procrastination

It is common for busy people to put off difficult or undesirable tasks until later. If taken to the extreme, however, **procrastination** can develop into a habit that causes serious problems. People who procrastinate may do so for a variety of different reasons, including miscalculation of how much time might be required to complete a task, lack of motivation, or plain laziness. Some common reasons people procrastinate are:

PROCRASTINATION
The act of putting off a task until another time.

Perfectionism. According to Jane B. Burka and Lenora M. Yuen, authors of *Procrastination: Why You Do It and What to Do About It*, habitual procrastinators often gauge their self-worth solely by their ability to achieve. In other words, "an outstanding performance means an outstanding person; a mediocre performance means a mediocre person."[8] To the perfectionist procrastinator, not trying at all is better than an attempt that falls short of perfection.

Fear of limitations. Some people procrastinate in order to avoid the truth about what they can achieve. By putting the task off to the last minute, this type of procrastinator can always attribute poor results to "not having enough time" rather than his or her own lack of ability. "As long as you procrastinate, you never have to confront the real limits of your ability, whatever those limits are,"[9] say Burka and Yuen.

Fear of expectations. Some procrastinators do so because of the expectations that may be placed on them. That is, if they work diligently and do very well at something, this may set up expectations, from others or even themselves, of a higher standard. The bar may be raised a bit higher for the future, and this would mean that they would have to continue to work harder and maintain this higher standard.

Even if you're on the right track, you'll get run over if you just sit there.

WILL ROGERS

Facing an overwhelming task. Some projects are so big that they seem too difficult or confusing. This can create immobilizing fear. If a person facing such a task fears failure, he or she may procrastinate to avoid confronting the fear.

How to avoid procrastination

Although it can bring relief in the short term, avoiding tasks almost always causes problems, such as a buildup of responsibilities and less time to complete them, work that is not up to par, the disappointment of others who are depending on your work, and stress brought on by the weight of the unfinished tasks. Particular strategies can help you avoid procrastination and the problems associated with it.

Analyze the effects of procrastinating. What may happen if you continue to put off a responsibility? Are the consequences serious enough to motivate you to stop procrastinating? Chances are you will benefit more in the long term from facing the task head-on and just getting it done.

Set reasonable goals. Unreasonable goals can intimidate and immobilize you. Set manageable goals and allow enough time to complete them.

Break tasks into smaller parts. If you concentrate on achieving one small step at a time, the task may become less burdensome. Setting concrete time limits for each task may help you feel more in control.

Get started whether or not you "feel like it." The motivation techniques from Chapter 1 might help you take the first step. Schedule a short period of time, even just 10 or 15 minutes, to get started. You don't have to work on it longer than that. Just getting it started is an accomplishment. However, once you start, you may find it easier to continue.

Ask for help. You don't have to go it alone. Once you identify what's holding you up, see who can help you face the task. Another person may come up with an innovative way to help you get moving.

Don't expect perfection. No one is perfect. Most people learn by starting at the beginning, making mistakes, and learning from those mistakes. It's better to try your best than to do nothing at all.

Reward yourself. Find ways to boost your confidence when you accomplish a particular task. Remind yourself—with a break, a movie, some kind of treat—that you are making progress.

Just say, "No." If you try all of the above strategies but still find yourself procrastinating, realize that every moment you procrastinate you are making a decision not to do the task. So be honest with yourself and admit that you are not going to do it. By making this decision, you will no longer be procrastinating.

Be flexible

No matter how well you plan your time, sudden changes can upend your plans. Any change, whether minor (a room change for a class) or major (a medical emergency), can cause stress. As your stress level rises, your sense of control dwindles.

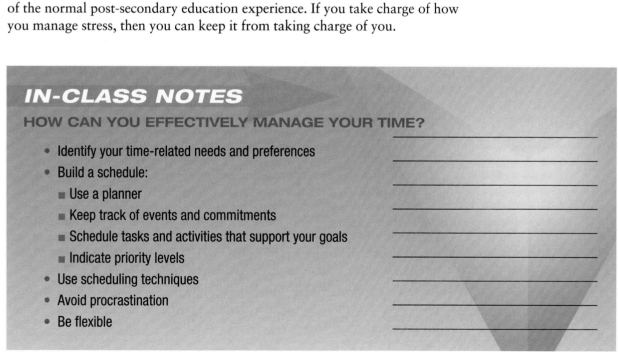

Although you can't always choose your circumstances, you have some control over how you handle them. Your ability to evaluate situations, come up with creative options, and put practical plans to work will help you manage the changes that you will inevitably encounter. For changes that occur frequently, think through a backup plan ahead of time. For surprises, the best you can do is keep an open mind about possibilities and rely on your internal and external resources.

When change involves serious problems—your car breaks down and you have no way to get to school; you fail a class; or a family member develops a medical problem and needs you to spend more time at home, for example—use problem-solving skills to help you through. As you will see in Chapter 4, problem solving involves identifying and analyzing the problem, brainstorming and exploring possible solutions, and choosing the solution you decide is best. Most educational institutions have resources available to help you throughout this process. Academic advisors, counsellors, financial aid advisors, and instructors may have ideas and provide assistance.

Change is one of many factors associated with stress. In fact, stress is part of the normal post-secondary education experience. If you take charge of how you manage stress, then you can keep it from taking charge of you.

IN-CLASS NOTES
HOW CAN YOU EFFECTIVELY MANAGE YOUR TIME?

- Identify your time-related needs and preferences
- Build a schedule:
  - Use a planner
  - Keep track of events and commitments
  - Schedule tasks and activities that support your goals
  - Indicate priority levels
- Use scheduling techniques
- Avoid procrastination
- Be flexible

How do you *cope with the stress* of being a student?

If you are feeling more stress in your everyday life as a student, you are not alone.[10] According to some surveys, stress levels among college or university students have increased dramatically in recent years. Stress factors for post-secondary students include being in a new and unfamiliar environment; facing increased workloads and making difficult decisions; and juggling school, work, family, and personal responsibilities.

Stress refers to the way in which your mind and body react to pressure. Pressure comes from situations like heavy workloads (exams and assignments), excitement (being a finalist for the lead in a play), change (new school, new courses), being short on time (working 20 hours a week at a job and trying to find time to study), or illness (having a head cold that wipes you out for a week).

The Social Readjustment Scale, developed by psychologists T. H. Holmes and R. H. Rahe, measures the intensity of people's reaction to change and the level of stress related to it (see Key 2.4). Holmes and Rahe found that people experience both positive and negative events as stressors. For example, whereas some events like the death of a relative are clearly negative, other stressors, like moving to a new home or even taking a vacation, are generally positive.

At their worst, stress reactions can make you physically ill (Chapter 10 will examine stress-related health issues—situations in which stress goes beyond normal levels, causing physical and emotional problems). But stress can also supply the heightened readiness you need to do well on tests, finish assignments on time, prepare for a class presentation, or meet new people. Your goal is to find a manageable balance. Key 2.5 (see p. 50) shows that stress can be helpful or harmful, depending on how much you experience.

Stress management strategies

Dealing with the stress of student life is, and will continue to be, one of your biggest challenges. But here's a piece of good news: Every goal-achievement and time-management strategy you have read in this chapter contributes to your ability to cope with stress. Remember that stress refers to how you react to pressure. When you make effective plans to move toward goals, you reduce pressure. When you set a schedule that works for you and stick to it, you reduce pressure. Less pressure results in less stress.

Here are some more specific practical strategies for coping with the day-to-day stress of being a student.

- **Eat right.** The healthier you are, the stronger you are and the more you will be able to cope with tough situations like studying for long hours, illnesses, and challenging academic work. Try to eat a balanced diet, low in sugar and fat, and maintain a healthy weight.
- **Exercise.** Physical exercise will help you manage your stress. Find a type of exercise you like and make it a regular part of your life. Schedule time for it in your planner.

Use the Holmes-Rahe scale to find your "stress score."

To find your current "stress score," add the values of the events that you experienced in the past year. The higher the number, the greater the stress. Scoring over 300 points puts you at high risk for developing a stress-related health problem. A score between 150 and 299 reduces your risk by 30 percent, and a score under 150 means that you have only a small chance of a problem.

EVENT	VALUE	EVENT	VALUE
Death of spouse or partner	100	Son or daughter leaving home	29
Divorce	73	Trouble with in-laws	29
Marital separation	65	Outstanding personal achievement	28
Jail term	63	Spouse begins or stops work	26
Personal injury	53	Starting or finishing school	26
Marriage	50	Change in living conditions	25
Fired from work	47	Revision of personal habits	24
Marital reconciliation	45	Trouble with boss	23
Retirement	45	Change in work hours, conditions	20
Changes in family member's health	44	Change in residence	20
Pregnancy	40	Change in schools	20
Sex difficulties	39	Change in recreational habits	19
Addition to family	39	Change in religious activities	19
Business readjustment	39	Change in social activities	18
Change in financial status	38	Mortgage or loan under $10,000	17
Death of a close friend	37	Change in sleeping habits	16
Change to different line of work	36	Change in # of family gatherings	15
Change in # of marital arguments	35	Change in eating habits	15
Mortgage or loan over $10,000	31	Vacation	13
Foreclosure of mortgage or loan	30	Christmas season	12
Change in work responsibilities	29	Minor violation of the law	11

Source: Reprinted from *Journal of Psychosomatic Research, 11(2)*, T. H. Holmes and R. H. Rahe, "The social readjustment rating scale," 1967, with permission from Elsevier Science Inc.

- **Get sleep.** Avoid the generalized dysfunction that sleep deprivation can create. Figure out how much sleep you need and do your best to get it.

- **Think positively.** Try to think of all the things you have to do as challenges, not problems.

- **Seek balance.** A balanced life includes time for work and time for play. It also includes time for yourself—for your thoughts, hopes, and plans—and time for relaxation, in whatever form you choose.

- **Address issues.** Try not to let things lie too long. Analyze stressful situations and use problem-solving strategies (see Chapter 4) to decide on a specific plan of action.

- **Set boundaries and learn to say no.** Try to delegate. Review obligations regularly; if you decide that something has become a burden, then consider dropping it from your roster of activities.

- **Surround yourself with people who are good for you.** Focus on friends who are good listeners and who will support you when things get rough. Friendship and humour go a long way toward reducing stress.

Stress levels can help or hinder performance.

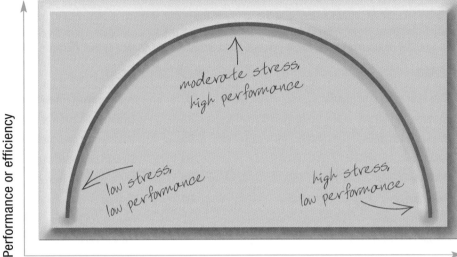

Source: From *Your Maximum Mind* by Herbert Benson, M.D., Copyright © 1987 by Random House, Inc., Used by permission of Time Books, a division of Random House.

Remember: *Any step toward a goal is a stress-management strategy because it reduces pressure.* In that sense, this entire book is a stress-management strategy. Every useful tool, from test-taking hints to job-hunting strategies, will help you reduce the pressure and allow you to start working toward your dreams.

IN-CLASS NOTES

HOW DO YOU COPE WITH THE STRESS OF BEING A STUDENT?

- Eating right
- Exercising
- Getting adequate sleep
- Thinking positively
- Seeking balance
- Addressing troubling issues
- Setting boundaries
- Finding support

_____

_____

_____

_____

_____

_____

In Hebrew, this word, pronounced "chai," means "life," representing all aspects of life—spiritual, emotional, family, educational, and career. Individual Hebrew characters have number values. Because the characters in the word *chai* add up to 18, the number 18 has come to be associated with good luck. The word *chai* is often worn as a good luck charm. The phrase *l'chaim* means "to life" and good luck.

As you plan your goals, think about the role luck may play in your success. If you work strategically and are open to new opportunities, you may find yourself in the right place at the right time to benefit from a "lucky break." Because you are prepared, you may find someone who is so impressed by your tenacity and focus that he or she offers to become your mentor. Or, after you complete your course work, you may meet someone with a business opportunity that is a perfect match for your skills, and you are hired on the spot. All your hard work in the direction of your goal will prepare you to take advantage of lucky breaks that come your way.

SUGGESTED READINGS

Allen, David. *Getting Things Done: The Art of Stress-Free Productivity*. New York: Penguin Books, 2003.

Burka, Jane B., and Lenora M. Yuen. *Procrastination*. Reading, MA: Perseus Books, 1983.

Buzan, Tony. *Make the Most of Your Mind*. New York: Fireside Books, 1988.

Covey, Stephen. *The Seven Habits of Highly Effective People*. New York: Simon & Schuster, 1995.

Emmett, Rita. *The Procrastinator's Handbook: Mastering the Art of Doing It Now*. New York: Walker & Co., 2000.

Gleeson, Kerry. *The Personal Efficiency Program: How to Get Organized to Do More Work in Less Time*. 2nd ed. New York: John Wiley & Sons, 2000.

Kidwell, Kirk, and Bob Reising. "Understanding the College First Year Experience." *Clearing House* 78 (2005): 253–255.

Lakein, Alan. *How to Get Control of Your Time and Your Life*. New York: New American Library, 1996.

Leyden-Rubenstein, Lori. *The Stress Management Handbook*. New York: McGraw-Hill, 1999.

Sapadin, Linda, and Jack Maguire. *Beat Procrastination and Make the Grade: The Six Styles of Procrastination and How Students Can Overcome Them*. New York: Penguin USA, 1999.

Timm, Paul R. *Successful Self-Management: A Psychologically Sound Approach to Personal Effectiveness*. Los Altos, CA: Crisp Publications, 1996.

INTERNET RESOURCES

Keys to Success Companion Website: www.pearsoned.ca/carter

Motivation and Goal Setting Worksheet. Counselling Dept., University of Victoria: www.coun.uvic.ca/learn/program/hndouts/goals.html

Strategies for Stress Management. Nancy Willihnganz, Counselling Dept., University of Victoria: www.coun.uvic.ca/personal/stresmgt.html

Links to Sites on Stress Management. Ministry of Training, Colleges and Universities, Gov't of Ontario: www.edu.gov.on.ca/eng/career/stress.html

Mind Tools (section on time management): www.mindtools.com/pages/main/newMN_HTE.htm

Top Achievement—goal-setting and self-improvement resources: www.topachievement.com

About.com stress-management resources: http://stress.about.com

Troubled With—information on stress management: www.troubledwith.com

Developing Successful Intelligence

PUTTING IT ALL TOGETHER

The Wheel of Life. This exercise uses a wheel—an image that has been used for centuries to promote understanding of the self and the world—to help you think about your strengths and weaknesses in eight important goal areas. Assess your level of proficiency in self-knowledge, study skills, personal life goals, finances, health and stress management, relationships, career, and time management by filling out the wheel as directed in Key 2.6.

Let this self-assessment help you make decisions about how you approach the material in this course. If you need work on study skills, for example, then focus specifically on the reading, note-taking, and test-taking chapters. At the end of the book you will have a chance to revisit the Wheel. If you learn all there is to know in this course, you should see improvement in your weaker goal areas over the course of the semester. Plus, you will have developed your ability to evaluate and manage yourself—a skill that is crucial to your success in school and at work.

Team Building

COLLABORATIVE SOLUTIONS

Multiple paths to a goal. This exercise will help you learn how to establish and commit to a goal. It will also show you how to develop ideas about how to approach one particular goal and realize how many possible paths you could follow to reach it.

1. In a group of three or four, brainstorm goals that focus on building a life skill—for example, leadership, teamwork, learning a foreign language.

_____

_____

_____

_____

52

(continued on page 54)

Build self-knowledge with the Wheel of Life.

Rate yourself in each area of the wheel on a scale of 1 to 10, 1 being least developed (near the center of the wheel) and 10 being most developed (the outer edge of the wheel). In each area, at the level of the number you choose, draw a curved line and fill in the wedge below that line. Be honest—this is for your benefit only. Finally, look at what your wheel says about the balance in your life. If this were a real wheel, how well would it roll?

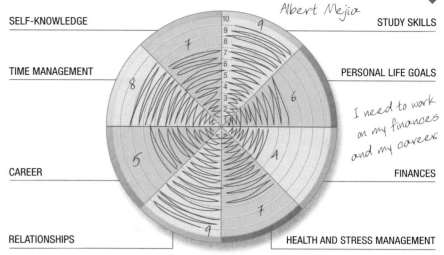

Sample Wheel

SELF-KNOWLEDGE
(learning styles, interests, abilities)

STUDY SKILLS
(reading, note taking, writing, test taking)

TIME MANAGEMENT

PERSONAL LIFE GOALS

Where do you need to improve?

CAREER

FINANCES

RELATIONSHIPS
(family, friends, significant other)

HEALTH AND STRESS MANAGEMENT

Source: Based on "The Wheel of Life" model developed by the Coaches Training Institute. © Co-Active Space 2000.

2. From that list, pick out one goal to explore together.

_____

3. Each group member takes two minutes alone to think about this goal in terms of the first goal-achievement step on page 37—defining a strategy. In other words, answer the question: "How would I do it?" Each person writes down all of the paths he or she can think of.

_____

_____

4. Each group member shares his or her strategy. The group considers each of the strategies and chooses one that seems effective.

_____

_____

5. Finally, as a group, brainstorm the rest of the goal-achievement process, for the chosen strategy or path:

- Set a timetable. When do you plan to reach your goal? Discuss different time frames and how each might change the path.

_____

_____

- Be accountable. What safeguards will keep you on track? Talk about different ways to make sure you are moving ahead consistently.

_____

_____

- Plan for obstacles. What will you do if you hit a roadblock? Brainstorm the kinds of roadblocks that could get in the way of this particular goal. For each, come up with ways to overcome the obstacle.

_____

_____

At the end of the process, you should now have a wealth of ideas about how to approach one particular goal—and an appreciation for how many possible paths you could follow to get there.

Writing

DISCOVERY THROUGH JOURNALING

Use the tables and spaces below to record data and answer questions. Write additional thoughts here or on a separate piece of paper or in a journal.

Discover how you spend your time.

1. Brainstorm everything you must accomplish this week. Include all activities, appointments, commitments, events, or responsibilities you must attend to this week. Be sure even to list routines like grooming, sleeping, eating, watching TV, etc.

_____

_____

_____

_____

_____

2. Use your list above to estimate the time you think you spend per week on each listed activity and enter the totals in the appropriate category under "Estimated Time Spent" on the chart below. Then add those hours to find an estimated grand total of hours you need this week to complete everything.

Activity	Estimated Time Spent	Adjusted Time to be Spent	Activity	Estimated Time Spent	Adjusted Time to be Spent
Class			Chores and personal business		
Work			Friends and important relationships		
Studying			Telephone/email time		
Sleeping			Leisure/entertainment		
Eating			Spiritual life		
Family time/child care			Other		
Commuting/traveling			**ESTIMATED GRAND TOTAL**		

3. There are only 168 hours per week. Are you over or under 168 hours? If your total is under 168 hours, yet it always seems as if you do not have enough time, go back over your list. Are there any activities missing, or have you underestimated the time required for some activities? If your number is over 168 hours, prioritize your activities and rethink your estimates so that the adjusted total of the hours is equal to or less than 168.

4. Now spend a few days recording exactly how you spend your time. You might just keep this by your bedside and record your day before going to bed. The chart on pages 58–59 has blocks showing half-hour increments. As you go through the week, write in what you do each hour, indicating when you started and when you stopped. Don't forget activities that don't feel like "activities," such as sleeping, relaxing, and watching TV. Finally, be sure to record your actual activities instead of how you want to have spent—or think you should have spent—your time. There are no wrong answers. Completing this exercise honestly will help you realize how you are actually spending your time and not just how you "think" you are spending it.

5. At the end of the week, go through the chart below and add up how many hours you spent on the activities for which you previously estimated your hours. Tally the hours in the boxes in the following table using straight tally marks; round off to half hours and use a short tally mark for each half hour. In the third column, total the hours for each activity. Leave the "Ideal Time in Hours" column blank for now.

Add the totals in the third column to find your grand total.

Activity	Time Tallied Over One-Week Period	Total Time in Hours	Ideal Time in Hours
Example: Class	~~HH~~ ~~HH~~ ~~HH~~ I₁	16.5	
Class			
Work			
Studying			
Sleeping			
Eating			
Family time/child care			
Commuting/traveling			
Chores and personal business			
Friends and important relationships			
Telephone/email time			
Leisure/entertainment			
Spiritual life			
Other			
ACTUAL GRAND TOTAL			

6. Compare your actual grand total to your estimated grand total. Then compare your actual time spent in hours for each category to your "Estimated Time Spent" totals (from the chart on page 55).

   - What matches and what does not? Describe the most interesting similarities and differences.

     _____

     _____

   - Where do you waste the most time? What do you think that is costing you?

     _____

     _____

7. On what activities do you think you should spend more or less time? Go back to the chart and fill in the "Ideal Time in Hours" column.

   _____

   _____

- What are you willing to do to change, and why?

  _____

  _____

- Describe what goal you are aiming for, and map out how you plan to put the changes into action.

  _____

  _____

Career Portfolio

PLAN FOR SUCCESS

Complete the following in the spaces below or in your electronic portfolio or on separate sheets of paper.

Career goals—knowledge and skills.

1. No matter what career goals you ultimately pursue, certain knowledge and skills are useful in any career area. Consider this list of the general skills that employers look for in people they hire:

Acceptance	Critical thinking	Leadership
Communication	Flexibility	Positive attitude
Continual learning	Goal setting	Teamwork
Creativity	Integrity	

   Choose and circle three of these that you want to focus on developing this year.

2. Map out a plan for your progress by indicating a series of smaller goals—from short-term to long-term—that will lead you toward developing these skills. For two of the three skills, use the spaces below to write what you hope to accomplish in the next year, the next six months, and the next month. For example:

   Skill: Leadership

   Next month: I will volunteer to lead a session with my Economics study group.

   In six months: I will look into leadership positions on the college newspaper.

   By the end of the year: I will have joined the newspaper team and expressed my interest in a leadership position.

Skill: _____

Next month I will _____

In six months I will _____

By the end of the year I will _____

Skill: _____

Next month I will _____

In six months I will _____

By the end of the year I will _____

Monday		Tuesday		Wednesday		Thursday	
TIME	ACTIVITY	TIME	ACTIVITY	TIME	ACTIVITY	TIME	ACTIVITY
6:00 A.M.		6:00 A.M.		6:00 A.M.		6:00 A.M.	
6:30 A.M.		6:30 A.M.		6:30 A.M.		6:30 A.M.	
7:00 A.M.		7:00 A.M.		7:00 A.M.		7:00 A.M.	
7:30 A.M.		7:30 A.M.		7:30 A.M.		7:30 A.M.	
8:00 A.M.		8:00 A.M.		8:00 A.M.		8:00 A.M.	
8:30 A.M.		8:30 A.M.		8:30 A.M.		8:30 A.M.	
9:00 A.M.		9:00 A.M.		9:00 A.M.		9:00 A.M.	
9:30 A.M.		9:30 A.M.		9:30 A.M.		9:30 A.M.	
10:00 A.M.		10:00 A.M.		10:00 A.M.		10:00 A.M.	
10:30 A.M.		10:30 A.M.		10:30 A.M.		10:30 A.M.	
11:00 A.M.		11:00 A.M.		11:00 A.M.		11:00 A.M.	
11:30 A.M.		11:30 A.M.		11:30 A.M.		11:30 A.M.	
12:00 P.M.		12:00 P.M.		12:00 P.M.		12:00 P.M.	
12:30 P.M.		12:30 P.M.		12:30 P.M.		12:30 P.M.	
1:00 P.M.		1:00 P.M.		1:00 P.M.		1:00 P.M.	
1:30 P.M.		1:30 P.M.		1:30 P.M.		1:30 P.M.	
2:00 P.M.		2:00 P.M.		2:00 P.M.		2:00 P.M.	
2:30 P.M.		2:30 P.M.		2:30 P.M.		2:30 P.M.	
3:00 P.M.		3:00 P.M.		3:00 P.M.		3:00 P.M.	
3:30 P.M.		3:30 P.M.		3:30 P.M.		3:30 P.M.	
4:00 P.M.		4:00 P.M.		4:00 P.M.		4:00 P.M.	
4:30 P.M.		4:30 P.M.		4:30 P.M.		4:30 P.M.	
5:00 P.M.		5:00 P.M.		5:00 P.M.		5:00 P.M.	
5:30 P.M.		5:30 P.M.		5:30 P.M.		5:30 P.M.	
6:00 P.M.		6:00 P.M.		6:00 P.M.		6:00 P.M.	
6:30 P.M.		6:30 P.M.		6:30 P.M.		6:30 P.M.	
7:00 P.M.		7:00 P.M.		7:00 P.M.		7:00 P.M.	
7:30 P.M.		7:30 P.M.		7:30 P.M.		7:30 P.M.	
8:00 P.M.		8:00 P.M.		8:00 P.M.		8:00 P.M.	
8:30 P.M.		8:30 P.M.		8:30 P.M.		8:30 P.M.	
9:00 P.M.		9:00 P.M.		9:00 P.M.		9:00 P.M.	
9:30 P.M.		9:30 P.M.		9:30 P.M.		9:30 P.M.	
10:00 P.M.		10:00 P.M.		10:00 P.M.		10:00 P.M.	
10:30 P.M.		10:30 P.M.		10:30 P.M.		10:30 P.M.	
11:00 P.M.		11:00 P.M.		11:00 P.M.		11:00 P.M.	
11:30 P.M.		11:30 P.M.		11:30 P.M.		11:30 P.M.	
12–6 A.M.		12–6 A.M.		12–6 A.M.		12–6 A.M.	

Friday		Saturday		Sunday		Notes
TIME	ACTIVITY	TIME	ACTIVITY	TIME	ACTIVITY	
6:00 A.M.		6:00 A.M.		6:00 A.M.		
6:30 A.M.		6:30 A.M.		6:30 A.M.		
7:00 A.M.		7:00 A.M.		7:00 A.M.		
7:30 A.M.		7:30 A.M.		7:30 A.M.		
8:00 A.M.		8:00 A.M.		8:00 A.M.		
8:30 A.M.		8:30 A.M.		8:30 A.M.		
9:00 A.M.		9:00 A.M.		9:00 A.M.		
9:30 A.M.		9:30 A.M.		9:30 A.M.		
10:00 A.M.		10:00 A.M.		10:00 A.M.		
10:30 A.M.		10:30 A.M.		10:30 A.M.		
11:00 A.M.		11:00 A.M.		11:00 A.M.		
11:30 A.M.		11:30 A.M.		11:30 A.M.		
12:00 P.M.		12:00 P.M.		12:00 P.M.		
12:30 P.M.		12:30 P.M.		12:30 P.M.		
1:00 P.M.		1:00 P.M.		1:00 P.M.		
1:30 P.M.		1:30 P.M.		1:30 P.M.		
2:00 P.M.		2:00 P.M.		2:00 P.M.		
2:30 P.M.		2:30 P.M.		2:30 P.M.		
3:00 P.M.		3:00 P.M.		3:00 P.M.		
3:30 P.M.		3:30 P.M.		3:30 P.M.		
4:00 P.M.		4:00 P.M.		4:00 P.M.		
4:30 P.M.		4:30 P.M.		4:30 P.M.		
5:00 P.M.		5:00 P.M.		5:00 P.M.		
5:30 P.M.		5:30 P.M.		5:30 P.M.		
6:00 P.M.		6:00 P.M.		6:00 P.M.		
6:30 P.M.		6:30 P.M.		6:30 P.M.		
7:00 P.M.		7:00 P.M.		7:00 P.M.		
7:30 P.M.		7:30 P.M.		7:30 P.M.		
8:00 P.M.		8:00 P.M.		8:00 P.M.		
8:30 P.M.		8:30 P.M.		8:30 P.M.		
9:00 P.M.		9:00 P.M.		9:00 P.M.		
9:30 P.M.		9:30 P.M.		9:30 P.M.		
10:00 P.M.		10:00 P.M.		10:00 P.M.		
10:30 P.M.		10:30 P.M.		10:30 P.M.		
11:00 P.M.		11:00 P.M.		11:00 P.M.		
11:30 P.M.		11:30 P.M.		11:30 P.M.		
12–6 A.M.		12–6 A.M.		12–6 A.M.		

Chapter Review Questions

Choose the option that BEST completes the statement or answers the question. After completing the questions, check your answers against the Answer Key at the back of this book (p. 314).

1. Values are
   a. ☐ Principles or qualities that one considers important.
   b. ☐ Unrelated to goals.
   c. ☐ Constant throughout life.
   d. ☐ Unrelated to choices and decisions made.

2. The most powerful influence on establishing a set of values is
   a. ☐ Family.
   b. ☐ Friends.
   c. ☐ Society.
   d. ☐ Yourself.

3. It is important to have academic integrity because
   a. ☐ Having integrity builds one's confidence, ability, knowledge, and reputation.
   b. ☐ It means that one has a code of honour that reflects one's personal values.
   c. ☐ Post-secondary institutions have strict policies on academic honesty and there are consequences for those who do not adhere to the policies.
   d. ☐ All of the above.

4. Developing cultural competence means
   a. ☐ Appreciating diversity.
   b. ☐ Knowing about your own culture.
   c. ☐ Respecting your own values.
   d. ☐ Forming opinions.

5. Long-term goals and short-term goals are similar in that they
   a. ☐ Should be set once and never changed.
   b. ☐ Must be determined by what people expect from you.
   c. ☐ Need to have an open-ended time frame.
   d. ☐ Require a plan of action.

6. The difference between short-term and long-term goals is
   a. ☐ Scope.
   b. ☐ Importance.
   c. ☐ Value.
   d. ☐ Necessity.

7. "Goals are dreams with _____."
   a. ☐ Commitments.
   b. ☐ Priorities.
   c. ☐ Deadlines.
   d. ☐ Strategies.

8. The more specific your plans, the more likely you are to
   a. ☐ Feel stifled and bogged down.
   b. ☐ Abandon them for something else.
   c. ☐ Fulfill them.
   d. ☐ Improve them.

9. Achieving your goals requires
   a. ☐ Defining your strategy.
   b. ☐ Setting a timeline.
   c. ☐ Checking your progress.
   d. ☐ All of the above.

10. The best time to study is
   a. ☐ First thing in the morning.
   b. ☐ Late at night.
   c. ☐ Right after class.
   d. ☐ Probably different for everyone.

11. The recommended amount of time for studying outside of class is

a. ☐ 1 hour of study for every 1 hour in class.

b. ☐ 1 hour of study for every 2 hours in class.

c. ☐ 2 hours of study for every 1 hour in class.

d. ☐ 2 hours of study for every 2 hours in class.

12. When using a planner, you should schedule

a. ☐ Every minute of your day.

b. ☐ Only Priority 1 tasks.

c. ☐ Only the tasks you are likely to forget.

d. ☐ None of the above.

13. An advantage of a daily planner is that it

a. ☐ Allows you to see what you are doing for a whole month at a glance.

b. ☐ Provides enough space for each day so that you can write detailed notes.

c. ☐ Is made to be posted up on a wall.

d. ☐ All of the above.

14. Alice has a major exam in one week. What would be the best schedule for study time?

a. ☐ 10 hours the day before the exam, including four 10-minute breaks.

b. ☐ 5 hours today and 5 hours the day before the exam, including four 10-minute breaks each day.

c. ☐ 90 minutes every day until the exam, including one 10-minute break each day.

d. ☐ 30 minutes every day until the exam, including one 10-minute break each day.

15. Effective time-management skills include

a. ☐ Spending as much time on a course outside of class as you spend in class.

b. ☐ Scheduling "holes" in your schedule to allow for the unexpected.

c. ☐ Using a day planner and planning every minute of your time with scheduled activities and sticking to your plan.

d. ☐ Not allowing any flexibility or spontaneity in your life.

16. Procrastination is the act of

a. ☐ Putting off something that can be done later.

b. ☐ Putting off something that needs to be done.

c. ☐ Asking someone else to do a task for you.

d. ☐ Accomplishing lower priority tasks after higher priority ones.

17. Breaking a difficult task into smaller parts is an effective strategy to

a. ☐ Procrastinate.

b. ☐ Avoid procrastination.

c. ☐ Prioritize goals.

d. ☐ Avoid prioritizing goals.

18. Which of the following is NOT an effective strategy for avoiding procrastination?

a. ☐ Analyzing the effects of procrastinating.

b. ☐ Asking for help.

c. ☐ Rewarding yourself.

d. ☐ Expecting perfection.

19. Some stress can be useful because it

a. ☐ Forces you to take time for relaxation.

b. ☐ Boosts the immune system.

c. ☐ Increases performance.

d. ☐ All of the above.

20. One useful stress-management strategy is

a. ☐ Eating chocolate.

b. ☐ Drinking alcohol.

c. ☐ Exercising regularly.

d. ☐ Sleeping more than you need.

Learning Styles, Education, and Careers

KNOWING YOUR TALENTS AND FINDING YOUR DIRECTION

This chapter is organized as follows:

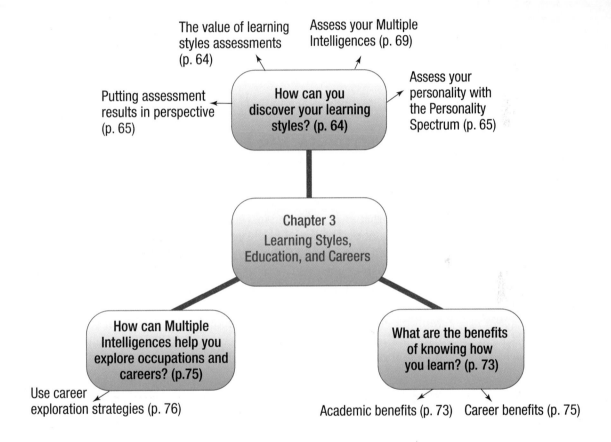

The value of learning styles assessments (p. 64)

Assess your Multiple Intelligences (p. 69)

Putting assessment results in perspective (p. 65)

How can you discover your learning styles? (p. 64)

Assess your personality with the Personality Spectrum (p. 65)

**Chapter 3
Learning Styles, Education, and Careers**

How can Multiple Intelligences help you explore occupations and careers? (p.75)

What are the benefits of knowing how you learn? (p. 73)

Use career exploration strategies (p. 76)

Academic benefits (p. 73)   Career benefits (p. 75)

TEST YOURSELF

- *What are the benefits of knowing how you learn?*
- *How is "intelligence" defined?*
- *What are characteristics of each intelligence?*
- *List study strategies most effective for each intelligence.*
- *What are four personality types according to the Personality Spectrum?*
- *Which of the personality types are "right-brained" dominant? Which are "left-brained"?*

- *Give an example of an effective study technique for each personality type.*
- *In what ways can information about your preferred way to learn benefit your career?*
- *What are some specific strategies you can use to explore your career options?*
- *How can multiple intelligences help you make career decisions?*

For the correct answers and additional questions on Chapter 3, visit www.pearsoned.ca/carter.

As a college or university student, you are investing valuable resources—time, effort, and money—in your education. Learning is the return on your investment. How well you learn depends in part on knowing yourself in two ways: knowing *how* you learn and knowing what you want to *do* with what you learn.

This chapter focuses first on helping you identify your learning styles, because when you understand how you learn, you will be a more effective student. Then you will read about occupations, because knowing where you want your education to take you will motivate you toward a goal.

How can you *discover* your learning styles?

Your style of taking in, processing, and remembering information is as unique as you are. Have you ever thought in detail about what that style is? Doing just that—working to understand your learning strengths and preferences and the primary ways in which you interact with others—will help you achieve your personal best in school and beyond.

This chapter presents two assessments designed to help you figure out how you learn and interact. The first—*Multiple Pathways to Learning*—focuses on learning strengths and preferences and is based on Professor Howard Gardner's Multiple Intelligences Theory. The second—the *Personality Spectrum*—is based on the Myers-Briggs Type Inventory® (MBTI) and helps you evaluate how you react to people and situations.

The value of learning styles assessments

There are some things that you do well and other things that you find difficult. To be a successfully intelligent learner, you need to maximize your strengths and compensate for your weaknesses. The first step toward that goal is to know what those strengths and weaknesses *are*—and that's what these assessments will help you discover. With the information you gain from the Multiple Pathways to Learning and the Personality Spectrum, you can choose your own best ways to study, manage time, remember material, and much more.

To be what we are, and to become what we are capable of becoming, is the only end of life.

ROBERT LOUIS STEVENSON

Knowing how you learn will help you set specific goals for positive change. For example, instead of saying, "I'm no good at math," you can strengthen your math skills with what you will learn from Multiple Pathways to Learning. There are strategies that you can adopt to fit your learning style. For example, you might draw diagrams of math problems if you are a visual learner or discuss solutions to problems with a study partner if you are an interpersonal learner. The better you know yourself, the better you are able to handle different learning situations and challenges.

Gaining an understanding of learning style will also enhance your ability to see and appreciate how people differ, because learning style is part of the diversity that originates within. When you sit in a classroom with a number of other students, you can be sure that each person is learning the material in a unique way. The more you know about how others approach learning, the more you can use that understanding to improve communication and teamwork.

LEARNING STYLE

A particular way in which the mind receives and processes information.

Putting results of assessments in perspective

First, remember that any assessment is simply a snapshot, a look at who you are at a given moment. Your answers can, and will, change as you and the circumstances around you change. These assessments help you look at the present—and plan for the future—by asking questions such as, Who am I right now? How does this compare with who I want to be?

Second, there are no "right" answers nor "best" set of scores. Think of your responses in the same way you would if you were trying on a new set of eyeglasses to correct blurred vision. The glasses will not create new paths and possibilities, but they will help you see more clearly the ones that already exist.

Following each assessment is information about the typical traits of, and appropriate study strategies for, each intelligence or personality spectrum dimension. As you will see from your scores, you have abilities in all areas, though some are more developed than others. Therefore, you will find useful suggestions under all the headings. Try different techniques and keep what works for you.

Assess your personality with the Personality Spectrum

Personality assessments help you understand how you respond to information, thoughts, feelings, people, and events in the world around you. The Personality Spectrum is the assessment tool used in this chapter. It is based on two of the most widely used personality inventories in the world—the Myers-Briggs Type Inventory, developed by Katharine Briggs and her daughter, Isabel Briggs Myers, and the Keirsey Temperament Sorter by David Keirsey and Marilyn Bates.

The Personality Spectrum adapts and simplifies the material from these two tools into four personality types—Thinker, Organizer, Giver, and Adventurer. The Personality Spectrum helps you identify the kinds of interactions that are most, and least, comfortable for you. For each of the four personality types, there are specific study techniques that help improve performance, learning, and ways of relating to others. Some examples of these are presented in Key 3.1 on page 68.

PERSONALITY SPECTRUM

STEP 1. Rank order all 4 responses to each question from most like you (4) to least like you (1) so that for each question you use the numbers 1, 2, 3, and 4 one time each. Place numbers in the boxes next to the responses.

4 most like me   **3** more like me   **2** less like me   **1** least like me

1. I like instructors who
   a. ☐ tell me exactly what is expected of me.
   b. ☐ make learning active and exciting.
   c. ☐ maintain a safe and supportive classroom.
   d. ☐ challenge me to think at higher levels.

2. I learn best when the material is
   a. ☐ well organized.
   b. ☐ something I can do hands-on.
   c. ☐ about understanding and improving the human condition.
   d. ☐ intellectually challenging.

3. A high priority in my life is to
   a. ☐ keep my commitments.
   b. ☐ experience as much of life as possible.
   c. ☐ make a difference in the lives of others.
   d. ☐ understand how things work.

4. Other people think of me as
   a. ☐ dependable and loyal.
   b. ☐ dynamic and creative.
   c. ☐ caring and honest.
   d. ☐ intelligent and inventive.

5. When I experience stress I would most likely
   a. ☐ do something to help me feel more in control of my life.
   b. ☐ do something physical and daring.
   c. ☐ talk with a friend.
   d. ☐ go off by myself and think about my situation.

6. I would probably not be a close friend with someone who is
   a. ☐ irresponsible.
   b. ☐ unwilling to try new things.
   c. ☐ selfish and unkind to others.
   d. ☐ an illogical thinker.

7. My vacations could be described as
   a. ☐ traditional.
   b. ☐ adventuresome.
   c. ☐ pleasing to others.
   d. ☐ a new learning experience.

8. One word that best describes me is
   a. ☐ sensible.
   b. ☐ spontaneous.
   c. ☐ giving.
   d. ☐ analytical.

STEP 2. Add up the total points for each letter.

TOTAL FOR   **a.** ☐ Organizer   **b.** ☐ Adventurer   **c.** ☐ Giver   **d.** ☐ Thinker

STEP 3. Plot these numbers on the brain diagram on page 67.

SCORING DIAGRAM FOR PERSONALITY SPECTRUM

Write your scores from p. 66 in the four squares just outside the brain diagram—Thinker score at top left, Giver score at top right, Organizer score at bottom left, and Adventurer score at bottom right.

Each square has a line of numbers that go from the square to the centre of the diagram. For each of your four

scores, place a dot on the appropriate number in the line near that square. For example, if you scored 15 in the Giver spectrum, you would place a dot between the 14 and 16 in the upper right-hand line of numbers. If you scored a 26 in the Organizer spectrum, you would place a dot on the 26 in the lower left-hand line of numbers.

Connect the four dots to make a four-sided shape. If you like, shade the four sections inside the shape using four different colors.

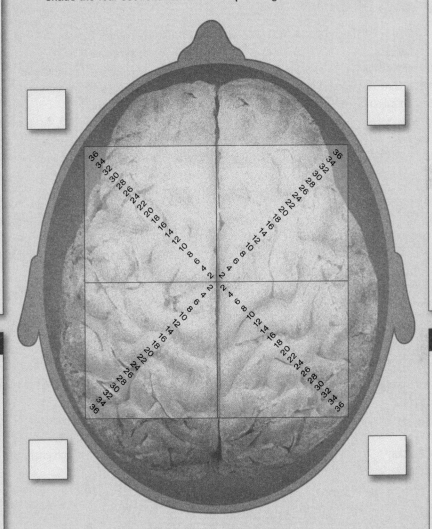

THINKER

Technical
Scientific
Mathematical
Dispassionate
Rational
Analytical
Logical
Problem Solving
Theoretical
Intellectual
Objective
Quantitative
Explicit
Realistic
Literal
Precise
Formal

GIVER

Interpersonal
Emotional
Caring
Sociable
Giving
Spiritual
Musical
Romantic
Feeling
Peacemaker
Trusting
Adaptable
Passionate
Harmonious
Idealistic
Talkative
Honest

ORGANIZER

Tactical
Planning
Detailed
Practical
Confident
Predictable
Controlled
Dependable
Systematic
Sequential
Structured
Administrative
Procedural
Organized
Conservative
Safekeeping
Disciplined

ADVENTURER

Active
Visual
Risking
Original
Artistic
Spatial
Skillful
Impulsive
Metaphoric
Experimental
Divergent
Fast-paced
Simultaneous
Competitive
Imaginative
Open-minded
Adventuresome

For the Personality Spectrum,
26–36 indicates a strong tendency in that dimension,
14–25 a moderate tendency,
and below 14 a minimal tendency.

Source for brain diagram: *Understanding Psychology*, 3/e, by Morris, © 1996. Adapted by permission of Prentice Hall, Inc., Upper Saddle River, NJ.

How to put your Personality Spectrum to work for you.

CHARACTERISTICS OF EACH PERSONALITY TYPE

Thinker
- Solving problems
- Developing models and systems
- Analytical and abstract thinking
- Exploring ideas and potentials
- Ingenuity
- Going beyond established boundaries
- Global thinking—seeking universal truth

Organizer
- Responsibility, reliability
- Operating successfully within social structures
- Sense of history, culture, and dignity
- Neatness and organization
- Loyalty
- Orientation to detail
- Comprehensive follow-through on tasks
- Efficiency

Giver
- Honesty, authenticity
- Successful, close relationships
- Making a difference in the world
- Cultivating your own potential and that of others
- Negotiation; promoting peace
- Communicating with others
- Openness
- Helping others

Adventurer
- High ability in a variety of fields
- Courage and daring
- Approaching problem solving in a hands-on fashion
- Living in the present
- Spontaneity and action
- Ability to negotiate
- Nontraditional style
- Flexibility
- Zest for life

STUDY TECHNIQUES TO MAXIMIZE PERSONALITY TYPES

Thinker
- Find time to reflect independently on new information
- Learn through problem solving
- Design new ways of approaching issues
- Convert material into logical charts
- Look for opportunities to work independently

Organizer
- Try to have tasks defined in clear, concrete terms so that you know what is required
- Look for a well-structured, stable environment
- Request feedback
- Use a planner to schedule tasks and dates
- Organize material by rewriting and organizing class or text notes, making flash cards, or carefully highlighting

Giver
- Study with others
- Teach material to others
- Seek out tasks, groups, and subjects that involves helping people
- Find ways to express thoughts and feelings clearly and honestly
- Put energy into your most important relationships

Adventurer
- Look for environments that encourage nontraditional approaches
- Find hands-on ways to learn
- Seek people whom you find stimulating
- Use or develop games and puzzles to help memorize terms
- Fight boredom by asking to do something extra or perform a task in a more active way

Joyce Bishop, *Keys to Success*, © 2001

Assess your Multiple Intelligences

In 1983, Howard Gardner, a Harvard University professor, changed the way people perceive (intelligence) and learning with his theory of Multiple Intelligences. Gardner believes that there are at least eight intelligences possessed by each person, and that every person has developed some intelligences more fully than others (see Key 3.2 for descriptions). According to this theory, when you find a task or subject easy, you are probably using a more fully developed intelligence. When you have trouble, you may be using a less developed intelligence.[1] Therefore, the question is not how smart you are, but how you are smart.

Gardner believes that the way you learn is a unique blend of intelligences, resulting from your distinctive abilities, challenges, experiences, and training. In addition, ability in the intelligences may develop or recede as your life changes. Gardner thinks that the traditional view of intelligence, based on mathematical, logical, and verbal measurements, doesn't reflect the entire spectrum of human ability.

The Multiple Pathways to Learning assessment helps you determine the levels to which your eight intelligences are developed. Key 3.3 (see p. 72), immediately following the assessment, describes specific skills associated with the eight intelligences as well as study techniques that maximize each. Finally, the Multiple Intelligence Strategies grids found throughout the textbook will demonstrate how to apply your learning style in your post-secondary education.

INTELLIGENCE

As defined by H. Gardner, an ability to solve problems or fashion products that are useful in a particular cultural setting or community.

Each intelligence is linked to specific abilities.   key 3.2

INTELLIGENCE	DESCRIPTION
Verbal-Linguistic	Ability to communicate through language (listening, reading, writing, speaking)
Logical-Mathematical	Ability to understand logical reasoning and problem solving (math, science, patterns, sequences)
Bodily-Kinesthetic	Ability to use the physical body skillfully and to take in knowledge through bodily sensation (coordination, working with hands)
Visual-Spatial	Ability to understand spatial relationships and to perceive and create images (visual art, graphic design, charts and maps)
Interpersonal	Ability to relate to others, noticing their moods, motivations, and feelings (social activity, co-operative learning, teamwork)
Intrapersonal	Ability to understand one's own behaviour and feelings (self-awareness, independence, time spent alone)
Musical	Ability to comprehend and create meaningful sound and recognize patterns (music, sensitivity to sound and patterns)
Naturalistic	Ability to understand features of the environment (interest in nature, environmental balance, ecosystem, stress relief brought by natural environments)

MULTIPLE PATHWAYS TO LEARNING

Each intelligence has a set of numbered statements. Consider each statement on its own. Then, on a scale from 1 to 4, rate how closely it matches who you are right now and write that number on the line next to the statement. Finally, total each set of six questions.

rarely	sometimes	usually	always
1	2	3	4

1. _____ I enjoy physical activities.
2. _____ I am uncomfortable sitting still.
3. _____ I prefer to learn through doing.
4. _____ When sitting I move my legs or hands.
5. _____ I enjoy working with my hands.
6. _____ I like to pace when I'm thinking or studying.

_____ TOTAL for BODILY–KINESTHETIC

1. _____ I enjoy telling stories.
2. _____ I like to write.
3. _____ I like to read.
4. _____ I express myself clearly.
5. _____ I am good at negotiating.
6. _____ I like to discuss topics that interest me.

_____ TOTAL for VERBAL–LINGUISTIC

1. _____ I use maps easily.
2. _____ I draw pictures/diagrams when explaining ideas.
3. _____ I can assemble items easily from diagrams.
4. _____ I enjoy drawing or photography.
5. _____ I do not like to read long paragraphs.
6. _____ I prefer a drawn map over written directions.

_____ TOTAL for VISUAL–SPATIAL

1. _____ I like math in school.
2. _____ I like science.
3. _____ I problem-solve well.
4. _____ I question how things work.
5. _____ I enjoy planning or designing something new.
6. _____ I am able to fix things.

_____ TOTAL for LOGICAL–MATHEMATICAL

1. _____ I listen to music.
2. _____ I move my fingers or feet when I hear music.
3. _____ I have good rhythm.
4. _____ I like to sing along with music.
5. _____ People have said I have musical talent.
6. _____ I like to express my ideas through music.

_____ TOTAL for MUSICAL

1. _____ I need quiet time to think.
2. _____ I think about issues before I want to talk.
3. _____ I am interested in self-improvement.
4. _____ I understand my thoughts and feelings.
5. _____ I know what I want out of life.
6. _____ I prefer to work on projects alone.

_____ TOTAL for INTRAPERSONAL

1. _____ I like doing a project with other people.
2. _____ People come to me to help settle conflicts.
3. _____ I like to spend time with friends.
4. _____ I am good at understanding people.
5. _____ I am good at making people feel comfortable.
6. _____ I enjoy helping others.

_____ TOTAL for INTERPERSONAL

1. _____ I enjoy nature whenever possible.
2. _____ I think about having a career involving nature.
3. _____ I enjoy studying plants, animals, or oceans.
4. _____ I avoid being indoors except when I sleep.
5. _____ As a child I played with bugs and leaves.
6. _____ When I feel stressed I want to be out in nature.

_____ TOTAL for NATURALISTIC

Developed by Joyce Bishop, Ph.D., and based upon Howard Gardner's *Frames of Mind: The Theory of Multiple Intelligences.*[2]

SCORING GRID FOR MULTIPLE PATHWAYS TO LEARNING

For each intelligence, shade the box in the row that corresponds with the range where your score falls. For example, if you scored 17 in Body–Kinesthetic intelligence, you would shade the middle box in that row; if you scored a 13 in Visual–Spatial, you would shade the last box in that row. When you have shaded one box for each row, you will see a "map" of your range of development at a glance.

A score of 20–24 indicates a high level of development in that particular type of intelligence, 14–19 a moderate level, and below 14 an underdeveloped intelligence.

	20–24 (Highly Developed)	14–19 (Moderately Developed)	Below 14 (Underdeveloped)
Bodily–Kinesthetic			
Verbal-Linguistic			
Visual-Spatial			
Logical–Mathematical			
Musical			
Intrapersonal			
Interpersonal			
Naturalistic			

How to put your Multiple Intelligences to work for you.

ABILITIES AND SKILLS ASSOCIATED WITH EACH INTELLIGENCE

Verbal-Linguistic
- Analyzing own use of language
- Remembering terms easily
- Explaining, teaching, learning, using humour
- Understanding syntax and meaning of words
- Convincing someone to do something

Musical-Rhythmic
- Sensing tonal qualities
- Creating or enjoying melodies and rhythms
- Being sensitive to sounds and rhythms
- Using "schemas" to hear music
- Understanding the structure of music

Logical-Mathematical
- Recognizing abstract patterns
- Reasoning inductively and deductively
- Discerning relationships and connections
- Performing complex calculations
- Reasoning scientifically

Visual-Spatial
- Perceiving and forming objects accurately
- Recognizing relationships between objects
- Representing something graphically
- Manipulating images
- Finding one's way in space

Bodily-Kinesthetic
- Connecting mind and body
- Controlling movement
- Improving body functions
- Expanding body awareness to all senses
- Coordinating body movement

Intrapersonal
- Evaluating own thinking
- Being aware of and expressing feelings
- Understanding self in relationship to others
- Thinking and reasoning on higher levels

Interpersonal
- Seeing things from others' perspectives
- Co-operating within a group
- Communicating verbally and non-verbally
- Creating and maintaining relationships

Naturalistic
- Deep understanding of nature
- Appreciation of the delicate balance in nature

STUDY TECHNIQUES TO MAXIMIZE EACH INTELLIGENCE

Verbal-Linguistic
- Read text and highlight no more than 10%
- Rewrite notes
- Outline chapters
- Teach someone else
- Recite information or write scripts/debates

Musical-Rhythmic
- Create rhythms out of words
- Beat out rhythms with hand or stick
- Play instrumental music/write raps
- Put new material to songs you already know
- Take music breaks

Logical-Mathematical
- Organize material logically
- Explain material sequentially to someone
- Develop systems and find patterns
- Write outlines and develop charts and graphs
- Analyze information

Visual-Spatial
- Develop graphic organizers for new material
- Draw mind maps
- Develop charts and graphs
- Use colour in notes to organize
- Visualize material

Bodily-Kinesthetic
- Move or rap while you learn
- Pace and recite
- Move fingers under words while reading
- Create "living sculptures"
- Act out scripts of material, design games

Intrapersonal
- Reflect on personal meaning of information
- Visualize information/keep a journal
- Study in quiet settings
- Imagine experiments

Interpersonal
- Study in a group
- Discuss information
- Use flash cards with others
- Teach someone else

Naturalistic
- Connect with nature whenever possible
- Form study groups of people with like interests

Source: Adapted from Lazear, *Seven Pathways of Learning,* 1994.

IN-CLASS NOTES
HOW CAN YOU DISCOVER YOUR LEARNING STYLES?

- Use learning styles assessments such as:
  - Multiple Pathways to assess Multiple Intelligences
  - Personality Spectrum to assess personality
- Put assessment results in perspective

What are the benefits of knowing *how you learn*?

Academic benefits

Knowing how you learn helps you choose study techniques that capitalize on your strengths. For example, if you learn successfully from a linear, logical presentation, you can look for order as you review notes, and you can organize information in a chronological, step-by-step, or a problem–solution structure. If you prefer to learn in a more interpersonal environment, you can try to work in study groups whenever possible.

Assessment of learning style also points you toward strategies that help with tasks and topics that don't come so easily. For example, "Adventurers," who may not respond well to linear information, have two choices when faced with logical presentations. They can apply their strengths to the material by finding a hands-on approach, for example, or they can improve on their ability to use study skills that work well for linear learners.

One of the best ways to understand the different learning styles is to work with others and experience the differences in how people take in and process information. This understanding of diverse learning styles will not only help you understand learning styles better but will also help you assign tasks effectively and learn more comprehensively when you study with others. For instance, an interpersonal learner, such as a "Giver," might take the lead in teaching information to others, whereas an "Organizer" might be the schedule coordinator for the group.

Your various instructors will most likely have different styles of teaching because an instructor's teaching style often reflects his or her dominant learning style. Therefore, your particular learning style may work well with some instructors and be a mismatch with others. After several class meetings, you should be able to assess an instructor's teaching styles (see Key 3.4). Then you can use what you know to maximize styles that suit you and compensate for those that don't.

Although presentation styles vary, the standard lecture is more common in theoretical based courses. For this reason, those whose preferred learning style is more verbal or logical, such as the Thinker or

Instructors often rely on one or more teaching styles.

TEACHING STYLE	WHAT TO EXPECT IN CLASS
Lecture, verbal focus	Instructor speaks to the class for the entire period, with little class interaction. Lesson is taught primarily through words, either spoken or written on the board, overhead projector, handouts, or text.
Group discussion	Instructor presents material but encourages class discussion.
Small groups	Instructor presents material and then breaks class into small groups for discussion or project work.
Visual focus	Instructor uses visual elements such as diagrams, photographs, drawings, transparencies.
Logical presentation	Instructor organizes materials in a logical sequence, such as by time or importance.
Random presentation	Instructor tackles topics in no particular order, and may jump around a lot or digress.

Organizer, are generally comfortable in these classes. However, applied courses, such as some science, trades or technology courses, tend to be more engaging to those who, like the Adventurers, prefer hands-on learning activities. Therefore, what can you do if your styles don't match with those of your instructor?

Play to your strengths. Find ways to incorporate strategies that fit with your preferred way to learn. For example, an Organizer learning from an instructor who delivers material in a random way might rewrite notes in a linear, outline format to bring structure to concepts and insert facts where they fit best. Likewise, a Giver taking a straight lecture course with no student-to-student contact might meet with a study group to go over the details and fill in factual gaps.

Work to strengthen weaker areas. Keep in mind that your learning style just indicates ways to learn that may be more comfortable for you, but you can learn in other ways too. It might just take a bit more effort, but be well worth it. For example, as visual learners review notes from a structured lecture course, they could outline them, allot extra time to master the material, and work with a study group. A Thinker, studying for a test from notes delivered by an Adventurer instructor, could find hands-on ways to review the material. It is often beneficial to take in and process information in more than one way.

Learning is not attained by chance, it must be sought for with ardour and attended to with diligence.

ABIGAIL ADAMS

Ask your instructor for additional help. If you are having trouble with coursework, communicate with your instructor through email or face-to-face during office hours. Share information with your instructor about how you learn best and ask for some suggestions on ways to master the course material.

The visual learner, for example, might ask the instructor to recommend graphs or figures that illustrate the lecture.

Instructors are unique. No instructor can give each of a diverse group of learners exactly what each one needs. The flexibility that you need to mesh your learning style with instructors' teaching styles is a tool for career and life success. Just as you can't hand-pick your instructors, you will not always be able to choose your colleagues or their work styles.

Career benefits

Knowing how you learn brings you these benefits in your career:

- **Better performance through self-awareness.** Since your learning styles are essentially the same as your working styles, knowing how you learn will help you identify career and work environments that suit you. Knowing your strengths will help you use and highlight them on the job. When a task involves one of your weaker skills, you can either take special care to accomplish it or suggest someone else who is a better fit.

- **Better teamwork.** The more attuned you are to abilities and personality traits, the better you will be at identifying the tasks you and others can best perform in team situations. For example, a Giver might enjoy helping new employees get used to the people and environment, or a supervisor directing an intrapersonal learner might offer him or her the chance to take material home to think about before a meeting.

- **Better career planning.** The more you know about how you learn and work, the more you will be able to focus on career paths that could work well for you. A better understanding of your learning strengths and preferences and personality traits will aid you in deciding upon a career path and choosing your courses or program of study.

IN-CLASS NOTES

WHAT ARE THE BENEFITS OF KNOWING HOW YOU LEARN?

- Academic benefits
- Career benefits

_____

_____

_____

_____

How can Multiple Intelligences help you *explore occupations and careers?*

Key 3.5 (see pp. 77–78) lists some possibilities for the eight intelligence types. This list is by no means complete. Rather, it represents only a fraction of the available opportunities. Use what you see here to inspire thought and spur investigation.

OCCUPATION

Profession, trade, or field of work.

CAREER

The sum of all of one's life work, whether paid or unpaid, at home, in the community, or at school.

Use career exploration strategies

Whatever your interests, you will benefit from starting to think about potential occupations early on. Use the following strategies to explore your career options.

Keep what you value in mind. Ask yourself what occupations support the principles that guide your life. What are the things that you really value in life? What things are really important to you when considering a job or occupational field? Some examples might be service to others, financial security, a broad-based education, time for family, etc.

Follow your passion. Find something you love doing more than anything else in the world, and then find a way to make money doing it. If you are sure of what you love to do, try to pinpoint a career niche. Open yourself to new ideas, and talk to others who are in the know who might help stimulate these ideas. Talk to people such as your instructors as well as people working in the field. What can they tell you about the daily work? Where is the profession headed in the future?

Use career resources. Visit your school's career centre to read current media, take an assessment, or explore the occupational fields that currently have good prospects. On the Internet, check out occupations, industries, and companies. A useful resource published by Human Resources and Skills Development Canada is the National Occupational Classification (NOC). It is available online at www23.hrdc-drhc.gc.ca. Another good resource is Job Futures, published by Service Canada and available online at www.jobfutures.ca. Both these resources are also available in hard copy at public libraries or post-secondary institutions in the library or career resource centre.

Explore educational requirements of occupations. Your choice of education may depend on the career direction you want to take. For example, pursuing a career in medicine requires education in the biological sciences. In contrast, pursuing a career in law may allow you to study political science, philosophy, and English. Some occupations will require many years of study; whereas others, only a few months. Consider the time and financial commitment required. Are you able to commit to at least four years of full-time study required for a degree, two years for a diploma, or less than that for a certificate? Consider the opportunities that will be available to you with each credential level. Will an apprenticeship in a skilled trade provide more job opportunities than a bachelor's degree, or vice versa?

Try hands-on exploration. Extracurricular activities and volunteering opportunities might provide experiences that help you decide. For example, a student interested in teaching may volunteer as a camp counsellor or an after-school tutor. This is a great way to learn what is involved in the daily work of a specific occupation. In addition, it also provides hands-on experience and training that you can add to your resumé and provides opportunity to build your network of people working in the field.

Multiple Intelligences may open doors to programs, co-op opportunities or student jobs, and occupations.

MULTIPLE INTELLIGENCES	CONSIDER MAJORING IN . . .	THINK ABOUT AN INTERNSHIP IN (A/AN) . . .	LOOK INTO A CAREER AS . . .
Bodily–Kinesthetic	Massage Therapy Physical Therapy Kinesiology Construction Engineering Chiropractics Sports Medicine Anatomy Dance Theatre	Sports Physician's Office Athletic Club Physical Therapy Centre Chiropractor's Office Construction Company Surveying Company Dance Studio Drafting Firm Theatre Company	Carpenter Draftsman Recreational Therapist Physical Therapist Mechanical Engineer Massage Therapist Dancer or Acrobat Exercise Physiologist Actor Athletic Trainer
Intrapersonal	Psychology Sociology English Finance Liberal Arts Biology Computer Science Economics	Research and Development Firm Accounting Firm Computer Company Publishing House Pharmaceutical Company Engineering Firm Biology Lab	Research Scientist Motivational Speaker Engineer Physicist Sociologist Computer Scientist Economist Author Psychologist
Interpersonal	Psychology Sociology Education Real Estate Public Relations Nursing Business Hotel/Restaurant Management Rhetoric/Communications	Hotel or Restaurant Travel Agency Real Estate Agency Public Relations Firm Human Resources Customer Service Marketing/Sales Group Counselling Social Service	Social Worker PR Rep/Media Liaison Human Resources Specialist Travel Agent Sociologist Anthropologist Counsellor Therapist Teacher or Teaching Assistant Nurse
Naturalistic	Forestry Astronomy Geology Biology Zoology Atmospheric Sciences Oceanography Agriculture Animal Husbandry Environmental Law Physics	Museum National Park Oil Company Botanical Gardens Environmental Law Firm Summer Camp Adventure Travel Agency Zoo Biological Research Firm	Forest Ranger Botanist or Herbalist Geologist Ecologist Marine Biologist Archaeologist Astronomer Adventure Travel Agent Wildlife Tour Guide Landscape Architect Camp Counsellor
Musical	Music Musical History Musical Theory Performing Arts Composition Voice Liberal Arts Entertainment Law	Performance Hall Radio Station Record Label Ballet or Theatre Company Recording Studio Children's Music Camp Orchestra or Opera Company Musical Talent Agency Entertainment Law Firm	Lyricist or Composer Singer or Musician Voice Coach Music Teacher or Critic Record Executive Conductor Radio DJ Sound Engineer Entertainment Lawyer

(continued)

Continued

MULTIPLE INTELLIGENCES	CONSIDER MAJORING IN . . .	THINK ABOUT AN INTERNSHIP IN (A/AN) . . .	LOOK INTO A CAREER AS . . .
Logical–Mathematical	Math Accounting Physics Economics Medicine Banking/Finance Astronomy Computer Science Systems Theory Law Chemistry Engineering	Law Firm Health Care Office Real Estate Brokerage Accounting Firm Animal Hospital Science Lab Consulting Firm Pharmaceutical Firm Bank	Doctor, Dentist, or Veterinarian Accountant Pharmacist Chemist Physicist Systems Analyst Investment Banker Financial Analyst Computer Scientist
Verbal–Linguistic	Communications Marketing English/Literature Journalism Foreign Languages Linguistic Theory Political Science Advertising/PR	Newspaper/Magazine Network TV Affiliate Publishing House Law Firm PR/Marketing Firm Ad Agency Training Company Human Resources Customer Service	Author Playwright Journalist TV/Radio Producer Literature Teacher Speech Pathologist Business Executive Copywriter or Editor Speech Therapist
Visual–Spatial	Visual Arts Architecture Interior Design Multimedia Design Film Theory Photography Art History	Art Gallery Museum Photography Studio Design Firm Advertising Agency Theatrical Set Designer Multimedia Firm Architecture Firm Film Studio	Graphic Artist Photographer Architect Cinematographer Art Therapist Designer Cartoonist/Illustrator Art Museum Curator Art Teacher

IN-CLASS NOTES

HOW CAN MULTIPLE INTELLIGENCES HELP YOU EXPLORE OCCUPATIONS & CAREERS?

- Use career exploration strategies together with information about your multiple intelligences
  - Keep what you value in mind
  - Follow your passion
  - Use career resources
  - Explore educational requirements of occupations
  - Try hands-on exploration

Sabiduría

In Spanish, the term *sabiduría* represents the two sides of learning: knowledge and wisdom. *Knowledge* involves gaining information, understanding concepts, and building what you know about how the world works. *Wisdom* is the collected meaning and significance gained from knowledge. The higher learning and life experiences you gain in post-secondary education will build your personal *sabiduría*, which, in turn, will help you make wise personal, educational, and career choices.

Think of this concept as you acquire knowledge in your classes. Try to transform the facts and concepts you study into the building blocks of wisdom.

SUGGESTED READINGS

Cobb, Joyanne. *Learning How to Learn: A Guide for Getting into College with a Learning Disability, Staying in, and Staying Sane.* Washington, DC: Child Welfare League of America, 2001.

College Board, ed. *The College Board Index of Majors and Graduate Degrees 2001.* New York: College Entrance Examination Board, 2000.

Gardner, Howard. *Intelligence Reframed: Multiple Intelligences for the 21st Century.* New York: Basic Books, 2000.

Fogg, Neeta, et al. *The College Majors Handbook with Real Career Paths and Payoffs: The Actual Jobs, Earnings, and Trends for Graduates of 60 College Majors.* Indianapolis, IN: Jist Works, 2004.

Johnston, Susan, M., and Sandra Moniz-Lecce. *The Career Adventure: Your Guide to Personal Assessment, Career Exploration and Decision Making.* Toronto: Pearson Education Inc., 2006.

Keirsey, David. *Please Understand Me II: Temperament, Character, Intelligence.* Del Mar, CA: Prometheus Nemesis Book Company, 1998.

Pearman, Roger R., and Sarah C. Albritton. *I'm Not Crazy, I'm Just Not You: The Real Meaning of the 16 Personality Types.* Palo Alto, CA: Consulting Psychologists Press, 1997.

Phifer, Paul. *College Majors and Careers: A Resource Guide for Effective Life Planning.* 4th ed. Chicago: Ferguson Publishing, 1999.

INTERNET RESOURCES

Keys to Success Companion Website: www.pearsoned.ca/carter

Understanding Learning Preferences, Getting There: Student Guide to the University of Toronto. Student Affairs Office, University of Toronto: www.sa.utoronto.ca/handbook.php?cid=11&sid=57

Learning Styles. Student Development Centre, University of Western Ontario: www.sdc.uwo.ca/learning/index.html?styles

Learning Styles: Cognitive Preference Inventory. Counselling and Career Coaching. Student Affairs. George Brown College: www.georgebrown.ca/saffairs/stusucc/learningstyles.aspx

Quiz: What Are My Multiple Intelligences? Canada Prospects 1999, Canada Career Consortium: www.careerccc.org/products/cp_99_e/section1/quiz.cfm

Keirsey Sorter and other Myers-Briggs information: www.keirsey.com

National Occupational Classification (NOC). Human Resources and Skills Development Canada: www23.hrdc-drhc.gc.ca

Job Futures. Service Canada: www.jobfutures.ca

BUILDING SKILLS

FOR ACADEMIC, CAREER, AND LIFE SUCCESS

Developing Successful Intelligence

PUTTING IT ALL TOGETHER

Learn from your experiences. Consider the experiences of your own life and what you have learned from them.

Step 1. Think it through: *Analyze your experiences by completing the following exercises.* What is a consistent challenge for you as a student?

_____

_____

How might this be explained by your learning styles?

_____

_____

Have you had an "aha" experience where you suddenly realized why you've struggled?

_____

_____

Step 2. Think out of the box: *Imagine strategies for learning.* Imagine you are a learning specialist assisting a student identical to yourself. By focusing on learning styles information, what possible challenges would you identify for this student?

_____

_____

What suggestions would you make to this student in order to handle these challenges?

_____

_____

create your future

Step 3. Make it happen: *Head off your own challenges with practical strategies.* You have named a consistent challenge and you have imagined what you would say as your own learning specialist. Now identify the steps you will take to help you face your challenge.

_____

_____

_____

_____

Team Building

COLLABORATIVE SOLUTIONS

Ideas about personality types. Divide into groups according to the four types of the Personality Spectrum—Thinker-dominant students in one group, Organizer-dominant students in another, Giver-dominant students in a third, and Adventurer-dominant students in the fourth. If you have scored the same in more than one of these types, join whatever group is smaller. With your group, brainstorm the following lists for your type:

1. Strengths of this type:

   _____

   _____

   _____

   _____

2. Struggles it brings:

   _____

   _____

   _____

   _____

3. Things that cause stress for this type:

   _____

   _____

   _____

   _____

4. Occupations that tend to suit this type:

   _____

   _____

   _____

   _____

5. Occupations that might be a challenge for this type:

_____

_____

_____

_____

6. Skills this type needs to develop:

_____

_____

_____

_____

Each group should present the information about their own type to the entire class. This will boost understanding and acceptance of diverse ways of relating to information and people.

Writing

Record your thoughts here or on a separate piece of paper or in a journal.

Strengths and weaknesses. What have the personal assessments in this chapter taught you about your strengths?

_____

_____

_____

Choose what you consider your greatest strength and discuss how you plan to use it to your advantage in your coursework.

_____

_____

_____

What areas of weakness did the assessments highlight?

_____

_____

_____

Choose a weakness that has given you difficulty in school and brainstorm ways to compensate for it.

_____

_____

_____

Career Portfolio

Complete the following exercise for your portfolio.

Self-portrait. Because self-knowledge helps you make the best choices about your future, a self-portrait is an important step in your career exploration. Use this exercise to synthesize everything you have been exploring about yourself into one comprehensive "self-portrait."

Use the style shown in the example in Key 3.6 or create your own visual to design your self-portrait. Use words and visual shapes to describe your dominant Multiple Intelligences and Personality Spectrum dimensions, values, abilities, career interests, and anything else that is an important part of who you are.

One example of a self-portrait.

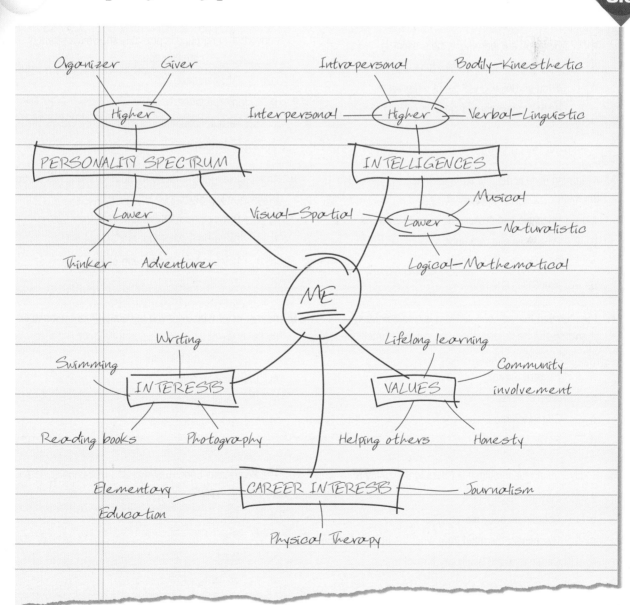

STUDY GUIDE
Chapter Review Questions

Choose the option that BEST completes the statement or answers the question. After completing the questions, check your answers against the Answer Key at the back of this book (p. 314).

1. Understanding how you learn best can help you
   a. ☐ Ignore your strengths and weaknesses.
   b. ☐ Ignore others' strengths and weaknesses.
   c. ☐ Avoid different learning challenges.
   d. ☐ Manage different learning challenges.

2. Learning styles assessments can help you understand
   a. ☐ How you are learning in the present.
   b. ☐ How you will learn in the future.
   c. ☐ What grades you will get in the present.
   d. ☐ What grades you will get in the future.

3. A learning style is defined as "a particular way in which the mind _____ information."
   a. ☐ Receives and processes.
   b. ☐ Processes and remembers.
   c. ☐ Remembers and retrieves.
   d. ☐ Processes and retrieves.

4. The idea that the way people learn is a combination of strengths and weaknesses in eight different "intelligences" was first developed by
   a. ☐ Howard Gardner.
   b. ☐ Albert Einstein.
   c. ☐ Sigmund Freud.
   d. ☐ Emily Stowe.

5. Bodily-kinesthetic intelligence refers to the ability to
   a. ☐ Play sports very well.
   b. ☐ Coordinate body movements.
   c. ☐ Disconnect the mind from what the body is feeling.
   d. ☐ Understand the bodily rhythms of music.

6. Howard Gardner defines an intelligence as an ability to
   a. ☐ Relate to others in a particular culture, setting or community, noticing their feelings and moods.
   b. ☐ Take in knowledge available in a particular culture, setting or community.
   c. ☐ Understand one's own behaviour and feelings and how they relate to one's particular culture, setting, or community.
   d. ☐ Solve problems or fashion products that are useful in a particular cultural setting or community.

7. A person who learns best by communicating verbally and nonverbally in groups is probably showing a strength in _____ intelligence.
   a. ☐ Intrapersonal.
   b. ☐ Interpersonal.
   c. ☐ Verbal–linguistic.
   d. ☐ Naturalistic.

8. An effective study strategy for someone who has a strength in visual–spatial intelligence would be to
   a. ☐ Draw colourful mind maps.
   b. ☐ Organize information in a linear manner.
   c. ☐ Discuss information with others.
   d. ☐ Rewrite notes.

9. An instructor who asks you to debate information in class is probably using _____ intelligence.
   a. ☐ Logical–mathematical.
   b. ☐ Intrapersonal.
   c. ☐ Visual–spatial.
   d. ☐ Verbal–linguistic.

10. The Personality Spectrum characterizes people into how many personality types?
   a. ☐ Two.
   b. ☐ Four.
   c. ☐ Eight.
   d. ☐ Sixteen.

11. Which personality types tend to be more "right-brained" thinkers?

- a. ☐ Thinkers and Givers.
- b. ☐ Organizers and Thinkers.
- c. ☐ Givers and Adventurers.
- d. ☐ Organizers and Givers.

12. Which personality types tend to be more "left-brained" thinkers?

- a. ☐ Thinkers and Givers.
- b. ☐ Organizers and Thinkers.
- c. ☐ Givers and Adventurers.
- d. ☐ Organizers and Givers.

13. Which of the following characteristics describe a "Giver"?

- a. ☐ Interpersonal.
- b. ☐ Active.
- c. ☐ Detailed.
- d. ☐ Analytical.

14. Adventurers need to look for opportunities to study in ways that are

- a. ☐ Quiet and independent.
- b. ☐ Well-structured and stable.
- c. ☐ Teaching others.
- d. ☐ Hands-on and stimulating.

15. One of the benefits of knowing how you learn best is that you can

- a. ☐ Choose instructors with a learning style opposite to yours so that you will be challenged to strengthen your weak areas.
- b. ☐ Choose courses that are completely taught by lecture because that is the style that suits every learning style.
- c. ☐ Study with others because someone in the group will help you master the material.
- d. ☐ Adapt your study strategies to suit the way you prefer to learn.

16. Knowing your preferred learning style and personality traits will help your career by

- a. ☐ Allowing you to find people to work with that share your exact style and traits.
- b. ☐ Staying away from jobs that require a less developed intelligence.
- c. ☐ Giving you information that you will use to choose one occupation you will fulfill for the rest of your life.
- d. ☐ Improving your teamwork skills.

17. A person who has a strength in bodily–kinesthetic intelligence might consider a career as a

- a. ☐ Carpenter.
- b. ☐ Forest Ranger.
- c. ☐ Nurse.
- d. ☐ Cartoonist.

18. A person whose personality type indicates a preference toward Adventurer and multiple intelligence toward Naturalistic might consider a career as a(n)

- a. ☐ Financial Analyst.
- b. ☐ Sound Engineer.
- c. ☐ Marine Biologist.
- d. ☐ Acrobat.

19. A(n) _____ can be defined as a profession, trade, or field of work.

- a. ☐ Skill.
- b. ☐ Job.
- c. ☐ Occupation.
- d. ☐ Career.

20. The accumulation of all of your life's work, whether paid or unpaid, at home, in the community, or at school, is considered to be your

- a. ☐ Work.
- b. ☐ Job.
- c. ☐ Occupation.
- d. ☐ Career.

Successfully Intelligent Thinking

ANALYTICAL, CREATIVE, AND PRACTICAL THINKING FOR SOLVING PROBLEMS AND MAKING DECISIONS

This chapter is organized as follows:

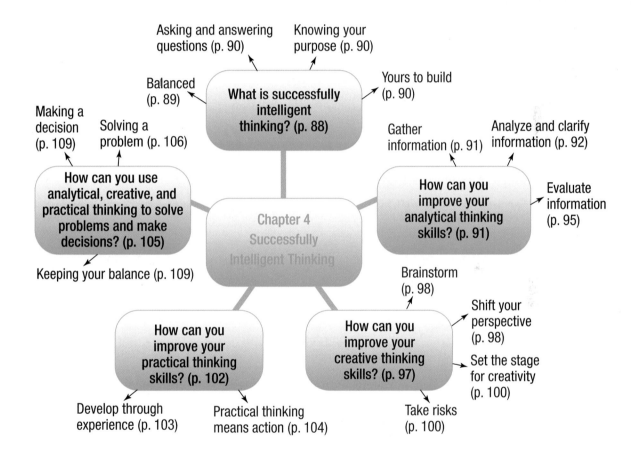

Asking and answering questions (p. 90)

Knowing your purpose (p. 90)

Balanced (p. 89)

Yours to build (p. 90)

What is successfully intelligent thinking? (p. 88)

Making a decision (p. 109)

Solving a problem (p. 106)

Gather information (p. 91)

Analyze and clarify information (p. 92)

How can you use analytical, creative, and practical thinking to solve problems and make decisions? (p. 105)

Chapter 4 Successfully Intelligent Thinking

How can you improve your analytical thinking skills? (p. 91)

Evaluate information (p. 95)

Keeping your balance (p. 109)

Brainstorm (p. 98)

Shift your perspective (p. 98)

How can you improve your practical thinking skills? (p. 102)

How can you improve your creative thinking skills? (p. 97)

Set the stage for creativity (p. 100)

Develop through experience (p. 103)

Practical thinking means action (p. 104)

Take risks (p. 100)

To survive and to thrive in environments of higher learning and beyond, you will need to use your thinking power to do more than remember formulas for a test. When problems or decisions arise on the road toward goals, how can you work through them successfully? The answer lies in how you combine your analytical, creative, and practical thinking skills—in other words, how you use your successful intelligence. As you remember from Chapter 1, successful intelligence is "the kind of intelligence used to achieve important goals."[1]

Thinking is a skill, just like other skills such as note taking or car repair, and it can be developed with practice. This chapter will help you build your ability to analyze information, come up with creative ideas, and put practical plans into action. With these skills you can become a better thinker, problem solver, and decision maker, able to reach the goals that mean the most to you.

What is *successfully intelligent thinking?*

Robert Sternberg uses this story to illustrate the impact of successful intelligence:

Two boys are walking in a forest. They are quite different. The first boy's teachers think he is smart, his parents think he is smart, and as a result, he thinks he is smart. He has good test scores, good grades, and other good paper credentials that will get him far in his scholastic life.

Few people consider the second boy smart. His test scores are nothing great, his grades aren't so good, and his other paper credentials are, in general, marginal. At best, people would call him shrewd or street smart.

As the two boys walk along in the forest, they encounter a problem—a huge, furious, hungry-looking grizzly bear, charging straight at them. The first boy, calculating that the grizzly bear will overtake them in 17.3 seconds, panics. In this state, he looks at the second boy, who is calmly taking off his hiking boots and putting on his jogging shoes.

The first boy says to the second boy, "You must be crazy. There is no way you are going to outrun that grizzly bear!"

The second boy replies, "That's true. But all I have to do is outrun you!"[2]

This story shows that successful problem solving and decision making require more than "book smarts." When confronted with a problem, using only analytical thinking put the first boy at a disadvantage. On the other hand, the second boy thought in different ways; he analyzed the situation, creatively considered the options, and took practical action. He asked and answered questions. He knew his purpose. And he lived to tell the tale.

Successfully intelligent thinking is balanced

Some tasks require only one thinking skill, or ability, at a time. You might use analytical thinking to complete a multiple-choice quiz, creative thinking to figure out how to get an assignment done on the same day you work a long shift, or practical thinking to put together a desk marked "some assembly required." However, when you need to solve a problem or make a decision, your analytical, creative, and practical thinking skills build upon one another to move you forward.[3] Envision it this way: Just as a pyramid needs three sides in order to stand, successful thinkers need all three thinking skills to develop the best solutions and decisions.

Each thinking skill adds an important dimension to accomplishing goals. Developing a balanced set of skills and knowing how and when to use each of them gives you more thinking power than having a strong aptitude in one ability only.[4] This kind of flexible thinking will help you connect your academic tasks to life goals—and show you where your hard work can take you (see Key 4.1).

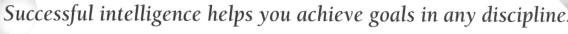

Successful intelligence helps you achieve goals in any discipline. Key 4.1

DISCIPLINE	ANALYTICAL THINKING	CREATIVE THINKING	PRACTICAL THINKING
Behavioural Science	Comparing one theory of child development with another	Devising a new theory of child development	Applying child development theories to help parents and teachers understand and deal with children more effectively
Literature	Analyzing the development of the main character in a novel	Writing alternative endings to the novel	Using the experience of the main character to better understand and manage one's own life situations
History	Considering similarities and differences between World War I and World War II	Imaging yourself as a German citizen, dealing with economic depression after WWI	Seeing what WWI and WWII lessons can be applied to current Middle East conflicts
Sports	Analyzing the opposing team's strategy on the soccer field	Coming up with innovative ways to move the ball downfield	Using tactics to hide your strategy from an opposing team—or a competing company

Source: Adapted from Robert J. Sternberg, *Successful Intelligence*, Plume: New York, 1997, p. 149.

Successfully intelligent thinking means asking and answering questions

What is thinking? According to experts, it is what happens when you ask questions and move toward the answers.[5] "To think through or rethink anything," says Dr. Richard Paul, director of research at the Center for Critical Thinking and Moral Critique, "one must ask questions that stimulate our thought. Questions define tasks, express problems and delineate issues. . . . only students who have questions are really thinking and learning."[6]

Successful intelligence depends on three thinking skills.

As you answer questions, you transform raw data into information that you can use. A *Wall Street Journal* article entitled "The Best Innovations Are Those That Come from Smart Questions" relays the story of a biology student, William Hunter, whose professor told him that "the difference between good science and great science is the quality of the questions posed." Later, as a doctor and the president and CEO of a pharmaceutical company, Dr. Hunter asked questions about new ways to use drugs. His questions led to the development of a revolutionary product—a drug-coated coronary stent that prevents scar tissue from forming. Through seeking answers to probing questions, Dr. Hunter reached a significant goal.[7]

You use questions in order to analyze (e.g., "How bad is my money situation?"), come up with creative ideas (e.g., "What ways could I earn money?"), and apply practical solutions (e.g., "How can I get a job that fits around my schooling?"). Later in the chapter, in the sections on analytical, creative, and practical thinking, you will find examples of the kinds of questions that drive each skill.

Like any other aspect of thinking, questioning is often not a straightforward process. Sometimes the answer doesn't come right away. Often the answer leads to more—and more specific—questions.

Successfully intelligent thinking requires knowing your purpose

To ask useful questions, you need to know *why* you are questioning. In other words, you need to define your purpose. A general question can be your starting point for defining your purposes: "What am I trying to accomplish, and why?" Then, within each stage of the process, you will find more specific purposes, or sub-goals, that help you generate analytical, creative, or practical questions along the way.

Successfully intelligent thinking is yours to build

Now and throughout your life, you can continually improve your ability to think. Studies have shown that the brain continues to develop throughout your life if you continue to learn new things.[8] Puzzle master Nob Yoshigahara has said, "As jogging is to the body, thinking is to the brain. The more we do it, the better we become."[9]

The mini-assessments within this chapter will help you get an idea of how you perceive yourself as an analytical, creative, and practical thinker. Every other chapter's set of *Get Analytical*, *Get Creative*, and *Get Practical* exercises then helps you to build your skills in those areas. Finally, the *Developing Successful Intelligence: Putting It All*

Together exercises at the ends of chapters encourage you to both build and combine your skills. *Your work throughout the book is geared toward building your successful intelligence.*

Begin by exploring the analytical thinking skills that you'll need in order to solve problems and make decisions effectively.

IN-CLASS NOTES

WHAT IS SUCCESSFULLY INTELLIGENT THINKING?

- Successfully intelligent thinking:
  - Is balanced
  - Means asking and answering questions
  - Requires knowing your purpose
  - Is yours to build

How can you improve your *analytical thinking skills?*

Analytical thinking—sometimes also referred to as critical thinking—is the process of gathering information, analyzing it in different ways, and evaluating it for the purposes of gaining understanding, solving a problem, or making a decision. It is as essential for real-life problems and decisions as it is for thinking through hypothetical questions on tests.

The first step in analytical thinking, as with all aspects of successful intelligence, is to define your purpose. What do you want to analyze, and why? Perhaps you need to analyze the plot of a novel in order to determine its structure; maybe you want to analyze your schedule in order to figure out whether you are arranging your time and responsibilities effectively.

Once you define your purpose, the rest of the analytical process involves gathering the necessary information, analyzing and clarifying the ideas, and evaluating what you've found.

Gather information

Information is the raw material for thinking. Choosing what to gather requires a careful analysis of how much information you need, how much time you should spend gathering it, and whether the information is relevant. Say, for instance, that your assignment is to write an essay on one style of music. If you gather every available resource on the topic, it might be next year before you get to the writing stage.

Here's how you might use analysis to effectively gather information for that essay:

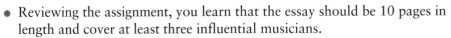

- Reviewing the assignment, you learn that the essay should be 10 pages in length and cover at least three influential musicians.
- At the library and online, you find lots of what appears to be relevant information.
- You choose a jazz movement, find five or six comprehensive pieces on it, and then select three in-depth sources on each of three musicians.

In this way you achieve a sub-goal—a selection of useful materials—on the way to your larger goal of writing a well-crafted essay.

Analyze and clarify information

Once you've gathered the information, the next step is to analyze it to determine whether the information is reliable and useful in helping you answer your questions.

Break information into parts

When analyzing information, you break information into parts and examine the parts so that you can see how they relate to each other and to information you already know. The following strategies help you break information down into pieces and set aside what is unclear, unrelated, or unimportant, resulting in a deeper and more reliable understanding.

Separate the ideas. Look at the information in pieces and look at each category of information separately. For example, if you are researching the rise of the Bebop movement, you might name events that influenced it, key musicians, information about the sound, and ideas behind it.

Compare and contrast. Look at how things are similar to, or different from, each other. For example, for the category on key musicians, you might explore how three bebop musicians are similar in style. You might also look at how they differ in what they want to communicate with their music.

Examine cause and effect. Look at the possible reasons why something happened (possible causes) and its consequences (effects, both positive and negative). Again, with the example of jazz music, you might examine the causes that led up to the bebop sound as well as its effects on other non-jazz musical styles.

There is one important caution to note here, though. You must be sure to analyze carefully and seek out *true causes* and not just apparent causes. That is, some apparent causes (often called "false causes") may not be actual causes. For example, events in the musical world and general society took place when the first musicians were developing the bebop style. Some may have led directly to the new style while some may simply have occurred at the same time.

Look for themes, patterns, and categories. Note connections that arise out of how bits of information relate to one another. A theme of freedom vs. structure, for example, might emerge out of an examination of bebop vs. swing jazz. Or you might notice a pattern of behaviour as you look at how different musicians broke off from the swing movement. Or musicians with different styles might fall into the bebop category based on their artistic goals.

Once the ideas are broken down, you can examine whether examples support ideas, separate fact from opinion, consider perspective, and investigate hidden assumptions.

> There is no expedient to which a [person] will not go to avoid the real labour of thinking.

THOMAS ALVA EDISON

Examine whether examples support ideas

When you encounter an idea or claim, examine how it is supported with examples or evidence (facts, expert opinion, research findings, personal experience, and so on). Ideas that aren't backed up with solid evidence or made concrete with examples are not useful. Be critical of the information you gather; don't take it at face value.

For example, an advertisement for a weight-loss pill, claiming that it allows users to drop a pound a day, quotes "Anne" who says that she lost 30 pounds in 30 days. The word of one person, who may or may not be telling the truth, is not adequate support. On the other hand, a claim that water once existed on Mars, backed up by measurements and photography from one of the Mars Exploration Rovers, may be based on evidence that is more reliable.

Distinguish fact from opinion

A *statement of fact* is information presented as objectively real and verifiable. For example, the statement "It's raining outside right now" can be easily verified as truth or not. In contrast, a *statement of opinion* is a belief, conclusion, or judgment that is inherently difficult, and sometimes impossible, to verify. For instance, "This is the most miserable rainstorm ever" is more likely to be a statement of opinion; it would be much more difficult, requiring much study and research, to ascertain it as a statement of fact. Key 4.2 defines important characteristics of fact and opinion. Even though facts may seem more solid, you can also make use of opinions if you determine that they are backed up with facts or even solid evidence. However, it is important to examine opinions for their underlying perspectives and assumptions.

Examine perspectives and assumptions

Perspective is a characteristic way of thinking about people, situations, events, and ideas. Perspectives can be broad, such as a generally optimistic or pessimistic view of life. Or they can be more focused, such as an attitude about whether students should work or not while they go to school.

Perspectives are associated with *assumptions*—judgments, generalizations, or biases influenced by experience and values. For example, the perspective that there are many different successful ways to be a family leads to assumptions such as "Single-parent homes can provide nurturing environments" and "Same-sex couples can rear well-adjusted children." Having a particular experience with single-parent homes or same-sex couples can build or reinforce a perspective.

Assumptions often hide within questions and statements, blocking you from considering information

Shifting your perspective helps you accept and understand different ways of living and interacting. Two students communicate via sign language while walking on campus.

Examine how fact and opinion differ.

OPINIONS INCLUDE STATEMENTS THAT...	FACTS INCLUDE STATEMENTS THAT...
... show evaluation. Any statement of value indicates an opinion. Words such as *bad, good, pointless,* and *beneficial* indicate value judgement. Example: "Bobby Orr is one of the best hockey players to play in the NHL."	*... deal with actual people, places, objects, or events.* Example: "Bobby Orr was the only defenceman to ever win the Art Ross trophy."
... use abstract words. Words that are complicated to define, like *misery* or *success,* usually indicate a personal opinion. Example: "The charity event was a smashing success."	*... use concrete words or measurable statistics.* Example: "The charity event raised $5,862."
... predict future events. Statements that examine future occurrences are often opinions. Example: "Mr. Maurin's course is going to set a new enrollment record this year."	*... describe current events in exact terms.* Example: "Mr. Maurin's course has set a new enrollment record this semester."
... use emotional words. Emotions are by nature unverifiable. Chances are that statements using such words as *delightful* or *miserable* express an opinion. Example: "That class is a miserable experience."	*... avoid emotional words and focus on the verifiable.* Example: "Citing dissatisfaction with the instruction, 7 out of the 25 students in that class withdrew in September."
... use absolutes. Absolute *qualifiers,* such as *all, none, never,* and *always,* often point to an opinion. Example: "All students need to have a job while in school.	*... avoid absolutes.* Example: "Some students need to have a job while in school."

Source: Adapted from Ben E. Johnson, *Stirring Up Thinking.* New York: Houghton Mifflin, 1998, pp. 268-270.

in different ways. Take this classic puzzler as an example: "Which came first, the chicken or the egg?" Thinking about this question, most people assume that the egg is a chicken egg. If you think past that assumption and come up with a new idea—such as, the egg is a dinosaur egg—then the obvious answer is that the egg came first!

Examining perspectives and assumptions is important for two reasons. First, they often affect your perception of the validity of materials you read and research. Second, your own perspectives and assumptions can cloud your interpretation of the information you encounter.

BIASED

Leaning in a particular direction; influenced by a point of view.

Perspectives and assumptions in information. Being able to determine the perspectives that underlie materials will help you separate biased from unbiased information. For example, the conclusions in two articles addressing private versus public education may differ radically if one is written with support and funding by the provincial government and the other with funds from private institutions. The bias would likely be reduced if the article was researched and written by a neutral source.

In addition to authors' perspectives, their assumptions often affect the validity of materials you read and research. It is important to assess your readings for underlying assumptions. For example, an article on private versus public education might assume that all private and all public education systems have similar characteristics. Clearly understanding such a document means separating the assumptions from the facts.

Personal perspectives and assumptions. Your own preferences, values, and biases—which influence your perspective—can affect how accurately you view information. For example, students who think that the death penalty is wrong may have difficulty analyzing the arguments in an article that supports it. Or, in a research situation, they might use only materials that agree with their own perspective. However, to do so would be misleading because all of the information is not accurately represented.

Consider the perspectives and assumptions that might follow from your values. Then, when you have to analyze information, try to set aside your personal perspectives and assumptions. "Anticipate your reactions and prejudices and then consciously resist their influence," says Colby Glass, a professor of information research and philosophy.[10]

In addition to helping you analyze accurately, opening yourself to new perspectives will help you build knowledge. According to Sternberg, "We need to . . . see issues from a variety of viewpoints and, especially, to see how other people and other cultures view issues and problems facing the world."[11]

Evaluate information

You've gathered and analyzed your information. You have examined its components, its evidence, its validity, its perspective, and any underlying assumptions. Now, based on an examination of evidence and careful analysis, you *evaluate* whether an idea or piece of information is good or bad, important or unimportant, right or wrong. You then set aside what is not useful and use the rest to form an opinion, possible solution, or decision.

For example, you're working on a group presentation on the effects of television watching on young children. You've gathered information that relates to your topic, developed a thesis, and analyzed whether the information supports this thesis. Now you evaluate all of the evidence, presenting what's useful in an organized and informative way. Key 4.3 provides a summary of questions you can ask in order to build and use analytical thinking skills.

Analytical thinking is only part of the picture. Pursuing your goals, in school and in the workplace, requires not just analyzing information but also thinking creatively about how to use it.

ASSESS ANALYTICAL THINKING SKILLS

get analytical!

How do you perceive yourself as an analytical thinker? For each statement, circle the number that feels right to you, from 1 for "least like me" to 5 for "most like me."

1. I tend to perform well on objective tests. ① ② ③ ④ ⑤
2. People say I'm a "thinker," "brainy," "studious." ① ② ③ ④ ⑤
3. I am not comfortable with grey areas—I prefer information to be laid out in black and white. ① ② ③ ④ ⑤
4. In a group setting, I like to tackle the details of a problem. ① ② ③ ④ ⑤
5. I sometimes over-think things and miss my moment of opportunity. ① ② ③ ④ ⑤

Total your answers here: _____

If your total ranges from 5–12, you consider your analytical thinking skills to be *weak*.

If your total ranges from 13–19, you consider your analytical thinking skills to be *average*.

If your total ranges from 20–25, you consider your analytical thinking skills to be *strong*.

Ask questions like these in order to analyze.

To gather information, ask:	• What requirements does my goal have?
	• What kinds of information do I need to meet my goal?
	• What information is available?
	• Where and when is it available? Where and when can I access it?
	• Of the sources I found, which ones will best help me achieve my goal?
To analyze, ask:	• What are the parts of this information?
	• What is similar to this information? What is different?
	• What are the reasons for this? Why did this happen?
	• What ideas or themes emerge from this material?
	• How would you categorize this information?
	• What conclusions can you make about this information?
To see if examples support an idea, ask:	• What examples, or evidence, support the idea?
	• Does the evidence make sense?
	• Does the evidence support the idea/claim?
	• Is this evidence key information that I need to answer my question?
	• Are there examples that might disprove the idea/claim?
To distinguish fact from opinion, ask:	• Do the words in this information signal fact or opinion? (See Key 4.2 on p. 94)
	• What is the source of this information? Is the source reliable?
	• How does this information compare to other facts or opinions?
	• If this is an opinion, is it supported by facts?
	• How can I use this fact or opinion?
To examine perspective and assumptions, ask:	• Who is the author? What perspectives might this person have?
	• What might be emphasized or left out as a result of the perspective?
	• How could I consider this information from a different perspective?
	• What assumptions might lie behind this statement or material?
	• How could I prove or disprove an assumption?
	• What contradictory assumptions might be equally valid?
	• How might a personal perspective or assumption affect the way I see this material?
To evaluate, ask:	• Do I agree with this information?
	• Does this information fit what I'm trying to prove or accomplish?
	• Is this information true or false, and why?
	• How important is this information?
	• Which ideas or pieces of information would I choose to focus on?

Adapted from www.ed.final.gov/trc/tutorial/taxonomy.html (Richard Paul, *Critical Thinking: How to Prepare Students for a Rapidly Changing World*, 1993) and from www.kcmetro.edu/longview/ctac/blooms.htm, Barbara Fowler, Longview Community College "Bloom's Taxonomy and Critical Thinking."

How can you improve your *creative thinking skills?*

Some researchers define creativity as combining existing elements in an innovative way to create a new purpose or result. For example, in 1970, 3M researcher Spencer Silver created a weak adhesive; four years later, another 3M scientist, Arthur Fry, used it for a hymnal marker. This led to what most people know today as Post-it® Notes, a basic necessity of almost every office. Other people define creativity as the art of generating ideas from taking a fresh look at how things are related. For instance, noting what ladybugs eat inspired organic farmers to bring them in to consume crop-destroying aphids.[12] Still other people, including Sternberg, define creativity as the ability to make unusual connections—to view information in quirky ways that bring about unique results.

To think creatively is to generate new ideas that often go against conventional wisdom and may bring change. Consider how, in the 1940s, mathematician Grace Murray Hopper pioneered the effort to create computer languages that non-mathematicians could understand; her efforts opened the world of computers to a wide audience.

Creativity is not limited to inventions. For example, one student used her creative mind in two ways. First, as part of her class on electrical circuits, she and her study group devised a solar-powered battery for a laptop computer. "We took the professor's laptop, put all the parts together, and sat outside watching it with a little device to see how much power it was saving. When it fully charged the battery, it was one of those times I felt that what I was learning was true, because I was putting it to use in real life."[13] Second, her experience led her to decide on a field of study and future career plan—engineering.

Creativity forms a bridge between analytical and practical thinking. You need to think analytically to evaluate the quality of your creative ideas. You also need to think practically to implement them.

Where does creativity come from? Some people, through luck or natural inclination, seem to come up with inspired ideas more often than others do.

Creativity connects analytical and practical thinking.

However, creative thinking, like analytical thinking, is a skill that can be developed. Creativity expert Roger von Oech says that mental flexibility is essential. "Like race-car drivers who shift in and out of different gears depending on where they are on the course," he says, you can enhance your creativity by learning to "shift in and out of different types of thinking depending on the needs of the situation at hand."[14]

The following strategies will help you make those shifts and build your ability to think creatively.

Brainstorm

Brainstorming can be defined as the practice of letting your mind free-associate to come up with different ideas or answers. This is also referred to as *divergent thinking*. In other words, you start with a question and then let your mind diverge—go in many different directions—in search of solutions. Think of brainstorming as *deliberate* creative thinking because you go into it fully aware that you are attempting to create new ideas. When you brainstorm, it is important to allow yourself to generate ideas without judging them or thinking about how useful they are. The point is just to generate ideas and then to evaluate each of them later. Brainstorming works well in groups because group members can become inspired by, and make creative use of, one another's ideas.[15]

While working through a problem for a course, these students demonstrate that successful problem solving often requires input from and teamwork by a group of people.

ANALOGY

A comparison based on a resemblance of things otherwise unlike.

One way to inspire ideas when brainstorming is to think of similar situations and to make an analogy. For example, the discovery of Velcro® is a product of analogy: When imagining how two pieces of fabric could stick to each other, the inventor thought of the similar situation of a burr sticking to clothing.

When you are brainstorming ideas, don't get hooked on finding the one right answer. Questions may have many "right answers," or many answers that have degrees of usefulness. The more possibilities you generate, the better your chance of finding the best one. Also, don't stop the process when you think you have the best answer, keep going until you are out of steam. You never know what may come up in those last gasps of creative energy.[16]

Shift your perspective

Just because everyone believes something, that doesn't make it so; just because something "has always been that way," that doesn't make it good. Changing how you look at a situation or a problem can inspire creative ideas. Here are some ways to do it:

Challenge assumptions. Consider the rationale behind assumptions or behaviours. Do they make sense? Are they based on logical or factual information? Is there another way? This is what Jacques Plante did in 1959. Up until that time, goalies playing hockey in the NHL did not wear masks during games.

Then during a game, Montreal Canadiens' goalie Jacques Plante was hit in the face by a puck and needed stitches. He returned to the game wearing a mask, much to the shock of the other players, coaches, and audience. However, Plante refused to play without it, and today he is credited as the one who introduced goalie masks as standard equipment in hockey.

> It is better to have enough ideas for some of them to be wrong, than to be always right by having no ideas at all.

EDWARD DE BONO

Take a new and different look. Try on new perspectives by asking others for their views, reading about new ways to approach situations, or deliberately going with the opposite of your first instinct.[17] Then use those perspectives to inspire creativity. For example, for your English course, analyze a novel from the point of view of one of the main characters. For Political Science, craft a position paper for a federal election candidate. Perception puzzles are a fun way to experience how looking at something in a new way can bring a totally different idea (see Key 4.4).

Ask "what if" questions. Set up hypothetical environments in which new ideas can grow: "What if I knew I couldn't fail?" "What if I had unlimited money or time?" Ideas will emerge from your "what if" questions. For example, the founders of Seeds of Peace, faced with generations of conflict in the Middle East, asked: What if Israeli and Palestinian teens met at a summer camp so that the next generation could develop greater understanding and respect than the last? And what if follow-up programs and reunions are set up to cement friendships so that relationships change the politics of the Middle East? Based on the ideas that were generated, they created an organization to prepare

Try these perception puzzles.

key 4.4

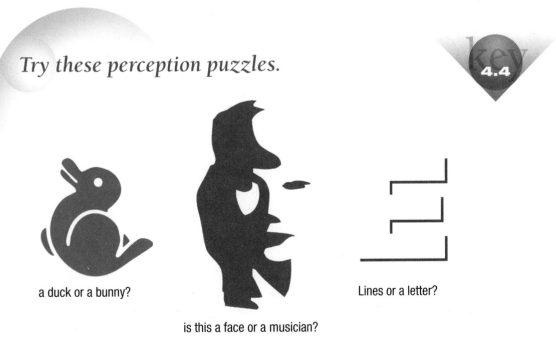

a duck or a bunny?

is this a face or a musician?

Lines or a letter?

Face puzzle: "Sara Nader" illustration from *Mind Sights* by Roger Shepard. Copyright © 1990 by Roger Shepard. Reprinted by permission of Henry Hold & Company.

teenagers from the Middle East with the leadership skills needed to coexist peacefully.

Set the stage for creativity

Use these strategies to give yourself the best possible chance at generating creative ideas.

Choose or create environments that free your mind. Find places that energize you. Play music that moves you. Paint your study walls your favourite colour. Seek out people who inspire you. Sternberg agrees: "Find the environment that rewards what you have to offer," he says, "and then make the most of your creativity and of yourself in that environment."[18]

Be curious. Try something you consider new and different. For example, take a course that is completely different from your others, try a new sport or game, listen to a new genre of music, or read a magazine or book that you know nothing about. Seeking out new experiences and ideas will broaden your knowledge, giving you more raw material with which to build creative ideas.[19]

Give yourself time to "sit" with a question. Generally speaking, North American society values speed, so much so that to say someone is "quick" is to say that person is intelligent.[20] Equating speed with intelligence can stifle creativity because many creative ideas come when you allow time for thoughts to percolate. Take breaks when figuring out a problem. Take the pressure off by getting some exercise, napping, talking with a friend, working on something else, or doing something fun. Creative ideas often come when you give your brain permission to "leave the job" for a while.[21]

Believe in yourself as a creative thinker. While it is normal to want critical approval and success for your creative efforts, you may not get it right away, especially if your ideas break new ground. When Gustav Mahler's *Symphony No. 2, "Resurrection,"* was performed in 1910, critics walked out of the concert hall because of its innovative sound. Today, the *"Resurrection"* symphony is considered one of the formative compositions of this era. Like Mahler, you must believe in your creative expression, no matter what others say. Critics, after all, can be wrong or simply a step or two behind.

Take risks

Creative breakthroughs can come from sensible risk taking. Two ways to take risks are to think unconventionally and to learn from mistakes.

Fly in the face of convention. Sometimes, to be creative and innovative, one must find a way to think, or to do things, in a way that is different from the usual accepted norm. Only by seeing things in another light might you come up with some idea that no one else has. For example, Entrepreneur Michael Dell, of Dell Computers, turned tradition on its ear when he took a "tell me what you want and I will build it for you" approach to computer marketing instead of a "build it and they will buy it" approach. The possibility of failure did not stop him from risking money, time, energy, and reputation to achieve a truly unique and creative goal.

Let mistakes be okay. Open yourself to the learning that comes from not being afraid to mess up. Sternberg reports that "in the course of their schooling... children learn that it's not all right to make mistakes. As a result, they become afraid to err and thus to risk the kind of independent, if sometimes flawed, thinking" that can promote creative ideas.[22] When Dr. Hunter, the successful inventor of the drug-coated coronary stent, and his company failed to develop a particular treatment for multiple sclerosis, he said, "You have to celebrate the failures. If you send the message that the only road to career success is experiments that work, people won't ask risky questions, or get any dramatically new answers."[23]

As with analytical thinking, asking questions powers creative thinking. See Key 4.5 for examples of the kinds of questions you can ask to get your creative juices flowing.

When you are working to solve a problem or make a decision, creative thinking allows you to generate possible choices and solutions. However, choices aren't enough, and potential solutions must be tried out. You need practical thinking in order to make the best choice or solution happen.

Ask these questions to jump-start creative thinking.

To brainstorm, ask:	• What do I want to accomplish?
	• What are the craziest ideas I can think of?
	• What are ten ways that I can reach my goal?
	• What ideas or strategies have worked before and how can I apply them?
	• How else can this be done?
To analyze, ask:	• How has this always been done—and what would be a different way?
	• What is another way to look at this situation?
	• How can I approach this task from a completely new angle?
	• How would others do this? How would they view this?
	• What if . . . ?
To shift your perspective, ask:	• Where and with whom do I feel relaxed and inspired?
	• What music helps me think out of the box?
	• When in the day or night am I most likely to experience a flow of creative ideas?
	• What do I think would be new and interesting to try, to see, to read?
	• What is the most outrageous outcome of a situation that I can imagine?
To take risks, ask:	• What is the conventional way of doing this? What would be a totally different way?
	• What would be a risky approach to this problem or question?
	• What choice would people caution me about and why?
	• What is the worst that can happen if I take this risk? What is the best?
	• What have I learned from this mistake?

ASSESS CREATIVE THINKING SKILLS

How do you perceive yourself as a creative thinker? For each statement, circle the number that feels right to you, from 1 for "least like me" to 5 for "most like me."

1. I tend to resist rules and regulations.   ① ② ③ ④ ⑤
2. People say I'm "expressive," "full of ideas," "innovative."   ① ② ③ ④ ⑤
3. I break out of my routine and find new experiences.   ① ② ③ ④ ⑤
4. In a group setting, I like to toss ideas into the ring.   ① ② ③ ④ ⑤
5. If you say something is too risky, I'm all for it.   ① ② ③ ④ ⑤

Total your answers here: _____

If your total ranges from 5–12, you consider your creative thinking skills to be *weak.*

If your total ranges from 13–19, you consider your creative thinking skills to be *average.*

If your total ranges from 20–25, you consider your creative thinking skills to be *strong.*

IN-CLASS NOTES

HOW CAN YOU IMPROVE YOUR CREATIVE THINKING SKILLS?

- Brainstorm
- Shift your perspective
- Set the stage for creativity
- Take risks

_____

_____

_____

_____

_____

How can you improve your *practical thinking skills?*

Practical thinking is sometimes also called "common sense" or "street smarts." It refers to how you adapt to your environment, or shape your environment to adapt to you, in order to pursue important goals. A basic example: Your goal is to pass a communications course. You are a visual learner in a verbally focused classroom. To achieve your goal, you can build your verbal skills (adapt to your environment) or you can ask the instructor and your study group to allow you to present information in visual terms (change your environment to adapt to you), or both.

Why do you need to think practically? Since many academic problems can be solved with analytical thinking alone, it's easy to get the impression that strong analytical thinking skills translate into life success. However, real-world problems are different from many academic problems. They are often less clear, related closely to your life and needs, and answerable in more than one way. In addition, real-life problems are usually more significant than are textbook problems. For example, the way you solve a financial dilemma has a more significant impact on your life than how you work through a geometry question. Therefore, successfully solving real-world problems demands a practical approach.[24]

Practical thinking allows you to bridge the gap between what makes a successful student and what brings real-world success. In other words, even if you ace the courses for your academic program, you also need to be able to apply what you learned in a specific job.

Experience helps develop practical thinking skills

You gain much of your ability to think practically (i.e., your common sense) from personal experience, rather than from formal lessons. This knowledge is an important tool in achieving goals.[25]

You can use what you learn from experience to answer "how" questions—how to talk, how to behave, how to proceed.[26] For example, after completing a few assignments for a particular course, you may pick up cues about how to impress that instructor. Following a couple of conflicts with a partner, you may learn how to avoid sore spots when the conversation heats up. Key 4.6 provides an example of "If . . . then . . ." statements in which this kind of knowledge can be used.

There are two key points to making practical knowledge work for you. First, make an active choice to learn from experience, and to pay attention to how things work at school, in personal relationships, and at work. Second, make sure you apply what you learn, assuring that you will not have to learn

Map out what you learn from experience.

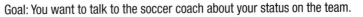

Goal: You want to talk to the soccer coach about your status on the team.

IF the team has had a good practice and IF you've played well during the scrimmage and IF the coach isn't rushing off somewhere, THEN grab a moment with him right after practice ends.

IF the team is having a tough time and IF you've been sidelined and IF the coach is in a rush and stressed, THEN drop in on his office hours tomorrow.

the same lessons over and over again. As Sternberg says, "What matters most is not how much experience you have had but rather how much you have profited from it—in other words, how well you apply what you have learned."[27]

Practical thinking means action

Learning different ways to take action and stay in motion builds your practical thinking ability. Strategies you learn throughout this course will keep you moving toward your goals.[28] These strategies include the following:

- **Stay motivated.** Use techniques from Chapter 1 to persevere when you face a problem. Get started on achieving results instead of dwelling on exactly how to start. Translate thoughts into concrete actions instead of getting bogged down in "analysis paralysis."

- **Make the most of your personal strengths.** What you've learned in Chapter 2 will help you see what you do best. Use those strengths as you apply practical solutions.

- **When things go wrong, accept responsibility and reject self-pity.** You know from Chapter 1 that failure is an excellent teacher. Learn from what happened, act on what you have learned, and don't let self-pity stall your momentum.

- **Manage time and tasks effectively.** Use what you know from Chapter 2 to plan your time in a way that promotes goal accomplishment. Avoid the pitfalls of procrastination. Accurately gauge what you can handle; avoid taking on too many projects, or too few.

See Key 4.7 for some questions you can ask in order to apply practical thinking to your problems and decisions.

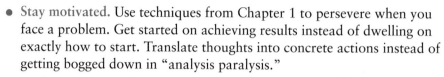
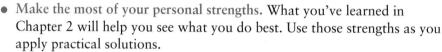

Ask questions like these to activate practical thinking.

Key 4.7

To learn from experience, ask:	• What worked well, or not so well, about my approach? My timing? My tone? My world?
	• What did others like or not like about what I did?
	• What did I learn from that experience, conversation, event?
	• How would I change things if I had to do it over again?
	• What do I know I would do again?
To apply what you learn, ask:	• What have I learned that would work here?
	• What have I seen others do, or heard about from them, that would be helpful here?
	• What does this situation have in common with past situations I've been involved in?
	• What has worked in similar situations in the past?
To boost your ability to take action, ask:	• How can I get motivated and remove limitations?
	• How can I, in this situation, make the most of what I do well?
	• If I fail, what can I learn from it?
	• What steps will get me to my goal, and what trade-offs are involved?
	• How can I manage my time more effectively?

ASSESS PRACTICAL THINKING SKILLS

How do you perceive yourself as a practical thinker? For each statement, circle the number that feels right to you, from 1 for "least like me" to 5 for "most like me."

1. I can find a way around any obstacle.   ① ② ③ ④ ⑤
2. People say I'm a "doer," the "go-to" person, "organized."   ① ② ③ ④ ⑤
3. When I have a vision, I translate it into steps from A to B to C.   ① ② ③ ④ ⑤
4. In a group setting, I like to set up the plan.   ① ② ③ ④ ⑤
5. I don't like to leave loose ends dangling—I'm a finisher.   ① ② ③ ④ ⑤

Total your answers here: _____

If your total ranges from 5–12, you consider your practical thinking skills to be *weak*.
If your total ranges from 13–19, you consider your practical thinking skills to be *average*.
If your total ranges from 20–25, you consider your practical thinking skills to be *strong*.

Your skills at a glance: In the sections of the triangle, write your assessment scores from *Get Analytical (p. 95), Get Creative (p. 102),* and *Get Practical (above).* Comparing the scores will give you an idea of how you perceive your skills in all three aspects of successful intelligence, and will help you think about where you may want to build strength.

CREATIVE

IN-CLASS NOTES

HOW CAN YOU IMPROVE YOUR PRACTICAL THINKING SKILLS?

- Experience helps develop practical thinking skills
- Practical thinking means action

_____
_____
_____
_____

How can you use *analytical, creative, and practical thinking together* to solve a problem or make a decision?

You have developed your understanding of what it means to think analytically, creatively, and practically. You have explored your perception of where your strengths and weaknesses lie. Now you will see how to put analytical, creative, and practical thinking together to solve problems and make decisions successfully—at school, in the workplace, or in your personal life.

A similar strategy can be used to either solve a problem or make a decision. Both solving a problem and making a decision require you to identify and analyze a situation, generate possibilities, choose a solution, follow through

Solve problems and make decisions using successful intelligence.

PROBLEM SOLVING	THINKING SKILL	DECISION MAKING
Define the problem—recognize that something needs to change, identify what's happening, look for true causes	STEP 1 DEFINE	Define the decision—identify your goal (your need) and then construct a decision that will help you get it
Analyze the problem—gather information, break it down into pieces, verify facts, look at perspectives and assumptions, evaluate information	STEP 2 ANALYZE	Examine needs and motives—consider the layers of needs carefully, and be honest about what you really want
Generate possible solutions—use creative strategies to think of ways you could address the causes of this problem	STEP 3 CREATE	Name and/or generate different options—use creative questions to come up with choices that would fulfill your needs
Evaluate solutions—look carefully at potential pros and cons of each, and choose what seems best	STEP 4 ANALYZE (EVALUATE)	Evaluate options—look carefully at potential pros and cons of each, and choose what seems best
Put the solution to work—persevere, focus on results, and believe in yourself as you go for your goal	STEP 5 TAKE PRACTICAL ACTION	Act on your decision—go down the path and use practical strategies to stay on target
Evaluate how well the solution worked—look at the effects of what you did	STEP 6 ANALYZE (RE-EVALUATE)	Evaluate the success of your decision—look at whether it accomplished what you had hoped
In the future, apply what you've learned—use this solution, or a better one, when a similar situation comes up again	STEP 7 TAKE PRACTICAL ACTION	In the future, apply what you've learned—make this choice, or a better one, when a similar decision comes up again

on it, and evaluate its success. Key 4.8 gives an overview of the paths, indicating the thinking process at each step.

Nevertheless, there are a few differences between the two paths of this strategy. So, how do you choose which path to follow? Understanding the differences will help. First of all, problem solving generally requires more focus on coming up with possible solutions; when you face a decision, your choices are often determined. Second, problem solving aims to remove or counteract negative effects; decision making aims to fulfill a need. See Key 4.9 for some examples. Also remember another difference: problem solving almost always requires you to make a decision (i.e., when you decide on a solution), but only some decision making requires you to solve a problem.

Solving a problem

A problem exists when a situation has negative effects. Recognizing that there is a problem requires being aware of those effects. It also requires knowing what is causing the problem. You need to determine what is causing the problem before you begin to solve it so that you are sure that the solutions

Examine how problems and decisions differ.

SITUATION	YOU HAVE A PROBLEM IF . . .	YOU NEED TO MAKE A DECISION IF . . .
Planning summer activities	Your low GPA means you need to attend summer school—and you've already accepted a summer job.	You've been offered two different summer jobs.
Entering a program of study	It's time to apply for a program of study, but you don't have all the prerequisites you need.	There are three programs that appeal to you and you qualify for them all.
Handling relationships with instructors	You are having trouble following the lecture style of a particular instructor.	Your business course has seven sections taught by different instructors; you have to choose one.

you come up with are addressing the root causes of the problem and not just the effects. In other words, your first move is to go from the effects—"I'm unhappy/uneasy/angry"—to determining why: "I have overcrowded my schedule." "I'm over my head in this course." "I have overspent on my credit card." Then you begin the problem-solving process in earnest.

What happens if you *don't* act in a successfully intelligent way? Take, for example, a student having an issue with an instructor. He may get into an argument with the instructor during class time, then may stop showing up to class and may not make an effort with assignments. All of these choices will most likely have bad consequences.

Now look at how this student might work through this problem using analytical, creative, and practical thinking skills. Key 4.10 shows how his effort can pay off.

As you go through the problem-solving process, keep these tips in mind.

Use probing questions to define problems. Focus on causes. If you are not happy in a class, for example, you could ask questions like these:

- What do I think about when I feel unhappy?
- Do my feelings involve my instructor? My classmates?
- Is the subject matter difficult? Is the volume of work too much?

Chances are that how you answer one or more of these questions may lead to a clear definition of the causes and ultimately to the right solution.

Analyze carefully. Gather all the information you can, so that you can consider the situation comprehensively. Consider what you can learn from the problem's similarity to, or difference from, other problems. Clarify facts. Note your own perspective, and ask others for theirs. Make sure you are not looking at the problem through the lens of an assumption.

No problem can stand the assault of sustained thinking.

VOLTAIRE

Work through a problem relating to an instructor.

DEFINE PROBLEM HERE:	ANALYZE THE PROBLEM
I don't like my instructor	We have different views and personality types— I don't feel respected or heard. I'm not motivated to learn the course material so my grades are suffering.

Use boxes below to list possible solutions:

POTENTIAL POSITIVE EFFECTS	SOLUTION #1	POTENTIAL NEGATIVE EFFECTS
List for each solution: Don't have to deal with that instructor Less stress	Drop the course	*List for each solution:* Grade gets entered on my transcript I'll have to take the course eventually; it's required for my program.
Getting credit for the course Feeling like I've honoured a commitment	**SOLUTION #2** Put up with it until the end of the semester	Stress every time I'm there Lowered motivation Probably not such a good final grade
A chance to express myself Could get good advice An opportunity to ask direct questions of the instructor	**SOLUTION #3** Schedule meetings with a counsellor and the instructor	Have to face instructor one-on-one Might just make things worse

Now choose the solution you think is best—circle it and make it happen.

ACTUAL POSITIVE EFFECTS	PRACTICAL ACTION	ACTUAL NEGATIVE EFFECTS
List for chosen solution: Got some helpful advice from counsellor Talking in person with the instructor actually promoted a fairly honest discussion I won't have to take the course again	I scheduled and attended meetings with both counsellor and instructor, and opted to stick with the course.	*List for chosen solution:* The discussion was difficult and sometimes tense I still don't know how much learning I'll retain from this course

FINAL EVALUATION: Was it a good or bad solution?

The solution has improved things. I'll finish the course, and even though the instructor and I aren't the best of friends, we have a mutual understanding now. I feel more respected and more willing to put my time into the course.

Generate possible solutions based on causes, not effects. Addressing a cause provides a lasting solution, whereas "fixing" an effect cannot. Say your shoulder hurts when you use your computer. Getting a friend to massage it is a nice but temporary solution, because the pain returns whenever you go back to work. Changing the height of your keyboard and mouse is a better idea, because it eliminates the cause of your pain.

Making a decision

Psychologists who have studied decision making have learned that many random factors influence the choices people make. For example, you may choose a career not because you love the work, but because you think others will approve of it. The goal is to make well-considered decisions despite factors that may derail your thinking.

What happens when you make important decisions quickly, without using your analytical, creative, and practical thinking skills? Consider a student trying to decide whether to transfer to another school. If she stays at her current school because a good friend says, "You can't leave me!" or transfers because she doesn't like her living situation, she may question her choice later—most likely because she didn't consider cause and effect carefully when deciding.

Now look at how this student might make a successfully intelligent decision. Key 4.11 shows how she worked through the analytical, creative, and practical parts of the process.

As you use the steps in Key 4.11 to make a decision, remember these hints:

Look at the given options—then try to think of more. Some decisions have a given set of options. For example, your school may allow you to choose a major, double major, or major and minor. However, when you are making your decision, you may be able to brainstorm with an advisor to come up with more options—such as an interdisciplinary major you create on your own.

Think about how your decision affects others. For example, the student thinking about a transfer considers the impact on friends and family. What she concludes about that impact may influence when she transfers and even the school she chooses.

Gather perspectives. Talk with others who have made similar decisions. There are more ways of doing things than one brain can possibly imagine on its own.

Look at the long-term effects. For important decisions, do a short-term evaluation and another evaluation after a period of time. See whether your decision has sent you down a path that has continued to bring positive effects.

Keeping your balance

No one has equal strengths in analytical, creative, and practical thinking. Adjusting your expectations to match what you can accomplish is a key principle of successful intelligence. It requires that you

- use what you've learned in this chapter and the rest of the text to maximize your analytical, creative, and practical abilities.
- reflect on what you do well, and focus on strengthening weaker skills.

Make a decision about whether to transfer to another school.

DEFINE THE DECISION	EXAMINE NEEDS AND MOTIVES
Whether or not to transfer to another school	I attend a small private college. My partner has changed jobs and we can no longer afford my tuition. My goal is to become a physical therapist, so I need a school with a full physical therapy program. My family needs to cut costs. I need to transfer credits.

Use boxes below to list possible choices:

POTENTIAL POSITIVE EFFECTS	CHOICE #1	POTENTIAL NEGATIVE EFFECTS
List for each solution:	Continue at the current college	*List for each solution:*
No need to adjust to a new place or new people		Need to finance most of my tuition or go into debt.
Ability to continue course work as planned		Difficult to find time for a job
		Might not qualify for student loan.

	CHOICE #2	
Opportunity to connect with other students	Transfer to a university	Need to earn some money or get financial aid
Cheaper tuition		Physical therapy program is difficult to get into.
Credits will transfer		

	CHOICE #3	
Many physical therapy courses available	Transfer to the community college	No personal contacts there that I know of
School is close so I could save commuting time and money		No bachelor's degree available so must eventually transfer to university
Reasonable tuition; credits will transfer		

Now choose the one you think is best—circle it and make it happen.

ACTUAL POSITIVE EFFECTS	PRACTICAL ACTION	ACTUAL NEGATIVE EFFECTS
List for chosen solution:	Go to community college for two years; then transfer to a university to get a B.A. and complete physical therapy course work.	*List for chosen solution:*
Money saved,		Less contact with friends
Opportunity to spend time on studies rather than on working to earn tuition money		Will eventually need to transfer to university
Availability of classes I need		Must keep grades up to compete

FINAL EVALUATION: Was it a good or bad choice?
I'm satisfied with the decision. It can be difficult to transfer to different schools, but I will also benefit from the experience. Plus the financial aspect of the decision is ideal. Saving on tuition and commuting costs now will help me save for my education later.

- combine all three thinking skills to accomplish your goals, knowing when and how to apply your analytical, creative, and practical abilities.
- believe in your skills as a thinker.

"Successfully intelligent people," says Sternberg, "defy negative expectations, even when these expectations arise from low scores on IQ or similar tests. They do not let other people's assessments stop them from achieving their goals. They find their path and then pursue it, realizing that there will be obstacles along the way and that surmounting these obstacles is part of the challenge."[29] Let the obstacles come, as they will for everyone, in all aspects of life. You can face and overcome them with the power of your successfully intelligent thinking.

Κρινειν

The word "critical" is derived from the Greek word *krinein*, which means to separate in order to choose or select. Successful intelligence requires that you separate, evaluate, and select ideas and information as you think through problematic situations. Says Sternberg, "It is more important to know when and how to use these aspects of successful intelligence than just to have them."[30]

Think of this concept as you use your analytical, creative, and practical thinking skills to solve problems, make decisions, innovate, and question. Consider information carefully, then separate out and select the best approaches. Successful intelligence gives you the power to choose how to respond to information, people, and events in ways that help you reach your goals.

SUGGESTED READINGS

Cameron, Julia with Mark Bryan. *The Artist's Way: A Spiritual Path to Higher Creativity.* 10th ed. New York: G.P. Putnam's Sons, 2002.

deBono, Edward. *Lateral Thinking: Creativity Step by Step.* New York: Perennial Library, 1990.

Goleman, Daniel. *Emotional Intelligence: Why It Can Matter More Than IQ.* New York: Bantam, 1995.

Moscovich, Ivan. *1000 Playthinks.* New York: Workman Publishing, 2001.

Noone, Donald J., Ph.D. *Creative Problem Solving.* New York: Barron's, 1998.

Sark. *Make Your Creative Dreams Real: A Plan for Procrastinators, Perfectionists, Busy People, and People Who Would Rather Sleep All Day.* New York: Fireside Press, 2004.

von Oech, Roger. *A Kick in the Seat of the Pants.* New York: Harper & Row Publishers, 1986.

von Oech, Roger. *A Whack on the Side of the Head.* New York: Warner Books, 1998.

INTERNET RESOURCES

Keys to Success Companion Website:
www.pearsoned.ca/carter

Critical Thinking and Information Use. Queen's University Library: http://library.queensu.ca/inforef/instruct/critical.htm

Creativity at Work (resources for workplace creativity):
www.creativityatwork.com

Creativity for Life (tips and strategies for creativity):
www.creativityforlife.com

BUILDING SKILLS

FOR ACADEMIC, CAREER, AND LIFE SUCCESS

Developing Successful Intelligence

PUTTING IT ALL TOGETHER

Make an important decision. Put the decision-making process to work on something that matters to you. You will apply your analytical, creative, and practical thinking skills.

Step 1. Analyze: *Define the decision.* Write an important long-term goal that you have. Then define the decision that will help you fulfill it. Example: "My goal is to become a nurse. My decision: What to specialize in."

Goal: _____

Decision: _____

Step 2. Analyze: *Examine needs and concerns.* Considering your goal and decision statements above, answer the following questions to analyze your related needs and wants. For example, the prospective nurse might list needs such as: "I need to feel that I'm helping people. I intend to help with the nursing shortage. I need to make a good living."

What do you want?

_____

_____

What are your needs and your related values?

_____

_____

What needs of others will you have to take into account?

_____

_____

create your future

113

What roadblocks might be involved?

_____

_____

Step 3. Be creative: *Generate options.* Generate some questions you might ask to imagine what's possible. For example, the nursing students might ask, "Where might I work? What might be the schedule and pace? Who might work with me? What would I see, smell, and hear on your job? What would I do every day?"

_____

_____

_____

_____

List all the options you know of and brainstorm other options that might not seem so obvious. The prospective nurse, for example, might list ER, pediatrics, surgery, oncology, geriatrics, and so on.

_____

_____

_____

_____

Step 4. Analyze: *Evaluate options.* Think about how well your options will fulfill your needs. Choose two of the options and write potential positive and negative effects (pros and cons) of each.

Option 1: _____

Potential pros: _____

Potential cons: _____

Option 2: _____

Potential pros: _____

Potential cons: _____

Step 5. Get practical: *Imagine acting on your decision.* Based on your thinking so far, describe one practical course of action that you might follow. List the specific steps you would take. For example, the prospective nurse might list actions that could help determine what type of nursing suits him/her best, such as interning, summer jobs, academic goals, and talking to working nurses.

_____

_____

Finally, plan to put your decision into action. Eventually you will need to complete the two final steps of the process.

Step 6 is to evaluate the decision: How did it work out? Analyze whether you, and others, got what you needed. **Step 7** is to practically apply what you've learned from the decision to other decisions you make in the future.

Team Building

Powerful group problem solving.

1. On an index card or a plain sheet of paper, each student in the class writes a school-related problem—this could be a fear, a challenge, a sticky situation, or a roadblock.

2. Students hand these in anonymously. The instructor writes the list up on the board.

3. The class divides into groups of two to four. Each group chooses one problem to work on (try not to have two groups working on the same problem). Students use the problem-solving flow chart (see Key 4.12 on page 117) to fill in their work. They should use the following steps:

Step 1. Analyze: *Define the problem.* As a group, look at the negative effects and state your problem specifically. Then, explore and write down the causes.

Step 2. Analyze: *Examine the problem.* Pick it apart to see what's happening. Gather information from all group members, verify facts, go beyond assumptions.

Step 3. Create: *Generate possible solutions.* From the most likely causes of the problem, derive possible solutions. Record all the ideas that group members offer. After 10 minutes or so, each group member should choose one possible solution to evaluate independently.

Step 4. Analyze: *Evaluate each solution.* In thinking independently through the assigned solution, each group member should (a) weigh the positive and negative effects, (b) consider similar problems, and (c) describe how the solution affects the causes of the problem. Evaluate your assigned solution. Is it a good one? Will it work?

Step 5. Get practical: *Choose a solution.* Group members then come together, share observations and recommendations, and then take a vote: Which solution is the best? You may have a tie or may want to combine two different solutions. Try to find the solution that works for most of the group. Then, together, come up with a plan for how you would put your solution to work.

Step 6. Analyze: *Evaluate your solution.* As a group, share and discuss what you had individually imagined the positive and negative effects of this solution would be. Try to come to an agreement on how you think the solution would work out.

Writing

Record your thoughts here or on a separate piece of paper or in a journal.

Wiser choices.
Think about a choice you made that, looking back, you wish you had handled differently.

_____

_____

Describe what the decision was, what option you chose, and what the consequences were.

_____

_____

Write about what you would do if you could make the decision again.

_____

_____

What did you learn from your experience that you can apply to other decisions?

_____

_____

How could being analytical, creative, and practical have helped you reach a more effective outcome?

_____

_____

Career Portfolio

PLAN FOR SUCCESS

Opportunities to gain experience.

People often put more time and effort into deciding what cell phone to buy than they do into making life-altering decisions like how to prepare for career success. Pursuing opportunities to gain job experience is part of a comprehensive career decision-making process. It's a practical way to get experience, learn what you like and don't like, and make valuable connections.

Occupations that I'm considering are:

1._____ _because_ _____

2._____ _because_ _____

3._____ _because_ _____

People whom I want to interview about their fields/professions are:

1._____ _because_ _____

2._____ _because_ _____

3._____ _because_ _____

Next, take practical steps to learn more about these occupations. Talk to the people you listed. Contact companies you would like to work for and see what opportunities are available.

Work through a problem using this flow chart.

DEFINE PROBLEM HERE: | ANALYZE THE PROBLEM

Use boxes below to list possible solutions:

| POTENTIAL POSITIVE EFFECTS | SOLUTION #1 | POTENTIAL NEGATIVE EFFECTS |

List for each solution: *List for each solution:*

SOLUTION #2

SOLUTION #3

Now choose the solution you think is best—circle it and make it happen.

| ACTUAL POSITIVE EFFECTS | PRACTICAL ACTION | ACTUAL NEGATIVE EFFECTS |

List for chosen solution: *List for chosen solution:*

FINAL EVALUATION: Was it a good or bad solution?

STUDY GUIDE
Chapter Review Questions

Choose the option that BEST completes the statement or answers the question. After completing the questions, check your answers against the Answer Key at the back of this book (p. 314).

1. Successfully intelligent thinking requires
   a. ☐ Stronger analytical skills than practical skills.
   b. ☐ Highly developed practical skills and less developed creativity.
   c. ☐ More creativity and less analytical skills.
   d. ☐ A balance among analytical, practical, and creative skills.

2. Studies have shown that the brain
   a. ☐ Does not change.
   b. ☐ Changes.
   c. ☐ Develops up to a certain age and then begins to deteriorate.
   d. ☐ Begins to deteriorate right after birth.

3. What is the first step in analytical thinking?
   a. ☐ Gathering information.
   b. ☐ Defining your purpose.
   c. ☐ Analyzing and clarifying the ideas.
   d. ☐ Evaluating the situation.

4. Consider the following statement:

   Twenty to thirty minutes of vigorous exercise three to five times a week is essential for good health.

   This statement is an example of:
   a. ☐ A fact.
   b. ☐ An opinion.
   c. ☐ A fact and an opinion.
   d. ☐ Neither a fact nor an opinion.

5. Which of the following is a good definition of critical thinking?
   a. ☐ Looking at the negative aspects of an idea.
   b. ☐ Accurately memorizing information and facts.
   c. ☐ Processing information to gain understanding, solve problems or make decisions.
   d. ☐ Making quick judgments about what one reads or hears.

6. Ideas that are *not* backed up with _____ are *not* useful.
   a. ☐ Solid evidence.
   b. ☐ An example.
   c. ☐ Solid evidence or an example.
   d. ☐ Assumptions.

7. It is important to examine opinions for their underlying
   a. ☐ Assumptions.
   b. ☐ Opinions.
   c. ☐ Assumptions and opinions.
   d. ☐ None of the above.

8. It is important to determine perspectives that underlie ideas because it will help you
   a. ☐ Separate biased from unbiased information.
   b. ☐ Adopt the same perspective.
   c. ☐ Reject the perspective.
   d. ☐ Formulate biases.

9. It is important to examine your own perspectives and assumptions because
   a. ☐ It can affect how accurately you view information.
   b. ☐ You can then use information that agrees only with your point of view.
   c. ☐ You can persuade others to adopt the same perspectives and assumptions.
   d. ☐ You can accept your own biases and prejudices.

10. Divergent thinking is another term for
    a. ☐ Brainstorming.
    b. ☐ Concentrating.
    c. ☐ Distracting.
    d. ☐ Analogy.

11. Brainstorming is characterized by

    a. ☐ Focusing on quality rather than quantity.

    b. ☐ Evaluating each idea as it comes up.

    c. ☐ Stopping when you find an idea that works.

    d. ☐ Generating ideas without evaluating them right away.

12. Creative ideas can come from

    a. ☐ Making mistakes.

    b. ☐ Sticking to conventional wisdom.

    c. ☐ Looking at things as you always have.

    d. ☐ Doing things correctly.

13. Which of the following is an accepted definition for creativity?

    a. ☐ The ability to make unusual connections between objects or information to bring about unique results.

    b. ☐ Combining existing elements in an innovative way to create a new purpose or result.

    c. ☐ The art of generating ideas by taking a fresh look at how things are related.

    d. ☐ All of the above.

14. What type of thinking skill allows you to bridge the gap between academics and real-world success?

    a. ☐ Analytical.

    b. ☐ Creative.

    c. ☐ Practical.

    d. ☐ Critical.

15. What are two key aspects to making practical knowledge work for you?

    a. ☐ Learn from experience and apply what you learn.

    b. ☐ Have many experiences and avoid making mistakes.

    c. ☐ Learn from others and avoid making mistakes.

    d. ☐ Stay motivated and manage time effectively.

16. The first step to solving a problem is

    a. ☐ Analyze the problem.

    b. ☐ Define the problem.

    c. ☐ Create solutions.

    d. ☐ Evaluate the pros and cons.

17. Which of the following is a difference between problem solving and decision making?

    a. ☐ Decision making requires more focus on analyzing the situation.

    b. ☐ Problem solving requires more focus on analyzing the situation.

    c. ☐ Decision making requires more focus on coming up with possible solutions.

    d. ☐ Problem solving requires more focus on coming up with possible solutions.

18. When analyzing a problem, it is important to develop solutions based on the _____ of the problem.

    a. ☐ Effects.

    b. ☐ Causes.

    c. ☐ Final evaluation.

    d. ☐ Side effects.

19. It is important to analyze or re-evaluate decisions once you've carried them out so that you can

    a. ☐ Prove yourself right.

    b. ☐ Prove to others you were right.

    c. ☐ Look at the effects of the decision.

    d. ☐ Look at the causes of the decision.

20. What is the key to successfully intelligent thinking?

    a. ☐ A balance among analytical, creative, and practical thinking.

    b. ☐ Always choosing between analytical, creative, or practical thinking and using just one to solve problems or make decisions.

    c. ☐ Using all three types of thinking in every situation.

    d. ☐ Using only the most developed thinking skill if you are weak in the others.

Reading and Learning

FOCUSING ON CONTENT

This chapter is organized as follows:

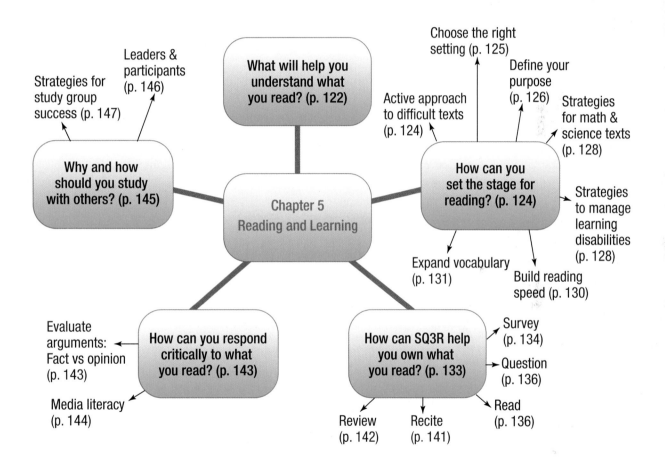

Strategies for study group success (p. 147)

Leaders & participants (p. 146)

What will help you understand what you read? (p. 122)

Choose the right setting (p. 125)

Define your purpose (p. 126)

Active approach to difficult texts (p. 124)

Strategies for math & science texts (p. 128)

Why and how should you study with others? (p. 145)

Chapter 5 Reading and Learning

How can you set the stage for reading? (p. 124)

Strategies to manage learning disabilities (p. 128)

Expand vocabulary (p. 131)

Build reading speed (p. 130)

Evaluate arguments: Fact vs opinion (p. 143)

How can you respond critically to what you read? (p. 143)

How can SQ3R help you own what you read? (p. 133)

Survey (p. 134)

Question (p. 136)

Read (p. 136)

Media literacy (p. 144)

Review (p. 142)

Recite (p. 141)

Your ability to read—and to understand, analyze, and use what you read—is one of the foundations of learning. However, your background as a reader may not have prepared you for how much reading you will be assigned in college or university, and the complexity of it. Almost all students need to adjust their habits in order to handle the increased demands of reading at the post-secondary level.

Taking a step-by-step approach linked to analytical, creative, and practical thinking techniques will help you get what you need from the materials you read and study. Most college or university courses require a lot of reading—sometimes 50 or more pages per class weekly. In addition to lectures, group activities, and hands-on assignments, reading is another means for you to acquire the learning necessary for the course. Therefore, you must approach this reading in a way that is different from how you might approach a novel or other book of interest. That is, when instructors assign that you *read* the textbook, what they really mean is that you *learn* the textbook for the course. This chapter introduces you to strategies to increase your speed and depth of understanding in order to increase your efficiency in learning from your textbooks. When you use these strategies to learn and retain more of what you read, every hour you spend with your books will be more valuable.

What will *help you understand* what you read?

Reading is an analytical process that requires you, the reader, to make meaning from written words. You do this by connecting what you know to what you read. Your understanding is affected by your familiarity with a subject, your cultural background and life experiences, and even the way you interpret words and phrases. Because these factors are different for every person, your reading experiences are uniquely your own.

Reading comprehension refers to your ability to understand what you read. True comprehension goes beyond parroting facts and figures to being able to assimilate and apply concepts to new ideas and situations. Improving your reading comprehension is especially important as assignments become longer and more difficult and as you have to complete them on your own. In addition, what you learn from introductory-level texts is the foundation for your understanding of advanced course material. Following are some general suggestions to help boost your comprehension. Keep them in mind as you work through this chapter and tackle reading assignments for your courses.

Read as much as you can. Read from other sources, not just your textbooks. Read novels, magazines, newspapers, and any other material you can get your hands on. Reading as much as you can will not only increase your vocabulary and reading speed, it will also help you become more informed. More than any other factor, what you already know influences comprehension by giving you a frame of reference for what you read.

Think analytically. Ask yourself questions: Do I understand the sentence, paragraph, or chapter I just read? Are the ideas and supporting examples clear? Could I explain the material to someone else? Could I apply the concepts to another topic or situation?

Build vocabulary. The larger your vocabulary, the more material you will understand without checking a dictionary or guessing. Challenge yourself to pick up reading material that is written at a level slightly higher than what you are used to. See if you can use some of the vocabulary in your everyday written and oral communication. Continually strive to learn and use new words.

Look for order and meaning in seemingly chaotic reading materials. The information in this chapter on the SQ3R reading technique (see p. 133) contains patterns that will help you learn new material. It is one of the most effective strategies for learning textbook material. Use it as much as you can.

Think positively. Instead of telling yourself that you cannot understand, tell yourself: *I will use the strategies I have learned, and with these strategies I can learn this material. I am determined to complete every reading assignment.*

BE THE AUTHOR OF YOUR LIFE

get creative!

Think about a book that made a difference for you.

Henry David Thoreau, a nineteenth-century author, poet, and philosopher, made the following observation: "How many a man has dated a new era in his life from the reading of a book." What do you think Thoreau meant by this statement?

_____

_____

Think about a book that influenced your education, or some other aspect of your life. Describe why it is important.

_____

_____

If you could write a book that would help others succeed in post-secondary learning, what would be the book's message? Why do you think your book would be important for others to read?

_____

_____

_____

_____

IN-CLASS NOTES

**WHAT WILL HELP YOU UNDERSTAND
WHAT YOU READ?**

- Read as much as you can
- Think analytically
- Build vocabulary
- Look for order and meaning
- Think positively

_____

_____

_____

_____

_____

_____

How can you *set the stage* for reading?

On any given day during your post-secondary studies, you may face reading assignments like these:

- A textbook chapter on the history of First Nations People in Canada (Canadian History)
- An original research study on the relationship between sleep deprivation and the development of memory problems (Psychology)
- Chapters 4 and 5 of a textbook on sales management (Marketing)
- A technical manual on the design of computer antivirus programs (Computer Science—Software Design)

This material is rigorous by anyone's standards. In fact, many students are surprised that so much reading is required in college and university, and that they may be expected to learn material on their own that is never covered in class.

To get through it all—and master what you read—you need a systematic approach that taps into your analytical and practical thinking skills. Without one, you may have trouble allocating your time and energy appropriately to each of your classes. Some material may make sense to you fairly quickly; some may require much more time and focus. A class may demand a lot of you one week and very little the next. The following strategies can help you begin gathering the tools you need for reading success. If you find you need further strategies, most post-secondary institutions in Canada provide learning services for students, including Learning Resource Centres or peer tutoring. Contact the Student Services or Counselling and Advising offices at your school to get more information.

Take an active approach to difficult texts

You are more likely to encounter unfamiliar concepts and terms as you advance in your post-secondary education. Often, students who are just beginning their post-secondary studies are overwhelmed by the level of difficulty of their textbooks and other reading. This happens often when assignments involve reading and interpreting complex technical manuals, or works from primary sources. *Primary sources* include historical or legal documents, works of literature (novels, poems, and plays), scientific studies, or journal articles. They are original documents rather than another writer's interpretation of these documents, and often they do not define terms or supply examples.

The following strategies may help you approach difficult material actively and positively:

Approach reading assignments with an open mind. Avoid prejudging material as impossible or boring before you start. Stay positive and realize that this material is important for the course you are taking.

Know that some texts require extra work and concentration. Set a goal to make your way through the material and learn it. Do whatever it takes. Consult resources—instructors, students, reference materials—for help.

Divide and conquer. Break the reading assignment into smaller tasks and distribute it over a few days. Plan to tackle small parts of it daily rather than attempting to learn the whole thing in one sitting. Work on learning and mastering each part before you move on to the next.

Own frequently used reference materials. Purchase a dictionary, a writer's style handbook, an atlas, and references in your area of study. "If you find yourself going to the library to look up the same reference again and again, consider purchasing that book for your personal library," advises library expert Sherwood Harris.[1]

Choose the right setting

Finding the best places and times to study will maximize your focus and discipline. Here are some suggestions:

Select the right location. Many students study at a library desk. Others prefer an easy chair or even the floor. Choose a spot that is comfortable but not so cushy that you fall asleep. Make sure you have adequate lighting and aren't too hot or cold. If you prefer to read alone, find an out-of-the-way spot at the library or use an empty classroom where interruptions are less likely. Even if you don't mind activity nearby, try to minimize distractions. If at any point you find it difficult to get motivated to study, try changing where you study. Rearrange the furniture in your study room, or find a different place to study in the library or on campus.

Reading is a means of thinking with another person's mind; it forces you to stretch your own.

CHARLES SCRIBNER JR.

Select the right time. Choose a time when you feel alert and focused. This time will be different for everyone. Recall from Chapter 2 what you learned about creating a schedule that suits your natural body rhythms—your goal is to study when your energy is high. Though night owls may be productive after 10:00 at night, morning people will be fuzzy during late-night sessions.

However, ideally you should try to complete reading assignments just before the related class and review it again just after the class. You will increase your understanding of the information presented in a class if you have pre-read the information. Also, your retention of the information will be higher if you review the information within 24 hours of the class.

Deal with internal distractions. Internal distractions—personal worries, anticipation of upcoming events, or even hunger—can get in the way of work. Try taking a break to tend to an issue that's bothering you, or use exercise, music, or silence to relax and refocus. If you're hungry, get a snack and come back to work.

Remember to take short breaks at least every 30 to 45 minutes. Instead of taking a break when your mind begins to wander, try to take a break before it does. This will make it easier for you to come back to your reading after a break. Also, it will reinforce the act of concentration because your mind will learn that concentration will be rewarded with a break.

Students with young children have an added factor when deciding when, where, and how to study. Key 5.1 explores ways that these students can maximize their study efforts.

Define your purpose for reading

Remember that textbooks are assigned to be *learned*, not just *read*. The readings that are assigned are another means of learning for the course. Before you start reading, define your purpose by asking yourself: "Why am I reading this? What do I need to learn from this?" You might answer by completing this sentence: "In reading this material, I intend to define/learn/answer/achieve. . . . " Defining your purpose helps you choose reading strategies and decide how much time and effort to spend. You will approach each of the four following purposes in different ways. Keep in mind that you may have one or more purposes for any "reading event."

Purpose 1: Read for understanding. Studying involves reading to comprehend general ideas and specific facts or examples. Facts and examples help explain or support ideas, and ideas provide a framework for remembering facts and examples.

Comparing notes to textbook chapters is an important part of reviewing and retaining material.

- General ideas. Reading for general ideas requires rapid reading of headings, subheadings, and summary statements to gain an overview—in other words, skimming the material (see marginal note on page 134).

- Specific facts or examples. At times, your focus may be on specific pieces of information—names and dates, chronologies, etc. At other times, your search may centre on examples that support general ideas—for example, the causes of economic recession. In both cases, scanning will help you rapidly find information (see marginal note on page 134).

Use these tools to manage children while studying.

Keep them up to date on your schedule.

Let them know when you have a big test or project due and when you are under less pressure, and what they can expect of you in each case.

Explain what your education entails.

Tell them how it will improve your life and theirs. This applies, of course, to older children who can understand the situation and compare it with their own schooling.

Find help.

Ask a relative or friend to watch your children or arrange for a child to visit a friend. Consider trading babysitting hours with another parent, hiring a sitter to come to your home, or using a day-care centre.

Keep them active while you study.

Give them games, books, or toys. If there are special activities that you like to limit, such as watching videos or TV, save them for your study time.

Study on the phone.

You might be able to have a study session with a fellow student over the phone while your child is sleeping or playing quietly.

Offset study time with family time and rewards.

Children may let you get your work done if they have something to look forward to, such as a movie night or a trip for ice cream.

SPECIAL NOTES FOR INFANTS

Study at night if your baby goes to sleep early, or in the morning if your baby sleeps late.

Study during nap times if you aren't too tired yourself.

Lay your notes out and recite information to the baby. The baby will appreciate the attention, and you will get work done.

Put baby in a safe and fun place while you study, such as a playpen, motorized swing, or jumping seat.

Purpose 2: Read to evaluate analytically. Analytical evaluation involves considering ideas and asking questions that test the writer's argument and assumptions. Analytical (or critical) reading brings an understanding of the material that goes beyond basic information recall (see pages 143–145 for more on analytical or critical reading).

Purpose 3: Read for practical application. When you read a computer manual or an instruction sheet on conducting a chemistry experiment, your goal is to learn how to do something. Reading and action usually go hand in hand.

Purpose 4: Read for pleasure. Some materials, such as popular magazines, stories, or novels are read for entertainment. These are read differently than you would read a textbook or other academic material.

Use special strategies with math and science texts

Different subjects present different reading challenges. Subjects vary, and your learning styles and preferences may make you more comfortable with some subjects than with others. For example, a calculus text will be very different from a text on world religions. Therefore, your strategies for learning these texts must also vary.

Math and science readings present unique challenges to many students. Try some of the following analytical, creative, and practical thinking techniques to meet the challenge:

- Interact with the material critically as you go. Math and science texts move sequentially (later chapters build on concepts introduced in previous chapters) and are often problem-and-solution based. Keep a notepad nearby to solve problems and take notes. Draw sketches to help visualize material. Try not to move on until you understand the example and how it relates to the central ideas. Write down questions to ask your instructor or classmates.

- Note formulas. Make sure you understand the principle behind every formula. That is, be sure you know why and how it works rather than just memorizing it. Read the assigned material to prepare for homework.

FORMULA
A general fact, rule, or principle usually expressed in mathematical symbols.

- Use memory techniques. Science textbooks are packed with specialized vocabulary that you will be expected to know. Mnemonic devices, flash cards, and rehearsing aloud or silently can aid memorization (for more on memory techniques, see Chapter 7). Selective highlighting and summarizing your readings in notes or table format will also help.

Develop strategies to manage learning disabilities

Students with reading-related learning disabilities (LD) may need to engage their practical thinking skills to manage reading assignments. The following are examples of how two students each accommodated their disability:

- Danielle received an A in her Art History course, in part because she chose some courses with heavy reading requirements and some with light requirements. This allowed her to complete all her assignments on time. In addition, she frequently sought instructors' advice about what they wanted her to learn from assigned texts and used tutors whenever she needed extra help.

- Chloe received an A in her Introduction to Psychology course, in part because she met twice weekly with a tutor who helped her prioritize her reading assignments and keep on top of her work. She also learned to tailor the amount of time she spent on different text sections to the importance of the sections on upcoming tests. Finally, when she felt comfortable with text concepts, she read them quickly or skipped them entirely, but when she had trouble with the material, she did extra reading or sought help.[2]

Reading ←

Use selected reading techniques in Multiple Intelligence areas to strengthen your ability to read for meaning and retention.

INTELLIGENCE	SUGGESTED STRATEGIES	WHAT WORKS FOR YOU? WRITE NEW IDEAS HERE
Verbal–Linguistic	• Mark up your text with marginal notes while you read. • When tackling a chapter, use every stage of SQ3R, taking advantage of each writing opportunity (writing Q-stage questions, writing summaries, and so on).	
Logical–Mathematical	• Read material in sequence. • Think about the logical connections between what you are reading and the world at large; consider similarities, differences, and cause-and-effect relationships.	
Bodily–Kinesthetic	• Take physical breaks during reading sessions—walk, stretch, exercise. • Pace while reciting important ideas.	
Visual–Spatial	• As you read, take particular note of photos, tables, figures, and other visual aids. • Make charts, diagrams, or think links illustrating difficult concepts you encounter in your reading.	
Interpersonal	• With a friend, have a joint reading session. One should read a section silently and then summarize aloud the important concepts for the other. Reverse the order of summarizer and listener for each section. • Discuss reading material and clarify important concepts in a study group.	
Intrapersonal	• Read in a solitary setting and allow time for reflection. • Think about how a particular reading assignment makes you feel, and evaluate your reaction by considering the material in light of what you already know.	
Musical	• Play music while you read. • Recite important concepts in your reading to rhythms or write a song to depict those concepts.	
Naturalistic	• Read and study in a natural environment. • Before reading indoors, imagine your favourite place in nature in order to create a relaxed frame of mind.	

Most post-secondary institutions offer services to accommodate disabilities or learning difficulties. If you have a disability or learning difficulty, investigate the services your institution offers. These services may be offered through reading and learning centres, tutoring programs, or counselling departments. Remember: The ability to succeed is often linked to the willingness to ask for help.

Build reading speed

Although comprehending is more important than reading quickly, a reasonable increase in reading speed saves time and effort. Though the average adult reads between 150 and 350 words per minute, faster readers are capable of speeds up to 1000 words per minute.[3] Contrary to what some people might believe, reading faster actually sometimes helps comprehension. This is because it is easier to link ideas before they leave your short-term memory. For example, if it takes you too long to read a paragraph, by the time you get to the end of the paragraph the information from the beginning will be gone from your memory. It will then be more difficult to link the ideas from the beginning and the end together.

Nevertheless, it is important to be able to vary your reading speed depending on what you are reading and your purpose for reading. Different reading materials will require different reading rates. For example, chemistry, biology, or physics textbooks will need to be read more slowly and carefully than newspapers, magazines, or novels which are meant to be read very quickly, at 350+ words per minute.

Raising your reading speed above 350 words per minute involves "skimming" and "scanning" (see the section on SQ3R on page 133). The following suggestions also increase speed without sacrificing comprehension:

- Try to read groups of words rather than single words. Just as a musician sees a group of notes together, train your eyes to see groups of words together.
- Avoid pointing your finger to guide your reading; use an index card or book marker to guide your eyes quickly down the page.
- When reading narrow columns, like those in newspapers, focus your eyes in the middle of the column. With practice, you'll be able to read the entire column width as you read down the page.
- Avoid sub-vocalization, which is speaking the words or moving your lips when reading. Your brain can take in information much faster than your lips can say words. If you read too slowly, your brain might get bored waiting and will begin to wander to look for other stimulation.

A key component to building speed is practice and more practice, says reading expert Steve Moidel. To achieve your goal of reading between 500 and 1000 words per minute, Moidel suggests that you start practicing at three times the rate you want to achieve, a rate that is much faster than you can comprehend.[4] For example, if your goal is 500 words per minute, speed up to 1500 words per minute. Reading at such an accelerated rate pushes your eyes and mind to adjust to the faster pace. When you slow down to 500 words per minute—a pace you can actually manage—your rate will feel comfortable even though it is much faster than your original speed. Self-paced computer software is available to help you gain speed.

Expand your vocabulary

A strong vocabulary increases speed and comprehension. The best way to build your vocabulary is to learn new and unfamiliar words as you encounter them. This involves the following steps.

Analyze word parts

Often, if you understand part of a word, you can figure out the entire word. This is true because many English words are made up of a combination of Greek and Latin prefixes, (roots,) and suffixes. *Prefixes* are word parts that are added to the beginning of a root. *Suffixes* are added to the end of the root.

Key 5.2 contains some common prefixes, roots, and suffixes. Knowing these verbal building blocks can dramatically increase your vocabulary. Key 5.3 shows how one root can be the stem of many words.

Using prefixes, roots, and suffixes, you can piece together the meaning of new words. For example, the word *prologue* is made up of the prefix *pro* (before) and the root *logue* (to speak). Thus, prologue refers to words spoken or written before the main text.

Use words in context

Although a definition tells you what a word means, it may not include a *context*—the part of a statement that surrounds a word and affects its meaning. Using a word in context after defining it helps anchor the information in

ROOT

The central part or basis of a word around which prefixes and suffixes can be added to produce different words.

Knowing common prefixes, roots, and suffixes expands your vocabulary.

key 5.2

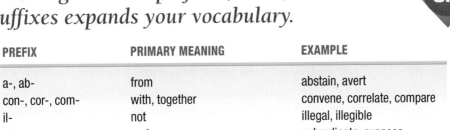

PREFIX	PRIMARY MEANING	EXAMPLE
a-, ab-	from	abstain, avert
con-, cor-, com-	with, together	convene, correlate, compare
il-	not	illegal, illegible
sub-, sup-	under	subordinate, suppose

ROOT	PRIMARY MEANING	EXAMPLE
-chron-	time	synchronize
-ann-	year	biannual
-sper-	hope	desperate
-voc-	speak, talk	convocation

SUFFIX	PRIMARY MEANING	EXAMPLE
-able	able	recyclable
-meter	measure	thermometer
-ness	state of	carelessness
-y	inclined to	sleepy

Knowing a single root can help you build different words.

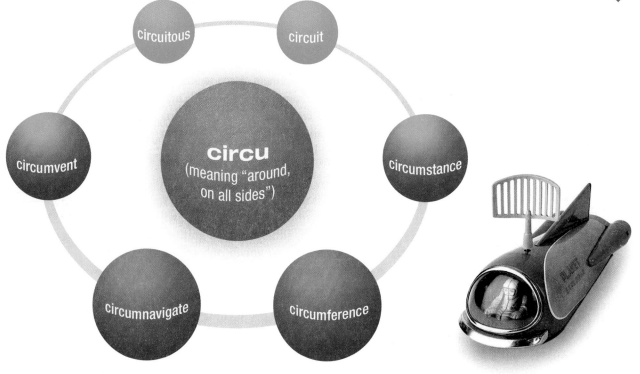

memory. Here are strategies for using context to solidify new vocabulary words.

- Use a new word in a sentence immediately after reading a definition, while the meaning is fresh.
- Reread a few times the sentence in which you originally saw the word to make sure you understand how the word is used.
- Use the word over the next few days whenever it may apply. Try it while talking with friends, writing emails or notes, or in your own thoughts.
- Once you finally learn what a word means, go back to information you previously didn't understand and solidify your comprehension.
- Talk about it. If after looking up a word you still have trouble with its meaning, ask an instructor or a friend to help you figure it out.

Use a dictionary

Dictionaries provide broad information such as word origin, pronunciation, parts of speech, and multiple meanings. Get a good quality dictionary and consult it when you encounter unfamiliar words. Electronic dictionaries are handy, although definitions are less complete. Dictionaries are also available on the Internet. Many textbooks include a *glossary* that defines terms found in the text. Scan the textbook chapter for new vocabulary before you begin to read, and then write the definition of the word in the margin with an arrow pointing to the word. That way, when you get down to reading, you do not need to interrupt your thought process to go and look up the word. You will have the definition right there and can carry on.

You may not always have time to use the following suggestions, but when you can, they will help you make the most of your dictionary.

- **Read every meaning of a word, not just the first.** Think critically about which meaning suits the context, then choose the one that is the best fit.
- **Replace the word in the sentence with the definition.** For example, imagine that you read the following sentence and do not know the word "*indoctrinated*": *The cult indoctrinated its members to reject society's values.*

  In the dictionary, you find several definitions, including "brainwashed" and "instructed." You decide that the one closest to the correct meaning is "brainwashed." With this term, the sentence reads: *The cult brainwashed its members to reject society's values.*

You have laid the groundwork for effective studying. You are now ready for the SQ3R process, which will give you tools for learning and mastering textbook material. As you will see next, SQ3R engages all three aspects of successful intelligence—analytical, creative, and practical.

IN-CLASS NOTES

HOW CAN YOU SET THE STAGE FOR READING?

- Take an active approach to difficult texts
- Choose the right setting
- Define your purpose for reading
- Use special strategies with math and science texts
- Develop strategies to manage learning disabilities
- Build reading speed
- Expand your vocabulary

How can SQ3R *help you own* what you read?

Even with all the time and energy you spend reading textbook chapters, there's no guarantee that you'll understand and remember what you read. The SQ3R study method will help you grasp ideas quickly, remember more, and review effectively for tests. SQ3R stands for *Survey, Question, Read, Recite,* and *Review.* These are the five steps of the studying process. This method was developed about 60 years ago by Francis Robinson. Since then, others have developed variations of this technique, but SQ3R remains the most popular and is still used today because it works well.[5] It is

SKIMMING

Rapid, superficial reading of material that involves glancing through to determine central ideas and main elements.

SCANNING

Reading material in an investigative way to search for specific information.

not merely a method of reading your textbooks. Rather, it is a method of *learning* your textbooks.

Moving through the stages of SQ3R requires that you know how to skim and scan and the differences between the two. Skimming involves the rapid reading of chapter elements, including introductions, conclusions, and summaries; the first and last lines of paragraphs; boldfaced or italicized terms; and pictures, charts, and diagrams. The goal of skimming is a quick construction of the main ideas. In contrast, scanning involves the careful search for specific ideas and facts. You might use scanning during the review phase of SQ3R to locate particular information, such as the answer to a specific question.

SQ3R is a studying framework, not a rigid system. You can follow the steps exactly as they are described or adjust them according to your preferences. You may decide, for example, to survey chapter elements in a different order than do your classmates, to write different questions, or to favour different review strategies. Explore the strategies, evaluate what works, and then make the system your own. Although SQ3R will help you as you study almost every subject, it is not suited for reading literature.

Step 1. Survey

Surveying involves previewing material before you actually study it. Compare it to looking at a map before a trip; taking a few minutes to analyze the route may save hours when you are on the road. You are combining your analytical and practical thinking skills to assess the material as quickly as possible.

When you survey, pay attention to the following text-wide and chapter-by-chapter elements:

Front matter. Before you even get to page 1, most textbooks have a table of contents, a preface, and other materials. The table of contents tells you about coverage, topic order, and features. The preface, in particular, can point out the book's unique approach. For example, the preface for this textbook discusses the purpose of the book and explains how the chapters are organized. It also highlights the main theme running through every chapter of the text: building successful intelligence.

Chapter elements. Chapters generally include devices that help you learn material. Among these are:

- Chapter title, which establishes the topic and perhaps the author's perspective on the topic.
- Chapter introduction, outline, list of objectives, or list of key topics.
- Headings, tables and figures, quotes, marginal notes, and photographs, which help you understand the structure and identify important concepts within the chapter.
- Special chapter features, often presented in boxes set off from the main text, that point to text-wide themes.
- Particular styles or arrangements of type (boldface, italics, underlining, larger fonts, bullet points, boxed text) that call attention to important words and concepts.

- Chapter summary, which reviews the concepts that were presented.
- Review questions and exercises, which help you review and think critically about the material.

Skimming these elements before reading the chapter will help you identify what is important. It will point out the key concepts in the chapter and how the author has organized the information.

Back matter. Some texts include a glossary at the back of the book, an index to help you locate topics, and a bibliography that lists additional readings.

During the Survey step of SQ3R, it is also very helpful to create an outline (discussed in Chapter 7) or concept map (also known as a mind map or think-link) to organize the headings of the chapter. This way, you can see how all key concepts in the chapter relate to one another, and all on one page. For examples, see the concept maps at the beginning of each chapter in this book.

Key 5.4 shows the many devices that texts employ. Think about how many of these devices you already use and which you will start using to boost comprehension.

Survey with text and chapter previewing devices.

key
5.4

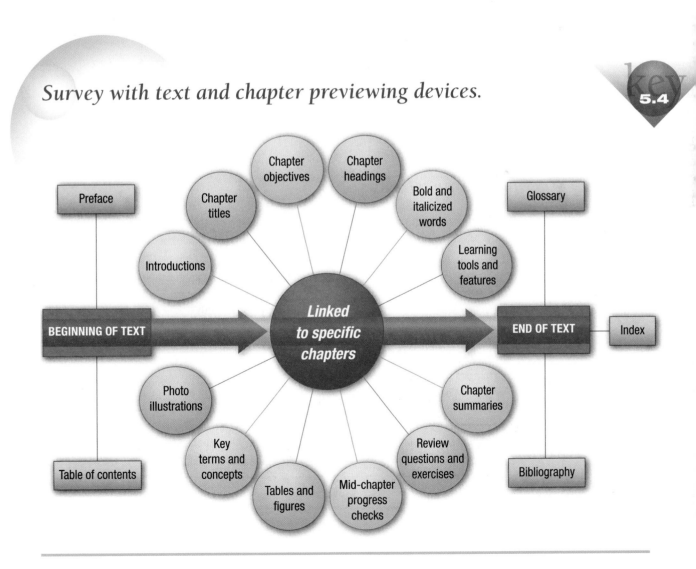

Step 2. Question

Your next step in the SQ3R process is to examine the chapter headings and, on a separate page or in the book margins, to *write questions* linked to them. If your reading material has no headings, develop questions as you read. These questions help you build comprehension and relate new ideas to what you already know. You can take questions from the textbook or from your lecture notes, or come up with them when you survey, based on the ideas you think are most important. This is not as difficult to do as you might think. Just attach the words "who," "what," "where," "when," "why," and "how" to the headings and turn them into questions.

Key 5.5 shows how this works. The column on the left contains secondary-level headings from a section of this chapter. The column on the right rephrases these headings in question form.

There is no "correct" set of questions. In fact, given the same headings, you could write many different questions. Try to think like your instructor and predict questions that might be asked on a test. This seems to be one strategy that is very closely related to success on tests, yet very few students know about it. As you predict test questions and develop the type of probing questions discussed in Chapter 4—questions that delve into the material and help you learn—you are engaging your creative and analytical abilities. Also, you become comfortable with seeing questions and answering them, so doing this on a test will not seem so threatening.

Step 3. Read

Once you have predicted questions and written them in the margin or elsewhere, your questions give you a starting point for *Reading*, the first R in

Use headings to form questions.

key
5.5

THIS EXAMPLE USES HEADINGS FROM THIS CHAPTER TO ILLUSTRATE HOW TO PREDICT TEST QUESTIONS

HEADING:	POSSIBLE TEST QUESTIONS:
Take an active approach.	How does one take an active approach to reading textbooks?
Choose the right setting.	When is the best time to study?
Define your purpose for reading.	Why is it important to define your purpose before you begin reading?
Use special strategies with math and science texts.	Give an example of a strategy you might use when studying math.
Develop strategies to manage learning disabilities.	Where can students who experience LD get assistance on campus to manage their learning disability?
Build reading speed.	Why is it useful to vary your reading speed?
Expand your vocabulary.	What is the best way to expand your vocabulary?

Use SQ3R to become an active reader.

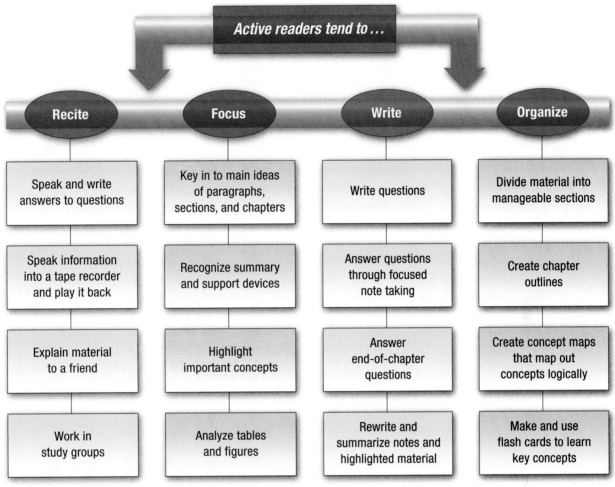

Active readers tend to ...

Recite	Focus	Write	Organize
Speak and write answers to questions	Key in to main ideas of paragraphs, sections, and chapters	Write questions	Divide material into manageable sections
Speak information into a tape recorder and play it back	Recognize summary and support devices	Answer questions through focused note taking	Create chapter outlines
Explain material to a friend	Highlight important concepts	Answer end-of-chapter questions	Create concept maps that map out concepts logically
Work in study groups	Analyze tables and figures	Rewrite and summarize notes and highlighted material	Make and use flash cards to learn key concepts

SQ3R. Learning from textbooks requires that you read actively. Active reading means engaging with the material through questioning, writing, note taking, and other activities. As you can see in Key 5.6, the activities of SQ3R promote active reading. Following are some analytical, creative, and practical strategies that encourage active involvement.

Focus on your Q-stage questions. Read the material with the purpose of answering each question. As you discover ideas and examples that relate to your question, write them down, underline them, or note them in the text.

Take notes on important concepts. As you read make notes of keywords, phrases, and concepts in your notebook. Some students divide the notebook page into two columns, writing questions on the left and answers on the right. This method is called the Cornell note-taking system and will be discussed further in Chapter 7.

Mark up your textbook. Writing notes in the text margins and circling or underlining key ideas will help you make sense of the material. Key 5.7 shows effective use of underlining and marginal notes on the page of a

Markets

The term *market* has acquired many meanings over the years. In its original meaning, a market is a physical place where buyers and sellers gather to exchange goods and services. Medieval towns had market squares where sellers brought their goods and buyers shopped for goods. In today's cities, buying and selling occur in shopping areas rather than markets. To an economist, a market describes all the buyers and sellers who transact over some good or service. Thus, the soft-drink market consists of sellers such as Coca-Cola and PepsiCo, and of all the consumers who buy soft drinks. To a marketer, a market is the set of all actual and potential buyers of a product or service.

Organizations that sell to consumer and business markets recognize that they cannot appeal to all buyers in those markets, or at least not to all buyers in the same way. Buyers are too numerous, too widely scattered, and too varied in their needs and buying practices. And different companies vary widely in their abilities to serve different segments of the market. Rather than trying to compete in an entire market, sometimes against superior competitors, each company must identify the parts of the market that it can serve best.

> *Definition of a market*

> *Companies can't appeal to everyone*

Sellers have not always practiced this philisophy. Their thinking has passed through three stages:

- *Mass marketing.* In mass marketing, the seller mass produces, mass distributes, and mass promotes one product to all buyers. At one time, Coca-Cola produced only one drink for the whole market, hoping it would appeal to everyone. The argument for mass marketing is that it should lead to the lowest costs and prices and create the largest potential market.

> *One-size-fits-all approach*

- *Product-variety marketing.* Here, the seller produces two or more products that have different features, styles, quality, sizes, and so on. Later, Coca-Cola produced several soft drinks packaged in different sizes and containers that were designed to offer variety to buyers rather than to appeal to different market segments. The argument for product-variety marketing is that consumers have different tastes that change over time. Consumers seek variety and change.

> *Offer variety to buyers*

- *Target marketing.* Here, the seller identifies market segments, selects one or more of them, and develops products and marketing mixes tailored to each. For example, Coca-Cola now produces soft drinks for the sugared-cola segment (Coca-Cola Classic and Cherry Coke), the diet segment (Diet Coke and Tab), the no-caffeine segment (Caffeine-Free Coke), and the noncola segment (Minute Maid sodas).

> *A tailored approach to specific market segments*

Today's companies are moving away from mass marketing and product-variety marketing toward target marketing. Target marketing can better help sellers find their marketing opportunities. Sellers can develop the right product for each target market and adjust their prices, distribution channels, and advertising to reach the target market efficiently. Instead of scattering their marketing efforts (the "shotgun" approach), they can focus on the buyers who have greater purchase interest (the "rifle" approach).

> *Current approach is usually TARGET MARKETING*

87

Source: Marketing: An Introduction, 4/E by Kotler/Armstrong, © 1997. Reprinted with permission of Pearson Education, Inc., Upper Saddle River, NJ.

marketing text. Owning your own textbooks and marking them up is an invaluable learning tool because it encourages you to be actively involved with the reading material. You are actively involved when you pick out the key points, and organize and summarize the information you read.

Some people prefer to highlight information using highlighter pens instead of underlining. However, it is usually better to keep a pencil in your hand when you are reading rather than a highlighter pen. Selective highlighting may help you pinpoint material to review, but most people tend to over-highlight. Excessive highlighting is not useful to learning and may actually interfere with comprehension. Furthermore, a highlighter pen does not allow you to do what you can do with a pencil.

If you use a pencil when you read, you can actively think about and organize the ideas for yourself. A pencil allows you to circle some things, and underline or double underline others. You can also number items in a list or sequence of events, and draw lines out to the margins where you can summarize, define, or make notes. With a highlighter, all the points you highlight just look the same, unless of course, you devise a system where you use different colours for different things; but changing pens can be cumbersome and confusing. In addition, the act of highlighting is often passive whereby you can fool yourself into thinking you are actively learning. In fact, what you might really be doing is saying, "I'm going to highlight this so that when I am ready to learn and remember it I'll know where to find it."

Here are tips on how to successfully mark up your texts:

- Mark the text after you read the material once through. Go back and mark the most important information. Only about 10% of the information should be underlined or highlighted.

- Highlight key terms and concepts. In addition to marking definitions and explanations, it is also useful to mark the examples that illustrate and support important ideas. Often similar examples will show up on tests.

- Avoid marking too much. A phrase or two in any paragraph is usually enough, since too much underlining may be overwhelming and of no use. If you must mark long passages, set them off with brackets rather than marking every line.

- Don't confuse highlighting for learning. You will not learn what you highlight unless you interact with it through careful review—asking questions and answering them, paraphrasing information, summarizing, and reciting what you have learned.

Divide your reading into digestible segments. If you are losing the thread of the ideas, try breaking up the reading into smaller segments. Try to avoid reading according to the clock, as in, "I'll read for 30 minutes and then quit." Instead, plan to take a small section and stick to it until you learn it and can explain it and answer questions about it. Divide the weekly readings so that you do a little every day rather than the whole thing in one day. Each day, review what you previously read before you begin to learn the next segment for that day.

Find the main idea. A crucial analytical skill in textbook reading is the ability to find the main idea—the thoughts that are at the heart of the writing, the ideas that create its essential meaning. Comprehension depends on your ability to recognize main ideas and to link the author's other thoughts to them. Although textbook chapters are usually very long, they often deal with just a few main ideas but give much detail about them. It can be difficult to pinpoint what is key and what is not. Here are places you are likely to find these core ideas:

- The major and minor headings almost always indicate the key points of the chapter. They are there to help you understand how the author has organized the ideas. Use the headings to create an outline of the chapter or a concept map (see Chapter 7).

- The sentence at the beginning of the paragraph typically states the topic of the paragraph and the author's perspective on the topic: in other words, what the author wants to communicate about that topic. The rest of the paragraph is usually made up of sentences adding support, further explanation, examples, or details.

- The end of the paragraph, following the supporting details that led up to it, is where you may find a sentence summarizing the main topic of the paragraph.

- Sometimes, the topic sentence is buried in the middle of the paragraph, sandwiched between supporting details. Finding it here is not as common as finding it in the beginning.

- Once in a while, the topic of the paragraph is found in a compilation of ideas from various sentences, each of which contains a critical element. It is up to the reader to piece these elements together to create the essence of meaning.

- It is also possible that the main idea is never explicitly stated, but only implied by the information presented in the paragraph. Then it is up to the reader to "read between the lines" to figure out the author's point.

How, then, do you decide just what is the main idea of a paragraph? Ophelia H. Hancock, a specialist in improving reading skills for post-secondary students, suggests a three-step approach:[6]

1. **Search for the topic of the paragraph.** The topic of the paragraph is the broad subject being discussed. This may include topics such as former Prime Minister Pierre Trudeau, hate crimes on campus, or the Internet, for example. This is not the same thing as the main idea, which is usually the author's perspective on the topic or what he or she wants you to get out of it.

2. **Identify the aspect of the topic that is the paragraph's focus.** If the general topic is former Prime Minister Pierre Trudeau, the author may choose to focus on any of thousands of aspects of that topic, such as his political career, government policies, or his effectiveness as a public speaker.

3. **Find what the author wants you to know about the specific aspect being discussed.** This is the main idea. The main idea of a paragraph dealing with Prime Minister Trudeau as a public speaker may be this: *Canadian Prime Minister Pierre Trudeau was a gifted, charismatic speaker.*

Knowledge is power they say. Knowledge is not only power, it is good fun.

E. M. FORSTER

Step 4. Recite

Once you finish reading a topic, stop and answer the questions you raised in the Q stage of SQ3R. Engage your practical thinking skills to choose the best way to do this. You may decide to *recite* each answer aloud, silently speak the answers to yourself, tell or teach the answers to another person, or write your ideas and answers in brief notes. Writing is often the most effective way to solidify what you have read because writing from memory checks your understanding. It also allows you to practice formulating your thoughts on paper as you will need to do in a testing situation.

Nevertheless, keep your learning styles in mind when you explore different strategies (see Chapter 3). For example, an intrapersonal learner may prefer writing, whereas an interpersonal learner might want to recite answers aloud to a classmate. A logical–mathematical learner may benefit from organizing material into detailed outlines, whereas a musical learner might want to chant information aloud to a rhythm.

After you finish one section, read the next. *Repeat the question–read–recite cycle until you complete the entire chapter.* If you find yourself fumbling for thoughts, you may not yet "own" the ideas. Read and learn the section that's giving you trouble until you master its contents. Understanding each section as you go is crucial because the material in one section often forms a foundation for the next.

get analytical!

FIND THE MAIN IDEA

Develop your ability to analyze the parts of a paragraph.

Use the three-step approach described on page 140 to find the main idea of the following paragraph:

> Tone relates not so much to what you say as to how you say it. The tone of your writing has a major impact on what you are trying to communicate to your audience. Tone involves your choice of words interacting with your message. Have you ever reacted to someone's understanding of what you wrote with "That's not what I meant to say"? Your tone can be what has thrown your readers off track, although you can only be misunderstood if your writing is unclear or imprecise.[7]

● What is the topic of this paragraph?

_____

_____

● What aspect of the topic is being discussed?

_____

_____

● What main idea is being communicated?

_____

_____

Now choose a paragraph from one of the texts you are currently studying, and use the same questions to find the paragraph's main idea. How do these questions help you focus on the paragraph's most important points?

Step 5. Review

Review soon after you finish a chapter—within 24 hours. Reviewing immediately and periodically in the days and weeks after you learn the information will solidify your understanding. Chances are good that if you close the book after you read, you will forget most of the material within 48 hours. Here are reviewing techniques that engage all three components of successful intelligence. Try many, and use what works best for you.

- Skim and reread your notes. Then try summarizing them from memory.
- Answer the text's end-of-chapter review, discussion, and application questions.
- Quiz yourself, using the questions you raised in the Q stage. If you can't answer any of your own or the text's questions, scan the text for answers.
- Create a chapter outline in standard outline or concept map form.
- Reread the preface, headings, tables, and chapter **summary.**
- Recite important concepts to yourself, or record important information on a cassette or digital recorder and play it in your car or on a portable player.
- Make flash cards that have an idea or word on one side and examples, a definition, or other related information on the other. Test yourself.
- Review and summarize in writing the material you have underlined, highlighted, or bracketed. Your goal is to create a summary that focuses on the central ideas, setting the stage for critical thinking.
- Think critically. Break ideas down into examples, consider similar or different concepts, recall important terms, evaluate ideas, and explore causes and effects.
- Discuss the concepts with a classmate or in a study group. Trying to teach study partners what you learned will pinpoint what material you know and what still needs work.

If a concept is still unclear, ask your instructor for help. Pinpoint the material you wish to discuss, schedule a meeting during office hours, and bring a list of questions.

Refreshing your knowledge is easier and faster than learning it the first time. Set up regular review sessions, perhaps once a week. Reviewing in different ways increases the likelihood of retention.

SUMMARY

A concise restatement of the material, in your own words, that covers the main points.

IN-CLASS NOTES

HOW CAN SQ3R HELP YOU OWN WHAT YOU READ?

- The SQ3R study method helps you:
  - Understand more quickly
  - Review more effectively
  - Remember more
- SQ3R stands for:
  - Survey
  - Question
  - Read
  - Recite
  - Review

How can you *respond critically* to what you read?

The fundamental purpose of all post-secondary reading is knowledge. Think of your reading process as an archaeological dig. The first step is to excavate a site and uncover the artefacts—that's your initial survey and reading of the material. As important as the excavation is, the process is incomplete if you stop there. The second step is to investigate each item, evaluate what they all mean, and derive knowledge from what you discover. Critical reading allows you to complete that crucial second step.

Like critical thinking, critical reading is a part of analytical thinking (see Chapter 4). Instead of simply accepting what you read, seek knowledge by questioning the material as you move from idea to idea. The best critical readers question every statement for accuracy, relevance, and logic. They also extend critical analysis to all information shared through all media.

Use knowledge of fact and opinion to evaluate arguments

Critical readers evaluate arguments to determine whether they are accurate and logical. In this context, *argument* refers to a persuasive case: a set of connected ideas supported by examples that a writer makes to prove or disprove a point.

It's easy to accept or reject an argument outright according to whether or not it fits with your point of view. If you ask questions, however, you can determine the argument's validity and understand it in greater depth. Evaluating an argument involves evaluation of the following:

- The quality of the evidence.
- Whether the support fits the concept.
- The logical connections.

When quality evidence combines with appropriate support and tight logic, the argument is solid.

What is the quality of the evidence? Ask the following questions to evaluate the evidence:

- What is the source of the information?
- Is the source reliable and free of bias?
- Who wrote this and what was their intent?
- What assumptions underlie this material?
- Is the argument based on opinion?
- How does the evidence compare with evidence from other sources?

How well does the evidence support the idea? Ask these questions to determine whether the evidence fits the concept:

- Is there enough evidence to support the central idea?
- Do examples and ideas logically connect to one another?

- Is the evidence convincing? Do the examples build a strong case?
- What different and perhaps opposing arguments seem just as valid?

Approach every argument with healthy skepticism. Have an open mind in order to assess whether you are convinced or have serious questions. Use critical thinking to make an informed decision.

If, for example, you read an article with this premise: "The dissolution of the traditional family unit (working father, stay-at-home mother, dependent children) is contributing to society's problems," you might examine the facts and examples the writer uses to support this statement, looking carefully at the cause-and-effect structure of the argument. You might question the writer's sources. You might think of examples that support the statement. You might find examples that disprove this argument, such as statistics regarding crime rates, education levels, or lifestyle satisfaction where nontraditional family units are common. Finally, you might think of opposing arguments, including the ideas and examples to support those arguments.

Increase media literacy

The agencies of mass communication—television, film, journalism (magazines and newspapers), books, and the Internet.

Use your analytical thinking skills to analyze the information you receive through the media, including television, radio, film, the Internet, newspapers, magazines, and books. By improving your *media literacy,* you will approach every media message with a healthy skepticism that leads you to ask questions, look for evidence, recognize perspectives, and challenge assumptions. This approach will help you decide which information you can trust and use.

The Center for Media Literacy explains "Five Core Concepts of Media Literacy":[8]

1. **All media are constructions.** All media are carefully constructed presentations designed for particular effect—to encourage you to feel certain emotions, to develop particular opinions, or to buy advertised products.

2. **Media use unique "languages."** Creators of media carefully choose wording, music, colours, timing, and other factors to produce a desired effect.

3. **Different audiences understand the same media message differently.** Individuals understand media in the context of their unique experiences. Someone who has climbed a mountain, for example, will experience a Mount Everest documentary differently from someone who has not.

4. **Media have commercial interests.** Creators of media are driven by the intent to sell products, services, or ideas. Advertising is chosen to appeal to the most likely audience. For example, beer and automobile ads are usually directed at 20- to 30-year-old men. These ads often appear during sporting events or other programs geared toward this same group.

5. **Media have embedded values and points of view.** Any media product reflects the values and biases of the people who created it.

Critical reading of texts and the media takes time and focus. You can learn from others by working in pairs or groups whenever you can.

Why and how should you *study with others*?

Use your practical thinking skills to find a study partner or set up a study group. When you study with others, you benefit from shared knowledge, solidified knowledge, increased motivation, and increased teamwork ability.

- **Shared knowledge.** It takes less time for study group members to pass on their knowledge to each other than for each member to learn all of the material alone.
- **Solidified knowledge.** When you discuss concepts or teach them to others, you reinforce what you know and strengthen your critical thinking. Part of the benefit comes from repeating information aloud, and part comes from how you think through information before you pass it on to someone else.
- **Increased motivation.** When you study by yourself, you are accountable to yourself alone. In a study group, however, others see your level of preparation, and this may increase your motivation.
- **Increased teamwork ability.** The more experience you have with group dynamics, the more effective your teamwork will be. Groups sometimes need to struggle through stages of development and solidify into an effective working group where members' skills, abilities, and learning styles complement one another.

Knowledge is of two kinds. We know a subject ourselves, or we know where we can find information upon it.

SAMUEL JOHNSON

When people in a group or study partnership complement one another, it can be beneficial to all. You might be able to find someone who has strengths in an area you need to work on, and weaknesses in an area that you are strong in, and then the two of you can support each other's learning. For example, someone who is easily distracted might find a study partner who is very focused to support staying on task. And perhaps the other can reciprocate by helping in another way, say with French or reading homework. In this way, it

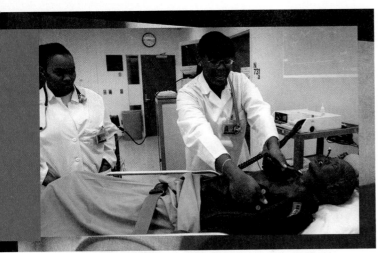

What you learn in your textbook is often enhanced and solidified by hands-on experience. These respiratory therapy students put their knowledge to work on a medical mannequin.

is beneficial to find study partners who have strengths in different learning styles than yours.

Group study can make a real difference if group members are dedicated. Choosing a leader, meeting at regular times, and setting goals all help groups accomplish their work.

Leaders and participants

Study groups and other teams rely on both leaders and participants to accomplish goals. Becoming aware of the roles each plays will increase your effectiveness.[9] Keep in mind that participants sometimes perform leadership tasks and vice versa. In addition, some teams shift their leadership frequently during a project.

Being an effective participant

Some people are most comfortable when participating in a group that someone else leads. Participants are "part owners" of the team process with a responsibility for, and a stake in, the outcome. The following strategies will help you become more effective in this role.

get practical! **FORM A STUDY GROUP**

Form a study group for one of your courses.

Get a group together and use this form to decide on and record the details.

- Course name: _____
- Study group members (names, phone numbers, e-mail addresses):

  Member #1 _____

  Member #2 _____

  Member #3 _____

  Member #4 _____

  Member #5 _____

- Regular meeting time(s): _____
- Regular meeting place(s): _____
- Three strategies you plan to use to make the most of group time:

  Strategy #1: _____

  Strategy #2: _____

  Strategy #3: _____

- **Get involved.** Let people know your views on decisions.
- **Be organized.** The more focused your ideas, the more others will take them seriously.
- **Be willing to discuss.** Be open to different opinions. Always be respectful.
- **Keep your word.** Carry out whatever tasks you promise to do.

Being an effective leader

Some people prefer to initiate the action, make decisions, and control how things proceed. Leaders often have a "big-picture" perspective that allows them to envision and plan group projects. The following strategies help a leader succeed.

- **Define and limit projects.** The leader should define the group's purpose (Is it to brainstorm, to make decisions, or to collaborate on a project?) and limit tasks so that the effort remains focused.
- **Assign work and set a schedule.** A group functions best when everyone has an assigned task and when deadlines are clear.
- **Set meeting and project agendas.** The leader should, with advice from other members, establish and communicate goals and define how the work will proceed.
- **Focus progress.** It is the leader's job to keep everyone headed in the right direction.
- **Set the tone.** If the leader is fair, respectful, encouraging, and hardworking, group members are likely to follow the example.
- **Evaluate results.** The leader should determine whether the team is accomplishing its goals on schedule. If the team is not moving ahead, the leader should make changes.

Strategies for study group success

Every study group is unique. The way a group operates may depend on members' personalities, the subject being studied, and the group's size. No matter the particulars, the following general strategies will foster success.

- **Choose a leader for each meeting.** Rotating the leadership helps all members take ownership of the group.
- **Set long-term and short-term goals.** At your first meeting, determine what the group wants to accomplish over the semester. At the beginning of each meeting, have one person compile a list of questions to address.
- **Adjust to different personalities.** The art of getting along will serve you well no matter what you do.
- **Share the work.** The most important factor is a willingness to work, not a particular level of knowledge.
- **Set a regular meeting schedule.** Try every week, every two weeks, or whatever the group can manage.
- **Create study materials for one another.** Give each group member the task of finding a piece of information to compile, photocopy or email, and to review for other group members.

- **Help each other learn.** Have group members teach pieces of information, make up quizzes for each other, or go through flash cards together.

- **Pool your note-taking resources.** Compare notes with your group members and fill in any information you don't have. Try different note-taking styles (see Chapter 7 for more on note taking).

- **Be aware of differences.** When members of a study group come from different backgrounds, the differing values and beliefs may impact how easily members get along. For example, whereas a student from a high-context culture such as Greece may want to begin every meeting with social talk, others from low-context cultures are likely to want to focus on assignments right away. Or students from a high-context culture like Japan may be uncomfortable talking about personal accomplishments in the way some others do and, instead, want to emphasize what the group does together. (For more on high-context and low-context cultures, see Chapter 2.)

Addressing the communication issues that result from these and other differences requires group members to talk openly about what they observe and to work to accommodate each other's style. Making such adjustments will prepare you well for the twenty-first-century workplace.

IN-CLASS NOTES

WHY AND HOW SHOULD YOU STUDYWITH OTHERS?

Why and how should you study with others?
Why:

- You can benefit from
  - Shared knowledge
  - Solidified knowledge
  - Increased motivation
  - Increased teamwork ability
- It encourages you to be an effective
  - Leader
  - Participant

How:

- Follow basic strategies for group success

читать

If you read Russian, you know that the word preceding this paragraph means "read." The brain's ability to process and group letters to form words, phrases, and sentences is the basis for reading and studying.

Think of the vast amounts of information your mind processes as you read and study your textbooks. Challenge yourself to raise the bar of achievement by reading often and using the strategies suggested in this chapter. You will understand more, remember more, and have more strategies to use as you work toward goals in school and beyond.

SUGGESTED READINGS

Armstrong, William H., and M. Willard Lampe II. *Barron's Pocket Guide to Study Tips: How to Study Effectively and Get Better Grades*. New York: Barron's Educational Series, 2004.

Chesla, Elizabeth. *Reading Comprehension Success: In 20 Minutes a Day*. 2nd ed. Florence, KY: Thomson Delmar Learning, 2002.

Frank, Steven. *The Everything Study Book*. Holbrook, MA: Adams Media, 1997.

Labunski, Richard E. *The Educated Student: Getting the Most Out of Your College Years*. Versailles, KY: Marley and Beck, 2003.

Luckie, William R., Wood Smethurst, and Sarah Beth Huntley. *Study Power Workbook: Exercises in Study Skills to Improve Your Learning and Your Grades*. Cambridge, MA: Brookline Books, 1999.

Silver, Theodore. *The Princeton Review Study Smart: Hands-on, Nuts and Bolts Techniques for Earning Higher Grades*. New York: Villard Books, 1996.

INTERNET RESOURCES

Keys to Success Companion Website: www.pearsoned.ca/carter

Learning Strategies for Specific Disabilities. Access Service Website, University of Ottawa: www.sass.uottawa.ca/access/professors/learning_strategies.php

Study Tips. Learning Strategies Development, Health, Counselling and Disability Services, Queen's University: www.bewell-dowell.org/sos/study_tips.html#

Academictips.org (study tips and links): www.academictips.org/

How to Study (study advice with valuable links): www.howtostudy.com

Prentice Hall Student Success Supersite. Academic Skills: www.prenhall.com/success/

BUILDING SKILLS

FOR ACADEMIC, CAREER, AND LIFE SUCCESS

SUCCESSFUL INTELLIGENCE

PRACTICAL · CREATIVE
ANALYTICAL

SUCCESSFUL INTELLIGENCE

Developing Successful Intelligence

PUTTING IT ALL TOGETHER

Learning from a textbook. The following page is from the chapter "Groups and Organizations" in the sixth edition of John J. Macionis' *Sociology*.[10] Apply SQ3R as you read the excerpt. Using what you learned in this chapter about study techniques, complete the questions that follow (some questions ask you to mark the page itself).

Step 1. Think it through: *Gather information and analyze it.*

a. Skim the excerpt. Identify the headings on the page and the relationships among them.

b. Mark primary-level headings with a #1, secondary headings with a #2, and tertiary (third-level) headings with a #3.

c. Analyze by answering the following questions.

Which heading serves as an umbrella for the rest?

_____

What do the headings tell you about the content of the page?

_____

What are three concepts that seem important to remember?

1._____

2._____

3._____

Step 2. Think out of the box: *Create useful study questions.* Based on the three concepts you pulled out, write three study questions that you can review with an instructor, tutor, or other student.

create your future

150

(continued on page 152)

SOCIAL GROUPS

Virtually everyone moves through life with a sense of belonging; this is the experience of group life. A **social group** refers to *two or more people who identify and interact with one another.* Human beings continually come together to form couples, families, circles of friends, neighborhoods, churches, businesses, clubs, and numerous large organizations. Whatever the form, groups encompass people with shared experiences, loyalties, and interests. In short, while maintaining their individuality, the members of social groups also think of themselves as a special "we."

Groups, Categories, and Crowds

People often use the term "group" imprecisely. We now distinguish the group from the similar concepts of category and crowd.

Category. A *category* refers to people who have some status in common. Women, single fathers, military recruits, homeowners, and Roman Catholics are all examples of categories.

Why are categories not considered groups? Simply because, while the individuals involved are aware that they are not the only ones to hold that particular status, the vast majority are strangers to one another.

Crowd. A *crowd* refers to a temporary cluster of individuals who may or may not interact at all. Students sitting in a lecture hall do engage one another and share some common identity as college classmates; thus, such a crowd might be called a loosely formed group. By contrast, riders hurtling along on a subway train or bathers enjoying a summer day at the beach pay little attention to one another and amount to an anonymous aggregate of people. In general, then, crowds are too transitory and impersonal to qualify as social groups.

The right circumstances, however, could turn a crowd into a group. People riding in a subway train that crashes under the city streets generally become keenly aware of their common plight and begin to help one another. Sometimes such extraordinary experiences become the basis for lasting relationships.

Primary and Secondary Groups

Acquaintances commonly greet one another with a smile and the simple phrase, "Hi! How are you?" The response is usually a well scripted, "Just fine, thanks, how about you?" This answer, of course, is often more formal than truthful. In most cases, providing a detailed account of how you are *really* doing would prompt the other person to beat a hasty and awkward exit.

Sociologists classify social groups by measuring them against two ideal types based on members' genuine level of personal concern. This variation is the key to distinguishing *primary* from *secondary* groups.

According to Charles Horton Cooley (1864–1929), a **primary group** is a *small social group whose members share personal and enduring relationships.* Bound together by primary relationships, individuals in primary groups typically spend a great deal of time together, engage in a wide range of common activities, and feel that they know one another well. Although not without periodic conflict, members of primary groups display sincere concern for each other's welfare. The family is every society's most important primary group.

Cooley characterized these personal and tightly integrated groups as *primary* because they are among the first groups we experience in life. In addition, the family and early play groups also hold primary importance in the socialization process, shaping attitudes, behavior, and social identity.

SOCIOLOGY

145

1._____

2._____

3._____

Step 3. Make it happen: *Read and remember*. Read the excerpt, putting SQ3R to work. Using a pencil, mark key phrases and sentences. Write short marginal notes to help you review the material later. After reading the excerpted page thoroughly, write a short summary paragraph.

_____

_____

_____

Team Building

COLLABORATIVE SOLUTIONS

Organizing a study group. Organize a study group with three or four members of your class. At the group's first meeting, discuss each of the following points and agree on the following:

- The goal for this group is _____
  (to prepare for an upcoming test, group project, etc.)

- We will meet weekly on _____ at _____ o'clock
           (day of the week) (time)
  in room _____.
     (where you will meet)

- We will work together by _____
  (e.g. listening openly, sharing ideas, discussing freely, providing constructive feedback, etc.)

- We agree to (check the ones you agree on):
  - pool and share our notes
  - teach each other difficult concepts
  - make up, administer, and grade quizzes for each other
  - create study flash cards
  - use SQ3R to review required readings

- We will be held accountable to each other by _____

_____

(Set specific guidelines for how group members will be held accountable.)

Writing

DISCOVERY THROUGH JOURNALING

Record your thoughts here or on a separate piece of paper or in a journal.

Reading challenges.

1. Which course this semester presents your most difficult reading challenge?

_____

2. What makes it difficult? Is it the type of material you have to read, the amount, the level of difficulty, or something else?

_____

3. By thinking about the strategies in this chapter, create and describe a plan that addresses this challenge.

_____

_____

_____

Career Portfolio

PLAN FOR SUCCESS

Complete the following here or in your electronic portfolio or on separate sheets of paper.

Reading skills on the job. North American society revolves around the written word. The focus on word processing and computerized documents has increased the need for computer-literate workers. The ability to communicate in various forms by reading and writing is one of the skills identified by The Conference Board of Canada as "need[ed] to enter, stay in, and progress in the world of work" and beyond in daily life.[11]

1. For each of the following skill areas listed, indicate all of the ways in which you use that skill on the job or know you will need to use it in your future career. Then, for each skill, rate your ability on a scale from 1 to 10, with 10 being highest.

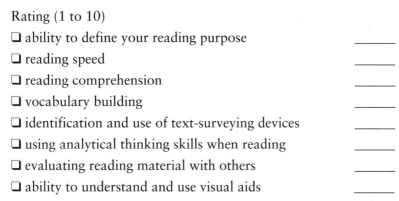

   Rating (1 to 10)
   ❑ ability to define your reading purpose _____
   ❑ reading speed _____
   ❑ reading comprehension _____
   ❑ vocabulary building _____
   ❑ identification and use of text-surveying devices _____
   ❑ using analytical thinking skills when reading _____
   ❑ evaluating reading material with others _____
   ❑ ability to understand and use visual aids _____

2. Circle the two skills that you think will be most important for your career as well as for your success as a learner.

3. For the two skill areas in which you rated yourself lowest, think about how you can improve your abilities. Make a problem-solving plan for each (you may want to use a flow chart like the one on page 117). Check your progress in one month and at the end of the semester.

Chapter Review Questions

Choose the option that BEST completes the statement or answers the question. After completing the questions, check your answers against the Answer Key at the back of this book (p. 314).

1. When instructors assign a chapter from a textbook, they want you to
   a. ☐ Read it.
   b. ☐ Skim it.
   c. ☐ Question it.
   d. ☐ Learn it.

2. Reading comprehension refers to your ability to
   a. ☐ Understand what you read.
   b. ☐ Read quickly for information.
   c. ☐ Ask analytical questions.
   d. ☐ Remember what you read.

3. Building your vocabulary will assist your reading comprehension because you
   a. ☐ Can use new words in your writing.
   b. ☐ Will not need to stop to look words up in a dictionary.
   c. ☐ Will be able to use a dictionary more efficiently.
   d. ☐ Can guess the meaning of words.

4. Which of the following would NOT be considered a primary source?
   a. ☐ An autobiography written by one of the survivors of the holocaust.
   b. ☐ A new play written by a popular playwright.
   c. ☐ A research study written by a scientific researcher.
   d. ☐ An article written by a journalist summarizing the latest studies on cancer.

5. Where is the best place to complete textbook readings?
   a. ☐ In the library where others are studying too.
   b. ☐ In a quiet room free from distractions.
   c. ☐ In a comfortable room where relaxing music is playing.
   d. ☐ The best location will be different for everyone.

6. When is the best time to complete textbook readings?
   a. ☐ First thing in the morning when you are fresh.
   b. ☐ Late at night when everyone is asleep and it is quiet.
   c. ☐ Just before the class in which the topic will be discussed.
   d. ☐ It will be different for everyone.

7. When is the best time to take a break?
   a. ☐ Before your mind begins to wander.
   b. ☐ After your mind begins to wander.
   c. ☐ After you complete the whole chapter.
   d. ☐ Every hour.

8. The purpose for reading textbooks is to read for
   a. ☐ Understanding.
   b. ☐ Analytical evaluation.
   c. ☐ Practical application.
   d. ☐ Any or all of the above.

9. Which of the following is true about reading?
   a. ☐ If you read too quickly, you will always sacrifice comprehension.
   b. ☐ All reading material should be read at the same rate.
   c. ☐ Increasing your reading speed takes practice.
   d. ☐ Sub-vocalization helps comprehension.

10. SQ3R is a method for
    a. ☐ Note taking.
    b. ☐ Reading.
    c. ☐ Reviewing.
    d. ☐ Summarizing.

11. The correct order for applying SQ3R technique is:

a. ☐ Summarize, question, read, recite, review.

b. ☐ Survey, question, recite, read, review.

c. ☐ Survey, question, read, review, retain.

d. ☐ Survey, question, read, recite, review.

12. When you are reading a paragraph for the first time, it is a good idea to underline the important information

a. ☐ As you read.

b. ☐ After you have read the entire paragraph.

c. ☐ After you have read the entire chapter.

d. ☐ When you preview the chapter.

13. When you survey a chapter, it is recommended that you _____ the lists, charts, graphs, and study questions.

a. ☐ Skip.

b. ☐ Copy.

c. ☐ Take notes on.

d. ☐ Skim.

14. How much of a text should you underline or highlight?

a. ☐ 10%

b. ☐ 20%

c. ☐ 30%

d. ☐ 50%

15. In order to increase retention, when is the best time after reading to review what you have learned?

a. ☐ Within 24 hours.

b. ☐ After 24 hours.

c. ☐ Within 48 hours.

d. ☐ After 48 hours.

16. Evaluating an argument DOES NOT include evaluation of

a. ☐ The quality of the evidence.

b. ☐ Whether support fits the concept.

c. ☐ The logical connections.

d. ☐ The time frame.

17. The term "media" includes

a. ☐ Television, film, magazines, newspapers, books, *but not* the Internet

b. ☐ Television, film, magazines, newspapers, the Internet, *but not* books.

c. ☐ Television, film, magazines, books, the Internet, *but not* newspapers.

d. ☐ Television, film, magazines, newspapers, books, *and* the Internet.

18. Improving your *media literacy* means you will approach every media message with healthy _____.

a. ☐ Respect.

b. ☐ Skepticism.

c. ☐ Disapproval.

d. ☐ Appreciation.

19. The most effective groups choose

a. ☐ One leader to lead all the meetings.

b. ☐ A different leader for each meeting.

c. ☐ Two leaders to share the task of leading the meetings.

d. ☐ No leader at all.

20. In order for a group to work well, participants need to

a. ☐ Keep their views and opinions to themselves.

b. ☐ Be concerned with only their own tasks, not anyone else's.

c. ☐ Be open to different opinions.

d. ☐ Tolerate it when others fail to carry out tasks they promise to do.

Research and Writing

GATHERING AND COMMUNICATING IDEAS

This chapter is organized as follows:

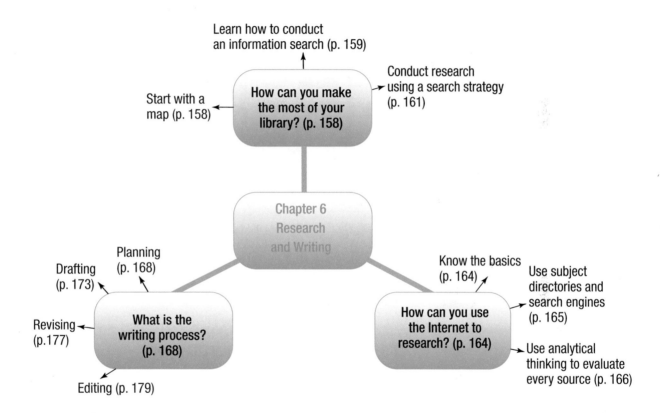

Learn how to conduct an information search (p. 159)

Conduct research using a search strategy (p. 161)

Start with a map (p. 158)

How can you make the most of your library? (p. 158)

Chapter 6
Research and Writing

Planning (p. 168)

Drafting (p. 173)

Revising (p.177)

What is the writing process? (p. 168)

Editing (p. 179)

Know the basics (p. 164)

Use subject directories and search engines (p. 165)

How can you use the Internet to research? (p. 164)

Use analytical thinking to evaluate every source (p. 166)

Research and writing, powerful tools that engage your successful intelligence, are at the heart of your education. Through library and Internet research, you gather and analyze information from sources all over the world. Through writing, you analyze ideas, think creatively about what they mean, and communicate information and perspectives to others. Whether you write an essay for an English course or a summary of a scientific study for Biology class, the writing process helps sharpen your thinking and your practical communication skills.

This chapter has two goals: to help you improve your skill in finding information at your college or university library and on the Internet, and to reinforce some of the writing basics that

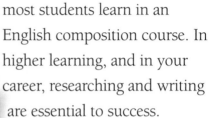

most students learn in an English composition course. In higher learning, and in your career, researching and writing are essential to success.

How can you *make the most* of your library?

A library is a home for information; consider it the "brain" of your post-secondary institution. Your practical thinking skills will help you find what you need quickly and efficiently.

Start with a map

Make your life easier right off the bat by learning how your library is organized:

Circulation desk. All publications are checked out at the circulation desk, which is usually near the library entrance.

Reference area. Here you'll find reference books, including encyclopedias, directories, dictionaries, almanacs, and atlases. You'll also find librarians and other library employees who can direct you to information. Computer terminals, containing the library's catalogue of holdings as well as online bibliographic and full-text databases, are usually part of the reference area.

Book area. Books, and sometimes magazines and journals in bound or boxed volumes, are stored in the stacks. A library with *open stacks* allows you to search for materials on your own. In a *closed-stack* system, a staff member retrieves materials for you.

Periodicals area. Here you'll find recent issues of popular and scholarly magazines, journals, and newspapers. Because you usually cannot check out unbound (periodicals,) you may find photocopy machines nearby where you can copy pages.

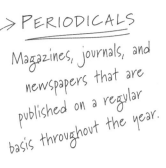

> PERIODICALS
>
> Magazines, journals, and newspapers that are published on a regular basis throughout the year.

Audiovisual materials areas. Many libraries have special areas for video, art and photography, and recorded music collections.

Computer areas. Computer terminals, linked to post-secondary library databases and the Internet, may be scattered throughout the building or set off in particular areas. You may be able to access these databases and the Internet from computer labs and writing centres. Some post-secondary library websites will even let you access some databases from your home computer.

Microform areas. Most libraries have microform reading areas. *Microforms* are materials printed in reduced size on film, either *microfilm* (a reel of film) or *microfiche* (a sheet or card of film), that is viewed through special machines.

Almost all college and university libraries offer orientation sessions on how to find what you need. In addition, library webpages usually allow access to online catalogues from your own institution and other local colleges and universities. You may also be able to access online databases from the websites, and phone numbers and email addresses for reference librarians. If you need assistance, take a real or virtual tour and sign up for training at the library.

While the library is still a major resource centre, online research has become a significant source of information for many students.

My library
Was dukedom large enough.

WILLIAM SHAKESPEARE

Learn how to conduct an information search

Narrow your topic

The most successful and time-saving search for information involves a specific *search strategy*—a practical, step-by-step method that takes you from general to specific sources. Starting with general sources provides an overview of your topic and can lead to more specific information and sources. For example, an encyclopedia article on the archaeological discovery of the Dead Sea Scrolls—manuscripts written between 250 BC and AD 68 that trace the roots of Judaism and Christianity—may mention that one of the most important

get practical!   DISCOVER YOUR COLLEGE OR UNIVERSITY LIBRARY

Learn the nuts and bolts of your school's library system.

Identify the following:

- Name and location of the library (or, if your college or university has more than one library, identify the branch you are most likely to use):

  _____

- Hours of operation:

  _____

- Library website address:

  _____

- Important email addresses and phone numbers, including those of the reference and circulation desks:

  _____

- Stack locations of the books and other publications you may need for your courses:

  _____

- Names and URLs of computer databases you are likely to use:

  _____

- Location of a library nook or chair that is ideal for studying:

  _____

books on the subject is *Understanding the Dead Sea Scrolls,* edited by Hershel Shanks. This book, in turn, leads you to 13 experts who wrote specialized text chapters.

It's important to narrow your topic, because broad topics yield too much data. Instead of using the topic "Dead Sea Scrolls" in your search, for example, consider narrowing it to any of the following:

- How the Dead Sea Scrolls were discovered by Bedouin shepherds in 1947
- The historical origins of the scrolls
- The process archaeologists used to reconstruct scroll fragments

Conduct a keyword search

To find materials related to your topic, conduct a *keyword search* of the library database. This is a method for locating sources through the use of topic-related words and phrases. By using words that are specific to your topic, you will filter out information that is not related and access only those sources that are relevant to what you are searching for. For example, if you search using the word "*art,*" you will receive a listing of hundreds or maybe thousands of sources. Instead, by using a keyword search that focuses on the topic you have narrowed in on, for example, "*nineteenth-century French impressionist art,*" you will get much more relevant and useful information.

Keyword searches are easier to use than some of the other search methods because they use natural language, rather than specialized classification vocabulary. Key 6.1 provides tips to help you use the keyword system.

How to perform an effective keyword search.

IF YOU ARE SEARCHING FOR...	DO THIS	EXAMPLE
A word	Type the word normally	aid
A phrase	Type the phrase in its normal word order (use regular word spacing) or surround the phrase with double quotation marks	financial aid *or* "financial aid"
Two or more keywords	Type the words in any order, surrounding the words with quotation marks (use *and* to separate the words)	"financial aid" *and* "scholarships"
Topic A or Topic B	Type the words in any order, surrounding the words with quotation marks (use *or* to separate the words)	"financial aid" *or* "scholarships"
Topic A but not Topic B	Type topic A first within quotation marks, and then topic B within quotation marks (use *not* to separate the words)	"financial aid" *not* "scholarships"

As you search, keep in mind that

- double quotes around a word or phrase will locate the exact term you entered ("financial aid").

- using uppercase or lowercase does not affect the search (*Scholarships* will find *scholarships*).

- singular terms will find the plural (*scholarship* will find *scholarships*).

- using the words "and," "or," and "not" will link or delineate two or more keywords and will result in a list of all sources that relate to the two terms (*financial aid and students*). Search systems are not equipped to understand phrases or sentences, so use only keywords.

Conduct research using a search strategy

Knowing where to look during each phase of your search helps you find information quickly and efficiently. A successful search strategy often begins with general references and moves to more specific references (see Key 6.2).

Use general reference works

Begin your research with general reference works. These works cover many different topics in a broad, general way. General reference guides are often available online or on CD-ROM. Works that fall into the general reference category include the following:

> **CD-ROM**
>
> A compact disc, containing words and images in electronic form, that can be read by a computer (CD-ROM stands for "compact disc read-only memory").

- Encyclopedias covering a range of topics, such as the multi-volume *Canadian Encyclopedia: Year 2000 Edition* or those specific to one field, such as the *Encyclopedia of Music in Canada* or *Canadian Encyclopedia of Gardening*

- Almanacs such as the *Scott's Canadian Sourcebook*, or *Canadian Almanac and Directory*

A library search strategy will help you find information.

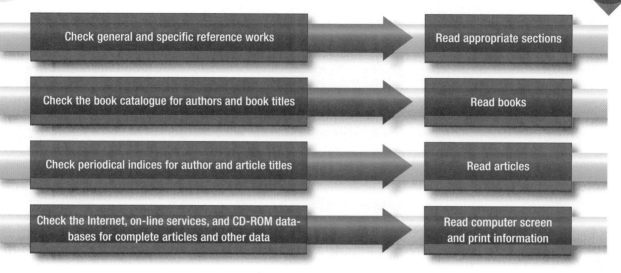

- Yearbooks such as the *Canada Yearbook* or those specific to a subject, such as the *Film Canada Yearbook*
- Dictionaries such as *Canadian Oxford Dictionary* or *Gage Canadian Dictionary*, or those specific to a field, such as *Canadian Dictionary of Finance and Investment Terms*
- Biographical reference works such as *Creative Canada: a Biographical Dictionary of Twentieth-Century Creative and Performing Artists*, or the *Who's Who* books on a variety of topics, such as *Who's Who in Fashion*, *Who's Who in Europe*, or *Who's Who in the Writers' Union of Canada*
- Bibliographies such as *Books in Print* (especially the *Subject Guide to Books in Print*)

Scan these sources for an overview of your topic. Bibliographies at the end of articles may also lead to important sources.

Browse through books on your subject

Use the computerized *library catalogue* to find books and other materials on your topic. The catalogue, searchable by author, title, and subject, tells you which publications the library owns. If the source you need is not available in your library, most colleges and universities have interlibrary loans services which can bring in materials for you from another institution's library.

Post-secondary libraries use the Library of Congress system to catalogue their holdings. This is different than the Dewey Decimal system typically used by elementary, high school, and public libraries. Each catalogue listing tells you exactly where the publication can be found in the library.

Use periodical indexes to search for periodicals

Periodicals are a valuable source of current information. They include journals, magazines, and newspapers, things that are published regularly, or "periodically," throughout the year, whether daily, weekly, monthly, or quarterly. *Journals* are written for readers with specialized knowledge and may be written for, and by, academics, whereas magazines are often written by journalists for the general public. That is, *Maclean's* magazine, for example, may run a general-interest article on AIDS research, whereas the *Journal of the American Medical Association* may print the original scientific study for an audience of scientists and others in the medical field.

Many libraries display periodicals that are up to a year or two old, and then they bind them and catalogue them into the stacks or convert older copies to microform. Many full-text articles are also available on computer databases or through the library's website link to article index databases.

> The outcome of any serious research can only be to make two questions grow where only one grew before.

THORSTEIN VEBLEN

Periodical indexes lead you to specific articles. There are a number of different index databases that you can search for articles on your topic of interest. Some databases, such as *Academic Search Premier* or the *Canadian Periodical Index* are general and multidisciplinary, and index articles on a variety of topics and disciplines. Others are specific to a certain field of study. There are indexes for articles specific to arts, humanities, business, science and technology, health sciences, and social sciences, for example. Most periodical databases index articles published in North America and abroad, but there are also databases that specialize in Canadian content, such as *Canadian Business and Current Affairs* or *Canadian Newsstand*.

Each database lists the periodicals, magazines, and/or newspapers it indexes. They include both popular and scholarly, or refereed, articles. The indexes include article abstracts (summaries of the articles), source information, and, in some cases, even the full text of the article. When the index indicates that the article is available in full-text, this means that you can read the article right there at the computer from the database. If it carries only the abstract, then you must either see if you can find the article in full-text format on a different periodical database or search for the paper copy of the journal or magazine on the shelf in the library.

Almost no library owns all of the publications listed in these and other specialized indexes. However, journals that are not part of your library's collection or that are not available in full-text form online may be available at another library. Interlibrary loans allow patrons to access materials from other libraries. Ask the librarian to help you arrange the interlibrary loan.

Ask the librarian

Librarians and other library staff can assist you in solving research problems. They can help you locate sources, navigate catalogues and databases, and uncover research shortcuts. Here are some tips that will help you get the advice you are seeking regarding your research.

- Be prepared and be specific. Instead of asking for information on Canadian politics, focus on the topic you expect to write about in your essay—for example, Pierre Trudeau and bilingualism in Canada.

- Ask for help when you can't find a specific source. For example, when a specific book is not on the shelf, the librarian may direct you to another source that works as well.

- Ask for help with computers and other equipment. Librarians are experts in using the computers and other equipment, so turn to them for help with technical problems.

The library is an indispensable tool in your efforts to gather information and build knowledge. It is the place to start when you have the quest for knowledge. In addition to library, catalogue, and periodical research, Internet research can also be an asset in connecting you almost instantaneously to billions of information sources.

How can you *use the Internet to research*?

The *Internet* is a computer network that links organizations and people around the world. To get what you need from it, you need to think analytically about what you want to know, conduct creative searches in which you explore topics from different perspectives, and use practical tools to locate information.

The first step in researching the Internet is to have some basic knowledge about it and how to use it effectively. Then, you need to understand the difference between search directories and search engines and to know how to use them. Finally, because just about anyone can "publish" information on the Internet, you need to know how to evaluate websites and the information they provide.

Know the basics

With a basic knowledge of the Internet, you can access facts and figures, read articles and reports, purchase products, download files, send messages electronically via email, and even "talk" to people in real time. Following is some basic information you should know:

- Access. Users access the Internet through Internet Service Providers (ISPs). Some ISPs are commercial, such as AOL Canada, Shaw, or Sympatico. Others are linked to companies, colleges, and other organizations.

- Information locations. Most information is displayed on *websites*, cyber-space locations developed by companies, government agencies, organizations, and individuals. Together, these sites make up the *World Wide Web (WWW)*.

- Finding locations. The string of text and numbers that identifies an Internet site is called a *URL* (Universal Resource Locator), or more commonly now, a *web address*. You can type in a URL to access a specific site. Many websites include *hyperlinks*—URLs, usually underlined and highlighted in color—that, when clicked on, will take you directly to another web location.

Use subject directories and search engines

Search engines and subject directories are your portal to the World Wide Web. They help you to search and access websites containing information. Search engines are different from directories in that they have millions of pages more. For example, Google (www.google.ca) is a search engine with over 4 billion pages, whereas Yahoo! (www.yahoo.com) and Lycos (www.lycos.com) are directories with about 2 million pages each.[1] A directory is useful to use when you have a broad topic to search but want fewer, more relevant, and rated or recommended sites, whereas you might prefer to use a search engine when you are looking for a specific site, have a very narrow topic, or want to view many different sites.

Some popular search engines include Google (www.google.ca), Alta Vista (www.altavista.com), and MetaCrawler (metacrawler.com). Some good directories are Yahoo! (www.yahoo.com), Lycos (www.lycos.com), Internet Public Library (www.ipl.org), Infomine (www.infomine.ucr.edu), and Librarians' Internet Index (www.lii.org).[2]

Information is accessible through search engines and subject directories by using keywords. Be specific and limit the number of words you use. Just as when you are searching library catalogues or periodical indexes, you will have better results if you use keywords rather than phrases or sentences.

The flood of unedited information on Google demands that users sharpen critical thinking skills, to filter the results. Google forces us to ask, "What do we really want to know?"

ESTHER DYSON

While the Internet can be a useful research tool, it is likely that the academic publications you may need in higher level post-secondary courses may be inaccessible through Google and other popular search tools, even though these publications are available online, free of charge, through college or university libraries. However, this is changing as Google, Yahoo!, and other search engines and directories are working with librarians and colleges to make digitized academic archives available to everyone.[3]

Internet search strategy

The World Wide Web has been called "the world's greatest library, with all its books on the floor." *Your goal is to find enough information without being overwhelmed by too much information.* With no librarian in sight, engage successful intelligence to use this basic search strategy:

1. Think carefully about what you want to locate. Professor Eliot Soloway recommends phrasing your search in the form of a question. For example, *What vaccines are given to children before age five?* Then he advises identifying the important words in the question (*vaccines, children, before age five*) as well as other related words (*chicken pox, tetanus, polio, shot, pediatrics,* and so on). This will give you a collection of terms to use in different combinations as you search.[4]

2. Use a search engine or subject directory to isolate sites under your desired topic or category. Save the sites that look useful. Most Internet software have a "bookmark" or "favourites" feature for recording sites you want to find again.

3. Explore these sites to get a general idea of what's available. If the search engine or directory takes you where you need to go, you're in luck. More often, in academic research, you will need to dig deeper. Use what you find to notice useful keywords and information locations.

4. Use your keywords in a variety of ways to uncover different possibilities. Make sure to spell keywords correctly.
   - Vary word order if you are using more than one keyword (for example, search under "*education, college or university, statistics*" and "*statistics, education, college or university*").
   - Use the words "and," "not," and "or" in ways that limit your search (see Key 6.1 on p. 161 for tips for using keywords in library searches).

5. Evaluate the list of links that appears. If there are too many, narrow your search by using more keywords or more specific keywords (e.g., Music Awards AND Juno AND 2007 AND nominees). If there are too few, broaden your search by using fewer or different keywords.

6. When you think you are done, start over. Choose another search engine or directory and perform your search again. Why? Because often different systems access different sites and sources.

Use analytical thinking to evaluate every source

It is up to you to evaluate the truth and usefulness of Internet information. Since the Internet is largely uncensored and unmonitored—a kind of "information free-for-all"—you must decide which sources to value and which to ignore. Use the following strategies to analyze the validity and usefulness of each source.[5]

- Ask questions about the source:

  Is the author a recognized expert?
  Does he or she write from a particular perspective that may bias the presentation?
  Is the source recent enough for your purposes?
  Where did the author get the information?

- Note the website's name and the organization that creates and maintains the site.

  Is the organization reputable?
  Is the organization known as an authority on the topic you are researching?

GOOGLE (YES, IT'S A VERB)

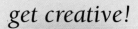

Explore ways to effectively use Google and other search engines and subject directories.

Google accesses billions of documents and has the capacity to return 750 000 Internet links in a third of a second. Because of this, it can overwhelm you with too much information, and some of it you'll find to be useless and unreliable. Therefore, you must use it skilfully.

With this in mind, use your creativity and analytical skills to complete the following:

- Choose a topic of interest to you, something common such as hockey, gardening, sports, or traveling. Google the topic to see how many websites you access. Write that number here. _____

  Now spend 10 minutes scanning the web listings. How many different topics did your search uncover *other* than the topic you intended?

- What does this tell you about the need for critical thinking when using Google and other search engines and subject directories in your research?

  _____

  _____

- Now, open your mind to the creative possibilities your research uncovered. Did any of the websites spark ideas about your topic that you had never considered? Write down two ideas you hadn't thought of before.

  1._____

  2._____

- If you are not sure of the source, the URL may give you a clue:

  .ca is used to indicate a site from Canada. Other countries (except for the United States) also use two-letter codes to indicate their country of origin (e.g., .uk from the United Kingdom)

  .edu originates at an American educational institution (e.g., www.harvard.edu) whereas Canadian post-secondary institutions use.ca (e.g., www.uvic.ca)

  .gc indicates Canadian federal government (e.g., www.hrsdc.gc.ca)

  .gov is a provincial government site, usually followed by the abbreviation for the province (e.g., www.gov.sk.ca)

  .org is used to indicate a non-commercial or non-profit organization (e.g., www.greenpeace.org)

  .com indicates a commercial site (e.g., www.hbc.com)

- Evaluate the material. Evaluate Internet sources the way you would other material:
  Is the source a published document (newspaper article, professional journal article, etc.)?
  Is it simply one person's views?
  Can you verify the data by comparing it to other material?
  Pay attention, also, to writing quality. Texts with grammatical and spelling errors, poor organization, or factual errors are likely to be unreliable.

  Take advantage of the wealth of material the Internet offers—but be selective. Always remember that your research will only be as accurate as your thinking. If you work hard to ensure that your research is solid and comprehensive, the product of your efforts will speak for itself.

Library and Internet research is often done as a step in writing a research paper. The success of your paper depends on the quality of your research and on your ability to write.

What is the *writing process*?

Knowing how to write well is so important for success, both academically and otherwise, that most post-secondary institutions require students to pass a language placement test or writing course. Many schools also have self-directed writing labs where students can practise and hone specific skills. This overview is intended to reinforce some of the basics you will learn in these settings.

The writing process for research papers and essays allows you to get your thoughts down on paper and rework them until you express yourself clearly. The four main parts of the process are planning, drafting, revising, and editing. Analytical, creative, and practical thinking play important roles throughout.

Planning

Planning gives you a chance to think about what to write and how to write it. Planning involves brainstorming for topic ideas, using (prewriting strategies) to define and narrow your topic, conducting research, writing a thesis statement, and writing a working outline. A good majority of the time you spend on your paper should be on these steps. Although the steps are listed in sequence, in real life they overlap one another and you will go back and forth between them as you plan your document. If you plan well, the drafting, revising, and editing will come easily.

PREWRITING STRATEGIES
Techniques for generating ideas about a topic and finding out how much you already know before you start your research and writing.

Open your mind through brainstorming

Brainstorming is a creative technique that involves generating ideas about a subject without making judgments (see Chapter 4). To begin brainstorming, write down anything on the assigned subject that comes to mind, in no particular order. Then, organize that list into an outline or concept map that helps you see the possibilities more clearly. To make the outline or concept map, separate the items you've listed into general ideas or categories and sub-ideas or examples. Then, associate the sub-ideas or examples with the ideas they relate to or support.

Key 6.3 shows a portion of an outline constructed from a brainstorming list. The assignment is a five-paragraph essay on a life-changing event. Here the student brainstormed the topic of "travel," then organized the ideas into categories.

Narrow your topic through prewriting strategies

Next, use one or more of the following prewriting strategies to narrow your topic, focusing on the specific sub-ideas and examples from your brainstorming session. As you narrow your topic, keep paper length, due date, and other requirements (such as topic range or purpose) in mind. These requirements influence your choice of a final topic.

Brainstorming. The same process you used to generate ideas also helps you narrow your topic. Write down your thoughts about the possibility you have

Brainstorm your topic and organize ideas in an outline.

A LIFE CHANGING EVENT
—family
—childhood
→ watching wrestling with my father
    — high-school sports
    → football, hockey, and amateur wrestling
        — wrestling camp in Alberta
            • a dream come true
            • Hart Brothers
        — physical conditioning
            • nightly training
            • 3—5 hour sessions
            • painful exercises
        — dream turned into a nightmare
            • drastic weight loss
            • a matter of survival
            • still have respect for wrestling

chosen, and then organize them into categories. See if any of the sub-ideas or examples might make good topics.

Preliminary researching. Use your textbook or do some preliminary research on the general topic to gain some background knowledge and information. If you do not know very much about the topic, this is a good way to gain some insight and ideas as to the focus and perspective you might take in your paper.

Freewriting. When you freewrite, you use your creative ability to write whatever comes to mind without censoring ideas or worrying about language or organization. Creative freewriting enables you to begin integrating what you know. Key 6.4 is a sample of freewriting.

Asking journalists' questions. Who? What? Where? When? Why? How? Ask these journalists' questions about any sub-idea or example to discover what you may want to write about (see Key 6.5).

Freewrite to integrate what you know.

key 6.4

> My chance to train at the Hart Brothers Wrestling Camp was an influence on my life. I used to watch wrestling with my dad when I was a kid. I was told that to be successful in wrestling, you had to be in really good shape. I figured my years of high school football, hockey, and amateur wrestling had me in shape. Boy, was I wrong! We trained on our own during the day. We met every night for several hours to jog, ride bikes and lift weights. Ed and Keith were in charge of training me. We had to practise doing knee bends: about 200 each night. We also had a chance to practise taking falls in a ring that they had set up at the gym. Being flexible was an important point for wrestlers at the camp. All these things made you tough. By the end of the first week of camp, I had lost a ton of weight and a lot of my enthusiasm for wrestling. Although I had been a fan of wrestling for a lot of years and had been planning to go to wrestling camp since I started high school, I had come to the conclusion that it wasn't for me. At least I can say that while I didn't finish the course, I did survive it.

Ask journalists' questions to focus your thinking.

Who?	Who was at wrestling camp? Who influenced me the most?
What?	What about wrestling changed my life? What did we do?
When?	When in my life did I go to wrestling camp, and for how long?
Where?	Where was camp located? Where did we spend our day-to-day time?
Why?	Why did I decide to go there? Why was it such an important experience?
How?	How did we train in the camp? How were we treated? How do I feel about not achieving my goal?

Prewriting helps you develop a topic broad enough to give you something with which to work but narrow enough to be manageable. Prewriting also helps you see what you know and what you don't know and where more research is required.

Conduct research and make notes

Try doing your research in stages. In the first stage, look for a basic overview that can lead to a thesis statement. In the second stage, go into more depth, tracking down information that helps you fill in gaps.

As you research, it is very important that you create notes not only on the content of the information you want to use but also on the source of this information (i.e., source notes). This will help you organize your work, keep track of your sources, and avoid plagiarism. Index cards are a good tool for note taking because you can write separate ideas on each card and then shuffle around and organize, eliminate, or add to them easily.

Source notes are the preliminary notes you take as you review research. Each source note should include the author's full name; the title of the work; the edition (if any); the publisher, year, and city of publication; issue and/or volume number when applicable (such as for a journal or magazine); and the page numbers you consulted. After this bibliographic information, write a short summary and a critical evaluation of the work. Key 6.6 shows an example of how you can write source notes on index cards.

Content notes can also be written on large index cards, in a notebook, or on your computer. These are taken during a thorough reading and provide an in-depth look at sources. Use them to record more detailed information you need to write your draft.

key 6.6

TUCKWELL, KEITH J. Canadian Advertising in Action,
Fifth Edition.

Scarborough: Prentice Hall, 2000, pp. 107–108.

Summary: Descriptions of how to identify a target market
for your product or service in Canada.

Evaluation: Detailed analysis of how to market your product.
Added pluses: Many examples and Web links.

WRITING
PURPOSE

The point of a paper,
which may be to
review or summarize
research, or to inform
or persuade readers.

AUDIENCE

The readers of your
work for whom your
purpose and content
must be clear.

Write a thesis statement

The pre-reading, research, and writing work is meant to prepare you to write a working *thesis statement*. The thesis statement is the central message you want to communicate in your document. It states the focus of your topic and point of view or perspective, and acts as the organizing principle of your paper. As you develop your thesis, take into consideration your **writing purpose** and **audience**, as these will affect your focus. Key 6.7 is an example from a student's essay.

The thesis statement acts as the organizing principle of your paper.

key 6.7

Topic:	Hart Brothers Pro Wrestling Camp
Purpose:	To inform
Audience:	Instructor who probably knows little about the topic
Thesis statement:	It may look easy on television, but it's not. Although I was a high school football and hockey player and a fan of wrestling for many years, nothing I had experienced prepared me for the longest week of my life: my week at the Hart Brothers Wrestling Camp.

Write a working outline

The final step in the preparation process is writing a working outline. An outline helps you to organize your thoughts and stay organized as you write. It allows you to make changes along the way but helps you stay focused on the points you want to include and how you will logically connect them. Use the outline as a loose guide and working document instead of a final structure, allowing changes to occur. This will help your paper evolve into its final form.

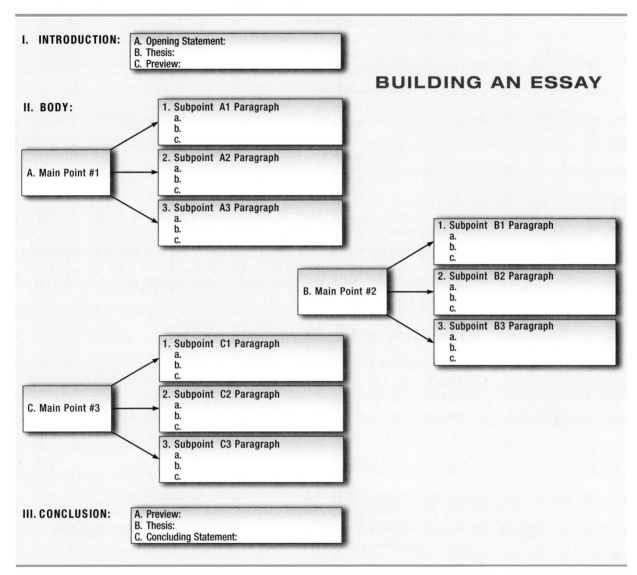

Create a checklist

Use the checklist in Key 6.8 to make sure your preparation is complete. Under Date Due, create your own writing schedule, giving each task an intended completion date. Work backward from the date the assignment is due, and estimate how long it will take to complete each step. Keep in mind that you'll probably move back and forth among the tasks on the schedule.

Drafting

A first draft involves putting ideas down on paper for the first time—but not the last. You may write many versions of the assignment until you are satisfied.

Use a preparation checklist to complete tasks and stay on schedule.

DATE DUE	TASK	IS IT COMPLETE?
	Brainstorm	
	Define and narrow	
	Use prewriting strategies	
	Conduct research if necessary	
	Write thesis statement	
	Write working outline	
	Complete research	

Each version moves you closer to saying exactly what you want in the way you want to say it.

When you think of drafting, it might help to imagine that you are creating a kind of "writing sandwich." The bottom slice of bread is the introduction, the top slice is the conclusion, and the sandwich stuffing is made of central ideas and supporting evidence.

Freewrite your draft

Take everything that you have developed in the planning stages and freewrite a rough draft. For now, don't consciously think about your introduction, conclusion, or the structure within the paper's body. Simply focus on getting your ideas onto paper. When you have something written, you can start to give it a more definite form. First, work on how you want to begin.

Write an introduction

The introduction tells readers what the essay is about. It usually begins with some general information about the topic and then focuses in on the thesis. It can also include a preview statement that briefly lists the main points or central ideas that will be covered in the body of the essay.

Create the body of a paper

The body of a paper contains the central ideas or main points and supporting details and evidence. *Evidence* consists of facts, statistics, examples, and expert opinions. Think about how you might group the evidence with the particular ideas it supports. Then try to find a structure that helps you organize your ideas and evidence into a clear pattern. Key 6.9 presents several organizational options.

Write the conclusion

A conclusion summarizes the information that is in the body of your paper, restates the thesis, and critically evaluates what is important about it. In

Find the best way to organize the body of the paper.

ORGANIZATIONAL STRUCTURE	WHAT TO DO
Arrange ideas by time	Describe events in order or in reverse order.
Arrange ideas according to importance	Start with the idea that carries the most weight and move to less important ideas. Or move from the least to the most important ideas.
Arrange ideas by problem and solution	Start with a problem and then discuss solutions.
Arrange ideas to present an argument	Present one or both sides of an issue.
Arrange ideas in list form	Group a series of items.
Arrange ideas according to cause and effect	Show how events, situations, or ideas cause subsequent events, situations, or ideas.
Arrange ideas through the use of comparisons	Compare and contrast the characteristics of events, people, situations, deas.

addition, you could conclude a paper by leaving a thought-provoking state-ment that:

- Relates a provocative story, statistic, quote, or question
- Calls the reader to action
- Looks to the future

Avoid introducing new information or repeating what you've already stated. Let your ideas in the body of the paper speak for themselves. Readers should feel that they have reached a natural point of completion.

Avoid plagiarism: Credit authors and sources

When you incorporate ideas from other sources into your work, you are using other writers' *intellectual property*. Using another writer's words, content, unique approach, or illustrations without crediting the author is called plagiarism and is illegal and unethical. Plagiarism is something that is taken very seriously by Canadian post-secondary institutions. It is important that you become familiar with your school's policy on academic honesty and that you fully understand what constitutes plagiarism so that you can be sure to avoid it. The following techniques will help you properly credit sources and avoid plagiarism:

PLAGIARISM

The act of using someone else's words, ideas, illustrations, unique approach, or specific reasoning without giving appropriate credit.

- Make source notes as you go. Plagiarism often begins accidentally during research. You may forget to include quotation marks around a quotation, or you may intend to cite or paraphrase a source but never do. To avoid forgetting, write detailed source and content notes as you research. Try writing something like "Quotation from original, rewrite later" next to quoted material you copy into notes, and add bibliographic information (title, author, source, page number, etc.) so you don't spend hours trying to locate it later.

- Learn the difference between a quotation and a paraphrase. A *quotation* repeats a source's exact words, which are set off from the rest of the text by quotation marks. A *paraphrase* is a restatement of the quotation in your own words. A restatement requires that you completely rewrite the idea, not just remove or replace a few words. As Key 6.10 illustrates, a paraphrase may not be acceptable if it is too close to the original.

- Use a citation even for an acceptable paraphrase. Take care to credit any source that you quote, paraphrase, or use as evidence. To credit a source, write a footnote or endnote that describes it, using the format preferred by your instructor. Writing handbooks explain the two standard documentation styles from the American Psychological Association (APA) and the Modern Language Association (MLA).

- Understand that copying material from the Internet is plagiarism. Words in electronic form belong to the writer just as words in print form do. If you cut and paste sections from a source document onto your draft, you are committing plagiarism.

Instructors consider work to be plagiarized when a student

- submits a paper from a website that sells or gives away research papers.

- buys a paper from a non-Internet service.

- hands in a paper written by a fellow student or a family member.

- copies material in a paper directly from a source without proper quotation marks or source citation.

- paraphrases material in a paper from a source without proper source citation.

Avoid plagiarism by learning how to paraphrase.

key 6.10

QUOTATION

From Searle, John R. "I Married a Computer." Rev. of *The Age of Spiritual Machines*, by Ray Kurzweil. *New York Review of Books* 8 Apr. 1999: 34+.

"We are now in the midst of a technological revolution that is full of surprises. No one thirty years ago was aware that one day household computers would become as common as dishwashers. And those of us who used the old Arpanet of twenty years ago had no idea that it would evolve into the Internet."

UNACCEPTABLE PARAPHRASE

The current <u>technological revolution</u> is <u>surprising</u>. <u>Thirty years ago, no one</u> expected computers to be <u>as common</u> today as air conditioners. What once was the Arpanet has <u>evolved into the Internet,</u> and no one expected that.

ACCEPTABLE PARAPHRASE

John Searle states that we live in a technologically amazing time of change in which computers have "become as common as dishwashers" (37). Twenty years ago, no one could have predicted the Arpanet would become the Internet (37).

Source: Lynn Quitman Troyka and Douglas Hesse, *Simon & Schuster Handbook for Writers*, Fourth Canadian Edition (Toronto, ON: Pearson Education Canada, 2006), 519–520.

get analytical!

Think about plagiarism and explore your views on this growing problem.

Complete the following:

- Why is plagiarism considered an offence that involves both stealing and lying? Describe how you look at it.

  _____

  _____

- Citing sources indicates that you respect the ideas of others. List two additional ways that accurately citing sources strengthens your writing and makes you a better student.

  1. _____

  2. _____

- What specific penalties for plagiarism are described in your school's policy? Explain whether you feel that these penalties are reasonable or excessive and whether they will keep students from plagiarizing.

  _____

  _____

  _____

- Many experts believe that researching on the Internet is behind many acts of plagiarism. Do you agree? Why or why not?

  _____

  _____

Students who plagiarize place their academic careers at risk, in part because the cheating is easy to discover. Increasingly, instructors are using anti-plagiarism software to investigate whether strings of words in student papers match those in a database. Make a commitment to hand in your own work and to uphold the highest standards of academic integrity. The potential consequences of cheating are not worth the risk.

Continue your checklist

Create a checklist for your first draft (see Key 6.11 on p. 178). The elements of a first draft do not have to be written in order. In fact, many writers recommend writing the introduction *after* the body of the paper, so the introduction reflects the paper's content and tone. Whatever order you choose, make sure your schedule gives you enough time for revisions.

Revising

When you revise, you critically evaluate the content, word choice, paragraph structure, and style of your first draft. Be thorough as you add, delete, replace, and reorganize paragraphs, sentences, and words. If your instructor evaluates an early draft of your paper, incorporate his or her ideas into the final product. If you disagree with a point, schedule a conference to talk it over.

Some classes include a peer review process in which students critique each other's work. Many schools also have tutors in writing or learning

Update your checklist for the first draft.

DATE DUE	TASK	IS IT COMPLETE?
	Freewrite a draft	
	Plan and write the introduction	
	Organize the body of the paper	
	Include research evidence in the body	
	Plan and write the conclusion	
	Check for plagiarism and rewrite passages to avoid it	
	Credit your sources	
	Solicit feedback	

centres who can provide feedback on your draft. It can be very useful to have other people read your paper and make suggestions for revision before you hand it in to your instructor, but just be sure that they do not make changes, edit, or revise it for you as this could be considered academic dishonesty.

During the revision process, you assess what you have done and revisit any part of your work that is off the mark. The best time to critically evaluate your writing is after you let it sit for a while, says Dr. Mel Levine, author of *The Myth of Laziness*. "The writing experience needs time to incubate. It is preferable to check something several days later or the night after it came to be. With time, it is much easier to evaluate your own work, to detect and correct its flaws with some objectivity, and to deftly surmount the impasses that felt insurmountable while you were immersed in the act of writing."[6]

Use analytical abilities as you revise

Engage your analytical thinking to evaluate the content and form of your paper. Ask yourself these questions as you revise:

- Does the paper fulfill the requirements of the assignment?
- Will my audience understand my thesis and how I've supported it?
- Does the introduction prepare the reader and capture attention?
- Is the body of the paper organized effectively?
- Is each idea fully developed, explained, and supported by examples?
- Are my ideas connected to one another through logical transitions?
- Do I have a clear, concise, simple writing style?
- Does the conclusion provide a natural ending to the paper?

Evaluate paragraph structure

Make sure that each paragraph has a *topic sentence* that states the paragraph's main idea (a topic sentence does for a paragraph what a thesis statement does for an entire paper). The remainder of the paragraph should support the idea with evidence. Most topic sentences are at the beginning of the paragraph, although sometimes topic sentences appear elsewhere. The topic sentence in the paragraph in Key 6.12 is underlined.

In addition, examine how paragraphs flow into one another by evaluating transitions—the words, phrases, or sentences that connect ideas.

Check for clarity and conciseness

Rewrite wordy phrases in a more straightforward, conversational way. For example, write "if" instead of "in the event that," and "now" instead of "at this point in time."

Editing

Editing involves correcting technical mistakes in spelling, grammar, punctuation, and gender-fair language, as well as checking for consistency in such elements as abbreviations and capitalization. Editing comes last, after you are satisfied with your ideas, organization, and writing style. If you use a computer, start with the grammar check and spell check to find mistakes, realizing that you still need to check your work manually as a spelling or grammar checker may not pick up all mistakes.

Take every opportunity you can to benefit from peer editing. Receiving feedback on your own papers, and reading other people's papers and giving them feedback, can be a valuable learning experience that helps you sharpen your writing skills.

Proofreading is the last editing stage and happens once your paper reaches its final form. Proofreading involves reading every word and sentence for accuracy. Look for technical mistakes, run-on sentences, and sentence fragments. Look for incorrect word usage and unclear references.

The topic sentence states the paragraph's main idea.

key
6.12

When I arrived at camp, I had little idea of what to expect. While I used to weight train, jog, and ride my bike for conditioning, nothing prepared me for the reality of the Hart camp. From the first day, they meant business. Each session began with a 2 km run through the Alberta foothills. Then the real fun began. The stretching and agility exercises were designed to improve stamina and improve balance while in the wrestling ring.

Writing

The techniques below allow you to access your power as a writer by uncovering valuable research sources and clearly communicating what you really want to say.

INTELLIGENCE	SUGGESTED STRATEGIES	WHAT WORKS FOR YOU? WRITE NEW IDEAS HERE
Verbal–Linguistic	• Read many resources and take comprehensive notes on them. Summarize the main points from your resources. • Interview someone about the topic and take notes.	
Logical–Mathematical	• Take notes on index cards and organize them according to topics and subtopics. • Create a detailed, sequential outline of your writing project, making sure that your argument is logical if your assignment requires persuasive writing.	
Bodily–Kinesthetic	• Pay a visit to numerous sites that hold resources you need or that are related to your topic—businesses, libraries, etc. • After brainstorming ideas for an assignment, take a break involving physical activity. During the break, think about your top three ideas and see what insight occurs to you.	
Visual–Spatial	• Create full-colour charts as you read each resource or interview someone. • Use concept maps or another visual organizer to map out your main topic, subtopics, and related ideas and examples. Use different colours for different subtopics.	
Interpersonal	• Discuss material with another student as you gather it. • Pair up with a classmate and become each other's peer editors. Read each other's first drafts and next-to-final drafts, offering constructive feedback.	
Intrapersonal	• Take time to mull over any assigned paper topic. Think about what emotions it raises in you, and why. Let your inner instincts guide you as you begin to write. • Schedule as much research time as possible.	
Musical	• Play your favourite relaxing music while you brainstorm topics for a writing assignment.	
Naturalistic	• Pick a research topic that relates to nature. • Build confidence by envisioning your writing process as a successful climb to the top of a mountain.	

Use a revising and editing checklist to finalize your paper.

DATE DUE	TASK	IS IT COMPLETE?
	Check the body of the paper for clear thinking and adequate support of ideas	
	Finalize introduction and conclusion	
	Check word spelling, usage, and grammar	
	Check paragraph structure	
	Make sure language is familiar and concise	
	Check punctuation and capitalization	
	Check transitions	
	Eliminate sexist language	
	Get feedback from peers and/or instructor	

A final checklist

You are now ready to complete your revising and editing checklist. All the tasks listed in Key 6.13 should be complete before you submit your paper. Key 6.14 shows the final version of the student's paper.

Writing is rewriting.

ERNEST HEMINGWAY

Your final paper reflects your efforts. Ideally, you have a piece of work that shows how you used your analytical, creative, and practical thinking to communicate ideas.

IN-CLASS NOTES

WHAT IS THE WRITING PROCESS?

- Planning
- Drafting
- Revising
- Editing

_____
_____
_____
_____

Sam Gordon   March 19, 2004

The Pain Isn't Fake

Bitten by the wrestling bug at an early age, I was determined to become a professional wrestler. As a child, I used to watch wrestling with my father Saturday afternoons. At school, my friends and I used to act out the role of "good guys" and "bad guys" during recess. As a teenager, I participated in a variety of contact sports. When I graduated from high school and the opportunity arose to attend a professional wrestling camp, I jumped at the chance. What I discovered was that, while it might look easy on television, in reality it's hard.

Located in the foothills of Alberta is the small town of Okotoks, home of the Hart Brothers Wrestling Camp. The Harts are recognized as some of the best trainers. They have built a strong reputation for running one of the most physically demanding schools in the world. Their philosophy comes from the patriarch of the family, Stu Hart. The wrestling world affectionately knows his training basement as the "dungeon." Many a spirit (and bone) has been broken here. His sons have continued his reputation for toughness, and, once a year, take in a new set of trainees. Any notion of wrestling camp as an acting school for "fakers" is quickly dismissed during the first training session. Let me explain.

When I arrived at camp, I, like most others, had little idea of what to expect. The camp itself is regimented in its methods. One of Stu Hart's sons, Keith, was in charge of my sessions, which were held five nights a week and lasted between three and five hours. Each session began with a 2 km run up and down the Alberta foothills. Once we returned to the camp, we had to do stretching exercises. Part of the workout was designed to improve our flexibility, and we would sit on the ground with the bottoms of our feet touching and our knees pointed out. Then, a 120-kg man would stand on our inner thighs, putting incredible pressure on the muscles and ligaments in our upper legs. As you can imagine, this stretching exercise brought tears to many eyes, mine included.

The session did not end there. From the stretching exercises, we began to learn how to take "bumps." The term "bump" refers to a wrestler falling down during a match. At the Hart camp, they teach many different ways of taking bumps. While it may sound simple to get into the ring and start falling down, there is a right way and a wrong way to take a bump without causing serious harm to yourself. When we first started taking bumps, many of my colleagues began to vomit. This is the body's natural reaction to the stress it takes when a person takes a bump. Adjusting to bumps, combined with the rigours of training, take their toll on the weight of the students. They told us that most students could expect to lose approximately 10 kg during the first week of camp. I lost 15 kg in my first four days alone.

Survival is a key word when describing the Hart wrestling camp. The Harts not only run a tough camp, they also run a professional and legitimate business. Most trainees, myself included, cannot get used to the punishment and decide to leave. The intensity of the training is physically taxing. The Harts were gracious enough to reimburse most of my money because I couldn't last a full week at their camp. I left Okotoks a little poorer, but a lot wiser. I had a new-found respect for those who wrestled professionally. I still watch wrestling with my father Saturday afternoons, but with a more critical eye and admiration for its participants, especially any wrestler with the last name "Hart."

Suà

Suà is a Shoshone Indian word, derived from the Uto-Aztecna language, that means "to think." Use your thinking skills to evaluate research sources as the basis for your positions, and communicate your conclusions effectively through writing and speaking. Through the power of thought, you will choose sources that support your thesis and express your insights.

SUGGESTED READINGS

Becker, Howard S. *Tricks of the Trade: How to Think About Your Research While You're Doing It.* Chicago: University of Chicago Press, 1998.

Booth, Wayne C., Gregory G. Columb, and Joseph M. Williams. *The Craft of Research.* 2nd ed. Chicago: University of Chicago Press, 2003.

Cameron, Julia. *The Right to Write: An Invitation into the Writing Life.* New York: Putnam, 2000.

Gibaldi, Joseph, and Phyllis Franklin. *MLA Handbook for Writers of Research Papers.* 6th ed. New York: Modern Language Association of America, 2003.

LaRocque, Paula. *Championship Writing: 50 Ways to Improve Your Writing.* Oak Park, IL: Marion Street Press, 2000.

Markman, Peter T., and Roberta H. Markman. *10 Steps in Writing the Research Paper.* 6th ed. New York: Barron's Educational Series, 2001.

Strunk, William, Jr., and E. B. White. *The Elements of Style.* 4th ed. New York: Allyn & Bacon, 2000.

Troyka, Lynn Quitman. *Simon & Schuster Handbook for Writers.* 7th ed. Upper Saddle River, NJ: Prentice Hall, 2004.

Walsch, Bill. *Lapsing into a Comma: A Curmudgeon's Guide to the Many Things That Can Go Wrong in Print—and How to Avoid Them.* New York: Contemporary Books, 2000.

Williams, Joseph M. *Style: Ten Lessons in Clarity and Grace.* Chicago: University of Chicago Press, 2003.

INTERNET RESOURCES

Keys to Success Companion Web site: www.pearsoned.ca/carter

Writing Kit. Academic Writing Help Centre, University of Ottawa: www.sass.uottawa.ca/writing/kit

Learning Skills Handouts. Learning Skills Program, Counselling Services, University of Victoria: www.coun.uvic.ca/learn/hndouts.html

Prentice Hall Student Success SuperSite—study skills section (valuable information on writing and research): www.prenhall.com/success

International Writing Centers Association: http://writingcenters.org/

The Writing Program @ Syracuse University: http://iwca.syr.edu

Online Writing Lab—Purdue University: http://owl.english.purdue.edu

How to Organize a Research Paper and Document It with MLA Citations (specific citation rules from the Modern Language Association): www.geocities.com/Athens/Oracle/4184

A Student's Guide to Research with the WWW: Web Searching, Web Page Evaluation, and Research Strategies (a comprehensive site developed at St. Louis University): www.slu.edu/departments/english/research

Developing Successful Intelligence

PUTTING IT ALL TOGETHER

Be a planner. Engage analytical, creative, and practical skills as you work through the planning stage of writing.

Step 1. Think it through: *Analyze your writing goal.* Imagine that you have been asked to write an essay about a time when you turned a difficulty into an opportunity.

A. Write a brief description of your topic:

_____

B. How might you frame your purpose if you were writing to a person who is going through a difficult time and needs inspiration?

_____

C. How would your purpose change if you were writing to an instructor who wanted to know what you learned from a difficult experience?

_____

D. Decide on your purpose and state it clearly:

_____

E. Decide on your intended audience. Who are you writing for?

_____

Step 2. Think out of the box: *Prewrite to create ideas.* On a separate sheet of paper, use prewriting strategies to start the flow of ideas.

- Brainstorm your ideas.
- Freewrite.
- Ask journalists' questions.

create your future

Step 3. Make it happen: Write a thesis statement. With the thesis statement, you make your topic as specific as possible and you clearly define your purpose.

Write your thesis statement here:

_____

_____

Team Building

Team research. Join with another classmate and decide on a relatively narrow research topic that interests both of you. Choose a topic you can investigate by spending no more than an hour in the library. The topic can be related to something current and in the news or be more academic and historical.

Topic: _____

Working together, use your school's library to research the topic and collect a list of sources for later investigation. When you are done, discuss the research process and answer the following questions together:

1. How did you "attack" and organize your research?

_____

_____

2. What research tools did you use to investigate the topic?

_____

3. Which research techniques yielded the best results?

_____

4. Which techniques led to dead ends?

_____

5. What did you learn about researching that might improve your approach to library and Internet research?

_____

_____

Writing

Record your thoughts here, or on a separate piece of paper or in a journal.

Learning from other writers. Identify a piece of powerful writing that you have recently read. (It could be a work of literature, a biography, a magazine or newspaper article, or even a section from one of your college or university textbooks.)

_____

Describe, in detail, why it was powerful. Did it make you feel something, think something, or take action? Why?

_____

_____

_____

_____

What can you learn about writing from this piece that you can apply to your own writing?

_____

_____

_____

Career Portfolio

PLAN FOR SUCCESS

Writing sample: A job interview cover letter. When you send your resumé, you should always send a cover letter along with it. A cover letter is used to introduce yourself, summarize your background, and explain your value to the company. For your portfolio, write a one-page, three-paragraph cover letter to a prospective employer. Be creative—you may use fictitious names, but select an occupation in an industry that interests you. Use the format shown in the sample letter in Key 6.15 to complete the following paragraphs:

- **Introductory paragraph:** Start with an attention getter—a statement that convinces the employer to read on. For example, name a person the employer knows who told you to write, or refer to something positive about the company that you read in the paper. Identify the position for which you are applying, and tell the employer that you are interested in working for the company.

_____

_____

- **Middle paragraph:** Sell your value. Try to convince the employer that hiring you will help the company in some way. Centre your "sales effort" on your experience in school and the workplace. If possible, tie your qualifications to the needs of the company. Refer indirectly to your enclosed resumé.

_____

_____

- **Final paragraph:** Close with a call to action. Ask the employer to call you, or tell the employer to expect your call to arrange an interview.

_____

_____

Exchange your first draft with a classmate. Read each other's paragraphs and provide feedback. Discuss each and make whatever corrections are necessary to produce a well-written, persuasive letter. Create a draft of your letter for your portfolio.

A cover letter should express your job interest and summarize why you are a strong candidate.

First name Last name
1234 Your Street
City, Prov. X1X 1G1

November 1, 2006

Ms. Prospective Employer
Prospective Company
5432 Their Street
City, Prov. X1X 1G1

Dear Ms. Employer:

On the advice of Mr. X, career centre advisor at Y College, I am writing to inquire about the position of production assistant at CWCW Radio. I read the description of the job and your company on the career centre's employment-opportunity bulletin board, and I would like to apply for the position.

I am completing my courses at Y College and will graduate this spring with a degree in communications. I have always wanted to pursue a career in radio. For the last year I have worked as a production intern at CCOL Radio, the college's station, and have occasionally filled in as a disc jockey on the evening news show. I enjoy being on the air, but my primary interest is production and programming. My enclosed resumé will tell you more about my background and experience.

I would be pleased to talk with you in person about the position. You can reach me anytime at 555/555-5555 or by email at xxxx@xx.com. Thank you for your consideration, and I look forward to meeting you.

Sincerely,

Sign Your Name Here

First name Last name

Enclosure(s) *(use this notation if you have included a resumé or other item with your letter)*

Chapter Review Questions

Choose the option that BEST completes the statement or answers the question. After completing the questions, check your answers against the Answer Key at the back of this book (p. 314).

1. Periodicals are

   a. ☐ Magazines.

   b. ☐ Magazines and journals.

   c. ☐ Magazines, journals, and newspapers.

   d. ☐ Magazines, journals, newspapers, and reference books.

2. Which is true about how a library is typically organized?

   a. ☐ Periodicals of the current year are shelved together with periodicals of past years.

   b. ☐ Books and current periodicals are shelved together.

   c. ☐ Audiovisual materials are shelved together with books.

   d. ☐ Encyclopedias, dictionaries, and atlases are shelved in the reference section.

3. A keyword search is a method for searching for information that uses

   a. ☐ A specialized language.

   b. ☐ Everyday language and topic-related words.

   c. ☐ Only very broad topic words.

   d. ☐ Phrases and sentences entered into a database.

4. Where can you access the best selection of periodical index databases?

   a. ☐ Bookstores.

   b. ☐ College and university bookstores.

   c. ☐ Community libraries.

   d. ☐ College and university libraries.

5. The library catalogue allows you to search for

   a. ☐ Articles found in journals, magazines, and newspapers.

   b. ☐ Books, magazines, journals, and videos.

   c. ☐ Books, articles, journals, and videos.

   d. ☐ Books, articles, journals, and magazines.

6. Periodical indexes allow you to search for

   a. ☐ Articles found in journals, magazines, and newspapers.

   b. ☐ Books, journals, and videos.

   c. ☐ Books, articles, and videos.

   d. ☐ Books, articles, journals, and magazines.

7. In a college or university library, where would you usually find periodicals that are more than a year old?

   a. ☐ Displayed on the shelf with the current editions.

   b. ☐ In the recycling bin because they are out-dated.

   c. ☐ In the stacks shelved with the other books.

   d. ☐ In the instructors' offices.

8. *Academic Search Premier* is an example of a

   a. ☐ Book.

   b. ☐ Website.

   c. ☐ Periodical index database.

   d. ☐ Search engine.

9. How are search engines and subject directories different?

   a. ☐ Search engines are useful when you have a very narrow topic, and subject directories are useful when you have a very broad topic.

   b. ☐ Search engines are useful when you have a very broad topic, and subject directories are useful when you have a very narrow topic.

   c. ☐ Subject directories will access millions more websites than search engines will.

   d. ☐ There is no difference between them.

10. Google (www.google.ca) is an example of a _____, and Librarians' Internet Index (www.lii.org) is an example of a _____.

    a. ☐ Subject directory; search engine.

    b. ☐ Subject directory; periodical index database.

    c. ☐ Search engine; subject directory.

    d. ☐ Search engine; periodical index database.

11. The four main parts of the writing process include

   a. ☐ Planning, drafting, revising, and editing.

   b. ☐ Researching, writing, revising, and editing.

   c. ☐ Researching, drafting, writing, and revising.

   d. ☐ Planning, researching, writing, and revising.

12. As you research for your assignments, it is very important that you create notes on the content of the information you want to use and also on the

   a. ☐ Source of the information.

   b. ☐ Library you used to find it.

   c. ☐ Keywords you used to search for it.

   d. ☐ Name of the librarian that helped you.

13. Which of the following is a good example of a thesis statement?

   a. ☐ What are effective interview skills?

   b. ☐ The advantages of effective communication.

   c. ☐ Interviews and communication.

   d. ☐ Effective communication skills are essential for interviews.

14. Writing a working outline is a necessary part of

   a. ☐ Planning.

   b. ☐ Drafting.

   c. ☐ Researching.

   d. ☐ Thesis.

15. What should be included in an introduction?

   a. ☐ Details about the main points.

   b. ☐ Information about the evidence supporting the points.

   c. ☐ Thesis.

   d. ☐ Summary and thought-provoking statement.

16. Plagiarism is defined as the act of using someone else's _____ without giving appropriate credit.

   a. ☐ Words or ideas.

   b. ☐ Words, ideas, or illustrations.

   c. ☐ Words, ideas, illustrations, or unique approach.

   d. ☐ Words, ideas, illustrations, unique approach, or specific reasoning.

17. Which of the following is true about plagiarism?

   a. ☐ It is considered an act of academic dishonesty that is taken very seriously by post-secondary institutions.

   b. ☐ It often happens by accident, and post-secondary institutions understand that, so they do not take it very seriously.

   c. ☐ There usually are no serious consequences attached to plagiarism.

   d. ☐ Plagiarism is not against the law.

18. Which of the following would usually NOT be considered plagiarism?

   a. ☐ Having a friend or family member help you with your paper.

   b. ☐ Buying a paper written by someone else and submitting it as your own.

   c. ☐ Using a paragraph or two from someone else's paper in your own paper.

   d. ☐ Having a peer tutor from your school's learning centre provide you with feedback on your draft.

19. A topic sentence does for a(n) _____ what a thesis statement does for a(n) _____.

   a. ☐ Essay; paragraph.

   b. ☐ Paragraph; essay.

   c. ☐ Introduction; conclusion.

   d. ☐ Conclusion; introduction.

20. It is suggested that the best time to evaluate and revise your writing is

   a. ☐ First thing in the morning.

   b. ☐ Immediately after you finish writing.

   c. ☐ After your assignment has been graded.

   d. ☐ A day or more after you wrote it.

Listening, Note Taking, and Memory

RECEIVING, RECORDING, AND REMEMBERING INFORMATION

This chapter is organized as follows:

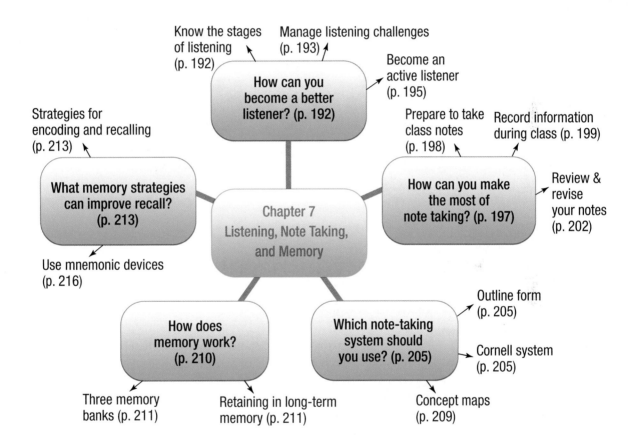

Know the stages of listening (p. 192)

Manage listening challenges (p. 193)

Become an active listener (p. 195)

How can you become a better listener? (p. 192)

Strategies for encoding and recalling (p. 213)

Prepare to take class notes (p. 198)

Record information during class (p. 199)

What memory strategies can improve recall? (p. 213)

Chapter 7 Listening, Note Taking, and Memory

How can you make the most of note taking? (p. 197)

Review & revise your notes (p. 202)

Use mnemonic devices (p. 216)

Outline form (p. 205)

How does memory work? (p. 210)

Which note-taking system should you use? (p. 205)

Cornell system (p. 205)

Three memory banks (p. 211)

Retaining in long-term memory (p. 211)

Concept maps (p. 209)

Higher learning exposes you daily to all kinds of information, and your job as a student is to receive it, sort and record it, and retain it. This chapter shows you how to do just that by building your skills in listening (receiving information), note taking (recording information), and memorizing (remembering information).

Compare these skills to using a camera: You start by locating an image through the viewfinder, then you carefully focus the lens (listening to the information you need), record the image on film or a digital card (taking notes on the information), and produce a print (remembering it when you need it). The whole process engages your analytical, creative, and practical abilities and helps you build knowledge you can use.

How can you become a better *listener*?

LISTENING

A process that involves sensing, interpreting, evaluating, and reacting to spoken messages.

The act of hearing isn't the same as the act of listening. Hearing refers to perceiving sounds or sensing spoken messages from their source. Listening, however, involves a complex process of communication. Successful listening occurs when the listener understands the speaker's intended message. The good news is that listening is a skill that can be learned and refined. It engages analytical and practical abilities.

Know the stages of listening

Listening is made up of four stages: sensing, interpreting, evaluating, and reacting. These stages happen instantaneously and build on one another. You move through these stages without conscious awareness as they take the message from the speaker to the listener and back to the speaker (see Key 7.1).

During the *sensation* stage, your ears pick up sound waves and transmit them to the brain. For example, you are sitting in class and hear your instructor say, "The only opportunity to make up last week's test is Tuesday at 5:00 p.m."

In the *interpretation* stage, you attach meaning to a message received. This involves understanding what is being said and relating it to what you

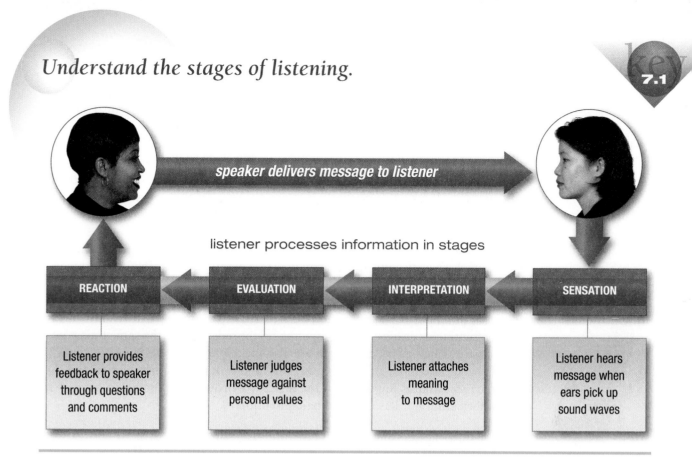

already know. You relate this message to your knowledge of the test, whether you need to make it up, and what you are doing on Tuesday at 5:00 p.m.

In the *evaluation* stage, you decide how you feel about the message—whether, for example, you agree or disagree with it, or like or dislike it—and decide how it relates to your needs and values. If the message goes against your values or does not fulfill your needs, you may reject it, stop listening, or argue in your mind with the speaker. Using the previous example, if you do need to make up the test but have to work on Tuesday at 5:00 p.m., you may evaluate the message as less than satisfactory.

The final stage of listening is a *reaction* to the message in the form of direct feedback. In a classroom, direct feedback comes in the form of questions and comments. Your reaction, in this case, may be to ask the instructor if he or she can schedule another test time.

Improving your listening skills involves two primary goals: managing listening challenges (maximizing the sensation stage) and becoming an active listener (maximizing the interpretation and evaluation stages).

Manage listening challenges

Classic studies have shown that immediately after listening, students are likely to recall only half of what was said. This is partly due to such listening challenges as divided attention and distractions, the tendency to shut out the message, the inclination to rush to judgment, and partial hearing loss or learning disabilities.[1] Fortunately, you can minimize these challenges. Here are some ways to do it.

Divided attention and distractions

At any one point in time there may be many things competing for your attention. Some of these things may be coming from within you and others from your environment. Anything that divides your attention or prevents you from focusing on what you need to concentrate on is considered a distraction.

Internal distractions include personal thoughts, feelings, behaviours, or attitudes that might distract you from receiving the full message. This may include things such as being hungry, having a headache, or worrying about a problem. It may also be that something the speaker says triggers a reaction that causes your mind to drift and begin thinking about something other than what you need to attend to at the time.

In contrast, *external distractions* include anything coming from your immediate environment that may interfere with your listening. These things are being picked up by your senses. For example, while you sit in class, your ears may be hearing the instructor speak or the competing sound of someone crumpling paper, your eyes may be looking at a visual the instructor is presenting or at his or her competing bright red shirt. At the same time your sense of smell, taste, and touch are also picking up information and calling for your attention. At every point, you need to filter this information and focus on what is important at the time. It is virtually impossible to remember information if it has not been paid attention to.

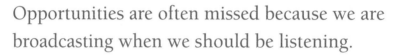

Opportunities are often missed because we are broadcasting when we should be listening.

AUTHOR UNKNOWN

There are practical strategies you can use to reduce distractions so that you can concentrate on what you're hearing. For example, sitting near the front of the room will help, as will moving away from chatting classmates. Work to concentrate when you're in class, reading, or studying, and save worrying about personal problems for later. Get enough sleep to stay alert, eat enough to avoid hunger, and dress comfortably.

Shutting out the message

If students perceive that a subject is difficult or uninteresting, they may tune out and miss material that forms the foundation for what comes next. To avoid this kind of listening lapse, remind yourself that instructors often use their lectures to supplement the text and then include that material on tests. If you pay attention to the entire lecture, you will be able to read over your notes later, compare your notes to the textbook, and use your analytical thinking skills to figure out how everything fits together.

If you experience a listening lapse, refocus your concentration quickly, instead of worrying about what you missed. Later, connect with a classmate to fill in the gaps in your notes.

Rushing to judgment

It is common for people to stop listening when they hear something they don't like. Their focus turns to their personal reactions and away from the message. For example, students who disagree with a point made during a lecture may spend valuable class time figuring out how to word a question or comment in response. While they work this out, they may miss the rest of the information presented.

Judgments may also involve reactions to the speakers themselves. If you do not like your instructors or if you have preconceived notions about their ideas or background, you may decide that you don't value what they have to say. Anyone whose words have ever been ignored because of race, ethnicity, gender, physical characteristics, or disability understands how prejudice can interfere with listening. Jumping to judgment prematurely can get in the way of your education.

Hearing loss or learning disabilities

Most Canadian post-secondary institutions provide services for students who have a disability. If you have a hearing loss that interferes with your listening in class, seek out services from your institution to provide accommodations to help you receive the information provided in class. These accommodations might include preferential seating, sign language interpreters, FM systems, a note taker, etc.

Other disabilities, such as attention deficit disorder (ADD) or a difficulty with processing spoken language, can add to listening difficulties. These difficulties may include trouble paying attention or understanding what is heard. If you have a disability that creates a listening challenge, seek accommodations through your institution. You can get information about the accommodations available to you through the office for services for students with a disability, the counselling or student health centre, an advisor, or an instructor.

Become an active listener

On the surface, listening seems like a passive activity: you sit back and take in information as someone else speaks. Effective listening, however, is an active process that involves setting a purpose for listening, paying attention to verbal cues, and asking questions for clarification.

Set purposes for listening. The first necessity for active listening is establishing why you are listening. Only by knowing what you want to achieve through listening will you become fully committed to the process. Your purpose for listening might be because you want to understand the material better or master a specific task. If you have a clear understanding of your purpose for listening, you will be more motivated to do so.

Pay attention to verbal cues. The words a speaker chooses to use can provide cues as to what information is important. This can help you predict test questions. For example, an idea described as "new and exciting" or "classic" is more likely to be on a test than one described as "interesting." In addition, verbal cues often involve transition words and phrases that help you organize information, connect ideas, and indicate what is noteworthy and what is not. Listen for phrases like those in Key 7.2, and pay attention to the material that follows those phrases.

VERBAL CUES

Spoken words or phrases that call your attention to the information that follows.

Ask questions. A willingness to ask questions shows a desire to learn and is the mark of an active, analytical thinker and listener. Among the most important

Verbal cues point out important information.

SIGNALS POINTING TO KEY CONCEPTS	SIGNALS OF SUPPORT
There are two reasons for this...	For example,...
A critical point in the process involves...	Specifically,...
Most importantly,...	For instance,...
The result is...	Similarly,...

SIGNALS POINTING TO DIFFERENCES	SIGNALS THAT SUMMARIZE
On the contrary,...	Finally,...
On the other hand,...	Recapping this idea,...
In contrast,...	In conclusion,...
However,...	As a result,...

types of questions you will ask are *clarifying questions*. Clarifying questions are those whereby you paraphrase what you heard the speaker say in order to check your understanding of what you heard and then ask whether that understanding is correct. For example, a clarifying question about verbal cues might be something like, "So a verbal cue is a word that provides a signal to an important point, is that correct?"

Although questions and comments turn you into an active, analytical listener and participant in the communication process, they can also distract you and the speaker if you are not careful. For example, too many questions and comments can interfere with the speaker's train of thought and flow of ideas, and formulating these questions could interfere with your getting the whole message, as stated previously. One practical way to avoid this is to jot down your questions quickly and come back to them during a question period. This strategy helps you continue to listen without worrying that you will forget your question or comment.

Effective listening skills prepare you to take effective notes. This is a necessary and powerful study tool.

IN-CLASS NOTES

HOW CAN YOU BECOME A BETTER LISTENER?

- Know the stages of listening
- Manage listening challenges
  - Divided attention and distractions
  - Shutting out the message
  - Rushing to judgment
  - Hearing loss or learning disabilities
- Become an active listener

_____

_____

_____

_____

_____

_____

_____

Take a look at your personal listening habits.

Complete the following:

- Analyze how present you are as a listener. Are you easily distracted, or can you focus well? Do you prefer to listen, or do you tend to talk?

- When you are listening, what tends to distract you?

- What happens to your listening skills when you become confused?

- How do you react when you strongly disagree with something your instructor says?

- Thinking about your answers and about your listening challenges, list two strategies from the chapter that can help you focus and improve your listening skills.

  1.

  2.

How can you make the most of *note taking?*

Many students make the mistake of not taking adequate notes in class. Some believe that they cannot listen to understand and take notes at the same time. Others think that if they understand what is being communicated in class, they do not need to note it down. However, *understanding something and remembering it are not the same thing.* For example, you can understand your shopping list, but it doesn't mean you will remember to buy everything on the list without writing it down. Usually, the information presented in classes is more detailed and complex than a shopping list, so writing it down can assist your understanding and memory. First, it gives you something to refer to in order to review to prevent forgetting. And second, in encouraging you to decide what is worth remembering, the act of note taking gets you thinking analytically and practically. In other words, note taking involves you in the learning process in the following ways:

- Having notes to read after class can help you process, learn, and remember information for recall later on tests and assignments.

- When you take notes, you listen more actively and become more involved in class.

- Notes help you think analytically and organize and synthesize ideas.

- When information presented in class is not found in your text, you will need to write this information down in order to review it.
- Note taking is a lifetime skill that you will use at work and in your personal life.

He listens well who takes notes.

DANTE ALIGHIERI

A useful set of notes allows you to review information you learned in class and/or from your textbook. Notes should be organized and detailed enough to help you complete assignments and review and prepare for exams. Making useful notes involves three steps. It requires effort before class (preparation), during class (focus and note-taking strategies), and after class (reviewing and revising notes).

Prepare to take class notes

Taking useful class notes requires some preparation before class. The following provides information about ways to prepare for note taking:

Preview your reading material before class. More than anything else you do, reading the assigned materials before class prepares you to understand the lecture and class discussion. This gives you the background knowledge you need to take effective notes. The class syllabus should tell you when specific reading assignments are due. If you have any questions, ask your instructor. You will follow the information presented in class much more effectively if you have already read something about it. Any information that you hear stressed in class that was also covered in the textbook is a red flag that this information is important.

Gather your supplies. Use separate notebooks or binders for each course you are taking, or divide a larger binder into sections, one for each course. Keep all notes for each course organized together. Binders are often more useful than notebooks because you can insert handouts immediately into your binder following your notes for that day. Taking notes using a laptop computer is also an effective way to keep notes organized and together. Print the notes, hole punch them, and keep them in a binder together with other notes and handouts.

Location, location, location. Choose your seat in class very carefully. Find one where you can see all visuals presented and can hear and see the instructor well. Be close enough that you can pick up on verbal and nonverbal cues from the speaker. Sitting near the front is usually the best choice as this will minimize distractions. Be ready to write when the instructor begins speaking, as instructors often give the most important information at the beginning of the class. They might relay important announcements, explain how the class will be organized, or state what they expect you to get from the class.

Choose the best note-taking system. Later in the chapter, you will learn about different note-taking systems. Take the following factors into account when choosing an appropriate format for your notes:

- **The instructor's style.** You'll be able to identify the instructor's style after a few classes and decide what note-taking system might fit best with this style. One instructor may deliver organized lectures covering one point after another in a linear format whereas another may jump from one point to another and back again.

- **The course material.** You may decide that a linear outline form works best for content in some courses, but that a concept map is better for others. Try a note-taking system for a few classes and make adjustments as necessary.

- **Your learning style.** Choose strategies that make the most of your learning strengths and help accommodate weaker ones. A visual–spatial learner, for example, might prefer concept maps over the Cornell system; a person who prefers to learn in a more linear, structured fashion might stick to outlines; an interpersonal learner might use the Cornell system and fill in the recall column in a study group setting (see Chapter 3 for a complete discussion of learning styles). You might even find that one system is best for some classes and another works best for others. Also, it can be very effective to review your notes by transposing them into a different format. For example, if you took notes in class in a linear, outline form, try creating a concept map for them as review.

Gather support. Set up a support system with two students in each class. You can agree to share notes after every class and compile them for a more complete set, or if you are absent, you can ask one of them for the notes you missed.

Record information effectively during class

Take notes in lectures

Because no one has time to write everything down, the following practical strategies will help you choose and record information that will be useful to you later in completing assignments or reviewing for exams. This is not a list of "musts." Rather, it is a list of ideas to try as you work to find the right note-taking strategy for you.

- Date and identify each page. If you take a few pages of notes in each class, date and number the pages as you go so that you can keep them in order.

- If your instructor jumps from topic to topic during a single class, it may help to start a new page of notes for each new topic.

- Record whatever an instructor emphasizes—key terms, definitions, ideas, and examples. (Key 7.3 shows methods an instructor might use to call attention to information.)

- Write down all questions raised by the instructor; these questions may appear on a test. Also write down answers that the instructor gets excited about or points out as good answers.

Writing down important information helps to keep you involved. As they take notes, these students are staying connected to what's happening in class.

- When taking notes in linear form, leave plenty of white space. Leave at least one or more blank spaces between major points. This white space will be more pleasing to the eye and will help you review your notes. You will be able to see things in segments and will also have room to add additional notes if required.

- Draw pictures and diagrams that help illustrate ideas. Add definitions or examples in the white space to help clarify the points.

- Write quickly but legibly, perhaps using a form of personal shorthand. Then immediately after class or during a break while the information is still fresh in your mind, revise them, and make improvements or additions.

- Mark key points with a star, by underlining, or using a highlighter pen, a different colour pen, or capital letters. Pens are available for sale that write in four different colours with the click of a finger. These are often a good investment as you can use colour in your notes to quickly and easily highlight different points.

- If you don't understand a concept, leave a space and place a question mark in the margin. Then take advantage of your resources—ask the instructor to explain the concept after class, discuss it with a classmate, or consult your textbook—and fill in the blank when the idea is clear.

- Try to use the same system throughout your notes. Be consistent in how you indicate importance and organize notes on each page. That is, use indenting, spacing, or underlining in a consistent manner. This will allow you to understand how your notes are organized and to perceive key information with a minimum of effort.

Instructors give verbal cues.

key
7.3

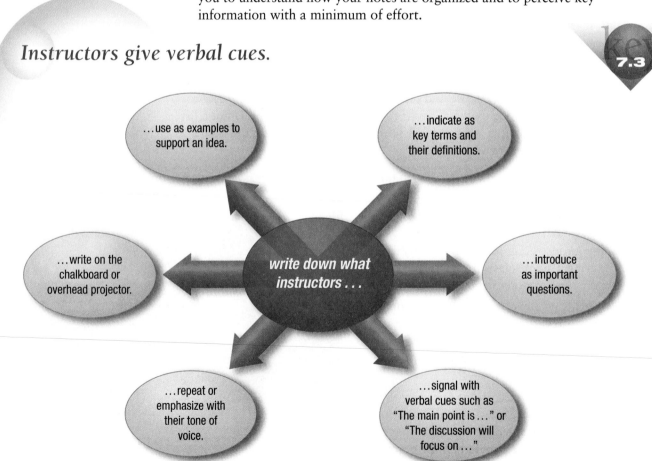

Take notes during class discussions

Often, students will stop taking notes during class discussion periods. Realize that a discussion is just another form of relaying information—and one that instructors may choose simply for variety or to engage the students. Therefore, it is important to continue to record information shared during discussions. It is often more difficult to take notes during these times, however, because one student may say something, then another, and finally the instructor may summarize the comments or link them together to make a point. Frequently, class discussions have tremendous value, but just as frequently information is presented in a disorganized, sometimes chaotic way. Here are suggestions for recording what you need to know during these discussions:

- Listen carefully to everyone. Jot down relevant points and ignore points that seem irrelevant.
- Listen for idea threads that weave through comments.
- Listen for ideas the instructor picks up on and emphasizes and for encouraging comments to students, such as "You make a great point," "I like your idea," and so on.
- Take notes when the instructor rephrases and clarifies a student's point.
- Try using a concept map as your note-taking system, since discussions often take the form of brainstorming sessions. A concept map will help you connect ideas that come at you from different perspectives and in different voices.
- Finally, if you are unsure, ask the instructor (during the discussion or in office hours) whether a student's statement is important.

FACE A NOTE-TAKING CHALLENGE

get practical!

Prepare to take notes in your most difficult class.

In the spaces below, record the specific steps you will take to prepare to take notes in what you consider to be your most challenging course.

- Course name and date of class:

  _____

- List all the readings you must complete before your next class (include pages from text-book and supplemental sources):

  _____

  _____

- Where will you sit in class to focus your attention and minimize distractions?

  _____

- Which note-taking system is best suited for the class, and why?

  _____

  _____

- Write the names and email addresses of two classmates who agree to share notes with you so you can improve your own notes:

  _____

  _____

Review and revise your notes

Reviewing your notes helps solidify information in memory. Reviewing also helps you link new information to information you already know, which is a key step in building new ideas. The review-and-revision stage of note taking should include time for planning, analyzing, synthesizing, adding information from other sources, summarizing, and working with a study group.

Plan a review schedule

Review within 24 hours of the class. You don't have to spend hours memorizing every word, just set some time aside to reread and improve your notes while the information is still fresh in your mind. Take some time to reorganize your notes, write questions and comments, add headings and underlining, etc. An hour between classes, for example, would be an ideal time for a quick review.

Review regularly. Schedule times during the week for reviewing notes from that week's classes. This can be a quick review that takes only a few minutes. Often, Friday afternoons or weekends are a good time to look back over the previous week's notes. Taking time for ongoing review of past classes will help prevent forgetting. Establish a regular routine for quick reviews and this will help assure that you will look at material often.

Review as preparation for tests. Step up your efforts before a test. Schedule longer review sessions, call a study group meeting, and review more frequently. Shorter sessions of intense review work interspersed with breaks may get more results than will long hours of continuous studying. Tony Buzan, in his book *Make the Most of Your Mind,* suggests taking short 2- to 10-minute breaks at least every 10 to 45 minutes, depending on the difficulty of the subject or your level of interest.[2] Frequent breaks give your mind time to process and file the information you reviewed. When you come back from your break, cover up the body of information in your notes that you just reviewed and see if you can recall and explain it without assistance from your notes. This is the best way to check if you really know something. This is usually more effective than simply recopying your notes.

Revise using other sources and successful intelligence

Instead of simply recopying your notes word for word, it is better to revise and reorganize them. You can do this by rewording or clarifying ideas using your own words; defining terms; adding headings, diagrams, or underlining; and adding information from your textbook or from other course readings and researched material. This is one of the best ways to link, synthesize, and apply new information to what you already know. Try using the following analytical, creative, and practical strategies to build understanding as you revise:

- Brainstorm and record examples from other sources that illustrate ideas in your notes. If you find your textbook or the class information difficult to understand, try getting another textbook on the same topic from the library and add explanations or examples from it into your notes.
- Pay attention to similarities between your textbook materials and class notes. Ideas that appear in both are probably important to know well and remember.

Note Taking

Note taking is a critical learning tool. The tips below will help you retain information for both the short and long term.

INTELLIGENCE	SUGGESTED STRATEGIES	WHAT WORKS FOR YOU? WRITE NEW IDEAS HERE
Verbal–Linguistic	• Rewrite important ideas and concepts in class notes from memory. • Write summaries of your notes in your own words.	
Logical–Mathematical	• Organize the main points of a lecture or reading using outline form. • Make charts and diagrams to clarify ideas and examples.	
Bodily–Kinesthetic	• Make note taking as physical as possible—use large pieces of paper and different coloured pens. • When in class, choose a comfortable spot where you have room to spread out your materials and shift body position when you need to.	
Visual–Spatial	• Take notes using coloured markers. • Rewrite lecture notes in think link format, focusing on the most important and difficult points from the lecture.	
Interpersonal	• Whenever possible, schedule a study group right after a lecture to discuss class notes. • Review class notes with a study buddy. See what you wrote that he or she missed and vice versa.	
Intrapersonal	• Schedule some quiet time as soon as possible after a lecture to reread and think about your notes. If no class is meeting in the same room after yours and you have free time, stay in the room and review there.	
Musical	• Play music while you read your notes. • Write a song that incorporates material from one class period's notes or one particular topic. Use the refrain to emphasize the most important concepts.	
Naturalistic	• Read or rewrite your notes outside. • Review notes while listening to a nature CD—running water, rain, forest sounds.	

- Think of material from the readings that supports and clarifies ideas in your notes. Join together your notes from the textbook or other readings with your notes from class.

- Consider what in your class notes differs from your readings and why. Consider whether these discrepancies might come up on a test.

- Write down new ideas that occur to you as you review. Include these in your notes.

- Extend and apply the concepts from your notes and other sources to new situations. See if you can make applications and come up with new examples from information presented in your notes. This will force you to think about, synthesize, and apply the information, thereby pushing you to a higher level of mastery over the information.

When you use your notes to inspire successfully intelligent thinking, your grades may reflect your efforts.

Summarize

Summarizing your notes involves critically evaluating which ideas and examples are most important and then rewriting the material in a shortened form. You may prefer to summarize as you review, with the notes in front of you, or immediately at the end of class. Some instructors suggest that students who summarize their notes right after class do better on exams than those who do not. If you use the Cornell system (see next page), you would summarize in the space at the bottom of the page.

Some students summarize from memory after review, to see how much they have retained. Others summarize as they read, then summarize from memory, and compare the two. Both ways are effective because they force you to check your knowledge of the information by summarizing and explaining it in your own words.

Work with study groups

When you work with a study group, you have the opportunity to review both your personal notes and those of your classmates. This can be an enormous

---

IN-CLASS NOTES

HOW CAN YOU MAKE THE MOST OF NOTE TAKING?

- Prepare to take class notes
- Record information effectively during class:
  - Take notes in lectures
  - Take notes during class discussions
- Review and revise your notes:
  - Plan a review schedule
  - Revise using other sources and successful intelligence
  - Summarize
  - Work with study groups

help if, for example, you lost concentration during part of a lecture and your notes don't make sense. You and another student may even have notes that have radically different information. When this happens, try to reconstruct what the instructor said and, if necessary, bring in a third person to clear up the confusion. See Chapter 5 for more information on effective studying in groups.

Which *note-taking system* should you use?

There are many different ways to take good notes. The form you use will be unique to your learning style or based on what you find effective and useful. Often, settling in on an effective note-taking style requires experimentation and practice. Begin with trying some of the more common note-taking systems, such as outlines, Cornell, or concept maps, and then revise and adapt them to meet your needs. Consider two factors when choosing which to use: what feels comfortable to you and what works best with course content. You might even use one system for some classes and another for others.

Take notes in outline form

When a reading assignment or class lecture seems well organized, you may choose to take notes in outline form. Outlining means constructing a line-by-line representation, with certain phrases set off by varying indentations, showing how concepts, facts, and examples are related.

Formal outlines indicate ideas and examples with Roman numerals, upper-case and lowercase letters, and numbers. In contrast, *informal outlines* show the same associations but replace the formality with a system of consistent indenting, bullets, and/or dashes. Key 7.4 illustrates the difference between formal and informal outlines. Keys 7.5 and 7.6 (see p. 207) provide examples of the two forms. Many students find informal outlines easier for taking notes in class, but then they revise their notes after class to create more formal notes.

Use the Cornell note-taking system

The Cornell note-taking system was developed by Walter Pauk at Cornell University. In the Cornell format, regular note paper is divided into sections.[3]

- The first section is the largest and is used for taking notes. It is the *note-taking column*. Use this column to record your notes in whatever form is most comfortable for you (formal or informal).

- The second section is a narrow column, about 5 cm in width, to the left of the notes. It is the *recall column*. This column is generally used, after the notes are completed, for predicting possible test questions or questions that can be used for review. By placing specific questions in the recall column, you can help yourself focus on critical details. Then when you review, you can cover up the body of notes on the right and see if you can

Choose between different outline structures.

FORMAL OUTLINE	INFORMAL OUTLINE
Topic	Topic
I. First Main Idea	First Main Idea
A. Major supporting fact	—Major supporting fact
B. Major supporting fact	—Major supporting fact
1. First reason or example	—First reason or example
2. Second reason or example	—Second reason or example
a. First supporting fact	—First supporting fact
b. Second supporting fact	—Second supporting fact
II. Second Main Idea	Second Main Idea
A. Major supporting fact	—Major supporting fact
1. First reason or example	—First reason or example
2. Second reason or example	—Second reason or example
B. Major supporting fact	—Major supporting fact

answer the questions without referring to the notes. Some students also use this recall column for highlighting main ideas or examples. For instance, for a math course, the formula or math question can be set out in the recall column and then the notes about the formula or the solution to the question can be recorded in the note-taking column.

- Across the bottom of the page is the third section. This is the area for the *summary*. Here you briefly summarize the notes on the page. You might choose not to include a summary section on every page of notes, but rather after a major section or at the end of the complete class notes. Completing the summary immediately after class or within 24 hours will reinforce concepts, provide an overview of what the notes say, and assist your retention of the information.

Key 7.7 (see p. 208) provides an example of how to set up your note paper and how to take notes in Cornell Format. Set up the Cornell Format in the following way:

- Start with a sheet of standard looseleaf paper. Look for note paper that has an extra-wide left-hand margin already drawn for you. This margin can be used for the recall column. If the margin on your paper is too narrow, just fold the paper over to create a wider margin.

- Label the top of the page with the date and title of the lecture. Also, it is useful to number your note pages in sequence so they don't get out of order.

- To create the summary area at the bottom, draw a horizontal line across the page, about 5 cm from the bottom.

Take notes in an informal outline form.

> October 3, 2005, p. 1
>
> UNDERSTANDING EMPLOYEE MOTIVATION
>
> Purpose of motivational theories
> — To explain role of human relations in motivating employee performance
> — Theories translate into how managers actually treat workers
> 2 specific theories
> — Human resources model, developed by Douglas McGregor, shows that
> managers have radically different beliefs about motivation.
> — Theory X holds that people are naturally irresponsible and uncooperative
> — Theory Y holds that people are naturally responsible and self-motivated

Use a formal outline to organize your notes.

> October 3, 2005, p. 1
>
> UNDERSTANDING EMPLOYEE MOTIVATION
>
> I. Purpose of motivational theories
>   A. To explain role of human relations in motivating employee performance
>   B. Theories translate into how managers actually treat workers
> II. specific theories
>   A. Human resources model
>   a. developed by Douglas McGregor
>   b. shows that managers have radically different beliefs about
>   motivation.
>   1. Theory X: people are naturally irresponsible and uncooperative
>   2. Theory Y: people are naturally responsible and self-motivated
>   B. Maslow's Hierarchy of Needs
>   a. developed by psychologist Abraham Maslow

The Cornell system provides space for notes, summary, and predicting test questions.

October 3, 2005, p. 1

UNDERSTANDING EMPLOYEE MOTIVATION

Why do some workers have a better attitude toward their work than others?

I. Purpose of motivational theories
   A. To explain role of human relations in motivating employee performance
   B. Theories translate into how managers actually treat workers

II. Specific theories
   A. Human resources model

How does the Human Resources model view motivation?

   a. developed by Douglas McGregor
   b. shows that managers have radically different beliefs about motivation.
      1. Theory X: people are naturally irresponsible and uncooperative
      2. Theory Y: people are naturally responsible and self-motivated
   B. Maslow's Hierarchy of Needs
      a. developed by psychologist Abraham Maslow

What are the 5 levels of Maslow's Hierarchy? Explain each level and give an example

      b. people have needs in 5 different areas, which they attempt to satisfy in their work.
         1. Physiological need: need for survival, including food and shelter
         2. Security need: need for stability & protection
         3. Social need: need for friendship & companionship
         4. Esteem need: need for status & recognition
         5. Self-actualization need: need for self-fulfillment
      c. Needs at lower levels must be met before a person tries to satisfy needs at higher levels.
      d.
         Self-Actualization Needs   eg. challenging job
         Esteem Needs   eg. job title
         Social Needs   eg. friends at work
         Security Needs   eg. health benefits
         Physiological Needs   eg. pay

Summary: Two motivational theories try to explain worker motivation. The human resources model includes Theory X and Theory Y. Maslow's Hierarchy of Needs suggests that people have needs in 5 different areas: physiological, security, social, esteem, and self-actualization

Create a concept map

A concept map, also known as a mind map or think-link, is a visual form of note taking. When you draw a concept map, you diagram ideas by using shapes and lines that link ideas and supporting details and examples. The visual design makes the connections easy to see, and the use of shapes and pictures extends the material beyond just words. Many learners respond well to the power of visualization. You can also use concept maps to brainstorm ideas for essay or presentation topics.

To create a concept map, start by writing your topic in the middle of a sheet of paper and circling or boxing it in. Next, draw a line from the topic and write the name of one major point or idea at the end of the line. Circle that idea also. Then, jot down specific facts related to the idea, linking them to the idea with lines. Continue the process, connecting thoughts to one another by using shapes, lines, and words. Key 7.8 illustrates how a student used concept mapping to create a diagram organizing information about

VISUALIZATION

The interpretation of verbal ideas through the use of visual images.

Concept maps provide a visual approach to note taking.

key
7.8

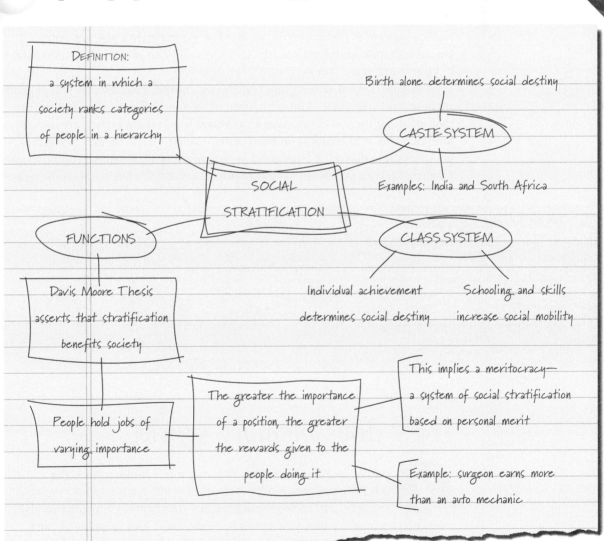

social stratification. Other mapping designs include stair steps showing connected ideas that build toward a conclusion, or a tree shape with roots as causes and branches as effects.

A concept map may or may not be your choice for in-class note taking. If your instructor uses a lot of visuals or provides information in a very linear form, this might not be the system to choose. However, if an instructor jumps from one topic to another frequently, this might be a useful way to take notes. If you prefer a more linear form for in-class notes, then try creating a concept map as part of your review process.

Concept maps have various advantages over other more linear forms of note taking. The first advantage is that it is a visual form whereby you create a map, or a distinct picture, for each set of notes. In some cases, pictures can be easier to remember than words. The second advantage is that because you do not have a lot of space to take notes, it forces you to think about the ideas and filter points down to just key words. If you are able to do this effectively, then you likely understand the concept well. In this way it becomes a way of checking your understanding of the information and of how the concepts relate to one another.

Related to this is another advantage. Concept mapping allows you to see all of your notes on one page. That is, often when you get to six or seven pages of notes, it becomes difficult to see how the information on the seventh page relates to that on the first. With a concept map, all of the information is there on one page and you can clearly see how all the concepts relate. And finally, concept maps can be fun to do. The more creative you get using colours, shapes, and diagrams, the easier it will be to picture that information in your mind when you need it.

No matter what note-taking system you choose, your success will depend on how well you use it. Although listening and attending to cues for important information and developing an effective note-taking system are important elements in this task, you must also be able to write quickly enough to get everything down (or have good keyboarding skills if using a computer). Coming up with your own system of abbreviations or shorthand might help.

IN-CLASS NOTES

WHICH NOTE-TAKING SYSTEM SHOULD YOU USE?

- Take notes in outline form
- Use the Cornell note-taking system
- Create a concept map

_____

_____

_____

_____

How does *memory* work?

Your Accounting instructor is giving a test tomorrow on the double-entry accounting system. You feel confident because you spent hours last week memorizing your notes. Unfortunately, by the time you take the test, you remember very little. This is not surprising, since most forgetting occurs within minutes after memorization.

In a classic study conducted in 1885, researcher Herman Ebbinghaus memorized a list of meaningless three-letter words such as CEF and LAZ. He then examined how quickly he forgot them. Within one hour he forgot more than 50 percent of what he had learned; after two days, he knew fewer than 30 percent of the material. Although Ebbinghaus's recall of the nonsense syllables remained fairly stable after that, his experiment shows how fragile memory can be—even when you take the time and expend the energy to memorize information.[4] This is why reviewing your notes within 24 hours of learning and then again weekly and monthly is so important for retention.

Three memory banks

Memories are stored in three different "storage banks" in your brain. The first, called *sensory memory*, is what holds the information coming in through your senses. Sensory memory lasts for only a second or less. If the information is focused on and paid attention to, it is then selected from sensory memory and moved into short-term memory.

Short-term memory is a temporary information storehouse that lasts no more than 10 to 20 seconds. It is any material that you can hold in conscious thought at any given moment. For example, when you look up a phone number in a phone book and then walk over to the phone and can't remember the number, that is short-term memory at play. To remember the phone number, you need to keep it in conscious thought by repeating it over and over until you get to the phone.

For information to be remembered for a longer time, the information must be transferred, or encoded, into *long-term memory*. This is the mind's more permanent storehouse. Although all three stages are important, targeting long-term memory will solidify learning the most. "Short-term memory is useful when we want to remember a phone number until we can dial," says biologist James Zull. "We use short-term memory for these momentary challenges, all the time, every day, but it is limited in capacity, tenacity, and time."[5] Zull explains that short-term memory can hold only small amounts of information for brief periods. In addition, it is unstable in that a distraction can easily dislodge information.

Retaining information in long-term memory

To retain information in long-term memory, your brain moves through a four-stage process, which relates directly to the stages of the listening process described in Key 7.1 on page 193. Key 7.9 illustrates the process.

1. Experiencing the material (concrete experience). Your brain takes in the information through one or more of your senses.

2. Relating the material to what you already know (reflective observation). You reflect on the new information and connect it to previous knowledge.

3. Forming new ideas (abstract hypothesis). You come up with new insights from the combination of what you knew before and what you are learning now.

4. Trying out and communicating new ideas (active testing). You explore your ideas to see if they make sense and work.

Long-term memory involves four stages.

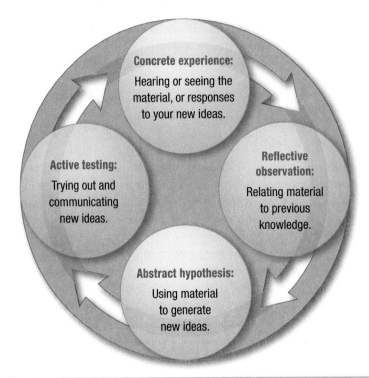

Here's an example to illustrate the process.

1. In your Introduction to Business course, you hear the following information during class: "During the economic bubble of the 1990s, ethical lapses were frequent at the highest levels of business. Among the corporations involved in ethical abuses were Enron and Tyco. Corporate executives at these companies bent the rules and ignored the law to maximize personal gain."

2. You think about the material in relation to what you know. First, you remember reading about the unethical practices of the billionaires of the 1930s, including J. P. Morgan and Andrew Carnegie, who built corporate empires—and amassed personal fortunes—through unethical business practices. Second, you think about ethical and unethical behaviour you have seen in people you know personally.

3. You form a new idea: Government regulations are necessary to curb the all-too-human tendency to bend rules for personal gain.

4. You try out your idea by talking to classmates and thinking further.

   Result: Information about business ethics is solidly anchored in long-term memory.

We rarely forget that which has made a deep impression on our minds.

TRYON EDWARDS

What memory strategies can improve *recall*?

If forgetting is so common, why do some people have better memories than others? Some may have an inborn talent for remembering. More often, though, they succeed because they have practised and mastered analytical, creative, and practical techniques for encoding information into long-term memory and for improving recall when they require the information. Both encoding the information and recalling it are necessary for memory to work effectively. These can be improved with specific strategies.

Develop strategies for encoding and recalling

Memory requires two things: encoding and recalling. *Encoding* is the process of storing information into your long-term memory. *Recalling* is the ability to retrieve it from long-term memory when you need it. Both are necessary because (1) if you do not get information into long-term memory, it will not be there to retrieve when you need it, and (2) if you get information in, but cannot find it and retrieve it when you need it, then you cannot remember it. The following strategies will help improve your encoding and recalling memory skills.

Have purpose and intention. Why can you remember the scoring stats for every player on your favourite hockey team but not the formulas for your math class? Perhaps this is because you want to remember the stats or you have a deep interest in them. To strengthen your intention to remember academic information, focus on why the information is important and how you can use it. Develop personal meaning and intention for learning and remembering the information.

Understand what you memorize. The best way to guarantee that concepts become part of your long-term memory is to use your analytical ability to understand them inside and out. With depth of learning comes the framework on which to place related concepts. Thus, if you are having trouble remembering something new, think about how the idea fits into what you already know. A simple example: If a new vocabulary word puzzles you, try to identify the word's root, prefix, or suffix. Knowing that the root *bellum* means "war" and the prefix *ante* means "before" will help you recognize and remember that *antebellum* means "before the war."

Recite, rehearse, and write. When you *recite* material, you repeat key concepts aloud, in your own words, to help you memorize them. *Rehearsing* is similar to reciting but is done silently. It is the process of mentally repeating, summarizing, and associating information with other information. *Writing* is reciting on paper. Organizational tools, such as an outline or concept map, will help you record material in ways that show the logical connections within its structure.

Study during short, frequent sessions. Research has shown that you can improve your chances of remembering material if you repeat it more than once. To get the most out of study sessions, spread them over time and rest in-between. You may feel as though you accomplish a lot by studying for an hour without a break; however, you'll probably remember more from three separate 20-minute sessions.

Get enough sleep. Sleep can actually aid memory because it reduces interference from new information. It also gives your mind and your body time to rest and recuperate. Studies have shown that sleep deprivation has a significant impact on memory and functioning, so be sure to get enough rest, especially in times of exertion or stress.

Avoid overburdening your memory with information that is too similar. When studying for several tests at once, avoid studying two similar subjects back to back, as the information can easily become confused. Your memory is likely to be more accurate when you study History right after Biology rather than, for example, Chemistry after Biology.

Limit and organize material. This involves two key activities:

● Separate main points from unimportant details. Ask yourself: What is the most important information? What is the main point and what is information providing details on this main point? Underline or highlight only the key points in your notes and textbooks, and jot down these main ideas. See the example in Key 5.7 on page 138.

● Divide material into manageable sections. Generally, when material is short and easy to understand, it is easier to recall. With longer material, however, you may benefit from dividing it into logical, smaller sections. Work on mastering each section, then put all the sections together, and test your memory of all the

Attending class with a clear, focused mind can help you retain what you hear. This professor begins and ends each class with a short meditation, with the goal of improving how he and his students perform.

material. Actors take this approach when learning their lines, and it can work just as well for students trying to learn new concepts.

Practice the middle. When you are trying to learn something, you usually study some material first, attack other material in the middle of the session, and approach still other topics at the end. Tony Buzan states that the information learned in the middle of a study session will be more difficult to recall than that at the beginning or the end.[6] Therefore, it pays to give this material special attention. Also, taking more frequent breaks creates more beginning and endings of a study session.

Create groupings. When items do not have to be remembered in any particular order, the act of grouping can help you recall them better. Say, for example, that you have to memorize these four 10-digit numbers:

   9806875087   9876535703   7636983561   6724472879

It may look impossible. If you group the numbers to look like telephone numbers, however, the job may become more manageable:

   (980) 687–5087   (987) 653–5703   (763) 698–3561   (672) 447–2879

In general, try to limit groups to 10 items or fewer. It's hard to memorize more than that at one time.

Use flash cards. Flash cards are a great visual memory tool. They give you short, repeated review sessions that provide immediate feedback, and they are portable, which gives you the flexibility to use them wherever you go. Use the front of an index card to write a word, idea, or phrase you want to remember. Use the back for a definition, an explanation, and other key facts. Key 7.10 shows two flash cards used to study for a Psychology exam.

Here are some suggestions for making the most of your flash cards:

- Carry the cards with you and review them frequently. Frequent quick 5-minute reviews spread out throughout the day are more useful than sitting down for a longer period only once.

- Shuffle the cards and learn the information in various orders. Information on a test will usually not be presented in any particular order, so flash cards are helpful in getting you accustomed to seeing material in various orders.

- Test yourself in both directions. First, look at the terms or questions and provide the definitions or explanations. Then turn the cards over and reverse the process.

Use a tape recorder. Use a tape recorder as an immediate feedback "audio flash card." Record short-answer study questions on tape, leave 10 to 15 seconds between questions to answer out loud, then record the correct answer after each pause. For example, a question for a writing class might be, "What are the three elements of effective writing? . . . (10- to 15-second pause) . . . topic, audience, and purpose."

Teach the information to someone else. Explaining the information in your own words will help you solidify your understanding and retain the information. In order to make it clear to someone else, you need to have it clear for yourself.

THEORY
- Definition: Explanation for a phenomenon based on careful and precise observations
- Part of the scientific method
- Leads to hypotheses

HYPOTHESIS
- Prediction about future behaviour that is derived from observations and theories
- Methods for testing hypotheses: case studies, naturalistic observations, and experiments

Also, people tend to remember more of what they say than what they hear or read, so speaking the information will help your memory of it. You may be able to improve your grades by sharing with a friend or family member what you learned in class that day. Explaining to someone what you have learned provides a quick and immediate review of the new learning you acquired in class, and allows you to check your understanding and paraphrase it into your own words to help retention.

Use mnemonic devices

Certain performers entertain their audiences by remembering the names of 100 strangers or flawlessly repeating 30 ten-digit phone numbers. Although these performers probably have superior memories, they also rely on memory techniques, known as mnemonic devices (pronounced neh-MAHN-ick), for assistance.

MNEMONIC DEVICES

Memory techniques that involve associating new information with information you already know.

Mnemonic devices depend on vivid associations, that is, relating new information to other information. Instead of learning new facts by rote (repetitive practice), associations give you a "hook" on which to hang these facts and retrieve them later. As you think of the "hook," it will remind you of the information you need to remember. Mnemonic devices make information familiar and meaningful through unusual, unforgettable mental associations and visual pictures; the more unusual or unforgettable, the easier to remember. Therefore, forming mnemonics relies on activating your creative ability.

There are different kinds of mnemonic devices, including visual images and associations, acronyms and acrostics, and songs and rhymes. Study how these devices work, then use your creative thinking skills to apply them to your own memory challenges.

Create visual images and associations

You are more likely to remember a piece of information if you link it to a visual image. The best mental images often involve bright colours, three dimensions, action scenes, and inanimate objects with human traits, ridiculousness, and humour.

Turning information into mental pictures helps improve memory, especially for visual learners. To remember that the Spanish artist Picasso painted *The Three Women*, you might imagine the women in a circle dancing to a Spanish song with a pig and a donkey (pig-asso). The more outlandish the image the better, since these images are the most memorable.

Memory is the stepping-stone to thinking, because without remembering facts, you cannot think, conceptualize, reason, make decisions, create, or contribute.

HARRY LORAYNE

Use visualization

Using visualization, you can take a "mental walk." As you picture yourself on a familiar walk, you imagine that you store new ideas in recognizable locations. Say, for example, that for a Biology course you have to remember the major endocrine glands. To do this, you can think of the route you take to the library. You pass the theatre on campus, the science centre, bookstore, cafeteria, athletic centre, and the social science building before reaching the library. At each spot along the route, you "place" the idea or concept you wish to learn. You then link the concept with a similar-sounding word that brings to mind a vivid image such as:

- At the campus theatre, you imagine bumping into the actor Brad *Pitt*, who is holding *two terriers* ("*Pitt-two terriers*" for pituitary gland).
- At the science centre, you visualize Mr. Universe with bulging *thighs*. When you are introduced, you learn that his name is *Roy* ("*thigh-Roy*" for thyroid gland).
- At the campus bookstore, you envision a second Mr. Universe with his *thighs* covered in *mus*tard ("*thigh-mus*" for thymus gland).
- In the cafeteria, you see an *ad* for *Dean Al* for president ("*ad-Dean Al*" for adrenal gland).
- At the athletic centre, you visualize a student throwing a ball into a *pan* and *creatures* applauding from the bleachers ("*pan-creatures*" for pancreas).
- At the social science building, you imagine receiving a standing *ovation* ("*ovation*" for ovaries).
- And at the library, you visualize sitting at a table taking a *test* that is *easy* ("*test-easy*" for testes).

Images such as these invoke your creative thinking skills. They are fun to come up with and will make remembering the information much easier.

Create acronyms

Another helpful association method involves the use of acronyms. Acronyms use the first letter of each word you need to remember and put them together to spell another word. For example, the acronym HOMES stands for the Canadian Great Lakes—Huron, Ontario, Michigan, Erie, and Superior. Or

> ACRONYM
> A word formed from the first letters of a series of words, created in order to help you remember the series.

you can remember the World War II Allies—Britain, the United States (America), and Russia—with the acronym BAR. When you are creating acronyms, the word (or words) spelled don't necessarily have to be real words. As you see in Key 7.11, the acronym Roy G. Biv will help you remember the colours of the spectrum.

Develop acrostics

Acrostics are similar to acronyms in that you use the first letter of each word, but instead of forming a word to remember, you form an entire sentence. The first letter of each word in the sentence stands for the first letter of the memorized term. For example, when science students want to remember the list of planets in order of their distance from the sun, they can remember the following sentence:

My very elegant mother just served us nine pickles.

Mercury Venus Earth Mars Jupiter Saturn Uranus Neptune Pluto

Use songs or rhymes

Some of the most classic mnemonic devices are rhyming poems that tend to stick in your mind. One you may have heard is the rule about the order of "i" and "e" in spelling:

I before E, except after C, or when sounded like "A" as in "neighbour" and "weigh." Four exceptions if you please: either, neither, seizure, seize.

Or, to remember the months of the year that have only 30 days:

Thirty days hath September, April, June, and November.

An acronym will help you recall the colours of the spectrum.

red
orange
yellow
green
blue
indigo
violet

R O Y G. B I V

Make up your own poems or songs, linking tunes or rhymes that are familiar to you with information you want to remember. Susan W. Fisher is an Introductory Biology instructor who uses this "biorap" to help everyone remember part of DNA replication. The rap is performed by class members and includes references to the football coach and student president:

A pairs with T and G pairs with C
It works 'cause the code's complementary
It lets you be you and me be me
From Coach Tressel to Eddie Pauline.

The chorus "DNA makes protein" is then repeated four times. David S. Waterman was a student in the class who said of this musical mnemonic, "Because the performances are entertaining, students are more apt to pay attention and remember what we see or hear."[7]

Improving your memory requires energy, time, and work. Using specific memory techniques will help you learn more in less time, and remember what you learn long after classes and exams are over.

IN-CLASS NOTES

WHAT MEMORY STRATEGIES CAN IMPROVE RECALL?

- Develop strategies for encoding and recalling
- Use mnemonic devices
  - Create visual images and associations
  - Use visualization (the mental walk strategy)
  - Create acronyms
  - Develop acrostics
  - Use songs or rhymes

In Sanskrit, the classical written language of India and other Hindu countries, these characters—pronounced as *sem ma yeng chik*—mean "do not be distracted." Think of this concept as you strive to improve your concentration for listening, note taking, and remembering. Focus on the ideas at hand. Try not to be distracted by other thoughts, negativity, or other people's ideas of what is correct, as you take in and record information and commit it to memory. Be present in the moment so you can apply your skills to learning as much as you can.

get creative! CRAFT YOUR OWN MNEMONIC

Make a mnemonic device to help you remember something important to you.

● As you review your textbooks in the next few weeks, identify a group of connected ideas that you have to memorize, for example, the names of all previous Canadian Prime Ministers or the characters in Shakespeare's *Romeo and Juliet.* Indicate what you will memorize here:

_____

_____

● Now create a mnemonic that will help you memorize the group. Use any of the mnemonic devices presented in this chapter, including visual images and associations, a mental walk, acronyms, acrostics, and/or songs and rhymes. Write the mnemonic here:

_____

_____

_____

SUGGESTED READINGS

Burley-Allen, Madelyn. *Listening: The Forgotten Skill: A Self-Teaching Guide.* New York: John Wiley & Sons, 1995.

Buzan, Tony. *Make the Most of Your Mind.* New York: Fireside (of Simon and Schuster), 1988.

DePorter, Bobbi, and Mike Hernacki. *Quantum Notes: Whole-Brain Approaches to Note-Taking.* Chicago: Learning Forum, 2000.

Dunkel, Patricia A., Frank Pialorsi, and Joann Kozyrez. *Advanced Listening Comprehension: Developing Aural & Note-Taking Skills.* 3rd ed. Boston: Heinle & Heinle, 2004.

Higbee, Kenneth L. *Your Memory: How It Works and How to Improve It.* New York: Marlowe & Co., 2001.

Lebauer, R. Susan. *Learn to Listen, Listen to Learn: Academic Listening and Note-Taking.* Upper Saddle River, NJ: Prentice Hall, 2000.

Levin, Leonard. *Easy Script Express: Unique Speed Writing Methods to Take Fast Notes and Dictation.* Chicago: Legend Publishing, 2000.

Lorayne, Harry. *Super Memory—Super Student: How to Raise Your Grades in 30 Days.* Boston: Little, Brown & Company, 1990.

Lorayne, Harry. *The Memory Book: The Classic Guide to Improving Your Memory at Work, at School, and at Play.* New York: Ballantine Books, 1996.

Robbins, Harvey A. *How to Speak and Listen Effectively.* New York: AMACOM, 1992.

Roberts, Billy. *Working Memory: Improving Your Memory for the Workplace.* London: Bridge Trade, 1999.

Roberts, Billy. *Educate Your Memory: Improvement Techniques for Students of All Ages.* London: Allison & Busby, 2000.

INTERNET RESOURCES

Keys to Success Companion Web site:
www.pearsoned.ca/carter

Learning Skills Handouts. Learning Skills Program, Counselling Services, University of Victoria:
www.coun.uvic.ca/learn/hndouts.html

Memory and Thinking Skills. Student Development Centre, University of Western Ontario:
www.sdc.uwo.ca/learning/index.html

ForgetKnot: A Source for Mnemonic Devices:
http://members.tripod.com/~ForgetKnot/

Prentice Hall Student Success Supersite—Study Skills:
www.prenhall.com/success/StudySkl/index.html

Helpful advice on listening from the Kishwaukee College Learning Skills Center:
http://kish.cc.il.us/lsc/ssh/listening.shtml

Developing Successful Intelligence

PUTTING IT ALL TOGETHER

Think it through: *Analyze your experience.*

- What is one long-term academic goal you are trying to fulfill?

- How long do you expect you will need to fulfill this goal?

- Why is this goal important to you?

- From your memory of reaching other important goals, what strategies will help you achieve it?

Think out of the box: *Let others inspire ideas.* Choose two people whom you respect and write their names here:

Put your listening skills to work: Spend a few minutes talking with each of them about your goal. Ask them about similar experiences they have had, and listen to the ideas that they used. Use what you've heard to begin brainstorming ideas about how you will achieve your goal.

create your future

_____

_____

Make it happen: *Put a practical plan together.* Map out how you will achieve your goal. Create a mnemonic device that will help you remember your plan. Envision your success as you put your plan into action.

_____

_____

_____

_____

_____

_____

Team Building

COLLABORATIVE SOLUTIONS

Create a note-taking team. Notes on both textbook material and class lectures are very important to your understanding of your coursework. Form a study group with two other people in your class and choose a reading assignment or class lecture to work on together. Agree to take notes independently. Then share your notes with each other and compare them, focusing on the following characteristics:

- Legibility (Can everyone read what is written?)
- Completeness (Did you all record the same information? If not, why not?)
- Organizational effectiveness (Does everyone get an idea of how ideas flow?)
- Value of the notes as a study aid (Will this help everyone remember the material?)

Based on what you've discussed with your group, describe specific ways to improve your personal note-taking skills:

_____

_____

_____

You can also work with your study group to compare notes taken in a particular class period and work on improving in-class note-taking techniques.

Writing

DISCOVERY THROUGH JOURNALING

Record your thoughts here or on a separate piece of paper or in a journal.

How people retain information. How do you react to the following statement? "We retain 10 percent of what we read, 20 percent of what we hear, 30 percent of what we see, 50 percent of what we hear and see, 70 percent of what we say, 90 percent of what we say and do."

Knowing this, what will you do differently in order to increase retention?

_____

_____

_____

Career Portfolio

PLAN FOR SUCCESS

Preparing for career success.

Your success in most career areas depends in part on your academic preparation. Some careers, such as medicine, require very specific curriculum choices (for example, specific biology and chemistry courses are required for medical school). Some careers require certain courses that teach basic competencies; for example, to be an accountant, you have to take accounting and book-keeping. Other career areas, such as many business careers, don't have specific requirements, but employers often look for certain curriculum choices that indicate the mastery of particular skills and knowledge.

1. Put your listening and note-taking skills to work as you investigate your options.

   - Name an occupation or career field that interests you:

     _____

   - Who are two people you could interview for information about that work?

     From an academic setting (e.g., instructor, counsellor, advisor, etc.):

     _____

     Working in the field: _____

2. Ask your interviewees questions about the following two points:

   - Education required for the work:
     What courses are required for this area?
     What courses are beneficial but not required?

   - Additional ways to prepare for work:
     How you can stretch yourself outside of class in ways that will help you stand out (e.g., extracurricular activities, leadership roles, part-time work, and any other helpful pursuits)?

   After the interviews, complete the following two lists:

RECOMMENDED COURSES *Mark the required ones with a star.*	RECOMMENDED ACTIVITIES
_____	_____
_____	_____
_____	_____
_____	_____
_____	_____

Chapter Review Questions

1. What are the four stages of listening?

   a. ☐ Sensing, interpreting, evaluating, and reacting.

   b. ☐ Selecting, interpreting, evaluating, and reacting.

   c. ☐ Sensing, interpreting, explaining, and reacting.

   d. ☐ Selecting, interpreting, explaining, and reacting.

2. Internal distractions are

   a. ☐ Anything coming from your immediate environment that may interfere with your listening.

   b. ☐ Anything coming from your immediate environment that needs to be controlled so that you can concentrate.

   c. ☐ Information being picked up from your environment through your senses.

   d. ☐ Personal thoughts, feelings, behaviours, or attitudes that might distract you from receiving the full message.

3. To be an active listener, you first need to

   a. ☐ Ask questions for clarification.

   b. ☐ Establish a reason for listening.

   c. ☐ Watch for cues.

   d. ☐ Find a comfortable chair.

4. What are verbal cues?

   a. ☐ Body gestures that indicate when something is important.

   b. ☐ Spoken words or phrases that call attention to the information that follows.

   c. ☐ Body gestures and words that work together to communicate a message.

   d. ☐ Body gestures and words that contradict one another.

5. Which of the following is true about memory?

   a. ☐ If you listen carefully to something, you will always be able to understand it.

   b. ☐ If you understand something, you will always be able to remember it.

   c. ☐ If you write something down, you will always be able to remember it.

   d. ☐ Understanding something and remembering it is not the same thing.

6. What are the three steps involved in the note-taking process?

   a. ☐ Previewing, note taking, recopying.

   b. ☐ Preparation, note taking, reviewing.

   c. ☐ Note taking, recopying, reviewing.

   d. ☐ Note taking, reviewing, reviewing again.

7. You will follow the information presented in class much more effectively if you

   a. ☐ Use a tape recorder to record it.

   b. ☐ Just sit and listen without the distraction of having to write it down.

   c. ☐ Have already read something about it.

   d. ☐ Copy only the visuals being presented.

8. The best seat in the class is usually at the

   a. ☐ Front.

   b. ☐ Back.

   c. ☐ Middle.

   d. ☐ It varies.

9. Which of the following would you NOT necessarily consider when choosing a note-taking method?

   a. ☐ The instructor's style.
   b. ☐ The course material.
   c. ☐ Your type of notebook.
   d. ☐ Your learning style.

10. Which of the following is true about note taking?

    a. ☐ You should choose one style of note taking and use that form for all your classes.
    b. ☐ The note-taking form you choose might vary from one class to another.
    c. ☐ The best note-taking system is the Cornell format.
    d. ☐ Concept mapping is the best note-taking system.

11. The Cornell system is a method for

    a. ☐ Reading textbooks.
    b. ☐ Taking notes.
    c. ☐ Retaining information.
    d. ☐ Improving your memory.

12. One advantage of concept mapping is that it allows you to

    a. ☐ View all your notes on a single page.
    b. ☐ Write your notes in detailed sentences.
    c. ☐ Predict test questions in the margin.
    d. ☐ Write your notes in a linear detailed format.

13. When listening for notes in class, you should

    a. ☐ Write down everything.
    b. ☐ Write down questions raised by the instructor.
    c. ☐ Use every bit of space on your paper.
    d. ☐ Avoid drawing diagrams.

14. When is the best time to review your notes?

    a. ☐ Within 24 hours after the class.
    b. ☐ Within 48 hours after the class.
    c. ☐ Within 24 hours before the next class.
    d. ☐ Within 48 hours before the next class.

15. The best way to study your notes is to

    a. ☐ Read them over and over again until you have them memorized.
    b. ☐ Read them aloud to someone else.
    c. ☐ Rewrite them word for word.
    d. ☐ Make up test questions and answer them without referring to your notes.

16. The Cornell system requires

    a. ☐ Only a recall column.
    b. ☐ A recall column and a note-taking column.
    c. ☐ A recall column, note-taking column, and summary section.
    d. ☐ A recall column, note-taking column, summary section, and definition section.

17. Concept maps provide a(n) _____ approach to note taking.

    a. ☐ Visual.
    b. ☐ Auditory.
    c. ☐ Linear.
    d. ☐ Simple.

18. How long does short-term memory last?

    a. ☐ 10 to 20 seconds.
    b. ☐ 10 to 20 minutes.
    c. ☐ 10 to 20 hours.
    d. ☐ 10 to 20 days.

19. Which of the following is NOT a strategy recommended for improving memory?

    a. ☐ Limit what you study.
    b. ☐ Recite and rehearse.
    c. ☐ Study in frequent short sessions.
    d. ☐ Study subjects that are similar one right after the other.

20. An example of an acrostic would be

    a. ☐ "Roy G. Biv" for the colours of the rainbow.
    b. ☐ "HOMES" for the names of the Great Lakes.
    c. ☐ "30 days hath September, April, June, and November" for the months that have only 30 days.
    d. ☐ "My very elegant mother just served us nine pickles" for the names of the planets in order from the sun.

Test Taking

SHOWING WHAT YOU KNOW

This chapter is organized as follows:

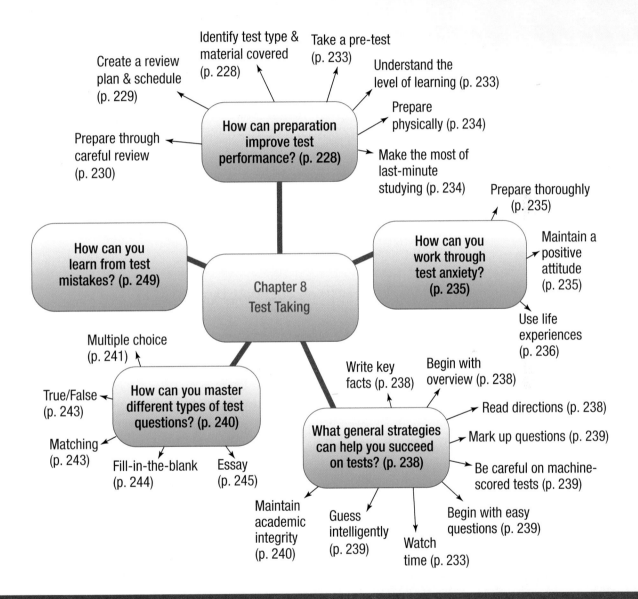

Create a review plan & schedule (p. 229)

Identify test type & material covered (p. 228)

Take a pre-test (p. 233)

Understand the level of learning (p. 233)

Prepare physically (p. 234)

Prepare through careful review (p. 230)

How can preparation improve test performance? (p. 228)

Make the most of last-minute studying (p. 234)

Prepare thoroughly (p. 235)

How can you learn from test mistakes? (p. 249)

How can you work through test anxiety? (p. 235)

Maintain a positive attitude (p. 235)

Chapter 8 Test Taking

Use life experiences (p. 236)

Multiple choice (p. 241)

Write key facts (p. 238)

Begin with overview (p. 238)

True/False (p. 243)

How can you master different types of test questions? (p. 240)

Read directions (p. 238)

Mark up questions (p. 239)

Matching (p. 243)

What general strategies can help you succeed on tests? (p. 238)

Be careful on machine-scored tests (p. 239)

Fill-in-the-blank (p. 244)

Essay (p. 245)

Begin with easy questions (p. 239)

Maintain academic integrity (p. 240)

Guess intelligently (p. 239)

Watch time (p. 233)

For a runner, a race is equivalent to a test because it measures ability at a given moment. Doing well in a race requires training similar to the learning and studying you do for exams. The best runners, and the best test takers, understand that they train not just for the race or test, but to achieve a level of competence that they will use elsewhere.

When you successfully show what you know on tests, you achieve educational goals and develop confidence that you can perform well again and again. Exams also help you gauge your progress and, if necessary, improve your efforts. Most important, smart test preparation results in real learning that you take with you from course to course and into your life and career.

As you will see in this chapter, test taking is about preparation, persistence, and strategy—all of which tap into your analytical, creative, and practical abilities. It is also about conquering fears, paying attention to details, and learning from mistakes.

How can preparation improve *test performance*?

Preparing for exams begins the very first day of the course and continues daily after that. By attending class, staying on top of assignments, completing readings and projects, participating in class discussions, and reviewing regularly, you are actively learning and retaining what you need to know in order to do well on exams. This knowledge is the most important test-preparation tool you have.

The following additional measures will help you to be as prepared as possible for an exam because they will help you put your analytical, creative, and practical thinking skills into action.

Ninety percent of life is just showing up.

WOODY ALLEN

Identify test type and material covered

Before you begin reviewing for a test, find out as much as you can about it, including:

- Topics that will be covered. Will it cover everything since the course began or will it be limited to a narrow topic?

- Types of questions. Will the types of questions be objective (multiple choice, true/false, sentence completion), subjective (essay), or a combination of these?
- Material you will be tested on. Will the test cover only what you learned in class and in the textbook, or will it also cover other readings and information?

If you ask your instructors, they may answer many of these questions. They may tell you the question format and the topics that will be on the test. Some instructors may even drop hints about possible questions, either directly (e.g., "I might ask a question on this subject on your next exam") or more subtly (e.g., "One of my favourite theories is. . . ."").

Here are other practical strategies for predicting what may be on a test.

Use SQ3R to identify what's important. As you will recall from Chapter 5, one of the steps in the SQ3R method of textbook reading is to predict and formulate test questions that you can use to review. Often, the questions you develop and ask yourself when you are reading assigned materials may be similar to those on the test. Textbook study questions are also good examples of questions that appear on tests.

Talk to people who already took the course. Try to get a sense of the types of questions you can expect on the test. Ask people who have taken the course to give you some indication of the level of difficulty, whether the tests focus primarily on assigned readings or class notes, what materials are usually covered, and what types of questions are asked. Also ask about instructors' preferences. If you learn that the instructor pays close attention to specific facts, for example, use flash cards to drill yourself on details. If the instructor emphasizes a global overview, focus on concepts.

Examine old tests. Often, if you ask instructors, they will provide you with examples of previous tests or direct you to where you might find examples of the types of test questions that will be asked. Make sure you consult these old tests only if you have the instructor's permission, so that you do not cross the lines of academic dishonesty or cheating.

Old tests will help you answer questions like:

- Do tests focus on examples and details, general ideas and themes, or a combination?
- Are the questions straightforward, or confusing and sometimes tricky?
- Will you be asked to integrate facts from different areas in order to draw conclusions?

Also, review the first test you take in the course with a focus on answering the above questions. This will give you a better idea of what to expect on future tests in that course.

Create a review plan and schedule

Start your test preparation by deciding what you will review. Go through your notes, texts, related primary sources, and handouts, and set aside materials you don't need. Then prioritize the remaining materials. Your goal is to focus on information that is most likely to be on the exam. Next, use the

WRITE YOUR OWN TEST

Prepare for an upcoming exam using a pre-test you create yourself.

Use the tips in this chapter to predict the material that will be covered, the types of questions that will be asked (multiple choice, essay, etc.), and the nature of the questions (a broad overview of the material or specific details).

Then be creative. Your goal is to write questions that your instructor is likely to ask—interesting questions that tap into what you have learned and make you think about the material in different ways. Go through the following steps:

1. Write on a separate sheet of paper each of the questions you create.
2. Use what you created as a pre-test. Set up test-like conditions—a quiet, timed environment—and see how well you do. Avoid looking at your text or notes unless the test is open book.
3. Evaluate your pre-test answers against your notes and the text. How did you do?
4. Finally, after you take your instructor's exam, evaluate whether you think this exercise improved your performance on the actual exam. Would you use this technique again when you study for another exam? Why or why not?

time-management and goal-setting skills from Chapter 2 to prepare a schedule. Consider all of the relevant factors—your notes and materials, the number of days until the test, and the time available for you to study each day.

A checklist like the one in Key 8.1 will help you organize and stay on track as you prepare. Use a checklist to assign specific tasks to particular study times and sessions. Make extra copies of the checklist so that you can fill out a new one each time that you have an exam.

Some courses require completion of a final exam, which usually takes place the last week of the semester. These exams are often cumulative, reviewing material covered from the beginning through to the end of the course. Preparation for these types of cumulative exams requires commitment and careful time management. Some institutions provide a few days without classes so that you can prepare for exams and/or finish papers. Others require you to complete this work and preparation while still attending classes.

Completing assignments and preparing for exams at the end of the course often requires stamina, organization, time management, and flexibility. If you have more than one exam to write within a few days of one another, you will likely need to review for them at the same time. Divide the total information you need to review into smaller chunks and plan when you will review each chunk. Organize your study schedule so that you begin with the most difficult content; each day, add another chunk of material to review. Before adding new material to review, go over the material you reviewed the previous days. Remember to schedule short breaks at least every 45 minutes throughout your study sessions.

Prepare through careful review

A careful review, using analytical and practical strategies like the following, will give you the best shot at remembering the material you study:

Use SQ3R. The reading method you studied in Chapter 5 provides an excellent structure for reviewing your reading materials.

Use a checklist to prepare for a test.

Course: _____   Instructor: _____

Date, time, and place of test: _____

Type of test (is it a major exam or a minor quiz?): _____

What the instructor said about the test, including the types of test questions, test length, and how much the test counts toward your final grade:

_____

_____

Topics to be covered on the test, in order of importance (information should also come from your instructor):

1. _____

2. _____

3. _____

4. _____

5. _____

Study schedule, including materials you plan to study (texts, class notes, homework problems, and so forth) and dates you plan to complete each:

MATERIAL   DATE OF COMPLETION

1. _____   _____

2. _____   _____

3. _____   _____

4. _____   _____

5. _____   _____

Materials you are expected to bring to the test (textbook, sourcebook, calculator, etc.):

_____

_____

_____

Special study arrangements (for example, plan study group meetings, ask the instructor for special help, get outside tutoring):

_____

_____

_____

Life-management issues (such as rearranging work hours):

_____

_____

_____

Source: Adapted from Ron Fry, *"Ace" Any Test,* 3rd ed. (Franklin Lakes, NJ: Career Press, 1996), 123–24.

- *Surveying* gives you an overview of topics. Notice the headings, subheadings, italics, summary, study questions, diagrams, charts, and figures, as these will point you toward the most important concepts in the chapter.

- *Questioning* helps you focus on important ideas and determine the meaning. Cover up the information and see if you can recall the answer to the questions you developed.

- *Reading* (or, in this case, rereading) reminds you of concepts and supporting information. You won't have time to reread and learn all of the information you covered in the course, though, so just concentrate on rereading the information you are not as comfortable with that you know will be on the test.

- *Reciting* helps to anchor the concepts in your head. It is the best way to check to see if you really know something. If you can explain it out loud to yourself or another person, or can explain it in writing, then you know you have an understanding of the information.

- *Reviewing,* such as quizzing yourself on the Q-stage questions, summarizing highlighted sections, making key-concept flash cards, and outlining chapters, helps solidify learning. If, from the beginning of the course, you get into the habit of continually reviewing course notes and textbook readings, your review just before an exam will go much more easily and smoothly because the information will already be very familiar to you.

Review your notes. Use the following techniques to review your notes before an exam:

- Time your reviews carefully. Review notes for the first time within 24 hours of the lecture, if you can, and then review again weekly, and monthly. Closer to the day of the test, condense your notes and do a more thorough review of all of them.

- Improve your notes. Go over your notes and fill in missing information, clarify points, write out abbreviations, and highlight key ideas.

- Organize the information. Consider adding headings and subheadings to your notes to clarify the structure of the information. Organize your notes using a different organizing structure. For example, if you originally took your notes in outline or Cornell format, try creating a concept map of the information. This is a great way to review because it will allow you to see if you understand how the concepts are organized and related. It will also force you to understand the concepts well enough to be able to pick out just a few key words for each point.

- Summarize the information. Evaluate which ideas and examples are most important, and then condense your notes in shortened form. Summarize your notes in writing or with a concept map. Try summarizing from memory as a self-test.

Learning is what most adults will do for a living in the 21st century.

BOB PERELMAN

Take a pre-test

Use end-of-chapter text questions and the questions you created when you read using SQ3R to create your own pre-test. If your course doesn't have an assigned text, develop questions from the questions you developed in the recall column of your Cornell-style notes. Don't forget to consider assigned outside readings as potential test material as well. Previous homework assignments will also help target areas you need to work on. Choose questions that are likely to be covered, then answer them under test-like conditions—in a quiet place, with no books or notes to help you (unless the exam is open book), and with a clock to tell you when to quit.

Answering mock test questions is one of the best ways to prepare for a test, and yet so few students know to do this. In comparison to reading and rereading your notes and textbook material, answering questions is by far a more effective use of your review time. When you just read and reread, you can never really be sure that you know the information well enough to explain it on a test. This is because reading and rereading puts you through a process of recognition. That is, as you see the information over and over again, you might fool yourself into thinking that you *know* the information when really all you are doing is *recognizing* it. The only way to check if you truly know it is to push yourself to recall it from memory and explain it for yourself by answering mock test questions. This will require you to understand the information, remember it, and check to see if you can explain it. Realize that understanding, remembering, and explaining are three separate questions.

Understand the level of learning required

Many students do not do well on tests because they do not target their learning at a high enough level. That is, they spend so much of their time learning and memorizing the information as it is presented to them. In some educational systems, all that is required is that students regurgitate the information as it was presented to them, but more often than not, the Canadian post-secondary system strives to have students who can "produce knowledge, not just reproduce it."

For this reason, assignments and exams will require students not only to recall and understand the information, but also to apply it, and to analyze, synthesize, and often even evaluate it, in ways that were not spelled out in class or in the textbook readings. For example, in one class the instructor for this course might describe what a daily planner is. Then on another day, he or she might describe what a long-term planner is. A very basic question on a test would just ask you to describe each of these as the instructor did. However, a more complex question might ask you to apply this learning by creating a schedule. Another question might ask you to analyze the pros and cons of each type of planner and evaluate which one you think is most effective. This information may not have been discussed directly in class or in the textbook, but the instructor wants to know that you are able to use your creative, analytical, and practical thinking skills to formulate your own ideas and opinions and to explain them.

The mistake that most students make is that they do not prepare for these more complex thinking types of questions. Be sure that you are learning concepts well enough so that you can not only recall and explain the information, but also apply, analyze, synthesize, and evaluate it when necessary on an exam.

Prepare physically

Most tests ask you to work at your best under pressure. There is an abundant amount of research indicating the relationship between adequate sleep and effective performance. A good night's sleep will leave you rested and alert and improve your ability to remember the material you have learned. Eating a light, well-balanced meal is also important. When time is short, grab a quick-energy snack such as a banana, orange juice, or a granola bar instead of a sugary snack such as a candy bar, cookie, or pop. For more ideas on getting adequate sleep and eating a balanced diet, look ahead to the material on Personal Wellness (Chapter 10).

Make the most of last-minute studying

Cramming is the process of studying intensively and around the clock right before an exam. Unfortunately, many students believe that this is an effective method of preparing for tests because they believe that they just need to have the information in short-term memory for the test. As you now know from the previous chapter on memory, short-term memory lasts only 10 to 20 seconds—this will never get you through an exam. In order to get through an exam, two things are necessary. First, the information must be encoded into long-term memory, and second, you need to be able to retrieve it from long-term memory when you need it. Therefore, if learning is your goal, cramming is not a good idea. It is best to give yourself enough time to prepare for an exam so that you can take time to encode the information and then practise retrieving it so that you know you will be able to do this in an exam environment.

Post-secondary students often learn very quickly that cramming is not an effective learning method at this level of education. However, the reality is that, at one point or another, nearly every student crams. If you do find your-self in a situation where you have no choice but to cram, use these hints to make the most of this intensive study time:

- Review your flash cards. If you use flash cards, review them one last time.
- Focus on crucial concepts. Resist reviewing notes or texts page by page.
- Create a last-minute study sheet. On a single sheet of paper, write down key facts, definitions, formulas, and so on. If you prefer visual notes, use concept maps to map out ideas and supporting examples.
- Arrive early. Study the sheet or your flash cards until you are asked to clear your desk.

After your exam, evaluate how cramming affected your recall. Within a few days, you will probably remember very little. This is a reality that will work against you in advanced courses that build on this knowledge and in occupations that require it. Think ahead about how you can start preparing earlier for your next exam.

Whether you cram or not, you may experience anxiety on test day. Many students do. Following are some ideas for how to handle test anxiety when it strikes.

How can you work through *test anxiety?*

Not all stress is bad; a certain amount of stress can be a good thing. Stress can make you more alert, and provide energy that motivates you to do your best. Some students, however, experience incapacitating levels of stress before and during exams.

Test anxiety can cause sweating, nausea, dizziness, headaches, and fatigue. It can reduce your ability to concentrate, make you feel overwhelmed, and cause you to "blank out." As a result, test anxiety often results in lower grades that may not reflect what you really know. Take two steps to minimize your anxiety: Prepare thoroughly and build a positive attitude.

TEST ANXIETY

A bad case of nerves that can make it hard to think or to remember.

Prepare thoroughly

The more confident you feel about the material, the better you will perform on test day. In this sense, consider all the preparation and study information in *Keys to Success* as assistance for test anxiety. Also, finding out what to expect on the exam will help you feel more in control. Seek out information about the material that will be covered, the question format, the length of the exam, and the points assigned to each question to eliminate the fear attached to the unpredictability of the test.

Creating and following a detailed review plan can also help you feel more in control, better prepared, and less anxious. Divide the plan into small, less overwhelming tasks. As you finish each, you will gain an increased sense of accomplishment, confidence, and control.

Maintain a positive attitude

Here are ways to maintain an attitude that will help you succeed.

- See the test as an opportunity to learn. Instead of thinking of tests as contests that you either "win" or "lose," think of them as signposts along the way to mastering the material. Learning is far more important than "winning."
- Understand that tests measure performance at a particular moment on a particular test. They do not measure personal value. Your grade could be

When you study in a group, you can compare your information, gain from what others know, and solidify your learning through teaching others.

different on another day or on a different set of questions, so how you do on a test does not reflect your ability to succeed. Whether you get an A or an F, you are the same person.

- **Appreciate your instructors' purpose.** Your instructors want to help you succeed. Don't hesitate to visit them during office hours and send email questions to clarify material.

- **Seek study partners who challenge you.** Find study partners who can inspire you to do your best. Try to avoid people who are also anxious because you both may pick up on each other's fears and negativity. (For more on study groups, see Chapter 5.)

- **Set yourself up for success.** Expect progress and success, not failure. Take responsibility for creating success through your work and attitude.

- **Practice relaxation.** When you feel test anxiety mounting, breathe deeply, close your eyes, and visualize positive mental images such as getting a good grade and finishing with time to spare. Try to ease muscle tension—stretch your neck, then tighten and release your muscles.

- **Practice positive self-talk.** Tell yourself that you can do well and that it is normal to feel anxious, particularly before an important exam. As you walk into the testing room, give yourself a pep talk that builds confidence. Try saying something like, "I know this stuff, and I'm going to show the instructor what I know." Also, slay your perfection monster by telling yourself, "I don't have to get 100% of the questions right."

Use life experiences

If you're returning to school after years away, you may wonder how well you will handle exams. To deal with these feelings, focus on what you have learned through life experience, including the ability to handle work and family pressures. Without even knowing it, you have developed time management, planning, and communication skills necessary for higher learning success.

In addition, your life experiences will give real meaning to abstract classroom ideas. For example, workplace relationships may help you understand concepts discussed in social psychology classes, and refinancing your home mortgage may help you grasp the importance of changes in interest rates, a key concept in economics.

Parents who have to juggle child care with study time can find the challenge especially difficult before a test. Here are some suggestions that might help:

- **Find help.** This is especially important with younger children. Enlist a neighbourhood teenager or family member or friend to look after children while you study.

- **Plan activities.** If you have younger children, have a supply of games, books, and videos on hand to use while you study.

- **Explain the time frame.** Tell school-aged children your study schedule and the test date. Plan a special activity to do together after your test.

Preparing for an exam sets the stage for taking the exam. You are now ready to focus on methods to help you succeed when the test begins.

Test Preparation

If the topic or format of a test challenges your stronger or weaker intelligences, these tips will help you make the most of your time and abilities.

INTELLIGENCE	SUGGESTED STRATEGIES	WHAT WORKS FOR YOU? WRITE NEW IDEAS HERE
Verbal–Linguistic	• Think of and write out questions your instructor may ask on a test. Answer the questions and then try rewriting them in a different format (essay, true/false, and so on). • Underline important words in review questions or practice questions.	
Logical–Mathematical	• Make diagrams of review or practice questions. • Outline the key steps involved in topics on which you may be tested.	
Bodily–Kinesthetic	• Use your voice to review out loud. Recite concepts, terms and definitions, important lists, dates, and so on. • Create a sculpture, model, or skit to depict a tough concept that will be on your test.	
Visual–Spatial	• Create a concept map to map out an important topic and its connections to other topics in the material. Study it and redraw it from memory a day before the test. • Make drawings related to possible test topics.	
Interpersonal	• Develop a study group and encourage each other. • In your group, come up with as many possible test questions as you can. Ask each other these questions in an oral-exam format.	
Intrapersonal	• Brainstorm test questions. Then, come back to them after a break or even a day's time. On your own, take the sample "test" you developed. • Make time to review in a solitary setting.	
Musical	• Play music while you read if it does not distract you. • Study concepts by reciting them to rhythms you create or to music.	
Naturalistic	• Bring your text, lecture notes, and other pertinent information to an outdoor spot that inspires you and helps you to feel confident, and review your material there.	

IN-CLASS NOTES

HOW CAN YOU WORK THROUGH TEST ANXIETY?

- Prepare thoroughly
- Maintain a positive attitude
- Use life experiences

_____

_____

_____

_____

What *general strategies* can help you succeed on tests?

Even though every test is different, there are general strategies that will help you handle almost all tests, including short-answer and essay exams.

Write down key facts

Before you even look at the test, write down key information, including formulas, rules, and definitions, that you studied recently and that you don't want to forget. Use the back of the question sheet or ask for some scrap paper for your notes. Be sure your instructor knows that you made these notes after the test began so that you do not find yourself accused of cheating or academic dishonesty.

Begin with an overview

Although exam time is precious, spend a few minutes at the start of the test gathering information about the questions. Check out how many questions there are in each section, their types, and point values. Then analyze the situation and think practically to schedule your time according to the type of questions and point value for each. For example, if a two-hour test is divided into two sections of equal point value—an essay section with four questions and a short-answer section with 60 questions—you might spend an hour on the essays (15 minutes per question) and an hour on the short answers (1 minute per question).

You may need to take level of difficulty into account as you come up with options for how to parcel out your time. For example, if you think you can get through the short-answer questions in 45 minutes and sense that you'll have more difficulty with the writing section, you can budget an hour and a quarter for the essays.

Read test directions

Reading test directions carefully can save you trouble. For example, although a test of 100 true/false questions and one essay may look straightforward, the directions may tell you to answer 80 of the 100 questions or that the essay is optional. If the directions indicate that you are penalized for incorrect answers, this means that for every answer that is incorrect, points will be deducted from the correct ones. For example, if a test has a total of 100 points and you get 50 right and 50 wrong, your mark on the test will be 0. In these cases, avoid guessing.

When you read the directions, you may learn that some questions or sections are weighted more heavily than others. For example, the short-answer questions may be worth 30 points, whereas the essays are worth 70. In this case, it's smart to spend more time on the essays than on the short answers. To stay aware of the specifics of the instructions, use the practical strategy of circling or underlining key information.

Mark up the questions

Highlight, underline, or circle instructions, and keywords in them, to avoid careless errors. As you read each question, circle qualifiers such as *always, never, all, none,* and *every,* and verbs that communicate specific test instructions. Underline concepts that are tricky or need special attention.

Take special care on machine-scored tests

Use the correct pencil (usually a number 2) on machine-scored tests, and mark your answers in the proper spaces, filling them completely. Periodically, use your practical thinking skills to check the answer number against the question number to make sure they match. If you mark the answer to question 4 in the space for question 5, not only will your response to question 4 be wrong, but your responses to all subsequent questions will be off by a line. To avoid this problem, put a small dot next to any number you skip and plan to return to later.

Neatness counts on these tests because the computer can misread stray pencil marks or partially erased answers. If you mark two answers to a question and partially erase one, the computer will read both responses and charge you with a wrong answer.

Work from easy to hard

Begin with the easiest questions, and answer them as quickly as you can without sacrificing accuracy. This will boost your confidence and leave more time for questions that require more focus and effort. Mark more difficult questions as you reach them, and return to them after answering the questions you know.

Watch your time

Keep track of how much time is left and how you are progressing. Some students are so concerned about time that they rush through the test and have time left over. If this happens to you, spend the remaining time refining and checking your work instead of leaving early. You may be able to correct mistakes, change answers, or add more information to an essay.

Master the art of intelligent guessing

When you are unsure of an answer, you have a choice between leaving it blank or completing it with a guess. As long as you are not penalized for incorrect answers, guessing can be beneficial. "Intelligent guessing," writes Steven Frank, an authority on student studying and test taking, "means taking advantage of what you do know in order to try to figure out what you don't. If you guess intelligently, you have a decent shot at getting the answer right."[1]

When you check your work at the end of the test, use your analytical ability to decide whether you would make the same guesses again. Chances are that you will leave your answers alone, but you may notice something that changes your mind. This might be a qualifier that affects meaning, a miscalculation in a math problem, or a cue in another question that helps you guess. It is also possible that when you go over the test, you might recall information that you drew a blank on the first time around.

Maintain academic integrity

Cheating as a strategy to pass a test or get a better grade robs you of the opportunity to learn the material, which, ultimately, is your loss. Cheating also jeopardizes your future if you are caught. You may be seriously reprimanded, or even expelled, if you violate your school's policy on academic integrity.

Now that you have explored these general strategies, you can use what you've learned to address specific types of test questions.

IN-CLASS NOTES

WHAT GENERAL STRATEGIES CAN HELP YOU SUCCEED ON TESTS?

- Write down key facts
- Begin with an overview
- Read test directions
- Mark up the questions
- Take special care on machine-scored tests
- Work from easy to hard
- Watch your time
- Master the art of intelligent guessing
- Maintain academic integrity

_____
_____
_____
_____
_____
_____
_____
_____
_____

OBJECTIVE QUESTIONS

Short-answer questions that test your ability to recall, compare, and contrast information and to choose the right answer from a limited number of choices.

How can you master *different types* of test questions?

Every type of test question has a different way of finding out how much you know about a subject. For **objective questions,** you choose or write a short answer, often making a selection from a limited number of choices. Multiple-choice, fill-in-the-blank, matching, and true/false questions fall into this category. (Subjective questions) require you to plan, organize, draft, and refine a response. All essay questions are subjective. In general, subjective questions tap your creative abilities more than short-answer questions do.

Key 8.2 shows samples of real test questions from a Western Civilization post-secondary textbook published by Pearson Education. Included are multiple-choice, true/false, fill-in-the-blank, matching, and essay and short-answer essay questions. Specific strategies are useful for each type of test question.

SUBJECTIVE
QUESTIONS

Essay questions that require you to express your answer in terms of your own personal knowledge and perspective.

Multiple-choice questions

Multiple-choice questions are the most popular type of question on standardized tests. These types of questions can often be easier than others because they provide the answer for you and you just have to recognize it among the options given. However, they can be tricky because they can test you on very specific information and provide options that are very similar to one another and misleading. The following analytical and practical strategies can help you answer them:

Carefully read the directions. Directions can be tricky. For example, whereas most test items ask for a single correct answer, some give you the option of marking several choices that are correct. For some tests, you might be required to answer only a certain number of questions.

Real test questions from a real post-secondary textbook.

key
8.2

From Chapter 29, "The End of Imperialism," in *Western Civilization: A Social and Cultural History,* 2nd edition.[2]

■ **MULTIPLE-CHOICE QUESTION**

India's first leader after independence was:

A. Gandhi   B. Bose   C. Nehru   D. Sukharno   *(answer: C)*

■ **FILL-IN-THE-BLANK QUESTION**

East Pakistan became the country of _____ in 1971.

A. Burma   B. East India   C. Sukharno   D. Bangladesh   *(answer: D)*

■ **TRUE/FALSE QUESTION**

The United States initially supported Vietnamese independence.   T   F   *(answer: false)*

■ **ESSAY QUESTION**

Answer one of the following:

1. What led to Irish independence? What conflicts continued to exist after independence?
2. How did Gandhi work to rid India of British control? What methods did he use?

Read each question thoroughly. Try to answer it without looking at the options. Then when you think you know the answer, look at the choices, and choose the option that most closely fits your answer. This strategy makes it less likely that you'll get confused.

Underline keywords and phrases. If the question is complicated, try to break it down into small sections that are easy to understand. Eliminate any filler words, or rephrase the question into your own words.

Pay attention to words that could throw you off. For example, it is easy to overlook negatives in a question (e.g., "Which of the following is NOT . . ."). Underline or circle these words so that you do not miss them.

If you don't know the answer, eliminate options that you know, or suspect, are wrong. If you can leave yourself with two possible choices, you will have a 50–50 chance of making the right choice. To narrow down, ask questions such as these about each of the choices:

- Is the choice accurate on its own terms? If there's an error in the choice—for example, a term that is incorrectly defined—the answer is wrong.

- Is the choice relevant? An answer may be accurate, but unrelated to the question.

- Are there any qualifiers? Absolute qualifiers, like *always, never, all, none,* or *every*, often signal an exception that makes a choice incorrect. For example, the word "always" makes the following statement incorrect: "Children always begin talking before the age of two." Very few things in life are absolute as always, never, all, none, or every. Most children begin talking before age two, but some start later. Analysis has shown that choices containing conservative qualifiers like *often, most, rarely,* or *may sometimes be* are often correct.

- Do the choices give clues? Does a puzzling word remind you of a word you know? Does any part of an unfamiliar word—its prefix, suffix, or root—ring a bell?

Make an educated guess by looking for patterns. Certain patterns tend to appear in multiple-choice questions and may help you make smart guesses. Although these patterns may not apply to the specific test questions you encounter, they're important to keep in mind. Experts advise you to:

- consider the possibility that a choice that is *more general* than the others is the right answer.

- consider the possibility that a choice that is *longer* than the others is the right answer.

- look for a choice that has a *middle value in a range* (the range can be from small to large or from old to recent). It is likely to be the right answer.

- look for two choices that have *similar meanings*. One of these answers is probably correct.

- look for answers that *agree grammatically* with the question. For example, a fill-in-the-blank question that has an "*a*" or "*an*" before the blank gives you a clue to the correct answer.

- as a last resort, for any questions for which you really do not know the answers, pick a letter option and choose this same option for all of them. Some suggest choosing either option B or C, or the option hidden between the others as the best guess. Odds are that if you pick one option consistently, sooner or later, it will come up as the correct answer.

Make sure you read every word of every answer. Instructors have been known to include answers that are almost right, except for a single word. Focus especially on qualifying words such as *always, never, tend to, most, often*, and *frequently*.

When questions are linked to a reading passage, read the questions first. This will help you read the passage more quickly and scan it for the answers. You can focus just on the information you need to answer the questions.

True/false questions

Read true/false questions carefully to evaluate what they are asking. If you're stumped, guess, unless of course you're penalized for wrong answers. With true/false questions, you have a 50–50 chance of guessing the right answer. If you must guess, try to assess, from the test and any previous tests, whether the instructor favours true or false. Do there seem to be more true answers or more false answers? Then, as a last resort, for any questions you have to guess, choose the option that the instructor seems to favour. Again, be consistent with your guesses; choose the same answer for any and all questions you must guess, and chances are at least one of them will be correct.

Look for qualifiers in true/false questions. Words such as *all, only*, and *always, never*, etc. are absolutes that often make a statement false because few things in life are all or none. On the other hand, words like *generally, often, usually*, and *sometimes* are conservatives that often make a statement true. Qualifiers can turn a statement that would otherwise be true into one that is false or vice versa. For example, "The grammar rule 'I before E except after C' is *always* true" is false, whereas "The grammar rule 'I before E except after C' is *usually* true" is true. The qualifier makes the difference.

Matching questions

Matching questions ask you to match the terms in one list with the terms in another list, according to the directions. For example, the directions may tell you to match a communicable disease with the germ that usually causes it. The following practical strategies will help you handle these questions.

Make sure you understand the directions. The directions tell you whether each answer can be used only once or more than once.

Work from the column with the longest entries. The left-hand column usually contains terms to be defined or questions to be answered, whereas the right-hand column contains definitions or answers. As a result, entries in the right-hand column are usually longer than those on the left. Reading the items on the right only once each will save time as you work to match them with the shorter phrases on the left.

Start with the matches you know. On your first run-through, mark these matches with a penciled line, waiting to finalize your choices after you've completed all the items. Keep in mind that if you can use an answer only once, you may have to change answers if you reconsider any of your original choices.

Finally, tackle the matches you're not sure of. On your next run-through, focus on the more difficult matches. Look for clues and relationships you might not have considered.

If one or more phrases seem to have no correct answer, look back at your easy matches to be sure that you did not jump too quickly. Consider the possibility that one of your sure-thing answers is wrong.

Fill-in-the-blank questions

Fill-in-the-blank questions, also known as sentence completion questions, ask you to supply one or more words or phrases with missing information that completes the sentence. These strategies will help you make successful choices.

Be logical. Insert your answer and then reread the sentence from beginning to end to be sure it is factually and grammatically correct and makes sense.

Note the length and number of the blanks. These are important clues but not absolute guideposts. If two blanks appear right after one another, the instructor is probably looking for a two-word answer. If a blank is longer than usual, the correct response may require additional space. However, if you are certain of an answer that doesn't seem to fit the blanks, trust your knowledge and instincts.

Pay attention to how blanks are separated. If there is more than one blank in a sentence and the blanks are widely separated, treat each one separately. Answering each as if it were a separate sentence-completion question increases the likelihood that you will get at least one answer correct. Here is an example:

> Tommy Douglas re-entered _____ politics in 1961 and became the leader of the _____ Party and _____ was introduced.
> (*Answer:* Tommy Douglas re-entered federal politics in 1961. He became the leader of the New Democratic Party and medicare was introduced.)

Think out of the box. If you can think of more than one correct answer, put them both down as long as you are definite that they are both right. If they are both correct, your instructor may be impressed by your assertiveness and creativity. However, if one is incorrect, he or she may mark the whole thing incorrect.

If you are uncertain of an answer, make an educated guess. Have faith that after hours of studying, the correct answer is somewhere in your subconscious mind and that your guess is not completely random. It is better to take a guess than to leave the question blank.

Essay questions

An essay question allows you to express your knowledge and views more extensively than does a short-answer question. With this freedom comes the challenge to organize and express that knowledge clearly.

The following steps will help improve your responses to essay questions. The process is basically a less extensive version of the writing process. That is, you need to plan, draft, revise, and edit your response. The primary differences between writing an essay in an exam and writing one as an assignment are that you are writing under time pressure and that you are working from memory.

1. **Read the question.** If there is a choice of essay questions, read them all before deciding which to tackle. Use your analytical ability to focus on what each question is asking. Then engage practical strategies as you read the directions carefully and do everything asked.

   Some essay questions may contain more than one part, so it is important to budget your time. For example, if you have one hour to answer three question sections, you might budget 20 minutes for each section. Then break each of the 20-minute sections into writing stages such as 3 minutes for planning, 15 minutes for drafting, 2 minutes for revising and editing.

2. **Watch for action verbs.** Certain verbs can help you figure out how to answer the question. Key 8.3 explains some words commonly used in essay questions. Realize, for example, that a question asking you to "discuss" is asking for something different than is one asking you to "analyze." Be sure you consider the action words used in the question to understand what is being asked. Underline these words as you read, and use them to guide your writing.

3. **Plan.** Use your creative thinking skills to brainstorm ideas and examples. Create an informal outline or a concept map to organize your ideas and list supporting examples.

4. **Draft.** Start with a thesis statement, one sentence that clearly states the overall point of your essay. Then devote one or more paragraphs to the main points that support your thesis. Back up the general statement that starts each paragraph with evidence in the form of examples, statistics, and so on. Use simple, clear language, and look back at your outline to make sure you cover everything. Wrap it up with a short, pointed conclusion that summarizes the main points, restates the thesis, and ends with a concluding statement. Since you probably won't have time for redrafting, try to be as complete and organized as possible.

5. **Revise.** Make sure you answer the question completely and include all of your points. Look for ideas you left out, general statements that need more support, paragraphs that don't hold together well, unnecessary material, and confusing sentences. Fix problems by adding new material in the margins and crossing out what you don't need. When adding material, you can indicate with an arrow where it fits or note that inserts can be found on separate pages. If you have more than one insert, label each to avoid confusion (e.g., Insert #1, Insert #2, etc.). A useful tool for essay exams is a pen that uses erasable ink. Some instructors also do not mind if the essay is written in pencil, but be sure to get approval for this beforehand.

6. **Edit.** Check for mistakes in grammar, spelling, punctuation, and usage. No matter your topic, being technically correct in your writing makes your work more impressive.

Focus on action verbs on essay tests.

Analyze—Break into parts and discuss each part separately.	**Explain**—Make the meaning of something clear, often by making analogies or giving examples.
Compare—Explain similarities and differences.	**Illustrate**—Supply examples.
Contrast—Distinguish between items being compared by focusing on differences.	**Interpret**—Explain your personal view of facts and ideas and how they relate to one another.
Criticize—Evaluate the positive and negative effects of what is being discussed.	**Outline**—Organize and present the main examples of an idea or sub-ideas.
Define—State the essential quality or meaning. Give the common idea.	**Prove**—Use evidence and argument to show that something is true, usually by showing cause and effect or giving examples that fit the idea to be proven.
Describe—Visualize and give information that paints a complete picture.	**Review**—Provide an overview of ideas and establish their merits and features.
Discuss—Examine in a complete and detailed way, usually by connecting ideas to examples.	**State**—Explain clearly, simply, and concisely, being sure that each word gives the image you want.
Enumerate/List/Identify—Recall and specify items in the form of a list.	**Summarize**—Give the important ideas in brief.
Evaluate—Give your opinion about the value or worth of something, usually by weighing positive and negative effects, and justify your conclusion.	**Trace**—Present a history of the way something developed, often by showing cause and effect.

Neatness is a crucial factor in essay writing. No matter how good your ideas are, if your instructor can't read them, your grade will suffer. If your handwriting is a problem, try printing your answers, skipping every other line, and writing on only one side of the paper. Students with illegible handwriting might ask to take the test using a laptop computer.

To answer the third essay question from the box below, one student created the informal planning outline shown in Key 8.4. Notice how abbreviations and shorthand help the student write quickly. It is much faster to write "Role of BL in IC" than "Role of Body Language in Interpersonal Communication." Key 8.5 (see p. 248) shows the student's essay, including the word changes and inserts she made while revising the draft.

Here are some examples of essay questions you might encounter in an Interpersonal Communication course. In each case, notice the <u>action verbs</u> from Key 8.3.

1. Summarize the role of the self-concept as a key to interpersonal relationships and communication.

2. Explain how internal and external noise affects the ability to listen effectively.

3. Describe three ways that body language affects interpersonal communication

get analytical!

Hone your ability to read and follow essay instructions accurately.

Focusing on the action verbs in essay test instructions can mean the difference between giving instructors what they want and answering off the mark.

- Start by choosing a topic you learned about in this text—for example, the concept of successful intelligence or internal and external barriers to listening. Write your topic here:

  _____

  _____

- Put yourself in the role of instructor. Write an essay question on this topic, using one of the action verbs in Key 8.3 to frame the question. For example, "Describe the three aspects of successful intelligence," or "Analyze the classroom-based challenges associated with internal barriers to listening."

  _____

  _____

- Now choose three other action verbs from Key 8.3. Use each one to rewrite your original question.

  1. _____
  2. _____
  3. _____

- Finally, analyze how each new verb changes the focus of the essay.

  1. _____
  2. _____
  3. _____

Create an informal outline during essay tests.

key 8.4

> Roles of BL in IC
>
> 1. To contradict or reinforce words
>
>   —e.g., friend says "I'm fine"
>
> 2. To add shades of meaning
>
>   —saying the same sentence in 3 diff. ways
>
> 3. To make lasting 1st impression
>
>   —impact of nv cues and voice tone greater than words
>
>   —we assume things abt person based on posture, eye contact, etc.

Revise your response to an essay question.

QUESTION: Describe three ways that body language affects interpersonal communication.

Body language plays an important role in interpersonal communication and helps shape the impression you make. Two of the most important functions of body language are to contradict and reinforce verbal statements. When body language contradicts verbal language, the message ~~conveyed~~ delivered by the body is dominant. For example, if a friend tells you that she is feeling "fine," but her posture is slumped, and her facial expression troubled, you have every reason to wonder whether she is telling the truth. If the same friend tells you that she is feeling fine and is smiling, walking with a bounce in her step, and has direct eye contact, her body language is ~~telling the truth~~.

The nonverbal cues that make up body language also have the power to add shades of meaning. Consider this statement: "This is the best idea I've heard all day." If you were to say this three different ways—in a loud voice while standing up; quietly while sitting with arms and legs crossed and looking away; and while ~~maintening~~ maintaining eye contact and taking the receiver's hand—you might send three different messages.

Finally, the impact of nonverbal cues can be greatest when you meet someone for the first time. When you meet someone, you tend to make assumptions based on nonverbal behaviour such as posture, eye contact, gestures, and speed and style of movement.

In summary, nonverbal communication plays a ~~crusial~~ crucial role in interpersonal relationships. It has the power to send an accurate message that may de-~~stroy~~ belie the speaker's words, offer shades of meaning, and set the tone of a first meeting.

Margin annotations:

, especially when ^ you meet someone for the first time

her eye contact minimal,

accurately reflecting and reinforcing her words.

Although first impressions emerge from a combination of nonverbal cues, tone of voice, and choice of words, nonverbal elements (cues and tone) usually come across first and strongest.

How can you learn from *test mistakes?*

The purpose of a test is to see how much you know, not merely to get a grade. Use the following strategies to analyze and learn from your mistakes so that you avoid repeating them.

Try to identify patterns in your mistakes. Look for the following:

- Careless errors. In your rush to finish, did you misread the question or directions, blacken the wrong box on the answer sheet, skip a question, or write illegibly?

- Conceptual or factual errors. Did you misunderstand a concept? Did you fail to master facts or concepts? Did you skip part of the text or miss classes in which ideas were covered?

Rework the questions you got wrong. Based on instructor feedback, try to rewrite an essay, recalculate a math problem from the original question, or redo questions following a reading selection. If you discover a pattern of careless errors, increase your efforts to be more careful and save time during the test to double-check your work.

Our greatest glory is not in never falling, but in rising every time we fall.

CONFUCIUS

After reviewing your mistakes, fill in your knowledge gaps. If you made mistakes because of a lack of understanding, develop a plan to learn the material. Solidifying your knowledge can help you on future exams and in life situations that involve the subject you're studying.

Talk to your instructors. Talk with your instructor about your specific mistakes on short-answer questions or about a weak essay. If you are not sure why you were marked down on an essay, ask what you could have done to

get practical!   LEARN FROM YOUR MISTAKES

Examine what went wrong on a recent exam to build knowledge for next time.

Look at an exam on which your performance fell short of expectations. If possible, choose one that contains different types of objective and subjective questions. With the test and answer sheet in hand, use your analytical and practical thinking skills to answer the following questions:

- Identify the types of questions on which you got the most correct answers (for example, matching, essay, multiple-choice, etc.).

  _____

- Identify the types of questions on which you made the greatest number of errors.

  _____

- Analyze your errors to identify patterns. For example, did you misread test instructions, or did you ignore qualifiers that changed the questions' meanings? What did you find?

  _____

  _____

- Finally, what are two practical actions you are committed to take during your next exam to avoid the same problems?

  Action 1: _____

  Action 2: _____

improve your grade. Take advantage of this opportunity to determine how to do better on the next exam.

If you fail a test, don't throw it away. Use it as a way to review material that you had trouble with or didn't know as well as you should have. You might also want to keep it as a reminder that you can improve if you have the will to succeed. When you compare a failure to later successes, you'll see how far you've come.

The willingness to learn from test mistakes is critical for all students. Often students who dismiss their instructors' feedback do not excel as much as those who take it seriously. Use what you learn from your mistakes on each test to improve your preparation and test-taking skill for future exams.

IN-CLASS NOTES

HOW CAN YOU LEARN FROM TEST MISTAKES?

- Avoid repeating mistakes by:
  - Identifying patterns in mistakes
  - Reworking wrong questions
  - Filling in knowledge gaps
  - Talking to instructors
  - Reviewing past tests

_____

_____

_____

_____

_____

_____

Sine qua non

Although Latin is no longer spoken and is considered a "dead" language, it plays an important role in modern English since many English words and phrases have Latin roots. The Latin phrase *sine qua non* (pronounced sihn-ay kwa nahn) means, literally, "without which not." In other words, a sine qua non is "an absolutely indispensable or essential thing."

Think of learning as the sine qua non of test taking. When you have worked hard to learn, review, and retain information, you will be well prepared for tests, no matter what form they take. Focus on knowledge to transform test taking from an intimidating challenge into an opportunity to demonstrate what you know.

SUGGESTED READINGS

Browning, William G., Ph.D. *Cliffs Memory Power for Exams*. Lincoln, NE: CliffsNotes Inc., 1990.

Frank, Steven. *Test Taking Secrets: Study Better, Test Smarter, and Get Great Grades*. Holbrook, MA: Adams Media Corporation, 1998.

Fry, Ron. *"Ace" Any Test*. 5th ed. Florence, KY: Thomson Delmar Learning, 2004.

Hamilton, Dawn. *Passing Exams: A Guide for Maximum Success and Minimum Stress*. New York: Continuum International, 2003.

Kesselman-Turkel, Judy, and Franklynn Peterson. *Test Taking Strategies*. Madison, WI: University of Wisconsin Press, 2004.

Luckie, William R., and Wood Smethurst. *Study Power: Study Skills to Improve Your Learning and Your Grades*. Cambridge, MA: Brookline Books, 1997.

Meyers, Judith N. *Secrets of Taking Any Test: Learn the Techniques Successful Test-Takers Know*. New York: Learning Express, July 2000.

INTERNET RESOURCES

Keys to Success Companion Web site: www.pearsoned.ca/carter

Exams: Preparing, Writing, and Beyond. Student Development Services. University of Western Ontario: http://www.sdc.uwo.ca/learning/index.html?topics

Learning Skills Handouts: Exam Prep and Writing. Learning Skills Program, Counselling Services, University of Victoria: www.coun.uvic.ca/learn/hndouts.html

Succeeding on Tests and Exams: Student Achievement Series Online. Centre for Student Development. McMaster University: http://csd.mcmaster.ca/student_achievement_series.htm

A Student Guide to Test Taking and Exams. Inter Universities North: Student Support. University College of the North: www.iun.mb.ca/ss.htm

Prentice Hall Student Success SuperSite (testing tips in academic skills section): www.prenhall.com/success

Test Taking Tips.com (test taking and study skills): www.testtakingtips.com

Study Strategies Homepage. University of Minnesota Duluth: www.d.umn.edu/student/loon/acad/strat/

BUILDING SKILLS

FOR ACADEMIC, CAREER, AND LIFE SUCCESS

Developing Successful Intelligence

PUTTING IT ALL TOGETHER

Test preparation and performance. Take a detailed look at your preparation for and performance on a recent test.

Step 1. Think it through: *Analyze how you did.* Were you pleased or disappointed with your performance and grade? Why?

_____

_____

_____

Thinking about your performance, look at the potential problems listed below. Circle any that you feel were a factor in this exam. Fill in the empty spaces with any key problems not listed.

- Incomplete preparation
- Fatigue
- Feeling rushed during the test
- Shaky understanding of concepts
- Poor guessing techniques

- Feeling confused about directions
- Test anxiety
- _____
- _____
- _____

If you circled any problems, explain why you made mistakes (if it was an objective exam) or why you didn't score well (if it was an essay exam).

_____

_____

_____

Step 2. Think out of the box: *Be creative about test-preparation strategies.* If you had absolutely no restrictions on time or on access to materials, how would you have prepared for this test?

create your future

Describe briefly what your plan would be and how it would minimize any problems you encountered.

_____

_____

Now think back to your actual preparation for this test. Describe techniques you used and note time spent.

_____

_____

How does what you would like to do differ from what you actually did?

_____

_____

Step 3. Make it happen: *Improve preparation for the future.* Think about the practical actions you will take the next time you face a similar test.

Actions I took this time, but do not intend to take next time:

_____

_____

Actions I did not take this time, but intend to take next time:

_____

_____

Team Building

COLLABORATIVE SOLUTIONS

Test study group. Form a study group with two or three other students. For the next exam, check off everything you do to prepare for it:

- ❑ learning what to expect on the test (topics and material that will be covered, types of questions that will be asked)
- ❑ examining old tests
- ❑ creating and following a study schedule and checklist
- ❑ using SQ3R to review material
- ❑ taking a pre-test
- ❑ getting a good night's sleep before the exam
- ❑ doing last-minute cramming
- ❑ mastering general test-taking strategies
- ❑ mastering test-taking strategies for specific types of test questions (multiple-choice, true/false, matching, fill-in-the-blank, essay)

After the exam, compare your preparation strategies with your study group. What important differences can you identify in the routines followed by group members?

_____

_____

How did learning styles play a role in those differences?

_____

_____

How do you think that different routines affected test performance and outcome?

_____

_____

What did you learn from the test-preparation habits of your group members that may help you as you prepare for upcoming exams?

_____

_____

Writing

DISCOVERY THROUGH JOURNALING

Record your thoughts here or on a separate piece of paper or in a journal.

Test anxiety. Do you experience test anxiety?

_____

Describe how tests generally make you feel (you might include an example of a specific test situation and what happened).

_____

_____

Identify your specific test-taking fears. Then brainstorm at least one idea for each on how to overcome this fear and any related self-defeating behaviours.

Test-Taking Fear   How to Overcome It

_____   _____

_____   _____

_____   _____

_____   _____

Career Portfolio

PLAN FOR SUCCESS

Complete the following here or in your electronic portfolio or on separate sheets of paper.

On-the-job testing. Depending on what future occupations you are considering, you may encounter one or more tests throughout your career. Some may be for entry into the field, some to test your proficiency on particular equipment, or others to move you to the next level of employment. Choose one occupation you are thinking about and investigate what tests may be involved as you advance through different stages of the field. Choose one of these tests that you will explore further and gather more information on. Answer the following questions:

- What does it test you on?

  _____

- In the course of pursuing this occupation, when would you need to take the test?

  _____

- What preparation is necessary for the test (including course work)?

  _____

- Does the test need to be retaken at any time (e.g., for recertification every few years)?

  _____

Finally, see if you can get an example of the test you will face if you pursue this occupation. For example, if your career choice requires proficiency on a specific computer program, your institution's career or computer centre may have the test available. Some examples of specific tests are also available through the Internet.

Chapter Review Questions

1. When is the best time to start preparing for exams?

   a. ☐ On the first day of the course.

   b. ☐ Two days before the exam.

   c. ☐ One week before the exam.

   d. ☐ Two weeks before the exam.

2. What reading strategy can you use to structure your review for tests?

   a. ☐ Cornell format.

   b. ☐ Concept mapping.

   c. ☐ Summarizing.

   d. ☐ SQ3R.

3. Which of the following is the least effective way to review for tests?

   a. ☐ Read and reread the information.

   b. ☐ Answer the study questions.

   c. ☐ Explain the information to someone else.

   d. ☐ Create a concept map from your linear-style notes.

4. Many students do not do well on tests because they

   a. ☐ Study too much.

   b. ☐ Have bad memories.

   c. ☐ Do not prepare for questions requiring more complex thinking.

   d. ☐ Prepare by answering study guide questions.

5. What is a positive effect of stress?

   a. ☐ It can make you more alert and provide energy to get things done.

   b. ☐ It can force you to slow down.

   c. ☐ It can cause sleep loss, which gives you more waking hours to get things done.

   d. ☐ There are no positive effects of stress.

6. What is the best way to relieve test anxiety?

   a. ☐ Over-prepare for the exam.

   b. ☐ Avoid the studying that causes the stress.

   c. ☐ Just accept the fact that you will fail.

   d. ☐ Seek out others who are just as anxious as you are.

7. When taking a test, the best way to proceed is to

   a. ☐ Read the directions quickly.

   b. ☐ Skim the whole test immediately.

   c. ☐ Answer the most difficult questions first.

   d. ☐ Spend most of the time on the essay question.

8. When budgeting your time on an exam, you should

   a. ☐ Spend most of the time on the essay question.

   b. ☐ Spend most of the time on the multiple-choice questions.

   c. ☐ Budget your time based on the number of points for each question.

   d. ☐ Budget your time so that you spend most of it on the questions you know.

9. Why is it a good idea to circle qualifiers in a test question?

   a. ☐ Qualifiers are important words that can change the meaning of the question.

   b. ☐ Words like "always" and "never" are clues that the answer is always right.

   c. ☐ Words like "often" and "sometimes" always indicate that the answer is right.

   d. ☐ Qualifiers are words you can skip over to get to the more important words.

10. How should you proceed in answering questions on a test?

    a. ☐ Start at the beginning and work straight through to the end.

    b. ☐ Start at the end where the essay usually is and work back to the beginning.

    c. ☐ Start with the most difficult questions first.

    d. ☐ Start with the easiest questions first.

11. Most post-secondary institutions

    a. ☐ Expect that students will find it necessary to cheat once in a while.

    b. ☐ Will turn a blind eye to situations of minor cheating.

    c. ☐ Will reprimand students with a warning when caught cheating.

    d. ☐ Have strict policies against cheating that may include expulsion.

12. When answering a multiple-choice question, it is best to read the

    a. ☐ Options before reading the question.

    b. ☐ Question first and then stop reading options when you find the right answer.

    c. ☐ Question first and try to answer it without reading the options.

    d. ☐ Options first and try to answer it without reading the question.

13. If you must guess the answer in a multiple-choice question, the best way to do so is to

    a. ☐ Eliminate the choices you suspect are wrong and then choose one of the others.

    b. ☐ Always choose option B or C as the answers are almost always hidden in the middle.

    c. ☐ Ignore whether the options are relevant to the question.

    d. ☐ Always eliminate options that use absolute qualifiers.

14. When completing matching questions

    a. ☐ Always stick with your first instinct.

    b. ☐ Use a pencil so you can change your answers.

    c. ☐ Work from the column with the shortest entries.

    d. ☐ Always match every item only once.

15. Which of the following is NOT a strategy recommended for completing fill-in-the-blank questions?

    a. ☐ Insert your answer and take time to reread the statement.

    b. ☐ Note the length of the blank lines.

    c. ☐ Note the number of blank lines.

    d. ☐ If you are uncertain of an answer, skip it.

16. The difference between writing an essay in an exam and writing one on your own time as an assignment is

    a. ☐ The writing process is completely different.

    b. ☐ In an exam, you should not take up time doing an outline.

    c. ☐ You are writing under time pressure and from memory.

    d. ☐ There is no opportunity to revise and edit.

17. What is the following essay question asking you to do?
Discuss the practice of cramming for exams.

    a. ☐ Evaluate the positive and negative effects.

    b. ☐ Give concrete examples.

    c. ☐ Visualize and paint a complete picture.

    d. ☐ Examine completely, connecting ideas to examples.

18. When you receive your test back after it has been graded, you should

    a. ☐ Just check out the grade and avoid looking at your answers.

    b. ☐ Analyze the errors that you made.

    c. ☐ Ignore the instructor's feedback so that you do not impose more stress on yourself.

    d. ☐ Ask others in the class what grade they received to see if you were graded fairly.

19. Often students who dismiss their _____ _____ do not _____ as much as those who take it seriously.

    a. ☐ Instructors' feedback; excel.

    b. ☐ Careless errors; stress.

    c. ☐ Simple successes; care.

    d. ☐ Own instincts; worry.

20. Which of the following is NOT a strategy for analyzing the mistakes you make on tests?

    a. ☐ Identify patterns.

    b. ☐ Rework the questions.

    c. ☐ Talk to your instructors.

    d. ☐ Summarize.

Relating to Others
COMMUNICATING IN A DIVERSE WORLD

This chapter is organized as follows:

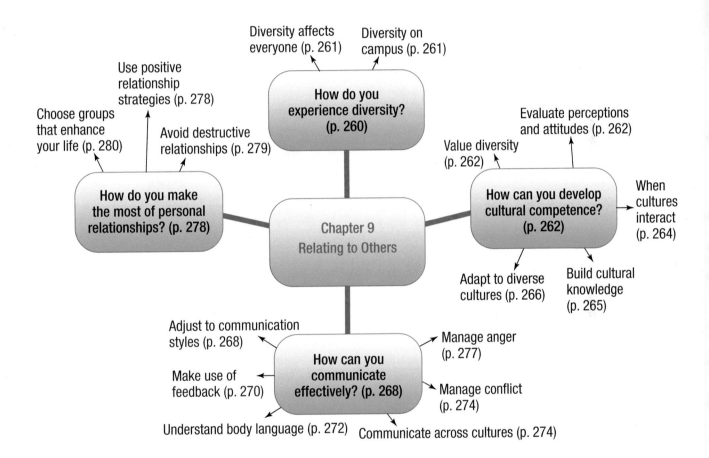

Diversity affects everyone (p. 261)

Diversity on campus (p. 261)

Use positive relationship strategies (p. 278)

Choose groups that enhance your life (p. 280)

Avoid destructive relationships (p. 279)

How do you experience diversity? (p. 260)

Evaluate perceptions and attitudes (p. 262)

Value diversity (p. 262)

How do you make the most of personal relationships? (p. 278)

Chapter 9 Relating to Others

How can you develop cultural competence? (p. 262)

When cultures interact (p. 264)

Adapt to diverse cultures (p. 266)

Build cultural knowledge (p. 265)

Adjust to communication styles (p. 268)

Manage anger (p. 277)

Make use of feedback (p. 270)

How can you communicate effectively? (p. 268)

Manage conflict (p. 274)

Understand body language (p. 272)

Communicate across cultures (p. 274)

TEST YOURSELF

- How is diversity experienced in your life?
- What are the five steps to developing cultural competence?
- How are prejudices and stereotypes perpetuated?
- Describe characteristics of the four basic types of communication styles.
- Give an example for each of non-constructive and constructive feedback.
- Explain four strategies for receiving feedback.
- Why is it important to understand body language?
- How could you use the problem-solving plan to resolve conflict?
- Explain the difference between passive, aggressive, and assertive communicators.
- What are three ways to develop positive relationships in your life?

For the correct answers and additional questions on Chapter 9, visit www.pearsoned.ca/carter.

Among your most meaningful, life-changing experiences at college or university will be those that take you out of your "comfort zone" and force you to question your thinking and even your basic beliefs. Encountering the diversity of the people around you can inspire this kind of questioning. As you read this chapter, you will explore how accepting differences and rejecting prejudice can lead to respect for others and strong teamwork skills, both of which are key ingredients for success in school and beyond.

In this chapter, you will investigate how analytical, creative, and practical abilities can help you build the cultural competence that will allow you to relate successfully to others. You will explore how to communicate effectively, investigating different communication styles and methods for handling conflict. Finally, you will look at how your personal relationships can inspire you and enhance your academic and personal life experiences.

How do you experience *diversity*?

Over the last century, Canada has become home to countless numbers of new immigrants from a multitude of countries and cultural backgrounds. The cultural portrait of Canada is continually changing. For instance, the 2001 census reported more that 200 different ethnic groups in Canada, and the number of people living in Canada that were born in other countries is the highest it has been in 70 years.[1] Technology and economic interdependence add to our growing cultural awareness. Television, the Internet, and the global marketplace link people from all over the world in ways that were unimaginable just a few years ago. We now have unprecedented access to information about what people do and how they live in nearly every corner of the globe.

Ethnicity and culture are just two aspects of diversity that we are enriched with in Canada. Diversity exists in many other ways too. It refers to the unique characteristics that all of us possess that both distinguish us as individuals and identify us as belonging to a group or groups. Diversity transcends concepts of race, ethnicity, socioeconomic status, gender, religion, sexual orientation, disability, and age.[2] All around you, there are opportunities to experience and learn from the uniqueness of others.

Diversity affects everyone

As you read in Chapter 1, diversity exists both within each person and among all people:

- **The diversity within each person.** Your physical being, personality, learning style, talents and skills, and analytical, creative, and practical abilities set you apart from everyone else. *No one else has been or ever will be exactly like you.*

- **The diversity among people.** Differences in skin colour, gender, ethnicity and national origin, age, physical characteristics and abilities, and sexual orientation are some of the major differences that exist among people. Differences in cultural and religious beliefs and practices, education and socioeconomic status, family background, and marital and parental status add to our country's cultural mosaic.

You may work with people from different backgrounds. You may encounter all kinds of people as you attend religious services, buy groceries and stamps, swim at a pool, or socialize. You may experience diversity within your family, often the kind of diversity that is not visible. Even if friends or family members have the same racial and ethnic background as you do, they might be completely different in how they learn, the way they communicate, what they value, and what they do well.

Diversity on campus

In college or university you are likely to meet class-mates or instructors who reflect Canada's growing diversity, including

- Biracial or multiracial individuals or those who come from families with more than one religious tradition.

- English as a foreign language speakers who may have immigrated from countries around the world.

- People making a career change and returning to school after years of working at the same occupation.

- Persons living with various kinds of disabilities.

- Persons practising different lifestyles—often expressed in the way they dress, their interests, their sexual orientation, and their leisure activities.

Being able to appreciate and adjust to differences among people is crucial to your success at school, at work, and in your personal relationships. You can accomplish this goal by using your analytical, creative, and practical abilities to develop cultural competence.

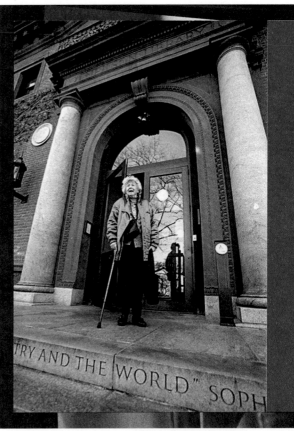

Workplaces and post-secondary campuses are filled with people of every age and stage of life. On track to receive her bachelor's degree, this 85-year-old student is determined to achieve her goal.

- Diversity affects everyone
  - Within each person
  - Among all people
- Diversity on campus
  - Appreciating and adjusting is crucial to success

_____

_____

_____

_____

How can you develop *cultural competence?*

As you learned in Chapter 2, *cultural competence* refers to the ability to understand and appreciate differences among people and change your behaviour in a way that enhances, rather than detracts from, relationships and communication. According to the National Center for Cultural Competence, to develop cultural competence you must act upon the following five steps:[3]

1. Value diversity.
2. Identify and evaluate personal perceptions and attitudes.
3. Be aware of what happens when different cultures interact.
4. Build knowledge about other cultures.
5. Use what you learn to adapt to diverse cultures as you encounter them.

As you develop cultural competence, you heighten your ability to analyze how people relate to one another. Most important, you develop practical skills that enable you to connect to others by bridging the gap between who you are and who they are.[4]

Value diversity

Valuing diversity means having a basic respect for, and acceptance of, the differences among people. Every time you meet someone new, you have a choice about how to relate. If you value diversity, you will choose to treat people with tolerance and respect, granting them the right to think, feel, and believe without being judged. Being open-minded in this way will help your relationships thrive, as shown in Key 9.1. Even though you won't like every person you meet, you can make an effort to show respect while focusing on the person as an individual.

Identify and evaluate personal perceptions and attitudes

Whereas people may value the *concept* of diversity, attitudes and emotional responses may influence how they act when they confront the *reality* of diver-

Approaching diversity with an open mind builds relationships.

YOUR ROLE	SITUATION	CLOSED-MINDED ACTIONS	OPEN-MINDED ACTIONS
Fellow student	For an assignment, you are paired with a student old enough to be your mother.	You assume the student will be clueless about the modern world. You think she might preach to you about how to do the assignment.	You get to know the student as an individual. You stay open to what you can learn from her experiences and knowledge.
Friend	You are invited to dinner at a friend's house. When he introduces you to his partner, you realize that he is gay.	You are turned off by the idea of two men in a relationship. You make an excuse to leave early. You avoid your friend after that.	You have dinner with the two men and make an effort to get to know more about them, individually and as a couple.
Employee	Your new boss is of a different racial and cultural background than yours.	You assume that you and your new boss don't have much in common. You think she will be distant and uninterested in you.	You rein in your stereotypes. You pay close attention to how your new boss communicates and leads. You adapt to her style and make an effort to get to know her better.

sity in their own lives. As a result, many people have prejudices that lead to damaging stereotypes.

Prejudice

Almost everyone has some level of **prejudice,** meaning that they prejudge others, usually on the basis of characteristics such as gender, race, sexual orientation, and religion. People judge others without knowing anything about them because of . . .

- **Influence of family and culture.** Children learn attitudes, including intolerance, superiority, and hate, from their parents, peers, and community.
- **Fear of differences.** It is human to fear and to make assumptions about the unfamiliar.
- **Experience.** One bad experience with a person of a particular race or religion may lead someone to condemn all people with the same background.

Stereotypes

Prejudice is usually based on **stereotypes**—assumptions made, without proof or critical thinking, about the characteristics of a person or group of people. Stereotyping emerges from . . .

- **A desire for patterns and logic.** People often try to make sense of the world by using the labels, categories, and generalizations that stereotypes provide.
- **Media influences.** The more people see stereotypical images—the airhead beautiful blonde, the jolly fat man—the easier it is to believe that stereotypes are universal.
- **Laziness.** Labeling group members according to a characteristic they seem to have in common takes less energy than exploring the qualities of individuals.

PREJUDICE

A preconceived judgment or opinion, formed without just grounds or sufficient knowledge.

STEREOTYPE

A standardized mental picture that represents an oversimplified opinion or uncritical judgment.

Stereotypes stall the growth of relationships, because pasting a label on a person makes it hard for you to see the real person underneath. Even stereotypes that seem "positive" may not be true and may get in the way of perceiving people as individuals. Key 9.2 shows some "positive" and "negative" stereotypes.

Use your analytical abilities to question your own ideas and beliefs and to weed out the narrowing influence of prejudice and stereotyping. Giving honest answers to questions like the following is an essential step in the development of cultural competence:

- How do I react to differences?
- What prejudices or stereotypes come to mind when I see people, in real life or the media, who are different than I am, who are from a different culture, or who make different choices?
- Where did my prejudices and stereotypes come from?
- Are these prejudices fair? Are these stereotypes accurate?
- What harm can having these prejudices and believing these stereotypes cause?

With the knowledge you build as you answer these questions, move on to the next stage: Looking carefully at what happens when people from different cultures interact.

Be aware of what happens when cultures interact

As history has shown, when people from different cultures interact, they often experience problems caused by lack of understanding, prejudice, and stereotypic thinking. At their mildest, these problems create roadblocks that obstruct relationships and communication. At their worst, they set the stage for acts of discrimination and hate crimes.

Discrimination

Discrimination refers to actions that deny people equal employment, educational, and housing opportunities, or treat people as second-class citizens. Canadian law assures that you cannot be denied basic opportunities and rights because of your race, creed, colour, age, gender, national or ethnic origin, religion, marital status, potential or actual pregnancy, or potential or actual illness or disability (unless the illness or disability prevents you from performing required tasks and unless accommodations are not possible).

Stereotypes involve generalizations that may not be accurate.

key 9.2

POSITIVE STEREOTYPE	NEGATIVE STEREOTYPE
Women are nurturing.	Women are too emotional for business.
White people are successful in business.	White people are cold and power hungry.
Gay men have a great sense of style.	Gay men are sissies.
People with disabilities have strength of will.	People with disabilities are bitter.
Older people are wise.	Older people are set in their ways.

EXPAND YOUR PERCEPTION OF DIVERSITY

Heighten your awareness of diversity by examining your own uniqueness.

Being able to respond to people as individuals requires that you become more aware of the diversity that is not always on the surface. Brainstorm 10 words or phrases that describe you. The challenge: Keep references to your ethnicity or appearance (brunette, gay, wheelchair dependent, First Nations, and so on) to a minimum, and fill the rest of the list with characteristics others can't see at a glance (laid-back, only child, 28 years old, drummer, marathoner, interpersonal learner, and so on).

1. _____
2. _____
3. _____
4. _____
5. _____

6. _____
7. _____
8. _____
9. _____
10. _____

Use a separate piece of paper to make a similar list for someone you know well—a friend or family member. Again, stay away from the most obvious visible characteristics. See if anything surprises you about the different image you create of this familiar person.

Despite these legal protections, discrimination is common and often appears on campuses. Students may not want to work with students of other races. Members of campus clubs may reject prospective members because of religious differences. Outsiders may harass students attending gay and lesbian alliance meetings. Instructors may judge students according to their weight, accent, or body piercing.

Minds are like parachutes. They only function when they are open.

SIR JAMES DEWAR

Hate crimes

The Canadian Criminal Code defines hate crimes as offences "motivated by bias, prejudice or hate based on race, national or ethnic origin, language, colour, religion, sex, age, mental or physical disability, sexual orientation, or any other similar factor." According to Statistics Canada's Pilot Survey, in 2001 to 2002, 57 percent of hate crimes were motivated by race or ethnicity, 43 percent by religion, and about 10 percent by sexual orientation The most common types of hate crimes included mischief or vandalism, assault, threats, and hate propaganda.[5] These statistics include only reported incidents, so they tell only a part of the story. Many more crimes likely go unreported by victims fearful of what might happen if they contact authorities.

HATE CRIME

A crime motivated by a hatred of a specific characteristic thought to be possessed by the victim.

Build cultural knowledge

The successfully intelligent response to discrimination and hate, and the next step in your path toward cultural competence, is to gather knowledge. You have a personal responsibility to learn about people who are different from you, including those you are likely to meet on campus.

What are some practical ways to begin?

- *Read* newspapers, books, magazines, and websites.
- *Ask questions* of all kinds of people, about themselves and their traditions.
- *Observe* how people behave, what they eat and wear, and how they interact with others.
- *Travel internationally* to unfamiliar places where you can experience first-hand different ways of living.
- *Travel locally* to equally unfamiliar, but close-by, places where you will encounter a variety of people.
- *Build friendships* with fellow students or co-workers you would not ordinarily approach.

Some post-secondary institutions have international exchange students who can help you appreciate the world's cultural diversity. In addition, talk with family, read, and seek experiences that educate you about your own cultural heritage. Building knowledge means learning about yourself and others. Then share what you know.

Adapt to diverse cultures

Adapting to diverse cultures is the process by which you take everything you have gathered about your value of diversity, your self-knowledge, your understanding of how cultures interact, and your information about different cultures and put it to work with practical actions. With these actions you can improve how you relate to others, and perhaps even change how people relate to one another on a larger scale. Think carefully, and creatively, about what kinds of actions feel right to you. Make choices that you feel comfortable with, cause no harm, and may make even a small difference.

Dr. Martin Luther King Jr. believed that careful thinking could change attitudes. He said:

The tough-minded person always examines the facts before he [she] reaches conclusions: in short, he [she] post-judges. The tender-minded person reaches conclusions before he [she] has examined the first fact; in short, he [she] prejudges and is prejudiced . . . . There is little hope for us until we become tough minded enough to break loose from the shackles of prejudice, half-truths, and down-right ignorance.[6]

Try the following suggestions. In addition, let them inspire your own creative ideas about what else you can do in your daily life to improve how you relate to others.

Look past external characteristics. If you meet someone who has a disability, get to know him or her. This person may be a professional who has children. He or she may love hockey, politics, or science fiction novels. These characteristics, not just physical, emotional or intellectual abilities, describe who people are.

When you meet different people, you discover many ways of being and learning. After having a stroke, this student learned how to write with her feet using a special device.

Put yourself in other people's shoes. Shift your perspective and try to understand what other people feel, especially if there's a conflict. For example, if you make a comment that someone interprets as offensive, think about why what you said was hurtful. If you can talk about it with the person, you may learn even more about how he or she heard what you said and why.

Adjust to cultural differences. When you understand someone's way of being and put it into practice, you show respect and encourage communication. If a friend's family is formal at home, dress appropriately and behave formally when you visit. If an instructor maintains a lot of personal space, keep a respectful distance when you visit during office hours. If a study group member takes offence at a particular kind of language, avoid it when you meet.

Help others in need. Newspaper columnist Sheryl McCarthy wrote about an African American man who, in the midst of the 1992 Los Angeles riots, saw an Asian American man being beaten and helped him to safety: "When asked why he risked grievous harm to save a man he didn't even know, he said, 'Because if I'm not there to help someone else, when the mob comes for me, will there be someone there to save me?'"[7]

Stand up against prejudice, discrimination, and hate. When you hear a prejudiced remark on campus or notice discrimination taking place, think about what you can do to encourage a move in the right direction. You may choose to make a comment, or to get help by approaching an authority such as an instructor or dean, because Canadian institutions have strict policies against discrimination and harassment. Sound the alarm on hate crimes. Let authorities know if you suspect that a crime is about to occur, join campus protests, and support organizations that encourage tolerance.

Recognize that people everywhere have the same basic needs. Everyone loves, thinks, hurts, hopes, fears, and plans. When you are trying to find common ground with diverse people, remember that you are united first through your essential humanity.

When people use successful intelligence to work through problems, changes can happen. Ada Maxwell, a student, believes that talking about intolerance is the key to eliminating it. "It doesn't have to be taboo," she said. "Half of the education . . . is the classes and the professors, but the other half—and it's a really important half—is what you can learn from other people. Your thinking can change and other people's thinking can change."[8]

Many minority students experience a dimension to post-secondary life unknown to other students. Examining their experiences and choices will help *all* students understand the complexity of what it means to be from a minority group in Canada.

get practical!

MAKE A DIFFERENCE

Find personal ways to connect with other cultures.

Rewrite three strategies in the "Adapt to Diverse Cultures" section on pages XXX–XXX as specific actions to which you can commit. For example, "Help others in need" might become "Sign up to tutor in the Writing Centre." Circle or check the number when you have completed each task or, if it is ongoing, when you have begun the change.

1. _____
   _____

2. _____
   _____

3. _____
   _____

IN-CLASS NOTES

HOW CAN YOU DEVELOP CULTURAL COMPETENCE?

- Value diversity
- Identify and evaluate personal perceptions and attitudes
  - Prejudice
  - Stereotypes
- Be aware of what happens when cultures interact
- Build cultural knowledge
- Adapt to diverse cultures

_____

_____

_____

_____

_____

_____

_____

How can you *communicate effectively?*

Clear-spoken communication promotes success at school, at work, and in personal relationships. Successfully intelligent communicators analyze and adjust to communication styles, learn to give and receive criticism, analyze and make practical use of body language, and work through communication problems.

Adjust to communication styles

When you speak, your goal is for listeners to receive the message as you intended. Problems arise when one person has trouble "translating" a message coming from someone using a different communication style. Your knowledge of the Personality Spectrum (see Chapter 3) will help you understand and analyze the ways diverse people communicate. Understanding the specific styles people have for communicating and the ways speakers and listeners must adjust in order to understand will help you communicate more effectively.

Identifying communication styles

The following are some communication styles that tend to be associated with the four dimensions in the Personality Spectrum. No one style is better than another. Successful communication depends on understanding your personal style and becoming attuned to the styles of others.

Thinker-dominant communicators focus on facts and logic. As speakers, they tend to rely on logical analysis to communicate ideas and prefer quantitative concepts to those that are conceptual or emotional. As listeners, they often do best with logical messages. Thinkers may also need time to process what they have heard before responding. These individuals may find it useful to communicate via written messages on paper or in email because writing can allow for time to put ideas together logically.

Organizer-dominant communicators focus on structure and completeness. As speakers, they tend to deliver well-thought-out, structured messages that fit into an organized plan. As listeners, they often appreciate a well-organized message that defines practical tasks in concrete terms. As with Thinkers, a written format is often an effective form of communication to or from an Organizer.

Giver-dominant communicators focus on concern for others. As speakers, they tend to cultivate harmony, analyzing what will promote closeness in relationships. As listeners, they often appreciate messages that emphasize personal connection and address the emotional side of an issue. Whether speaking or listening, Givers often favour in-person talks over written messages.

Adventurer-dominant communicators focus on the present. As speakers, they focus on creative ideas, tending to convey a message as soon as the idea arises and move on to the next activity. As listeners, they appreciate up-front, short, direct messages that don't get sidetracked. Like Givers, Adventurers tend to communicate and listen more effectively in person.

Use this information as a starting point for your self-exploration, but don't be limited by it. Just as people tend to demonstrate characteristics from more than one Personality Spectrum dimension, communicators may demonstrate different styles. Analyze your style by thinking about the communication styles associated with your dominant Personality Spectrum dimensions. Compare them to how you tend to communicate and how others seem to respond to you. Then use creative and practical thinking skills to decide what works best for you as a communicator.

Speakers adjust to listeners

Listeners may interpret messages in ways you never intended. Think about practical solutions to this kind of problem as you read the following example involving a Giver-dominant instructor and a Thinker-dominant student (the listener).

Instructor: "Your essay didn't communicate any sense of your personal voice."

Student: "What do you mean? I spent hours writing it. I thought it was on the mark."

- **Without adjustment:** The instructor ignores the student's need for detail and continues to generalize. Comments like, "You need to elaborate. Try writing from the heart. You're not considering your audience," might confuse or discourage the student.

- **With adjustment:** Greater logic and detail will help. For example, the instructor might say: "You've supported your central idea clearly, but you didn't move beyond the facts into your interpretation of what they mean. Your essay does not convey your understanding of the facts. The language doesn't sound like it is coming directly from you."

Listeners adjust to speakers

As a listener, improve understanding by being aware of stylistic differences and translating the message into one that makes sense to you. The following example of an Adventurer-dominant employee speaking to an Organizer-dominant supervisor shows how adjusting can pay off.

> Employee: "I'm upset about the e-mail you sent me. You never talked to me directly and you let the problem build into a crisis. I haven't had a chance to defend myself."

- **Without adjustment:** If the supervisor is annoyed by the employee's insistence on direct personal contact, he or she may become defensive: "I told you clearly what needs to be done. I don't know what else there is to discuss."

- **With adjustment:** In an effort to improve communication, the supervisor responds by encouraging immediate in-person exchange that is favoured by the employee. "Let's meet after lunch so you can explain to me how you believe we can improve the situation."

Although adjusting to communication styles helps you speak and listen more effectively, you also need to understand—and learn how to effectively give and receive—feedback.

Make use of constructive feedback

CONSTRUCTIVE

Promoting improvement or development.

Feedback can be either constructive or non-constructive. Constructive feedback is a practical problem-solving strategy, involving goodwill suggestions for improving a situation. In contrast, non-constructive feedback focuses on what went wrong, doesn't offer alternatives or help that might help solve the problem, and is often delivered negatively, creating bad feelings.

When offered constructively and carefully, feedback can help bring about important changes. Consider a case in which someone has continually been late to study group sessions. The group leader can comment in one of two ways. Which comment would encourage you to change your behaviour?

- **Constructive.** The group leader talks privately with the student: "I've noticed that you've been late quite a few times. We count on you, because our success depends on what each of us contributes. Is there a problem that is keeping you from being on time? Can we help?"

- **Non-constructive.** The leader watches the student arrive late and says, in front of everyone, "If you can't start getting here on time, there's really no point in your coming."

Communication ◀

Using techniques corresponding to your stronger intelligences boosts your communication skills both as a speaker and as a listener.

INTELLIGENCE	SUGGESTED STRATEGIES	WHAT WORKS FOR YOU? WRITE NEW IDEAS HERE
Verbal–Linguistic	• Find opportunities to express your thoughts and feelings to others—either in writing or in person. • Remind yourself that you have two ears and only one mouth. Listening is more important than talking.	
Logical–Mathematical	• Allow yourself time to think through solutions before discussing them—try writing out a logical argument on paper and then rehearsing it orally. • Accept the fact that others may have communication styles that vary from yours and that may not seem logical.	
Bodily–Kinesthetic	• Have an important talk while walking or performing a task that does not involve concentration. • Work out physically to burn off excess energy before having an important discussion.	
Visual–Spatial	• Make a drawing or diagram of points you want to communicate during an important discussion. • If your communication is in a formal classroom or work setting, use visual aids to explain your main points.	
Interpersonal	• Observe how you communicate with friends. If you tend to dominate the conversation, brainstorm ideas about how to communicate more effectively. • Remember to balance speaking with listening.	
Intrapersonal	• When you have a difficult encounter, take time alone to evaluate what happened and to decide how you can communicate more effectively next time. • Remember that in order for others to understand clearly, you may need to communicate more than you expect to.	
Musical	• Play soft music during an important discussion if it helps you, making sure it isn't distracting to the others involved.	
Naturalistic	• Communicate outdoors if that is agreeable to all parties. • If you have a difficult exchange, imagine how you might have responded differently had it taken place outdoors.	

While at school, your instructors will provide feedback on your class work, assignments, and exams. On the job, feedback may come from supervisors, co-workers, or customers. No matter the source, constructive comments can help you grow as a person. Be open to what you hear, and use the information to help you grow and succeed.

Offering constructive feedback

When offering constructive feedback, use the following strategies to be effective:

- Comment on the behaviour rather than the person. Avoid personal attacks. "You've been late to five group meetings" is much preferable to "You're irresponsible."
- Define the problematic behaviour specifically. Try to focus on the facts, substantiating with specific examples and minimizing emotions. Avoid additional complaints as people can hear feedback better if it is focused on one thing at a time.
- Suggest new approaches and offer assistance. Talk about practical ways of handling the situation. Work with the person to develop creative options. Help the person feel supported.
- Use a positive approach and hopeful language. Express the conviction that changes will occur and that the person can turn the situation around.

Receiving feedback

When you find yourself on the receiving end of feedback, use the following techniques:

- Analyze the comments. Listen carefully before you evaluate what you heard. What does it mean? What is the intent? Try to let non-constructive comments go without responding.
- Request suggestions on how to change the situation. Ask, "How would you like me to handle this in the future?"
- Summarize the feedback and your response to it. Make sure everyone understands the situation.
- Use a specific strategy. Use problem-solving skills to analyze the problem, brainstorm ways to change, choose a strategy, and take practical action to make it happen.

Feedback, as well as other thoughts and feelings, may be communicated verbally or nonverbally. In addition to communicating well verbally, you will become a more effective communicator if you understand how you, and others, communicate through the use of body language.

Understand body language

Body language has an extraordinary capacity to express people's real feelings through gestures, eye movements, facial expressions, body positioning and posture, touching behaviours, vocal tone, and use of personal space. It is important to know how to analyze body language because:

Nonverbal cues shade meaning. What you say can mean different things depending on body positioning or vocal tone. The statement, "That's a great

GIVE CONSTRUCTIVE FEEDBACK

Imagine how you would offer constructive feedback.

Briefly describe a situation in your life that could be improved if you were able to offer constructive feedback to a friend or family member. Describe the improvement you want:

_____

_____

_____

Imagine that you have a chance to speak to this person. First describe the setting—time, place, atmosphere—where you think you would be most successful:

_____

_____

_____

Now develop your "script." Keeping in mind what you know about constructive feedback, analyze the situation and decide what you think would be the best approach. Write freely what you would say. Keep in mind the goal you want your communication to achieve.

_____

_____

_____

Finally, if you can, make your plan a reality. Will you do it?   Yes   No

If you do have the conversation, note here: Was it worth it?   Yes   No

---

idea" sounds positive. However, said while sitting with your arms and legs crossed and looking away, it may communicate that you dislike the idea. Said sarcastically, the tone may reveal that you consider the idea a joke.

Culture influences how body language is interpreted. For example, in North America, looking away from someone may be a sign of anger or distress; in Japan, the same behaviour is usually a sign of respect.

Nonverbal communication strongly influences first impressions. First impressions emerge from a combination of verbal and nonverbal cues. Nonverbal elements, including tone of voice, posture, eye contact, and speed and style of movement, usually come across first and most obvious.

Although reading body language is not an exact science, the following practical strategies will help you use it to improve communication.

- Pay attention to what is said through nonverbal cues. Focus on your tone, your body position, and whether your cues reinforce or contradict your words. Then do the same for those with whom you are speaking. Look for meaning in the physical.

- Note cultural differences. Cultural factors influence how an individual interprets nonverbal cues. In cross-cultural conversation, discover what seems appropriate by paying attention to what the other person does on a consistent basis, and by noting how others react to what you do.

- Adjust body language to the person or situation. What body language might you use when making a presentation in class? Meeting with your advisor? Confronting an angry co-worker? Think through how to use your physicality to communicate successfully.

Communicate across cultures

As you meet people from other countries and try to form relationships with them, you may encounter communication issues that are linked to cultural differences.[9] As you recall from Chapter 2, these problems often stem from the different communication styles that are found in high-context and low-context cultures.

You cannot shake hands with a clenched fist.

INDIRA GANDHI

In low-context cultures, communication is linked primarily to words and to the explicit messages sent through these words. In contrast, in high-context cultures, words are often considered less important than such factors as context, situation, time, formality, personal relationships, and nonverbal behaviour.

Key 9.3 will help you see how 12 world cultures fit on the continuum of high- to low-context communication styles. Key 9.4 summarizes some major communication differences you should be aware of when talking with someone from a different culture. Being attuned to culture-based communication differences will help you interact comfortably with people who come from different parts of the world.

Language barriers may also arise when communicating cross-culturally. When speaking with someone who is struggling with your language, make the conversation easier by choosing words the person is likely to know, avoiding slang expressions, being patient, and using body language to fill in what words can't say. Also, invite questions from the other, and ask questions yourself, so that you both can be as clear as possible.

One of the main barriers to successful communication is conflict, which can result in anger and even violence. With effort, you can successfully manage conflict and stay away from those who cannot.

Manage conflict

Conflicts arise when there is a clash of ideas or interests. You may have small conflicts, such as one with a housemate over a door left unlocked, or you may have major conflicts with your partner about finances, or with an

The continuum of high- and low-context cultures.

key **9.3**

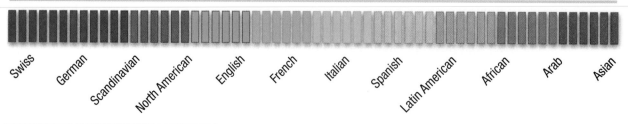

LOW-CONTEXT CULTURES   **HIGH-CONTEXT CULTURES**

Swiss   German   Scandinavian   North American   English   French   Italian   Spanish   Latin American   African   Arab   Asian

Some ways communication differs in high- and low-context cultures. **key 9.4**

FACTORS AFFECTING COMMUNICATION	LOW-CONTEXT CULTURES	HIGH-CONTEXT CULTURES
Personal Relationships	The specific details of the conversation are more important than what people know about each other.	Personal trust is the basis for communication, so sharing personal information forms a basis for strong, long-lasting relationships.
Time	People expect others to be punctual and to meet schedules.	Time is seen as a force beyond the person's control. Therefore lateness is common, and not considered rude.
Formality	A certain degree of civility is expected when people meet, including handshakes and introductions.	People often require formal introductions that emphasize status differences. As a result, a student will speak with great respect to an instructor.
Eye Contact	Expect little direct eye contact.	• Arabs may use prolonged, direct eye contact. • Students from Japan and other Far Eastern countries are likely to turn their eyes away from instructors as a sign of respect.
Personal Space	In North America, people converse while remaining between 4 and 12 feet apart.	People from Latin America and the Middle East may sit or stand between 18 inches and 4 feet away from you.

Source: Adapted from Louis E. Boone, David L. Kurtz, and Judy R. Block, *Contemporary Business Communication,* 2nd ed. (Upper Saddle River, NJ: Prentice Hall, 1997), 72.

instructor about a failing grade. Conflict, as unpleasant as it can be, is a natural element in the dynamic of getting along with others. Prevent it when you can, and when you can't, use problem-solving strategies to resolve it.

Conflict prevention

These two strategies can help you prevent conflict from starting in the first place.

Being assertive. No matter what your dominant learning styles, you tend to express yourself in one of three ways—aggressively, assertively, or passively. Aggressive communicators focus primarily on their own needs and can become impatient when needs are not satisfied. Assertive communicators are likely both to get their message across and to give listeners the opportunity to speak, without attacking others or sacrificing their own needs. Passive communicators focus primarily on the needs of others and often deny themselves power, causing frustration.

Key 9.5 contrasts the characteristics of these three. Assertive behaviour strikes a balance between aggression and passivity and promotes the most productive communication. Aggressive and passive communicators can use practical strategies to move toward a more assertive style of communication.

- Aggressive communicators could benefit from taking more time before speaking, using "I" statements, listening to others, and avoiding the urge to give orders.

> ASSERTIVE
>
> Able to declare and affirm one's own opinions while respecting the rights of others to do the same.

Assertiveness fosters successful communication.

AGGRESSIVE	ASSERTIVE	PASSIVE
Loud, heated arguing	Expressing feelings without being nasty or overbearing	Concealing one's own feelings
Blaming, name-calling, and verbal insults	Expressing oneself and giving others the chance to express themselves	Feeling that one has no right to express anger
Walking out of arguments before they are resolved	Using "I" statements to defuse arguments	Avoiding arguments
Being demanding: "Do this"	Asking and giving reasons: "I would appreciate it if you would do this, and here's why . . ."	Being noncommittal: "You don't have to do this unless you really want to . . ."

- Passive communicators might become more assertive by acknowledging anger, expressing their opinions, exercising the right to make requests, and knowing that their ideas and feelings are important.

Sending "I" messages. "I" messages help you communicate your needs rather than attacking someone else. Creating these messages involves stating how you feel and being clear about the behaviour that evoked that reaction from you. For instance, the following statements are rephrased by using the simple formula, "I feel (or felt) . . . when . . . ." "You didn't lock the door!" becomes "I felt nervous when I came to work this morning and the door was unlocked." Similarly, "You didn't call last night" becomes "I felt worried when I didn't hear from you last night."

"I" statements soften the conflict by highlighting the effects that the other person's actions have on you, rather than focusing on the person or the actions themselves. These statements help the receiver feel freer to respond, perhaps offering help and even acknowledging mistakes.

Conflict resolution

All too often, people deal with conflict through avoidance (a passive tactic that shuts down communication) or escalation (an aggressive tactic that often leads to fighting). Conflict resolution demands calm communication, motivation, and careful thinking. Use your analytical, creative, and practical thinking skills to apply the problem-solving process (see Chapter 4):

- Define and analyze the problem.
- Brainstorm possible solutions.
- Analyze potential solutions.
- Choose a solution and make it happen with practical action.

Trying to calm anger is an important part of resolving conflict. All people get angry sometimes—at people, events, and themselves. However, excessive anger can contaminate relationships, stifle communication, and turn friends and family away.

Manage anger

Strong emotions can get in the way of happiness and success. It is hard to concentrate on your studies if you are raging over being cut off in traffic or can't let go of your anger with a friend. Psychologists report that angry outbursts may actually make things worse. When you feel yourself losing control, try some of these practical anger-management techniques.

- **Relax.** Breathe deeply. Slowly repeat a calming phrase like "Take it easy" or a word such as "Relax."

- **Change your environment.** Take a break from what's upsetting you. Go for a walk, to the gym, or to a movie. Come up with some creative ideas about what might calm you down.

- **Think before you speak.** When angry, most people tend to say the first thing that comes to mind, even if it's hurtful. Inevitably, this escalates the feelings and intensity of the argument. Instead, wait until you are in control before you say something.

- **Do your best to solve a problem, but remember that not all problems can be solved.** Instead of blowing up, think about how you can handle what's happening. Analyze a challenging situation, make a plan, resolve to do your best, and begin. If you fall short, you will know you made an effort and be less likely to turn your frustration into anger.

- **Get help if you can't keep your anger in check.** If you consistently lash out, you may need the help of a counsellor. Most colleges and universities have counsellors available to students with personal, academic, or career counselling.

Your ability to communicate and manage conflict has a major impact on your relationships with friends and family. Successful relationships are built on self-knowledge, good communication, and hard work.

IN-CLASS NOTES

HOW CAN YOU COMMUNICATE EFFECTIVELY?

- Adjust to communication styles
  - Identifying communication styles
  - Speakers adjust to listeners
  - Listeners adjust to speakers
- Make use of constructive feedback
  - Offering constructive feedback
  - Receiving feedback
- Understand body language
- Communicate across cultures
- Manage conflict
  - Conflict prevention
  - Conflict resolution
- Manage anger

How do you make the most of *personal relationships?*

Personal relationships with friends, classmates, parents, spouses and partners can be sources of great satisfaction and inner peace. Good relationships can motivate you to do your best in school, on the job, and in life. When relationships fall apart, however, nothing may seem right. You may be unable to eat, sleep, or concentrate. Relationships have enormous power.

Use positive relationship strategies

Here are some strategies for improving personal relationships.

Make personal relationships a high priority. Life is meant to be shared. In some marriage ceremonies, the bride and groom share a cup of wine, symbolizing that the sweetness of life is doubled by tasting it together and the bitterness is cut in half when shared by two.

Invest time. You devote time to education, work, and sports. Relationships benefit from the same investment. In addition, spending time with people you like can relieve stress.

Spend time with people you respect and admire. Life is too short to spend it with people who bring you down or encourage you to ignore your values. Maintain relationships with people you care about and respect.

If you want a friend, be a friend. If you treat others with the kind of loyalty and support that you appreciate yourself, you are likely to receive the same in return.

Work through tensions. Negative feelings can fester when left unspoken. Get to the root of a problem by discussing it, compromising, forgiving, and moving on.

Take risks. It can be frightening to reveal your deepest dreams and frustrations, to devote yourself to a friend, or to fall in love. However, if you open yourself up, you stand to gain the incredible benefits of companionship, which for most people outweigh the risks.

Find an arrangement that suits you. Some people have many acquaintances and others have only a few close friends. Some people prefer to socialize in large groups and some in small groups. Some people date exclusively and commit early. Others date casually. Be honest with yourself, and others, about what you want in a relationship and communicate that openly.

If a relationship fails, find ways to cope. When an important relationship becomes strained or ends, analyze the situation and choose practical strategies to help you move on. Some people need time alone; others need to be with friends and family. Some seek counselling. Some throw their energy into school or exercise. Some cry. Whatever you do, believe that in time you will emerge from the experience stronger.

Avoid destructive relationships

On the far end of the spectrum are relationships that turn destructive. University and college campuses see their share of violent incidents. The more informed you are, the less likely you are to add to the sobering statistics.

Sexual harassment

Although the most common targets are women, both men and women can be victims of sexual harassment. Sexual harassment basically consists of these two types:

- *Quid pro quo harassment* refers to a request for a sexual favour or activity in exchange for something else. "If you do X for me, I won't fail you/fire you/make your life miserable."

- *Hostile environment harassment* indicates any situation in which sexually charged remarks, behaviour, or items cause discomfort. Examples include lewd jokes, pictures, and pornography.

How to cope. If you feel degraded by anything that goes on at school or work, address the person whom you believe is harassing you. If you do not feel comfortable or safe confronting that person, then speak to a person in authority who can help. On campus, that might be a counsellor, instructor, or student ombudsperson.

Violence in relationships

Violence in relationships is disturbingly common. In academic settings, violence can be found as early as elementary school in the form of bullying. High school and post-secondary students often also experience bullying, harassment, and abuse. Dating violence occurs among adolescents in high school and among adults in college or university. According to the 1998 Canadian Campus Survey, which included a sample of 7800 students, 13 percent of students reported that they had experienced a sexual assault during their lifetime and 20 percent reported a physical assault.[10] Another study reported that 25 percent of women who were attending school had experienced either sexual assault or physical assault at the hands of a dating partner.[11]

These numbers may be even higher if experiences of physical or sexual coercion or verbal or emotional threats and abuse were included. Also, the numbers focus only on dating relationships and might be higher if people who were married or living together were also surveyed. Furthermore, there is no way of knowing how many people experience violence without reporting it.

How to cope. Analyze your situation and use problem-solving skills to come up with options. If you see warning signs such as controlling behaviour, unpredictable mood swings, personality changes associated with alcohol and drugs, and outbursts of anger, consider ending the relationship. If you are being abused, call a shelter or abuse hotline or seek counselling at school or at a community centre. If you need medical attention, go to a clinic or hospital emergency room. If you believe that your life is in danger, leave and obtain a restraining order that requires your abuser to stay away from you.

Rape and date rape

Any intercourse or anal or oral penetration by a person against another person's will is defined as rape. Rape is primarily an act of rage and control, not a sexual act. Acquaintance rape, or date rape, refers to sexual activity during a date that is against one partner's will, including situations where one partner is too drunk or drugged to give consent. A drug called Rohypnol, known as roofies, is sometimes used by date rapists to sedate victims and is difficult to detect in a drink. Rape and sexual assault are illegal.

How to cope. When you are on a date with someone, communicate clearly what you want and don't want to do. Listen to your instincts if you are not feeling safe or comfortable, and remove yourself from the situation. If you are with someone who seems unstable or angry, stick to safe, public places. Always get your own drink and keep an eye on it to be sure no one has the opportunity to slip anything into it. Avoid alcohol or drugs that might make it difficult for you to stay in control, and keep a cell phone handy.

If you are raped, whether by an acquaintance or a stranger, seek medical attention immediately. Do not shower or change your clothes until after you have seen a doctor because this may destroy the evidence. Next, talk to a close friend or counsellor and report the incident to the police. Whether or not you take legal action, continue to get help through counselling, a rape survivor group, or a hotline.

Choose communities that enhance your life

Personal relationships often take place within communities, or groups, that include people who share your interests, such as recreation groups, hobby or interest clubs, athletic clubs, and political groups, etc. So much of what you accomplish in life is linked to your network of personal contacts.

If you affiliate with communities that are involved in positive activities, you are more likely to surround yourself with responsible and interesting people who may become your friends and colleagues. You may find among them your future spouse or partner, your best friend, a person who helps you land a job, your doctor, accountant, real estate agent, and so on.

Finding and working with a community of people with similar interests can have positive effects in personal relationships and in workplace readiness, as one university student, Kasey Doyle, explains:

> A friend persuaded me to join a service sorority on campus. I was hesitant at first, but once I began to get involved, I realized that I had missed out on many opportunities. Not only have I made many friends, I have also become more outgoing and personable. . . . I found a place where I fit in. Joining this organization also prepared me for my major and my job at [the campus newspaper] *The Progress*. As a reporter, you are expected to be outgoing and personable, and before joining an organization, I was extremely shy. I'm definitely not timid anymore, and I have matured and become more self-confident.[12]

If you find yourself drawn toward gangs or groups that encourage negative and even harmful behaviour, stop and think before you get involved. Analyze why you are drawn to these groups. It may be fear, loneliness, or insecurities that have you seeking out destructive relationships. Consider the consequences

DATE RAPE

Sexual assault perpetrated by the victim's escort during an arranged social encounter.

of involvement and resist the temptation. If you are already involved and want out, stand up for yourself and be determined. Look for relationships with people and groups that are positive, supportive and will help you reach your potential.

Kente

The African word *kente* means "that which will not tear under any condition." Kente cloth is worn by men and women in African countries such as Ghana, Ivory Coast, and Togo. There are many brightly coloured patterns of kente, each beautiful, unique, and special.

Think of how this concept applies to people. Like the cloth, all people are unique, with brilliant and subdued aspects. Despite mistreatment or misunderstanding by others, you need to remain strong so that you don't tear, allowing the weaker fibres of your character to show through. The kente of your character can help you endure, stand up against injustice, and fight peacefully, but relentlessly, for the rights of all people.

SUGGESTED READINGS

Dublin, Thomas, ed. *Becoming American, Becoming Ethnic: College Students Explore Their Roots.* Philadelphia: Temple University Press, 1996.

Feagin, Joe R., Hernan Vera, and Nikitah O. Imani. *The Agony of Education: Black Students at White Colleges and Universities.* New York: Routledge, 1996.

Gonzales, Juan L., Jr. *The Lives of Ethnic Americans.* 2nd ed. Dubuque, IA: Kendall/Hunt, 1994.

Hockenberry, John. *Moving Violations.* New York: Hyperion, 1996.

Levey, Marc, Michael Blanco, and W. Terrell Jones. *How to Succeed on a Majority Campus: A Guide for Minority Students.* Belmont, CA: Wadsworth Publishing Co., 1997.

Qubein, Nido R. *How to Be a Great Communicator: In Person, on Paper, and at the Podium.* New York: John Wiley & Sons, 1996.

Schuman, David. *Diversity on Campus.* Dubuque, IA: Kendall/Hunt, 2001.

Suskind, Ron. *A Hope in the Unseen: An American Odyssey from the Inner City to the Ivy League.* New York: Broadway Books, 1999.

Takaki, Ronald. *A Different Mirror: A History of Multicultural America.* Boston: Little, Brown & Company, 1994.

Tannen, Deborah. *You Just Don't Understand: Women and Men in Conversation.* New York: Perennial Currents, 2001.

Tatum, Beverly Daniel. *"Why Are All the Black Kids Sitting Together in the Cafeteria?" and Other Conversations About Race: A Psychologist Explains the Development of Racial Identity.* Philadelphia: Basic Books, 2003.

Terkel, Studs. *Race: How Blacks and Whites Think and Feel About the American Obsession.* New York: Free Press, 1995.

Trotter, Tamera, and Joycelyn Allen. *Talking Justice: 602 Ways to Build and Promote Racial Harmony.* Saratoga, FL: R & E Publishers, 1993.

INTERNET RESOURCES

Keys to Success Companion Web site:
www.pearsoned.ca/carter

Culture.ca: Canada's Cultural Gateway. Department of Canadian Heritage: www.culture.ca

Learning Disabilities Association of Canada:
www.ldac-taac.ca

Canadian Federation of Students Fact Sheets and Advisories. No Means No: Anti-Date Rape Campaign: http://www.cfs-fcee.ca/html/english/research/fact_sheets.php

Prentice Hall Student Success Supersite (success stories from students from a diversity of backgrounds):
www.prenhall.com/success

The Sociology of Race and Ethnicity (with multiple links to other resources):
http://www.trinity.edu/mkearl/race.html

BUILDING SKILLS

FOR ACADEMIC, CAREER, AND LIFE SUCCESS

Developing Successful Intelligence

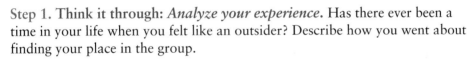

PUTTING IT ALL TOGETHER

Learn from experience.
Consider experiences that you have had in the past and learn from them.

Step 1. Think it through: *Analyze your experience.* Has there ever been a time in your life when you felt like an outsider? Describe how you went about finding your place in the group.

_____

_____

_____

Step 2. Think out of the box: *Create a challenge.* Think about the activities and organizations at your school and name one organization or activity that you might choose to take part in. Describe what you think you could gain from your experience.

_____

_____

_____

Step 3. Make it happen: *Use practical strategies to connect with others.* Contact the organization or activity coordinator and ask for details, such as when the group meets, what they do, what the time commitment would likely be, what the benefit would be. Record this information here.

_____

_____

_____

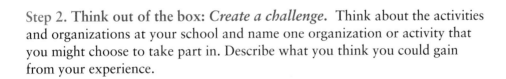
create your future

Would you consider joining the organization or activity?

_____

Writing

DISCOVERY THROUGH JOURNALING

Record your thoughts here or on a separate piece of paper or in a journal.

Opening your mind. What human characteristic is the most difficult for you to accept? Describe your difficulty with race, culture, ethnic origin, weight, gender, sexual orientation, or any other human characteristic.

_____

_____

What do you think is the source of your uneasiness—parents, peers, experience, any other source?

_____

_____

Describe what you can do now to think more openly, and think about why it may help you to combat your prejudices.

_____

_____

Team Building

COLLABORATIVE SOLUTIONS

Problem solving close to home. Divide into groups of two to five students. Assign one group member to take notes. Discuss the following questions, and summarize your discussion:

1. What are three major problems the world faces about how people get along with and accept others?

   1. _____

   2. _____

   _____

   3. _____

   _____

2. What could we do to deal with these three problems?

   _____

   _____

3. What can each individual student do to make improvements? (Talk about what you specifically feel that you can do.)

   _____

   _____

   _____

When all groups have finished, gather as a class and hear each group's responses. Observe the variety of problems and solutions. Notice whether more than one group came up with one or more of the same problems. If there is time, one person in the class, together with your instructor, could gather the responses to question 3 into an organized document that you can send to your school or local paper.

Career Portfolio

PLAN FOR SUCCESS

Complete the following here or in your electronic portfolio or on separate sheets of paper.

Compiling a resumé. What you have accomplished in various academic and work situations will be important for you to emphasize as you strive toward a career that is right for you. Your roles on the job, in school, at home, or in the community help you gain knowledge and experience.

Below, list your education and skills information. Also give details about your job experience such as job title, the dates of employment, and the tasks that this job entailed. Be as detailed as possible and write down everything you remember. When you compile your resumé, you can make this material more concise. Keep this list current by adding experiences and accomplishments as you go along.

Education	Skills	Job Experience		
		Job Title	Dates of Employment	Job Responsibilities

Using the information you have gathered and Key 9.6 as a model, draft a resumé for yourself. Remember that there are many ways to construct a resumé; consult other resources, such as those listed in the Suggested Readings, for different styles. You may want to format your resumé according to a style that best highlights your skills and accomplishments. Keep your resumé draft on hand—and on a computer disk. When you need to submit a resumé with a job application, update the draft and print it on high-quality paper.

Here are some general tips for writing a resumé:

- Always put your name and contact information at the top. Make it stand out.

- State an objective if it is appropriate—if your focus is specific or you are designing this resumé for a particular interview or occupational field.

- List your post-secondary education, starting from the most recent and working backward. This may include summer school, night school, seminars, and accreditations.

- List jobs with the most recent job first. Include all types of work experience (full-time, part-time, volunteer, etc.)

- When you describe your work experience, use action verbs and focus on what you have accomplished, rather than on the description of assigned tasks.

- Include keywords that are linked to the description of the jobs for which you will be applying.

- List references on a separate sheet and, rather than submitting them with your resumé, take this reference sheet to the interview and submit it then. You may want to write "References upon request" at the bottom of your resumé.

- Use formatting (larger font sizes, different fonts, italics, bold, and so on) and indents selectively to make the important information stand out.

- Get several people to look at your resumé before you send it. Perhaps an instructor or counsellor can give you some suggestions. Other readers may have ideas that you haven't thought of and may find errors that you have missed.

Manon Leblanc

237 Custer Street, Surrey, BC V4A XXX • 604/555-5252 (w) or 778/555-7865 (h) • fax: 604/555-2735 • e-mail: manon@zzz.com

EDUCATION

2001 to present Kwantlen University College, Surrey, BC

Pursuing a B.A. in the Spanish BCLAD (Bilingual, Cross-Cultural Language Acquisition Development) Education and Multiple Subject Credential Program. Expected graduation: June, 2005

PROFESSIONAL EMPLOYMENT

10/02 to present **Research Assistant, Knowledge Media Lab**

Developing ways for teachers to exhibit their inquiry into their practice of teaching in an on-line, collaborative, multimedia environment.

5/01 to present **Webmaster/Web Designer**

Work in various capacities at QuakeNet, an Internet Service Provider and Web Commerce Specialist in Surrey, BC. Designed several sites for the Kwantlen Student Activity Coordinator as well as private clients such as A Body of Work and Yoga Forever.

9/01 to 6/02 **Literacy Coordinator**

Coordinated, advised, and created literacy curriculum for a literacy project at Prescott School in West Langley. Worked with non-reader 4th graders on writing and publishing, incorporating digital photography, Internet resources, and graphic design.

8/01 **Bilingual Educational Consultant**

Consulted for The Learning Channel, field-testing bilingual materials. With a research team, designed bilingual educational materials for adult beginner French students.

1/01 to 6/01 **Technology Consultant**

Worked with 24 Hours in Cyberspace, an on-line worldwide photojournalism event. Coordinated participation of schools, translated documents, and facilitated public relations.

SKILLS

Languages: Fluent in French.
Proficient in Italian.

Computer: Programming ability in HTML, Javascript, Pascal, and Lisp. Multimedia design expertise in Adobe Photoshop, Netobjects Fusion, Adobe Premiere, Macromedia Flash, and many other visual design programs.

Personal: Perform professionally in Mary Schmary, a women's a cappella quartet. Have climbed Mt. Kilimanjaro.

Choose the option that BEST completes the statement or answers the question. After completing the questions, check your answers against the Answer Key at the back of this book (p. 314).

1. Which of the following is NOT included in the definition of diversity?

a. ☐ Ability.

b. ☐ Sexual orientation.

c. ☐ Age.

d. ☐ Career.

2. Cultural competence refers to the ability to understand and appreciate differences among

a. ☐ People, and to change your behaviour in a way that enhances, rather than detracts from, relationships and communication.

b. ☐ Countries, and to change your values in a way that is in keeping with your own particular culture.

c. ☐ Your own culture and others, and to act in ways that maintain your cultural history and values.

d. ☐ People within your own culture, and to change their behaviour so that everyone's behaviour is in keeping with the values of your culture.

3. Prejudice is defined as

a. ☐ A judgment or opinion.

b. ☐ A judgment or opinion formed without just grounds.

c. ☐ A judgment or opinion formed without just grounds or sufficient knowledge.

d. ☐ A judgment or opinion formed without just grounds or sufficient knowledge that is acted on or expressed to others.

4. *"Women are caring and nurturing."* This statement is an example of a

a. ☐ Positive fact.

b. ☐ Negative fact.

c. ☐ Positive stereotype.

d. ☐ Negative stereotype.

5. In order to adapt to college or university, students will find it useful to

a. ☐ Spend all of their social time only with people who have the same backgrounds, experiences, or beliefs as they do.

b. ☐ Cut their ties with people who have the same backgrounds, experiences, or beliefs as they do and develop new relationships with people from other groups.

c. ☐ Spend some of their time among people who share their background and some with people from other groups, attempting to find a balance.

d. ☐ Spend all of their time alone so that they can focus and concentrate on their studies.

6. Of the four different communication styles, Adventurer-dominant communicators tend to

a. ☐ Focus on creative ideas as speakers, and appreciate short, direct messages as listeners.

b. ☐ Promote harmony as speakers, and emphasize personal closeness as listeners.

c. ☐ Deliver well-thought-out messages as speakers, and appreciate practical, concrete messages as listeners.

d. ☐ Rely on conceptual ideas as speakers, and emphasize logical messages as listeners.

7. Which of the following statements are true of feedback?

a. ☐ All feedback is constructive and useful.

b. ☐ All feedback is non-constructive and damaging.

c. ☐ Feedback needs to be limited.

d. ☐ Feedback can help bring about necessary changes.

8. Which of the following is NOT useful for providing constructive feedback?

a. ☐ Comment on the person rather than the behaviour.

b. ☐ Be specific about the problem behaviour.

c. ☐ Suggest new approaches.

d. ☐ Offer assistance.

9. It is important to know how to analyze body language because

a. ☐ All cultures use the same gestures and body language.

b. ☐ Men and women differ in their body language.

c. ☐ Body language is more honest than verbal language.

d. ☐ What a person says can mean different things, depending on their body language.

10. In North America, direct eye contact and an "open" body posture tends to communicate

a. ☐ Interest.

b. ☐ Submission.

c. ☐ Power.

d. ☐ Aggression.

11. Aggressive communicators focus primarily on _____ needs and passive communicators focus primarily on _____ needs.

a. ☐ Their own; their own.

b. ☐ Their own; others'.

c. ☐ Others'; others'.

d. ☐ Others'; their own.

12. The most productive communication is

a. ☐ Aggressive.

b. ☐ Passive.

c. ☐ Assertive.

d. ☐ Passive–Aggressive.

13. Which of the following is the most effective way to communicate your needs?

a. ☐ "You don't spend any time with me."

b. ☐ "I feel that you don't like me."

c. ☐ "I think we should spend more time together."

d. ☐ "I feel disappointed when I cannot spend time with you."

14. What is the most effective conflict resolution strategy?

a. ☐ Communicate aggressively how you feel.

b. ☐ Stand firm in your convictions and don't back down until you get your way.

c. ☐ Avoid conflicts at any cost in order to maintain peace in the relationship.

d. ☐ Identify the problem, then brainstorm and assess possible solutions.

15. While you are a student it is best to

a. ☐ Avoid conflicts in your relationships because they will create stress that will interfere with your studies.

b. ☐ Invest time in relationships with people you care for, respect, and admire.

c. ☐ Inform your friends and family that school is now of a higher priority than they are.

d. ☐ Avoid relationships altogether.

16. Victims of sexual harassment are

a. ☐ Always women.

b. ☐ Only gay men.

c. ☐ Men and women.

d. ☐ People of all ages and genders.

17. Quid pro quo and hostile environment are two examples of _____ harassment.

a. ☐ Sexual.

b. ☐ Verbal.

c. ☐ Physical.

d. ☐ Emotional.

18. Which of the following constitutes an act of violence?

a. ☐ Bullying.

b. ☐ Rape.

c. ☐ Physical abuse.

d. ☐ All of the above.

19. Acquaintance rape, or date rape, refers to sexual activity during a date that is against one partner's will,

a. ☐ Including situations where one partner is too drunk or drugged to give consent.

b. ☐ Not including situations where one partner is too drunk or drugged to give consent.

c. ☐ Not including situations where the assailant is someone a person knows well.

d. ☐ Not including sexual activity that involves only anal or oral penetration.

20. Which of the following is the LEAST effective way to build positive relationships in one's life?

a. ☐ Join community groups that share interests similar to yours.

b. ☐ Find work with people with whom you have things in common.

c. ☐ Get involved in campus events and activities to meet other students and faculty.

d. ☐ Seek out the attention of individuals and groups that are destructive to others in order to feel more powerful.

10

Creating Your Life

BUILDING A SUCCESSFUL FUTURE

This chapter is organized as follows:

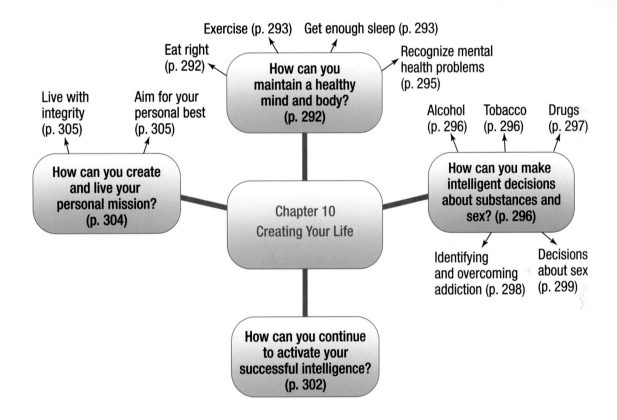

Exercise (p. 293)   Get enough sleep (p. 293)

Eat right (p. 292)

How can you maintain a healthy mind and body? (p. 292)

Recognize mental health problems (p. 295)

Live with integrity (p. 305)

Aim for your personal best (p. 305)

Alcohol (p. 296)   Tobacco (p. 296)   Drugs (p. 297)

How can you create and live your personal mission? (p. 304)

Chapter 10 Creating Your Life

How can you make intelligent decisions about substances and sex? (p. 296)

Identifying and overcoming addiction (p. 298)

Decisions about sex (p. 299)

How can you continue to activate your successful intelligence? (p. 302)

TEST YOURSELF

- *What are the symptoms of depression?*
- *Explain the difference between the three main types of eating disorders.*
- *Define what an addiction is.*
- *What is binge drinking?*
- *What is the highly addictive drug found in tobacco?*

- *Why are synthetic drugs so hazardous?*
- *Besides helping to prevent pregnancy, what method of birth control also helps protect against STIs?*
- *List at least 10 of the 20 common characteristics found in successfully intelligent people.*
- *How does one formulate a personal mission statement?*

For the correct answers and additional questions on Chapter 10, visit www.pearsoned.ca/carter.

As you come to the end of your work in this course, you have built up a wealth of knowledge. You are facing important academic and career decisions and starting to think about where the choices you make will ultimately lead you.

This chapter will continue to help you build life skills that can fuel your future success. It will look at how to maintain wellness in body and mind, how to continue to activate your successful intelligence, and how to create and live your personal mission.

How can you maintain a healthy *mind and body*?

The healthier you are, the more you'll be able to reach your potential. You can make your physical health a priority by eating right, exercising, and getting enough sleep. Make your mental health a priority by recognizing mental health problems, related to stress or other causes, and understanding ways to get help.

Eat right

The requirements of post-secondary education can make it a challenge to always eat well. Students spend hours sitting in class or studying and tend to eat on the run. Social events are often built around less-than-nutritious food, and eating junk food can become a habitual reaction to stress.

Nevertheless, making healthier choices about what you eat can lead to more energy, better general health, and an improved quality of life. Some research has also shown that what you eat has an effect on your learning and even on your grades. These practical tips will help you pay attention to how you eat, and make changes when you need to, so that you can stay healthy and academically fit.

- Eat a diet consisting of a variety of foods, including plenty of vegetables, fruits, and grain products. The more natural and less processed, the better.

- Reduce portion size and consume sugar and salt in moderation.

- Choose a diet low in fat and cholesterol.

- Plan your meals and avoid skipping meals. Eat three meals and at least two healthy snacks a day.

- Eat because you're hungry; avoid using food for stress relief.

- Drink at least six to eight glasses of water a day to stay hydrated. Your brain needs water to work. Avoid sugary drinks, like soft drinks and even some juices, and limit your intake of coffee and tea.

- If you need to lose weight, find a support group, such as Weight Watchers® or an on-campus organization, that can help you stay on target.

Exercise

Being physically fit enhances your general health, increases your energy, and helps you cope with stress. During physical activity, the brain releases endorphins, chemical compounds that have a positive and calming effect on the body.

College athletes use daily exercise as a stress reliever. Larisa Kindell, a co-captain of a swimming team, credits her athletic routine with helping her balance her life. "If I didn't have swimming, a place to release my academic stress, I don't think I'd be as effective in the classroom or studying at night," she said. Swimming has taught her "discipline, time management, and motivation" and has contributed to her academic success.[1] Always check with a physician before beginning an exercise program.

Types of exercise

There are three general categories of exercises. The type you choose depends on your exercise goals, available equipment, your time, fitness level, and other factors.

- **Cardiovascular training** strengthens your heart and lung capacity. Examples include running, swimming, in-line skating, aerobic dancing, and biking.

- **Strength training** strengthens different muscle groups. Examples include using weight machines and free weights and doing push-ups and abdominal crunches.

- **Flexibility training** increases muscle flexibility. Examples include stretching, pilates, and yoga.

Busy students often have trouble getting to the gym, even when there is a fully equipped athletic centre on campus. Even in the busiest weeks, you can stay on the move by walking to classes and meetings, using the stairs in your buildings, or using home exercise equipment such as weights, a treadmill, or an elliptical trainer.

Get enough sleep

Post-secondary students are infamous for being sleep deprived. While research indicates that students need eight to nine hours of sleep a night to function well, recent studies show that students average six to seven hours, and often get much less.[2]

Students, overwhelmed with responsibilities, often feel that they have no choice but to prioritize schoolwork over sleep. It is not uncommon for students to stay up regularly until the wee hours of the night getting readings and assignments done. Many students have to balance school with work and family commitments, and end up sacrificing sleep and health for it.

The groundwork of all happiness is health.

LEIGH HUNT

For the sake of both your health and your grades, find a way to get the sleep you need. Sleep expert Gregg D. Jacobs, Ph.D., recommends the following practical suggestions for improving sleep habits:[3]

- Reduce consumption of alcohol and caffeine.
- Exercise regularly, especially in the afternoon or early evening.
- Take naps.
- Be consistent with wake times and bed times.
- Complete tasks an hour or so before sleep.
- Establish a comfortable sleeping environment.

In addition, it is recommended that you do not regularly study or read textbooks while sitting or lying in bed. Although initially, reading a boring textbook might actually help you fall asleep, eventually, your mind will begin to associate your bed with studying rather than relaxation and sleep, and it may become more and more difficult for you to fall asleep.

get practical!   IMPROVE YOUR PHYSICAL HEALTH

Make a change in how you eat, exercise, or sleep.

First, decide what you most need to change. What's most important to your health right now—to eat better, exercise more, or get more sleep? Name it: _____

Now, considering your individual situation and looking at the strategies in this chapter, list five practical actions you can take right away to improve upon this part of your life. Word them as action statements. *Examples:* "I will leave earlier so that I can walk to my first class." "I will stop keeping candy bars in my room." "I will take a nap whenever I'm tired in the afternoon."

1. _____

2. _____

3. _____

4. _____

5. _____

The final step: Just do it!

Recognize mental health problems

No one is happy all the time. However, some people experience emotional disorders that make it more difficult than usual to cope with life's ups and downs. If you recognize yourself in any of the following descriptions, take practical steps to improve your health. Most student health centres and campus counselling centres can provide both medical and psychological help for students with emotional disorders. Treatment may range from counselling and psychotherapy to drug therapy and, if necessary, hospitalization or residence in a treatment centre.

Depression. A depressive disorder is a treatable illness that requires medical evaluation and attention. Symptoms include constant sadness or anxiety, loss of interest in activities that you normally like, eating too much or too little, and low self-esteem. Depression can be caused by genetic, psychological, physiological, environmental, or a combination of causes. In extreme cases, severe depression can lead to serious consequences and even suicide.

Anorexia nervosa. This condition, occurring mainly in young women, creates an intense desire to be thin. People with anorexia become dangerously thin even though they continually believe they are overweight. They may habitually restrict food intake, exercise constantly, and use laxatives to lose weight. An estimated five to seven percent of post-secondary students in North America suffer from anorexia.[4] Effects of anorexia-induced starvation include loss of menstrual periods in women, impotence in men, organ damage, heart failure, and death.

Bulimia. People who binge on excessive amounts of food, usually sweets and fattening foods, and then purge through self-induced vomiting, have bulimia. They may also use laxatives or exercise obsessively. Effects of bulimia include damage to the digestive tract and even heart failure due to the loss of important minerals.

Binge eating. Like people who have bulimia, people with binge eating disorder have difficulty controlling how much food they eat. They eat large amounts of food and have difficulty stopping; however, they do not purge afterwards. Binge eaters are often overweight and may suffer from health problems associated with obesity.

Maintaining a healthy mind and body requires eating right, exercising, getting enough sleep and recognizing difficulties related to mental health. In addition, it requires making successfully intelligent decisions about substances and sex.

IN-CLASS NOTES

HOW CAN YOU MAINTAIN A HEALTHY MIND AND BODY?

- Eat right
- Exercise
- Get enough sleep
- Recognize mental health problems

How can you make *successfully intelligent decisions* about substances and sex?

You are responsible for the choices you make regarding alcohol, tobacco, drugs, and sexual practices. As you read, think about the effects of your actions on yourself and others, and consider how to make positive, life-affirming choices.

Alcohol

Alcohol is a depressant that slows vital body functions and is the most frequently abused drug on campuses. Even a few drinks affect thinking and muscle coordination. Heavy drinking can damage the liver, the digestive system, and brain cells and can impair the central nervous system. Prolonged use also leads to **addiction**, making it seem impossible to quit. In addition, alcohol contributes to the deaths of thousands of people every year through both alcohol-related illnesses and accidents involving drunk drivers.[5]

Of all alcohol consumption, **binge drinking** is associated with the greatest problems. Here are statistics from a recent survey of Canadian university students:[6]

- Sixty-three percent of the students surveyed labeled themselves as binge drinkers, drinking about twice a month.
- Over a third of the students who binge drink reported hangover as the most common consequence of alcohol consumption, followed by memory loss, missing classes, unplanned or unsafe sex, and driving while intoxicated.[7]
- On an average day, four post-secondary students die in accidents involving alcohol, 1370 are injured, and 192 are raped or sexually assaulted by their dates after drinking.[8]

Even though these numbers are high, a recent study reported that students are now becoming much more responsible about alcohol use.[9] This may be because it is getting more and more difficult to be accepted into post-secondary institutions and students are having to complete studies with more responsibilities, so students are now taking their academic success more seriously. Also, some researchers suggest that students often overestimate how much their peers drink; once they realize this, they are not as likely to continue drinking as much.[10]

ADDICTION

Compulsive physiological need for a habit-forming substance.

BINGE DRINKING

Having five or more drinks at one sitting.

Tobacco

When people smoke, they inhale nicotine, one of the most highly addictive drugs and one which is found in all tobacco products. Nicotine's immediate effects may include an increase in blood pressure and heart rate, sweating, and throat irritation. Long-term effects may include high blood pressure, bronchitis, emphysema, stomach ulcers, and heart disease. Pregnant women who smoke increase their risk of having infants with low birth weight, premature births, or stillbirths. Furthermore, inhaling tobacco smoke damages the cells that line the air sacs of the lungs and can cause lung cancer. Lung cancer causes more deaths than any other type of cancer.[11]

Quitting smoking is difficult and should be attempted gradually, ideally with the support of friends and family. The positive effects of quitting include increased life expectancy, greater lung capacity, and more energy. This may inspire any smoker to consider making a lifestyle change. Consider your options and make a responsible choice.

Drugs

Students may use drugs to relieve stress, to be accepted by peers, or just to try something new. In most cases, the negative consequences of drug use outweigh any temporary high.

There are many ways to have a good time in college or university. Many students take entertaining short courses such as ballroom dancing, which is a social event as well as an educational experience.

Illicit drugs are against Canadian law, and you may be arrested, tried, and imprisoned for possessing even a small amount of drugs. You can jeopardize your reputation, your student status, and your ability to get a job if you are caught using drugs or if drug use impairs your performance. Finally, long-term drug use can damage your body and mind. Key 10.1 shows commonly used drugs and their potential effects.

In Canada, there has been a rise in the use of synthetic drugs, in particular MDMA, better known as ecstasy, and crystal meth. These drugs are highly addictive, and yet the use of these drugs is on the rise at parties, raves, and concerts. Ecstasy is a combination stimulant and hallucinogen, and its immediate effects include diminished anxiety and relaxation. When the drug wears off, nausea, hallucinations, shaking, vision problems, anxiety, and depression replace these highs. Long-term users risk permanent brain damage in the form of memory loss, chronic depression, and other disorders.[12]

Crystal meth has seen increased use in recent years and seems to be replacing ecstasy as the drug used by teenagers and young adults. It is cheaper and more accessible and, in some cases, is disguised as ecstasy. The RCMP has reported that some of the drugs seized at parties or dances that were sold as ecstasy were, in fact, crystal meth. As well, the police say that some dealers give out "free samples" at parties or in the dance scene, in hopes of hooking new customers.[13] It is one of the most highly addictive drugs and one of the hardest to treat and to withdraw from. Use of crystal meth can lead to brain damage, including memory impairment and an increasing inability to grasp abstract thoughts.

You are responsible for analyzing the potential consequences of what you introduce into your body. Ask questions like the following: Why do I want to do this? What positive and negative effects might my behaviour have? Why do others want me to take drugs? What do I really think of these people? How would my drug use affect the people in my life? The more carefully you analyze your situation, the more likely you will be to make choices that are in your own best interest.

Drugs affect body and mind.

DRUG CATEGORY	DRUG TYPES	HOW THEY MAKE YOU FEEL	PHYSICAL EFFECTS	DANGER OF PHYSICAL DEPENDENCE	DANGER OF PSYCHOLOGICAL DEPENDENCE
Stimulants	Cocaine, amphetamines	Alert, stimulated, excited	Nervousness, mood swings, stroke or convulsions, psychoses, paranoia, coma at large doses	Relatively strong	Strong
Depressants	Alcohol, Valium, Xanax, Rohypnol	Sedated, tired, high	Cirrhosis; impaired blood production; greater risk of cancer, heart attack, and stroke; impaired brain function	Strong	Strong
Opiates	Heroin, codeine, other pain pills	Drowsy, floating, without pain	Infection of organs, inflammation of the heart, hepatitis	Yes, with high dosage	Yes, with high dosage
Cannabinols	Marijuana, hashish	Euphoria, mellowness, little sensation of time	Impairment of judgment and coordination, bronchitis and asthma, lung and throat cancers, anxiety, lack of energy and motivation, reduced ability to produce hormones	Moderate	Relatively strong
Hallucinogens	LSD (acid), mushrooms	Heightened sensual perception, hallucinations, confusion	Impairment of brain function, circulatory problems, agitation and confusion, flashbacks	Insubstantial	Insubstantial
Inhalants	Glue, aerosols	Giddiness, lightheadedness	Damage to brain, heart, liver, and kidneys	Insubstantial	Insubstantial

Source: Adapted from *Educating Yourself about Alcohol and Drugs: A People's Primer* by Marc Alan Schuckit, M.D. New York: HarperCollins, 1998.

Identifying and overcoming addiction

Substances such as alcohol, tobacco, or drugs often cause physical and chemical changes and psychological dependence. These habits can be difficult to break, and quitting may involve a painful withdrawal. If you think you may be addicted, take the initiative to seek help. Asking for help is a courageous move to reclaim your life. The following resources can help you generate options and generate practical plans for recovery.

Counselling and medical care. You can find help from school-based, private, government-sponsored, or workplace-sponsored resources. Ask your school's counselling or health centre, your personal physician, or a local hospital for a referral.

Detoxification ("detox") centres. If you have a severe addiction, you may need a controlled environment where you can separate yourself completely from drugs or alcohol. Some are live-in programs, while others are day programs to help you get through the withdrawal process.

Support groups. Alcoholics Anonymous (AA) is the premier support group for alcoholics. AA has led to other support groups for addicts such as Overeaters Anonymous (OA) and Narcotics Anonymous (NA). Many post-secondary institutions and community organizations have AA, NA, or other group sessions on-site.

Decisions about sex

Another important aspect of both physical and mental health involves being comfortable with your sexuality and making wise sexual decisions. Choosing birth control and knowing how to avoid sexually transmitted infections have short- and long-term consequences for the rest of your life.

What sexuality means to you and the role it plays in your life are your own business. However, the physical act of sex goes beyond the private realm. Individual sexual conduct can result in an unexpected pregnancy and in contracting or passing on a sexually transmitted infection (STI). These consequences affect everyone involved in the sexual act and, often, their loved ones.

Your self-respect depends on making choices that maintain health and safety—yours as well as those of the person with whom you are involved. Think carefully about sexual issues, weighing the positive and negative effects of your choices. Knowing about birth control options and sexually transmitted infections can help you make well-informed decisions.

Birth control

Some people choose to use birth control in order to prevent pregnancy. Some birth control methods also protect against sexually transmitted infections. Key 10.2 describes established methods, with effectiveness percentages and STI prevention based on proper and regular use.

If you choose to use birth control, evaluate the pros and cons of each option for yourself as well as for your partner. Consider cost, ease of use, reliability, comfort, and protection against STIs. You may want to communicate with your partner and together make a choice that is comfortable for both of you. For more information, check your library, the Internet, or a bookstore; talk to your doctor; or ask a counsellor at the student health centre.

Sexually transmitted infections

Sexually transmitted infections (STIs) spread through sexual contact (intercourse or other sexual activity that involves contact with the genitals). All are highly contagious. The only birth control methods that offer protection are male and female condoms (latex or polyurethane only) that prevent skin-to-skin contact. Most STIs can also spread to infants of infected mothers during birth. Have a doctor examine any irregularity or discomfort as soon as you detect it.

Make an educated decision about birth control.

METHOD	APPROXIMATE EFFECTIVENESS	PREVENTS STIs?	DESCRIPTION
Abstinence	100%	Only if no sexual activity occurs	Just saying no. No intercourse means no risk of pregnancy. However, alternative modes of sexual activity can still spread STIs.
Condom (male)	94%	Yes, if made of latex	A sheath that fits over the penis and prevents sperm from entering the vagina.
Condom (female)	90%	Yes	A sheath that fits inside the vagina, held in place by two rings, one of which hangs outside. Made of polyurethane.
Diaphragm or cervical cap	85%	No	A bendable rubber cap that fits over the cervix and pelvic bone inside the vagina (the cervical cap is smaller and fits over the cervix only). Both must be fitted initially by a gynecologist and used with a spermicide.
Oral contraceptives (the pill)	97%	No	A dosage of hormones taken daily by a woman, preventing the ovaries from releasing eggs. Side effects can include headaches, weight gain, and increased chances of blood clotting. Various brands and dosages; must be prescribed by a gynecologist.
Spermicidal foams, jellies, inserts	84% if used alone	No	Usually used with diaphragms or condoms to enhance effectiveness, they have an ingredient that kills sperm cells (but not STIs). They stay effective for a limited period of time after insertion.
Intrauterine device (IUD)	94%	No	A small coil of wire inserted into the uterus by a gynecologist (who must also remove it). Prevents fertilized eggs from implanting in the uterine wall. Possible side effects include bleeding.
Depo-Provera (the shot)	Nearly 100%	No	An injection that a woman must receive from a doctor every few months. Possible side effects may resemble those of oral contraceptives.
Tubal ligation	Nearly 100%	No	Surgery for women that cuts and ties the fallopian tubes, preventing eggs from traveling to the uterus. Difficult and expensive to reverse. Recommended for those who do not want any, or any more, children.
Vasectomy	Nearly 100%	No	Surgery for men that blocks the tube that delivers sperm to the penis. Like tubal ligation, difficult to reverse and recommended only for those who don't want any, or any more, children.
Rhythm method	Variable	No	Abstaining from intercourse during the ovulation segment of the woman's menstrual cycle. Can be difficult to time and may not account for cycle irregularities.
Withdrawal	Variable	No	Pulling the penis out of the vagina before ejaculation. Unreliable, because some sperm can escape in the fluid released prior to ejaculation. Dependent on a controlled partner.

To stay safe, know these facts about sexually transmitted infections.

DISEASE	SYMPTOMS	HEALTH PROBLEMS IF UNTREATED	TREATMENTS[14,15]
Chlamydia	Discharge, painful urination, swollen or painful joints, change in menstrual periods for women	Can cause pelvic inflammatory disease (PID) in women, which can lead to sterility or ectopic pregnancies; infection; miscarriage or premature birth.	Curable with full course of antibiotics; avoid sex until treatment is complete.
Gonorrhea	Discharge, burning while urinating	Can cause PID, swelling of testicles and penis, arthritis, skin problems, infections.	Usually curable with antibiotics; however, certain strains are becoming resistant to medication.
Genital herpes	Blister-like itchy sores in the genital area, headache, fever, chills	Symptoms may subside and then reoccur, often in response to high stress levels; carriers can transmit the virus even when it is dormant.	No cure; some medications such as Acyclovir reduce and help heal the sores and may shorten recurring outbreaks.
Syphilis	A genital sore lasting one to five weeks, followed by a rash, fatigue, fever, sore throat, headaches, swollen glands	If it lasts over four years, it can cause blindness, destruction of bone, insanity, or heart failure; can cause death or deformity of a child born to an infected woman.	Curable with full course of antibiotics.
Human Papilloma Virus (HPV, or genital warts)	Genital itching and irritation, small clusters of warts	Can increase risk of cervical cancer in women; virus may remain in body and cause recurrences, even when warts are removed.	Treatable with drugs applied to warts or various kinds of wart removal surgery.
Hepatitis B	Fatigue, poor appetite, vomiting, jaundice, hives	Some carriers will have few symptoms; others may develop chronic liver disease that may lead to other diseases of the liver.	No cure; some will recover, some will not. Bed rest may help ease symptoms. Vaccine is available.
HIV/AIDS	Four main phases of progression of HIV to AIDS; initial symptoms can resemble the flu or go completely unnoticed; symptoms, which become more serious as the infection progresses and the immune system becomes weaker, include persistent fever and diarrhea, weight loss, fatigue, and other symptoms	Phase 4 is AIDS. As the immune system becomes weaker it can no longer defend against other diseases and infections, resulting in death.	No cure; individual drug treatments vary to prolong lives, but can cause severe side effects.

Key 10.3 on page 301 describes common STIs. The most serious of the STIs is AIDS (acquired immune deficiency syndrome), which is caused by the human immunodeficiency virus (HIV). Not everyone who tests positive for HIV will develop AIDS, but AIDS has no cure and results in eventual death. Medical science continues to develop drugs to combat HIV and AIDS and its related illnesses. The drugs can cause severe side effects, however, and none are cures.

HIV is transmitted through two types of bodily fluids: fluids associated with sex (semen and vaginal fluids) and blood. People have acquired HIV through sexual relations, by sharing hypodermic needles for drug use, and by receiving infected blood transfusions. You cannot become infected unless one of those fluids is involved. Therefore, it is unlikely you can contract HIV from toilet seats, hugging, kissing, or sharing a glass. Other than not having sex at all, a latex condom is the best defence against AIDS. Although some people dislike using condoms, it's a small price to pay for preserving your life.

To be safe, have an HIV test done at your doctor's office or at a health clinic. If you are infected, first inform all sexual partners and seek medical assistance. Then, contact support organizations in your area.

Health, both mental and physical, is one asset that will serve you well as you move along your life path. Continue to care for yourself and use your successful intelligence along the way.

IN-CLASS NOTES

HOW CAN YOU MAKE SUCCESSFULLY INTELLIGENT DECISIONS ABOUT SUBSTANCES AND SEX?

Consider the effects on yourself and others regarding:

- Alcohol
- Tobacco
- Drugs
- Addiction
- Decisions about sex
  - Birth control
  - Sexually transmitted infections (STIs)

_____

_____

_____

_____

_____

_____

_____

_____

How can you continue to activate your *successful intelligence?*

Robert Sternberg has found that successfully intelligent people, despite differences in thinking and in personal goals, have several particular characteristics in common. He calls them "self-activators." These are things that get successfully intelligent people moving and keep them going. According to Sternberg, successfully intelligent people:[16]

1. Motivate themselves. They make things happen, spurred on by a desire to succeed and a love of what they are doing.

2. **Learn to control their impulses.** Instead of going with their first quick response, they sit with a question or problem. They allow time for thinking and let ideas surface before making a decision.

3. **Know when to persevere.** When it makes sense, they push past frustration and stay on course, confident that success is in their sights. They also are able to see when they've hit a dead end, and in those cases, they know when to stop pushing.

4. **Know how to make the most of their abilities.** They understand what they do well and capitalize on it in school and in work.

5. **Translate thought into action.** Not only do they have good ideas; they are able to turn those ideas into practical actions that bring ideas to fruition.

6. **Have a product orientation.** They want results; they focus on what they are aiming for rather than on how they are getting there.

7. **Complete tasks and follow through.** With determination, they finish what they start. They also follow through to make sure all the loose ends are tied and the goal has been achieved.

8. **Are initiators.** They commit to people, projects, and ideas. They make things happen rather than sitting back and waiting for things to happen to them.

9. **Are not afraid to risk failure.** Because they take risks and sometimes fail, they often enjoy greater success and build their intellectual capacity. Like everyone else, they make mistakes, but they learn from them and tend not to make the same mistake twice.

10. **Don't procrastinate.** They are aware of the negative effects of putting things off, and they avoid them. They create schedules that allow them to accomplish what's important on time.

11. **Accept fair blame.** They strike a balance between never accepting blame and taking the blame for everything. If something is their fault, they accept the responsibility and don't make excuses.

12. **Reject self-pity.** When something goes wrong, they find a way to solve the problem. They don't get caught in the energy drain of feeling sorry for themselves.

13. **Are independent.** They can work on their own and think for themselves. They take responsibility for their own schedule and tasks.

14. **Seek to surmount personal difficulties.** They keep things in perspective, looking for ways to remedy personal problems and separate them from their professional lives.

15. **Focus and concentrate to achieve their goals.** They create an environment in which they can best avoid distraction, and they focus steadily on their work.

16. **Spread themselves neither too thin nor too thick.** They strike a balance between doing too many things, which results in little progress on any of them, and too few things, which can reduce the level of accomplishment.

17. **Have the ability to delay gratification.** While they enjoy the smaller rewards that require less energy, they focus the bulk of their work on the goals that take more time but promise the most gratification.

18. **Have the ability to see the forest and the trees.** They are able to see the big picture and to avoid getting bogged down in tiny details.

19. **Have a reasonable level of self-confidence and a belief in their ability to accomplish their goals.** They believe in themselves enough to get through the tough times, while avoiding the kind of overconfidence that stalls learning and growth.

20. **Balance analytical, creative, and practical thinking.** They sense what to use and when to use it. When problems arise, they combine all three skills to arrive at solutions.

Make these characteristics your personal motivational tools. Return to them when you need reactivation. Use them to make sure that you move ahead toward the goals that mean most to you.

How can you *create and live* your personal mission?

If the trees are your goals, the forest is the big picture of what you are aiming for in life—your personal mission. To define your mission, craft a *personal mission statement*.

Dr. Stephen Covey, author of *The Seven Habits of Highly Effective People*, defines a mission statement as a philosophy outlining what you want to be (character), what you want to do (contributions and achievements), and the principles by which you want to live (your values). He describes the statement as "a personal constitution, the basis for making major, life-directing decisions."[17]

Here is a mission statement written by Carol Carter, one of the authors of *Keys to Success*:

> My mission is to use my talents and abilities to help people of all ages, stages, backgrounds, and economic levels achieve their human potential through fully developing their minds and their talents. I aim to create opportunities for others through work, service, and family. I also aim to balance work with people in my life, understanding that my family and friends are a priority above all else.

How can you start formulating a mission statement? Try using Covey's three aspects of personal mission as a guide. Think through the following:

- **Character.** What aspects of character do you think are most valuable? When you consider the people you admire most, which of their qualities stand out?

- **Contributions and achievements.** What do you want to accomplish in your life? Where do you want to make a difference?

- **Values.** How do the values you established in your work in Chapter 2 inform your life goals? What in your mission could help you live according to what you value most highly? For example, if you value community involvement, your mission may reflect a life goal of holding elected office, which may translate into an interim goal of taking on a leadership role with your school's student association.

Because what you want out of life changes as you move from one phase to the next—for example, from single person to partner, from student to working citizen—your personal mission should remain flexible and open to revision. If you frame your mission statement carefully so that it truly reflects your goals, it can be your guide in everything you do, helping you to live with integrity and to work to achieve your personal best.

Live with integrity

Having integrity puts your (ethics) into day-to-day action. When you act with integrity, you earn trust and respect from others. If people can trust you to be honest, to be sincere in what you say and do, and to consider the needs of others, they will be more likely to encourage you, support your goals, and reward your work.

Seeking experiences that broaden your horizons may be part of your personal mission. These students are learning both academic and life lessons during their travel in China.

Living with integrity helps you believe in yourself and in your ability to make good choices. A person of integrity isn't a perfect person, but is one who makes the effort to live according to values and principles, continually striving to learn from mistakes and to improve. Take responsibility for making the right moves, and you will follow your mission with strength and conviction.

> ETHICS
> A system of moral values; a sense of what is right to do.

Aim for your personal best

Your personal best is simply the best that you can do, in any situation. It may not be the best you have ever done. It may include mistakes, for nothing significant is ever accomplished without making mistakes and taking risks. It may shift from situation to situation. As long as you aim to do your best, though, you are inviting growth and success.

Aim for your personal best in everything you do. As a lifelong learner, you will always have a new direction in which to grow and a new challenge to face. Seek constant improvement in your personal, educational, and professional life. Dream big, knowing that incredible things are possible for you if you think positively and act with successful intelligence. Enjoy the richness of life by living each day to the fullest, developing your talents and potential into the achievement of your most valued goals.

IN-CLASS NOTES

HOW CAN YOU CREATE AND LIVE YOUR PERSONAL MISSION?

- Live with integrity
- Aim for your personal best

EXPLORE YOUR PERSONAL MISSION

Work toward a description of your most important life goals.

As a way of exploring what you most want out of life, consider one or more of the following questions, which ask you to look at the life you imagine you will have. Write freely and record your thoughts in the spaces below or on a separate piece of paper.

1. You are at your retirement dinner. You have had an esteemed career in whatever you ended up doing in your life. Your best friend stands up and talks about the five aspects of your character that have taken you to the top. What do you think they are?

   _____

   _____

   _____

2. You are preparing for a late-in-life job change. Updating your resumé, you need to list your contributions and achievements. What would you like them to be?

   _____

   _____

3. You have been told that you have one year to live. Talking with your family, you reminisce about the values that have been central to you in your life. Based on that discussion, how do you decide you want to spend your time in this last year? How will your choices reflect what is most important to you?

   _____

   _____

   _____

Thinking about your answers, draft a personal mission statement, up to a few sentences long, that reflects what you want to achieve in life. Focus on what you want to do and the effects you want to have on the world.

   _____

   _____

   _____

   _____

Kaizen

Kaizen is the Japanese word for "continual improvement." Striving for excellence, finding ways to improve on what already exists, and believing that you can effect change are at the heart of the industrious Japanese spirit. The drive to improve who you are and what you do provides the foundation for a successful future.

   Think of this concept as you reflect on yourself, your goals, your lifelong education, your career, and your personal pursuits. Create excellence and quality by continually asking yourself, "How can I improve?" Living by *kaizen* helps you to be a respected friend and family member, a productive and valued employee, and a truly contributing member of society. You can affect the world.

SUGGESTED READINGS

Adams, Robert Lang, et al. *The Complete Resume and Job Search Book for College Students*. Holbrook, MA: Adams Publishing, 1999.

Beatty, Richard H. *The Resume Kit*. 5th ed. New York: John Wiley & Sons, 2003.

Bolles, Richard Nelson. *What Color Is Your Parachute? 2003: A Practical Manual for Job Hunters and Career Changers*. Berkeley, CA: Ten Speed Press, 2003.

Detweiler, Gerri. *The Ultimate Credit Handbook*. 3rd ed. New York: Plume, 2003.

Duyff, Roberta Larson. *The American Dietetic Association's Complete Food and Nutrition Guide*. Hoboken, NJ: Wiley, 2003.

Health Canada. Sexually Transmitted Infections. 2006. http://www.hc-sc.gc.ca/dc-ma/sti-its/index_e.html.

Jones, Laurie Beth. *The Path: Creating Your Mission Statement for Work and for Life*. New York: Hyperion, 1998.

Kadison, Richard D., and Theresa Foy DiGeronimo. *College of the Overwhelmed: The Campus Mental Health Crisis and What to Do About It*. San Francisco: Jossey-Bass, 2004.

Kuhn, Cynthia, et al. *Buzzed: The Straight Facts About the Most Used and Abused Drugs from Alcohol to Ecstasy*. 2nd ed. New York: W. W. Norton, 2003.

Selkowitz, Ann. *The College Student's Guide to Eating Well on Campus*. Bethesda, MD: Tulip Hill Press, 2000.

Tyson, Eric. *Personal Finance for Dummies*. Foster City, CA: IDG Books Worldwide, 2000.

Ward, Darrell. *The Amfar AIDS Handbook: The Complete Guide to Understanding HIV and AIDS*. New York: W. W. Norton, 1998.

INTERNET RESOURCES

Keys to Success Companion Web site: www.pearsoned.ca/carter

Health Encyclopedia. Student Services, University of British Columbia: www.students.ubc.ca/health/encyclopedia.cfm

Hot Health Links. U of A Health Info Site, University Health Centre, University of Alberta: www.uofaweb.ualberta.ca/healthinfo

Canada's Food Guide to Healthy Eating. Health Canada: www.hc-sc.gc.ca/fn-an/food-guide-aliment/index_e.html

Canadian Centre on Substance Abuse: www.ccsa.ca

Prentice Hall Student Success Supersite (fitness and well-being information): www.prenhall.com/success

Columbia University's Health Education Program: www.alice.columbia.edu

Federal Centers for Disease Control and Prevention (disease prevention and health information): www.cdc.gov

MayoClinic.com (medical information from this world-renowned medical centre): www.mayoclinic.com

HIV Prevention: www.thebody.com/safesex.html

Fifth Estate program on crystal meth: www.cbc.ca/fifth/darkcrystal/index.html

BUILDING SKILLS

FOR ACADEMIC, CAREER, AND LIFE SUCCESS

Developing Successful Intelligence

PUTTING IT ALL TOGETHER

Learn from experience. Consider experiences that you have had in the past and learn from them.

Step 1. Think it through: *Analyze your past experiences.* What do you consider a missing piece in your life, and how do you think you could fill the gap?

_____

_____

Step 2. Think out of the box: *Imagine ways to contribute.* Think about the ways in which you could serve. How might your talents and skills give something to others? Brainstorm ideas about how you could use what you do well to make a difference.

_____

_____

_____

Step 3. Make it happen: *Make a practical plan to get involved.* Decide on a specific way to help others, then form a plan to pursue this goal. As you think about your decision, consider your "missing piece": Is there a way to contribute that also somehow fills that missing piece? Write down what you intend to do and the specific steps you will take to do it.

_____

_____

create your future

Team Building

Build communication skills. This exercise will help you prepare for situations when you meet someone new and want to learn about them, and share about yourself. This might be a social event or a job interview.

1. Interviews versus social situations: In both these situations, you would be sharing information about yourself. How would the questions and your responses differ between these two situations?

   _____

   _____

   _____

2. Choose between an interview and a social situation.

   Take a few minutes to brainstorm questions you think you might be asked in one of the above situations. Write your questions here and then the answer to each beneath it.

   Question: _____

   Answer: _____

   Question: _____

   Answer: _____

   Question: _____

   Answer: _____

   Question: _____

   Answer: _____

3. Role play the situation you chose. Find someone to practise with. Have them ask you questions and answer them as if you were meeting for the first time. Then switch places and ask them questions about themselves.

4. Share with each other what interesting ideas stand out to you from the role play. Practise receiving feedback from the other person about how you responded to the questions about yourself.

This exercise will build your ability to glean information from others and to answer questions during an interview or in a social situation. You will use this skill throughout your professional life. Probe respectfully when learning about others so that you develop the ability to draw out the best in someone. Be as interested, and as interesting, as you can.

Writing

Record your thoughts here or on a separate piece of paper or in a journal.

Addiction. At one time or another, many people have had to cope with some kind of addiction. Describe how you feel about addiction in any form. It could be addiction to alcohol, drugs, food, sex, the Internet, gambling, or anything else.

_____

_____

_____

Have you ever faced an addiction or been close to someone who did? Describe how you coped. If not, describe how you think you would work through the problem if it ever happened to you.

_____

_____

_____

Career Portfolio

PLAN FOR SUCCESS

Complete the following here or in your electronic portfolio or on separate sheets of paper. When you have finished, read through each of the exercises you completed for your career portfolio. You have gathered information to turn to again and again on your path to a fulfilling, successful career.

A Wheel for Life. In Key 10.4 you see a blank Wheel of Life. It is similar to one you completed in Chapter 2. Without looking at the first wheel you completed, fill in this wheel and use it to evaluate yourself as you are right now, after completing this course. Then answer the following questions:

1. Where would you rank yourself in the eight categories?

_____

_____

2. Now look back at your previous wheel and compare the two. Are there any changes?

- Where have you grown?

_____

- How has your self-perception changed?

_____

- What can you learn from this new wheel about what you have accomplished and what you plan for the future?

_____

_____

3. Are there any areas you think may still stand in the way of your success in the future? If so, what specific steps are you willing to take to change them?

_____

_____

Use this new wheel to evaluate your progress.

Rate yourself in each area of the wheel on a scale of 1 to 10, 1 being least developed (near the center of the wheel) and 10 being most developed (the outer edge of the wheel). In each area, at the level of the number you choose, draw a curved line and fill in the wedge below that line. Be honest—this is for your benefit only. Finally, look at what your wheel says about the balance in your life. If this were a real wheel, how well would it roll?

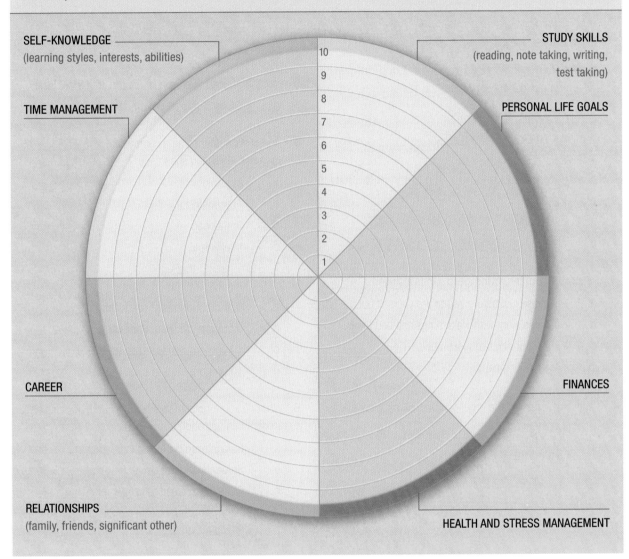

SELF-KNOWLEDGE (learning styles, interests, abilities)

STUDY SKILLS (reading, note taking, writing, test taking)

TIME MANAGEMENT

PERSONAL LIFE GOALS

CAREER

FINANCES

RELATIONSHIPS (family, friends, significant other)

HEALTH AND STRESS MANAGEMENT

Source: Based on "The Wheel of Life" model developed by the Coaches Training Institute, © Co-Active Space 2000.

Chapter Review Questions

Choose the option that BEST completes the statement or answers the question. After completing the questions, check your answers against the Answer Key at the back of this book (p. 314).

1. Which of the following helps you maintain a healthy body?
   a. ☐ Eating highly processed foods.
   b. ☐ Eating 2 meals a day.
   c. ☐ Eliminating snacks.
   d. ☐ Drinking plenty of water.

2. Swimming is an example of a _____ training exercise.
   a. ☐ Cardiovascular.
   b. ☐ Strength.
   c. ☐ Flexibility.
   d. ☐ Stress.

3. Suggestions for improving sleep habits include:
   a. ☐ Exercise just before bed to tire yourself out.
   b. ☐ Be consistent with wake times and bed times.
   c. ☐ Read a boring textbook in bed.
   d. ☐ Avoid taking naps.

4. Leigh Hunt stated, "The groundwork of all happiness is _____"
   a. ☐ Money.
   b. ☐ Success.
   c. ☐ Health.
   d. ☐ Love.

5. Which is true about depression?
   a. ☐ It is a sign of weakness.
   b. ☐ It is always caused by stress.
   c. ☐ Everyone experiences depression, and it is not serious.
   d. ☐ Depression can be caused by any number of different reasons.

6. A person who eats excessive amounts of food and then purges through self-induced vomiting has
   a. ☐ Binge eating disorder.
   b. ☐ Bulimia.
   c. ☐ Anorexia nervosa.
   d. ☐ Binge eating disorder and bulimia.

7. Addiction is defined as a compulsive _____ need for a habit-forming substance.
   a. ☐ Physiological.
   b. ☐ Psychological.
   c. ☐ Emotional.
   d. ☐ Intellectual.

8. Binge drinking is defined as having
   a. ☐ 5 or more drinks in one week.
   b. ☐ 5 or more drinks in one sitting.
   c. ☐ 10 or more drinks in one week.
   d. ☐ 10 or more drinks in one sitting.

9. What do some researchers believe about post-secondary students and alcohol?
   a. ☐ Students are becoming more irresponsible about drinking.
   b. ☐ Students underestimate how much their peers drink.
   c. ☐ Students overestimate how much their peers drink.
   d. ☐ Rarely do students drink enough to affect their academic grades.

10. Nicotine is
    a. ☐ A highly addictive drug found in tobacco.
    b. ☐ A form of tobacco that is not addictive.
    c. ☐ Rarely found in cigarettes sold in Canada.
    d. ☐ Not related to any type of health problems.

11. Which is not a potential effect of smoking?

   a. ☐ Emphysema.

   b. ☐ Lung cancer.

   c. ☐ Increased blood pressure.

   d. ☐ Cirrhosis.

12. Which of the following is an example of a drug categorized as a depressant?

   a. ☐ Marijuana.

   b. ☐ Cocaine.

   c. ☐ Heroin.

   d. ☐ Alcohol.

13. Crystal meth is a synthetic drug that is

   a. ☐ Highly addictive and very difficult to treat.

   b. ☐ Highly addictive but very easy to treat.

   c. ☐ Addictive only after many uses.

   d. ☐ Not addictive unless used regularly.

14. Which of the following is the least effective way to handle an addiction?

   a. ☐ Counselling.

   b. ☐ Support groups.

   c. ☐ Detoxification

   d. ☐ Substitution.

15. The only birth control method that is 100 percent effective against pregnancy is

   a. ☐ A condom.

   b. ☐ The pill.

   c. ☐ An IUD.

   d. ☐ Abstinence.

16. Besides helping to prevent pregnancy, what method of birth control also helps protect against STIs?

   a. ☐ Spermicidal foams or jellies.

   b. ☐ An IUD.

   c. ☐ A condom.

   d. ☐ Depo-Provera.

17. How is the human immunodeficiency virus (HIV) transmitted from one person to another?

   a. ☐ Hugging and kissing.

   b. ☐ Toilet seats.

   c. ☐ Semen, vaginal fluid, or blood.

   d. ☐ Sharing a drink.

18. Robert Sternberg defines successfully intelligent people as "self-_____."

   a. ☐ Motivators.

   b. ☐ Controllers.

   c. ☐ Acceptors.

   d. ☐ Activators.

19. What aspects are included in a mission statement?

   a. ☐ Character, contributions/achievements, values.

   b. ☐ Character, contributions/achievements, personality.

   c. ☐ Personality, contributions/achievements, values.

   d. ☐ Intelligence, character, values.

20. A person with integrity makes an effort to live

   a. ☐ Life to the fullest.

   b. ☐ According to values and principles.

   c. ☐ Within the boundaries of expectations.

   d. ☐ According to what others believe.

Answer Key

For Study Guide Questions

Chapter 1, pages 26–27	Chapter 3, pages 84–85	Chapter 5, pages 154–155	Chapter 7, pages 224–225	Chapter 9, pages 288–289
1. d	1. d	1. d	1. a	1. d
2. a	2. a	2. a	2. d	2. a
3. c	3. a	3. b	3. b	3. c
4. b	4. a	4. d	4. b	4. c
5. a	5. b	5. d	5. d	5. c
6. c	6. a	6. c	6. b	6. a
7. c	7. b	7. b	7. c	7. d
8. d	8. a	8. d	8. a	8. a
9. a	9. d	9. c	9. c	9. d
10. d	10. b	10. b	10. b	10. a
11. d	11. c	11. d	11. b	11. b
12. c	12. b	12. b	12. a	12. c
13. c	13. a	13. d	13. b	13. d
14. a	14. d	14. a	14. a	14. d
15. b	15. d	15. a	15. d	15. b
16. d	16. d	16. d	16. c	16. d
17. c	17. a	17. d	17. a	17. a
18. b	18. c	18. b	18. a	18. d
19. c	19. c	19. b	19. d	19. a
20. a	20. d	20. c	20. d	20. d

Chapter 2, pages 60–61	Chapter 4, pages 118–119	Chapter 6, pages 188–189	Chapter 8, pages 256–257	Chapter 10, pages 312–313
1. a	1. d	1. c	1. a	1. d
2. d	2. b	2. d	2. d	2. a
3. d	3. b	3. b	3. a	3. b
4. a	4. b	4. d	4. c	4. c
5. d	5. c	5. b	5. a	5. d
6. a	6. a	6. a	6. a	6. b
7. c	7. c	7. c	7. b	7. a
8. c	8. a	8. c	8. c	8. b
9. d	9. a	9. a	9. a	9. c
10. d	10. a	10. c	10. d	10. a
11. c	11. d	11. a	11. d	11. d
12. d	12. a	12. a	12. c	12. d
13. b	13. d	13. d	13. a	13. a
14. c	14. c	14. a	14. b	14. d
15. b	15. a	15. c	15. d	15. d
16. b	16. b	16. d	16. c	16. c
17. b	17. d	17. a	17. d	17. c
18. d	18. b	18. d	18. b	18. d
19. c	19. c	19. b	19. a	19. a
20. c	20. a	20. d	20. d	20. b

Chapter 1

1. Minister of Human Resources Development Canada, "Education and Skills are the Key to Getting Work," *Job Futures: World of Work*, www.jobfutures.ca/en/brochure/more.html (accessed September 2006).
2. Robert J. Sternberg, *Successful Intelligence* (New York: Plume, 1997), 11.
3. Ibid., 12.
4. Ibid., 127–128.
5. Rick Pitino, *Success Is a Choice* (New York: Broadway Books, 1997) 40.
6. From student essay submitted by the First Year Experience students of Patty Parma, Palo Alto College, San Antonio, Texas, January 2004.
7. "Are the Classes Really That Much Harder Than High School?" New Mexico State University, June 1999 [online], www.nmsu.edu/aggieland/students/faq_classes.html (accessed March 2004).
8. Jamilah Evelyn, "A Clean Slate: Many Colleges Start Programs to Forgive Poor Grades," *The Chronicle of Higher Education*, October 11, 2002 [online], http://chronicle.com/weekly/v49/i07a03901.htm (accessed March 2004).
9. Rita Lenken Hawkins, Baltimore City Community College, 1997.
10. Cited in Colin Rise and Malcolm J. Nicholl, *Accelerated Learning for the 21st Century* (New York: Dell, 1997) 5–6.
11. From student essay submitted by the First Year Experience students of Patty Parma, Palo Alto College, San Antonio, Texas, January 2004.

Chapter 2

1. *Code of Student Conduct*, Office of Student Conduct, Mount Royal College, September 2003 [online], www.mtroyal.ca/codeofstudentconduct/index.shtml (accessed March 2006).
2. Background information for information on cultural diversity from Afsaneh Nahavandi and Ali Malekzadeh, *Organizational Behavior: The Person-Organization Fit* (Upper Saddle River, NJ: Prentice Hall, 1999).
3. Louis E. Boone, David L. Kurtz, and Judy R. Block, *Contemporary Business Communication*, 2nd ed. (Upper Saddle River, NJ: Prentice Hall, 1997) 68–72.
4. Louis E. Boone and David L. Kurtz, *Contemporary Business Communication* (Englewood Cliffs, NJ: Prentice Hall, 1994) 643.
5. Paul Timm, *Successful Self-Management: A Psychologically Sound Approach to Personal Effectiveness* (Los Altos, CA: Crisp Publications, 1987), 22–41.
6. "Why don't students study more?" *Recruitment & Retention in Higher Education* 19 (2005): 3–4.
7. Kirk Kidwell and Bob Reising, "Understanding the College First Year Experience," *Clearing House* 78 (2005): 253–255.
8. Jane B. Burka and Lenora M. Yuen, *Procrastination* (Reading, MA: Perseus Books, 1983) 21–22.
9. Ibid.
10. The following articles were used as sources in this section: Glenn C. Altschuler, "Adapting to College Life in an Era of Heightened Stress," *New York Times*, Education Life, Section 4A, August 6, 2000, 12; Carol Hymowitz and Rachel Emma Silverman, "Can Workplace Stress Get Worse?" *Wall Street Journal*, January 16, 2001, B1; Robert M. Sapolsky, "Best Ways to Reduce Everyday Levels of Stress . . . Bad Ol' Stress," *Bottom Line Personal*, January 15, 2000, 13; Kate Slaboch, "Stress and the College Student: A Debate" [online], www.jour.unr.edu/outpost/voices/voi.slaboch.stress.htm (accessed April 4, 2001); University of South Florida, The Counseling Center for Human Development, "Coping with Stress in College" [online], http://usfweb.usf.edu/counsel/self-hlp/stress.htm (accessed April 4, 2001); Jodi Wilgoren, "Survey Shows High Stress Levels in College Freshmen," *New York Times*, January 23, 2000, NA.

Chapter 3

1. Howard Gardner, *Multiple Intelligences: The Theory in Practice* (New York: HarperCollins, 1993) 5–49.
2. Developed by Joyce Bishop, Ph.D., Golden West College, Huntington Beach, CA, based on Howard Gardner, *Frames of Mind: The Theory of Multiple Intelligences* (New York: HarperCollins, 1993).

Chapter 4

1. Robert J. Sternberg, *Successful Intelligence* (New York: Plume, 1997) 12.
2. Ibid., 127.
3. Matt Thomas, "What Is Higher-Order Thinking and Critical/Creative/Constructive Thinking?" The Center for Studies in Higher-Order Literacy [online], http://members.aol.com/MattT10574/Higher OrderLiteracy.htm#What (accessed April 2004).
4. Sternberg, *Successful Intelligence*, 128.
5. Vincent Ruggiero, *The Art of Thinking*, 2001, quoted in "Critical Thinking," Oregon State University [online], http//success.oregonstate.edu/study/learning.cfm (accessed April 2004).
6. Richard Paul, "The Role of Questions in Thinking, Teaching, and Learning," The Center for Thinking and Learning, 1995 [on-line], www.criticalthinking.org/University/univclass/roleofquest.html (accessed April 2004).
7. "The Best Innovations Are Those That Come from Smart Questions," *Wall Street Journal*, April 12, 2004, B1.
8. Lawrence F. Lowery, "The Biological Basis of Thinking and Learning," Full Option Science System at the University of California at Berkeley, 1998 [online], http://lhsfoss.org/newsletters/archive/pdfs/FOSS_BBTL.pdf (accessed April 2004).
9. Ivan Moscovich, *1000 Playthinks* (New York: Workman Publishing, 2001) 7.
10. Colby Glass, "Strategies for Critical Thinking," March 1999 [online], www.accd.edu/pac/philosop/phil1301/ctstrategies.htm (accessed April 2004).
11. Sternberg, *Successful Intelligence*, 49.
12. Charles Cave, "Definitions of Creativity," August 1999 [online], http://members.ozemail.com.au/ caveman/Creative/Basics/definitions.htm (accessed April 2003).
13. Elizabeth F. Farrell, "Engineering a Warmer Welcome for Female Students," *The Chronicle of Higher Education*, February 22, 2002 [online], http://chronicle.com/weekly/v48/i24/24a03101.htm (accessed March 2004).
14. Roger von Oech, *A Kick in the Seat of the Pants* (New York: Harper & Row Publishers, 1986), 5–21.
15. Dennis Coon, *Introduction to Psychology: Exploration and Application*, 6th ed. (St. Paul: West Publishing Company, 1992) 295.
16. Roger von Oech, *A Whack on the Side of the Head* (New York: Warner Books, 1990), 11–168.
17. J. R. Hayes, *Cognitive Psychology: Thinking and Creating* (Homewood, IL: Dorsey, 1978).
18. Sternberg, *Successful Intelligence*, 219.
19. Adapted from T. Z. Tardif and R. J. Sternberg, "What Do We Know About Creativity?" in *The Nature of Creativity*, ed. R. J. Sternberg (London: Cambridge University Press, 1988).
20. Sternberg, *Successful Intelligence*, 212.
21. Hayes, *Cognitive Psychology*.
22. Sternberg, *Successful Intelligence*, 202.
23. "The Best Innovations Are Those That Come from Smart Questions," *Wall Street Journal*, April 12, 2004, B1.
24. Sternberg, *Successful Intelligence*, 229–230.
25. Ibid., 236.
26. Robert J. Sternberg and Elena L. Grigorenko, "Practical Intelligence and the Principal," *Yale University: Publication Series No. 2*, 2001: 5.
27. Sternberg, *Successful Intelligence*, 241.
28. Ibid., 251–269.
29. Ibid., 19.
30. Ibid., 128.

Chapter 5

1. Sherwood Harris, *The New York Public Library Book of How and Where to Look It Up* (Englewood Cliffs, NJ: Prentice Hall, 1991) 13.
2. Roxanne Ruzic, CAST, "Lessons for Everyone: How Students with Reading-Related Learning Disabilities Survive and Excel in College Courses with Heavy Reading Requirements," Paper presented at the Annual Meeting of the American Educational Research Association, April 13, 2001 [online], www.cast.org/udl/index.cfm?i=1540 (accessed February 2004).
3. Steve Moidel, *Speed Reading* (Hauppauge, NY: Barron's Educational Series, 1994) 18.
4. Ibid.
5. Francis P. Robinson, *Effective Behavior* (New York: Harper & Row, 1941).
6. Ophelia H. Hancock, *Reading Skills for College Students*, 5th ed. (Upper Saddle River, NJ: Prentice Hall, 2001) 54–59.
7. Excerpted from Lynn Quitman Troyka, *Simon & Schuster Handbook for Writers*, 5th ed. (Upper Saddle River, NJ: Prentice Hall, 1999) 12.
8. Center for Media Literacy, 1998.
9. Louis E. Boone, David L. Kurtz, and Judy R. Block, *Contemporary Business Communication* (Englewood Cliffs, NJ: Prentice Hall, 1994) 489–499.
10. John J. Macionis, *Sociology*, 6th ed. (Upper Saddle River, NJ: Prentice Hall, 1997) 174.
11. The Conference Board of Canada, *Employability Skills 2000+* Brochure (Ottawa, ON: The Conference Board of Canada, 2000).

Chapter 6

1. Kwantlen University College Library Website, "Precision Web Search" [online] (Kwantlen University, 2006), http://www.kwantlen.ca/library/guides/internet.html (accessed September 2006).
2. Ibid.
3. Jeffrey R. Young, "Libraries Try to Widen Google's Eyes," *The Chronicle of Higher Education*, May 21, 2004, A1.
4. Lori Leibovich, "Choosing Quick Hits Over the Card Catalog," *New York Times*, August 10, 2000, 1.
5. Floyd H. Johnson, "The Internet and Research: Proceed with Caution" [online] (May 1996), http://showcase.netins.net/web/nwc-iowa/InternetResearch.html (accessed September 2006).
6. Mel Levine, *The Myth of Laziness* (New York: Simon & Schuster, 2003) 183.

Chapter 7

1. Ralph G. Nichols, "Do We Know How to Listen? Practical Helps in a Modern Age," *Speech Teacher* (March 1961): 118–124.
2. Tony Buzan, *Make the Most of Your Mind* (New York: Fireside [of Simon and Schuster], 1988) 42.
3. Walter Pauk, *How to Study in College*, 7th ed. (Boston: Houghton Mifflin, 2001) 236–241.
4. Herman Ebbinghaus, *Memory: A Contribution to Experimental Psychology*, trans. H. A. Ruger and C. E. Bussenius (New York: New York Teacher's College, Columbia University, 1885).
5. James Zull, *The Art of Changing the Brain: Enriching Teaching by Exploring the Biology of Learning* (Sterling, VA: Stylus Publishing, 2002).
6. Buzan, *Make the Most*, 41–43.
7. Vyacheslav Kandyba, "Professor Uses Music to Bring Biology to Life," *The Chronicle of Higher Education*, March 30, 2003 [online], http://chronicle.com/weekly/v49/i38/38a01002.htm (accessed March 2004).

Chapter 8

1. Steven Frank, *The Everything Study Book*. (Holbrook, MA: Adams Media Corporation, 1996) 208.
2. Margaret L. King, *Instructor's Manual with Tests for Western Civilization: A Social & Cultural History*, 2nd Edition. (Upper Saddle River, NJ: Pearson Education Inc., 2003) Reprinted with permission.

Chapter 9

1. "Canada's Ethnocultural Portrait: The Changing Mosaic," Statistics Canada, 2001 [online], www12.statcan.ca.
2. Ibid.
3. "Conceptual Frameworks/Models, Guiding Values and Principles," National Center for Cultural Competence, 2002 [online] http://gucchd. georgetown.edu//nccc/framework.html (accessed May 2004).
4. Information in the sections on the five stages of building competency is based on Mark A. King, Anthony Sims, and David Osher, "How Is Cultural Competence Integrated in Education?" *Cultural Competence* [online], www.air.org/cecp/cultural/Q_integrated.htm#def (accessed May 2004).
5. "Pilot Survey of Hate Crime," The Daily, June 1, 2004, Statistics Canada [online], www.statcan.ca.
6. Martin Luther King Jr., from his sermon "A Tough Mind and a Tender Heart," *Strength in Love* (Philadelphia: Fortress Press, 1986) 14.
7. Sheryl McCarthy, *Why Are the Heroes Always White?* (Kansas City, MO: Andrews and McMeel, 1995) 137.
8. Doug Gavel, "Students Speak Out at Hate Crime Forum," *Harvard University Gazette*, www.news.harvard.edu/gazette/2001/02.15/01-hatecrime.html.
9. Information for this section from Philip R. Harris and Robert T. Moran, *Managing Cultural Differences*, 3rd ed. (Houston, TX: Gulf Publishing Company, 1991); and Lennie Copeland and Lewis Griggs, *Going International: How to Make Friends and Deal Effectively in the Global Marketplace* (New York: Random House, 1985).
10. Centre for Addiction and Mental Health, *Canadian Campus Survey* Executive Summary Online, as cited in "Dating Violence: A Fact Sheet from the Department of Justice Canada" [online], http://www.justice.gc.ca/en/ps/fm/datingfs.html#head.
11. Holly Johnson, *Dangerous Domains: Violence Against Women in Canada* (Toronto: Nelson, 1996) 112–115, as cited in "Dating Violence: A Fact Sheet from the Department of Justice Canada" [online], http://www.justice.gc.ca/en/ps/fm/datingfs.html#head2
12. Kasey Doyle, "Getting Involved on Campus Important," *The Eastern Progress*, November 4, 2004 [online], http://www.easternprogress.com/media/storage/paper419/news/2004/11/04/Perspective/Getting.Involved.On.Campus.Important-792180.shtml.

Chapter 10

1. Jennifer Jacobson, "How Much Sports Is Too Much? Athletes Dislike Conferences' Efforts to Give Players More Time to Be Students," *The Chronicle of Higher Education*, December 6, 2002 [online], http://chronicle.com/weekly/v49/i15a03801.htm (accessed March 2004).
2. CBS News, "Help for Sleep-Deprived Students," Durham, NC, April 19, 2004 [online], www.cbsnews.com/stories/2004/04/19/health/main612476.shtml (accessed May 2004).
3. Herbert Benson, M. D., Eileen M. Stuart, R.N., C.M.S., et al., *The Wellness Book* (New York: Simon & Schuster, 1992), 292; and Gregg Jacobs, Ph.D., "Insomnia Corner," *Talk About Sleep*, 2004 [online], www.talkaboutsleep.com/sleepdisorders/insomnia_corner.htm (accessed May 2004).
4. Kim Hubbard, Anne-Marie O'Neill, and Christina Cheakalos, "Out of Control," *People*, April 12, 1999, 54.
5. J. McGinnis and W. Foege, "Actual Causes of Death in the United States," *Journal of the American Medical Association* *(JAMA)* 270 (1993): 2208.
6. M. De La Hey, "Survey Highlights Problem of Binge Drinking at Canadian Universities (Canadian Campus Survey)," *Journal of Addiction and Mental Health*, 3(4) (2000): 3. Retrieved July 11, 2006 from CBCA Reference database in full-text.
7. Ibid.
8. "A Matter of Degree: Social Norming Strategy Challenges Campus Drinking Culture," *CrossCurrents*, 6(4) (2003): 10. Retrieved July 11, 2006 from CBCA Reference database in full-text.

9. Ibid.
10. Ibid.
11. David Stout, "Direct Link Found Between Smoking and Lung Cancer," *New York Times,* October 18, 1996, A1, A19.
12. National Institute on Drug Abuse, "National Survey Results on Drug Abuse from Monitoring the Future Study," Bethesda, MD: National Institutes of Health, 1994.
13. "Dark Crystal," *The Fifth Estate*, CBC News, March 23, 2005 [online], http://www.cbc.ca/fifth/darkcrystal/index.html.
14. Health Canada, *It's Your Health: HIV/AIDS,* 2004, http://www.hc-sc.gc.ca/iyh-vsv/diseases-maladies/hiv-vih_e.html.
15. CPAVIH: Committee of People Living with HIV in Quebec, *AIDS 101,* 2nd ed., 2000, http://pubs.cpha.ca/PDF/P22/18942.pdf.
16. List and descriptions based on Robert J. Sternberg, *Successful Intelligence* (New York: Plume, 1997) 251–269.
17. Stephen Covey, *The Seven Habits of Highly Effective People* (New York: Simon & Schuster, 1989), 70–144, 309–318.

Credits

Successful intelligence excerpts and themes reprinted with permission of Simon & Schuster Adult Publishing Group from SUCCESSFUL INTELLIGENCE by Robert J.Sternberg. Copyright © 1996 by Robert J. Sternberg.

Photo Credits

Unless otherwise specified, all photo objects throughout this text are provided by HeremaTechnology, © 2001.

By page number: 2, Richard Perry/New York Times; **16,** Marilynn K. Yee/NY Times; **28,** Michael Stravato/NY Times; **62,** Edward Keating/NY Times; **86,** NY Times; **93,** Jonathan Wiggs/Boston Globe; **98,** Michael Quan/NY Times; **120,** Marilynn K. Yee/ NY Times; **126,** Stephanie Klein-Davis/NY Times; **146,** Ruby Washington/NY Times; **156,** Joyce Dopkeen/NY Times; **159,** Michelle V. Agins/NY Times; **190,** Suzanne DeChillo/ NY Times; **199,** Angel Franco/NY Times; **214,** Suzanne Kreiter/Boston Globe; **226,** Stephanie Klein-Davis/NY Times; **236,** Suzanne Kreiter/Boston Globe; **258,** Keith Meyers/NY Times; **261,** Joyce Dopkeen/NY Times; **266,** Michelle V. Agins/NY Times; **290,** Digital Vision; **297,** Librado Romero/NY Times; **305,** NY Times.

Index

A

academic integrity, 32–33, 240
academic path, 8
Academic Search Premier, 163
access, 164
acquaintance rape, 280
acronyms, 217–218
acrostics, 218
action
    focus on, 7–8
    and practical thinking, 104
    taking action, 13
active approach, 124–125
active listener, 195–196
active reading, 136
adapting to diverse cultures,
        266–267
addiction, 298–299
adventurer-dominant
        communicators, 269
aggressive communicators, 275
AIDS (acquired immune deficiency
        syndrome), 301, 302
alcohol, 296
Alcoholics Anonymous (AA), 299
almanacs, 161
Alta Vista, 165
American Psychological Association
        (APA), 176
analogy, 98
analytical evaluation, 127
analytical thinking
    analysis of information, 92–95
    assessment of skills, 95
    assumptions, 93–95
    break information into parts, 92
    clarification of information,
        92–95
    decision making, 109
    define your purpose, 91
    described, 7, 91
    evaluation of information, 95
    evaluation of Internet sources,
        167–168
    fact *versus* opinion, 93
    first step, 91
    improvement of skills, 91–95
    information gathering, 91–92
    media literacy, 144
    perspectives, 93–95
    problem solving, 106–107
    reading comprehension, 123
    revising, 178
    support for ideas, 93
anger management, 277
anorexia nervosa, 295
answering questions, 90
arguments, 143–144
asking questions, 90, 95–96, 101,
        104
assertive communicators, 275
assumptions, 93–95, 98–99
attention deficit disorder (ADD),
        195
attitudes, 262–265
audience, 172
audiovisual materials, 159

B

back matter, 135
balance, 89, 109–111
basic needs, 267
Bates, Marilyn, 65
behavioural patterns, 33
believe in yourself, 100
biased information, 94
bibliographies, 162
binge drinking, 296
binge eating, 295
biographical reference works, 162
birth control, 299
Bishop, Joyce, 70
body language, 272–273
body of the paper, 174, 175
book area, 158
brainstorming, 98, 168, 169
breaks, 44–45
Briggs, Katharine, 65
bulimia, 295
bullying, 279
Burka, Jane B., 45
Burns, Daniel, 16
Buzan, Tony, 44, 215

C

calendars, 42–43
Canadian Criminal Code, 265
Canadian Periodical Index, 163
cardiovascular training, 293
career, 76
career exploration strategies, 76
career goal, 8
career planning, 75
career resources, 76
career success, 5
Carter, Carol, 35, 304
categories, 92
cause and effect, 92
CD-ROM, 161
celebrating success, 18
Center for Media Literacy, 144
chai, 50
changing world, 18–20
chaos, 20
chapter elements, 134–135
checklist
    drafting, 177
    final checklist, 181
    planning, 173, 174
    revising and editing checklist, 181
    test preparation, 230
    updating, 178
circulation desk, 158
citation, 176
clarifying questions, 196
clarity, 179
class discussions, 201
closed-stack system, 159
code of moral values, 32
commitment, 13
communication. *See* effective
        communication
communication styles, 268–270
communities, 280–281
community involvement, 5
compare, 92
comprehension, 122–123
computer areas, 159
concept maps, 135, 209
conciseness, 179
conclusion, 174–175
conflict management, 274–276
conflict prevention, 275–276
conflict resolution, 276
conquering fears, 14–16, 15
constructive feedback, 270–271,
        273
content notes, 171
context, 131–132
contrast, 92

coping with stress, 48–50
Cornell note-taking system, 205–206
counselling, 298
Covey, Stephen, 304
cramming, 234
creative thinking
    asking questions, 101
    assessment of skills, 102
    brainstorm, 98
    decision making, 109
    deliberate creative thinking, 98
    described, 7
    improvement of skills, 97–102
    problem solving, 106–107
    risk taking, 100–101
    shift your perspective, 98–99
    strategies, 100
creativity, 97–98
credit authors and sources, 175–177
"critical," 111
critical reading, 143–144
critical thinking, 7
crystal meth, 297
cultural appreciation, 5
cultural competence, 34, 262–267
cultural differences, 267
cultural diversity. *See* diversity
cultural knowledge, 265–266
culture
    see also diversity
    adapting to diverse cultures, 266–267
    and body language, 273
    communication across cultures, 274–275
    defined, 33
    high-context cultures, 33, 274–275
    interaction of cultures, 264–265
    low-context cultures, 34, 274–275
curiosity, 100

D
daily tasks, 43
databases, 163
date rape, 280
decision making, 106, 109
define your purpose, 90, 91, 126–128
Dell, Michael, 100
depression, 295
destructive relationships, 279–280
detoxification, 299
Dewey Decimal system, 162
dictionaries, 132–133, 162
difficult reading material, 124–125

discrimination, 264–265, 267
distractions, 194
divergent thinking, 98
diversity
    experiencing, 260–261
    perception of, 265
    and values, 33–34
    valuing diversity, 16–17, 262
divided attention, 194
"do not be distracted," 219
down time, 44
drafting
    avoiding plagiarism, 175–177
    body of the paper, 174, 175
    checklist, 177
    conclusion, 174–175
    credit authors and sources, 175–177
    described, 173–174
    freewriting, 174
    introduction, 174
    "writing sandwich," 174
drugs, 297

E
earning potential, 4–5
eating disorders, 295
eating right, 292–293
Ebbinghaus, Herman, 211
ecstasy, 297
editing, 179–181
education, and income, 5
educational requirements, 76
effective communication
    adjustment to communication styles, 268–270
    adjustment to listeners, 269–270
    adjustment to speakers, 270
    anger management, 277
    assertive communicators, 275
    body language, 272–273
    communication across cultures, 274–275
    conflict management, 274–276
    constructive feedback, 270–271, 273
electronic planner, 40
employability, 4–5
encoding, 180–213
encyclopedias, 161
essay questions, 245, 246–247, 246–247, 246–248
ethical values, 32–33
ethics, 305
ethnicity, 260
evaluation stage, 193
evidence, 143–144
exercise, 293
expectations, fear of, 46

experience, 105, 236
external characteristics, 266
external distractions, 194
extracurricular activities, 76

F
fact, 93
failure, 17–18
fairness, 33
false causes, 92
fear of expectations, 46
fear of limitations, 46
fears, 14–16, 15
feedback, 270–271, 273
fill-in-the-blank questions, 244
first impressions, 273
flash cards, 215
flexibility, 47, 293
formal outlines, 205
formula, 128
freewriting, 170, 174
front matter, 134
Fry, Arthur, 97

G
Gardner, Howard, 64, 69
general ideas, 126
general reference works, 161–162
giver-dominant communicators, 269
glossary, 132
goalie masks, 99
goals
    achievement, 6–9, 37–38, 89
    career goal, 8
    defined, 35
    long-term goals, 35–36
    mapping out, 38
    prioritize, 36–37
    reinforcement of one another, 37
    setting goals, 35–38
    short-term goals, 36
    successful intelligence and, 90
    tasks and activities supporting, 41–42
Google, 165, 167
groupings, 215

H
habits, 14
hands-on exploration, 76
hate, 267
hate crimes, 265
headings, 136, 140
healthy mind and body
    eating right, 292–293
    exercise, 293
    mental health problems, 295
    sleep, 293–294
hearing loss, 195

high-context cultures, 33, 274–275
higher learning
  celebrating success, 18
  changing world, 18–20
  learning from failure, 17–18
  life success goals, 4–6
  and success, 16–20
  valuing diversity, 16–17
highlighting information, 139
HIV (human immunodeficiency
    virus), 301, 302
Holmes, T.H., 48–49
Holmes-Rahe scale, 49
honesty, 33
hostile environment harassment,
    279
Human Resources and Skills
    Development Canada, 76
Hunter, William, 90
hyperlinks, 165

I
"I" messages, 276
inert intelligence, 6
Infomine, 165
informal outlines, 205, 246–247
information
  analysis of, 92–95
  biased information, 94
  break into parts, 92
  clarification of, 92–95
  evaluation of, 95
  gathering information, 91–92
  highlighting information, 139
  perspectives and assumptions in,
      94
  search (library), 159–161
  support for ideas, 93
  too similar, 214
instructors, 73–75
integrity, 32–33, 305
intellectual property, 175
intelligence
  see also successful intelligence
  defined, 6, 69
  multiple intelligences, 64, 69,
      75–77
  types of, 75, 77–78
intelligent guessing, 239–240
intention, 213
internal distractions, 126, 194
Internet access, 164
Internet Public Library, 165
Internet research
  analytical thinking, 167–168
  bookmark, 166
  copying material, and plagiarism,
      176
  evaluation of sources, 167–168

favourites, 166
first step, 164
hyperlinks, 165
information locations, 165
keywords, 166
know the basics, 164–165
search engines, 165
search strategy, 165–166
subject directories, 165
web address, 165
websites, 165
Internet Service Providers (ISPs),
    164
interpretation stage, 192
introduction, 174
IQ, 6

J
Job Futures, 76
journalists' questions, 170–171
journals, 162
judgment, 194–195

K
kaizen, 306
Keirsey, David, 65
Keirsey Temperament Sorter, 65
keyword search, 160–161
Kindell, Larisa, 293
know your purpose, 90, 91
  see also define your purpose
knowledge
  shared knowledge, 145
  solidified knowledge, 145
krinein, 111

L
last-minute studying, 234
Latin, 251
learning disabilities, 128–130, 195
learning from failure, 17–18
learning style
  academic benefits of knowing
      your style, 73–75
  assessment results, 65
  benefits of knowing your style,
      73–75
  career benefits of knowing your
      style, 75
  defined, 65
  discover your learning style,
      64–65
  exploration of strategies, 141
  Multiple Pathways to Learning,
      69, 72
  and note-taking style, 199
  Personality Spectrum, 65, 68
  value of learning styles
      assessments, 64–65

lectures, 199–200
level of learning, 233
librarian, 163–164
Librarians' Internet Index, 165
library catalogue, 162
Library of Congress system, 162
library research
  ask the librarian, 163–164
  books on your subject, 162
  general reference works, 161–162
  information search, 159–161
  keyword search, 160–161
  library catalogue, 162
  narrow your topic, 159–160
  organization of your library,
      158–159
  orientation sessions, 159
  periodical indexes, 162–163
  search strategy, 161–164
life-enhancing communities,
    280–281
life experiences, 105, 236
life success goals, 4–6
limit material, 214–215
limitations, fear of, 46
listening
  active listener, 195–196
  clarifying questions, 196
  defined, 192
  distractions, 194
  divided attention, 194
  evaluation stage, 193
  hearing loss, 195
  interpretation stage, 192
  learning disabilities, 195
  management of listening
      challenges, 193–195
  purposes, 195
  reaction stage, 193
  rushing to judgment, 194–195
  sensation stage, 192
  shutting out the message, 194
  stages of, 192–193
  verbal cues, 195, 196
living with integrity, 305
long-term goals, 35–36
long-term memory, 211, 212
low-context cultures, 34, 274–275
lucky breaks, 50–51
Lycos, 165

M
machine-scored tests, 239
Mahler, Gustav, 100
main idea, 139–140, 141
Make the Most of Your Mind
    (Buzan), 44
marginal notes, 139
mark up your textbooks, 139

matching questions, 243–244
math texts, 128
Maxwell, Ada, 267
McCarthy, Sheryl, 267
MDMA, 297
media, 144
media literacy, 144
medical care, 298
memory
    long-term memory, 211, 212
    sensory memory, 211
    short-term memory, 211
    storage banks, 211
memory strategies
    encoding, 213–216
    mnemonic devices, 216–219, 220
    recalling, 213–216
memory techniques, 128
mental health problems, 295
MetaCrawler, 165
microfiche, 159
microfilm, 159
microform reading areas, 159
mission statement, 304–305
mistakes, 101
mnemonic devices, 128, 216–219,
    220
Modern Language Association
    (MLA), 176
Moidel, Steve, 130
monthly calendars, 42–43
motivation, 12–16, 145
multiple-choice questions, 241–243
multiple intelligences, 75–77
Multiple Intelligences Theory, 64, 69
Multiple Pathways to Learning, 64,
    65, 69, 72
Myers, Isabel Briggs, 65
Myers-Briggs Type Inventory
    (MBTI), 64, 65

N
Narcotics Anonymous (NA), 299
narrow your topic, 159–160,
    169–171
National Occupational
    Classification (NOC), 76
negative talk, 12
non-constructive feedback,
    270–271
nonverbal cues, 273
note taking
    class discussions, 201
    content notes, 171
    and the learning process,
        197–198
    lectures, 199–200
    location in class, 198
    marking up your textbook, 139

preparation for, 198–199
preview reading material, 198
during research, 171
review, 202
revising your notes, 202–204
source notes, 171
study groups, 204–205
summarizing, 204
supplies, 198
support system, 199
and test preparation, 232
verbal cues, 200
note-taking system
    choosing a system, 198–199
    concept maps, 135, 209
    Cornell note-taking system,
        205–206
    outline form, 205

O
objective questions, 240
occupations, 76
old tests, 229
open stacks, 158
opinion, 93
opportunity, 20
organize material, 214
organizer-dominant communicators,
    269
other languages, 148
outline, 173
outline form of note taking, 205
Overeaters Anonymous (OA), 299
overwhelming tasks, 46

P
paragraph structure, 178–179
paragraph topics, 140
paraphrase, 176, 177
passion, 76
passive communicators, 276
patterns, 92
Pauk, Walter, 205
perception puzzles, 99
perceptions, 262–265
perfectionism, 45
performance, and stress, 50
periodical indexes, 162–163
periodicals, 159
personal best, 305
personal digital assistant (PDA), 40
personal goal plan, 38
personal mission statement,
    304–305
personal perspectives and
    assumptions, 95
personal relationships
    avoidance of destructive
        relationships, 279–280

date rape, 280
life-enhancing communities,
    280–281
rape, 280
sexual harassment, 279
strategies, 278
violence, 279
personal time profile, 39
personality assessments, 65
Personality Spectrum, 64, 65, 68
perspectives, 93–95, 98–99
physical preparation for tests, 234
Pilot Survey, 265
plagiarism, 175–177
planners, 40
planning
    brainstorming, 168–169
    checklist, 173–174
    freewriting, 170
    journalists' questions, 170–171
    narrow your topic, 169–171
    note taking, 171
    preliminary researching, 170
    prewriting strategies, 168,
        169–171
    research, 171
    thesis statement, 172
    working outline, 173
Plante, Jacques, 98–99
pleasure reading, 128
positive attitude, 235–236
positive habits, 14
positive self-talk, 12, 236
positive thinking, 123
practical application, 127
practical thinking
    as action, 104
    assessment of skills, 105
    decision making, 109
    experience and, 105
    improvement of skills, 102–105
    meaning of, 7
    problem solving, 106–107
    questions to ask, 104
practice the middle, 215
prefixes, 131
prejudice, 263, 267
preliminary researching, 170
preparation checklist, 173, 174
preparation for tests
    careful review, 230–232
    checklist, 230
    cramming, 234
    create a pre-test, 230
    identification of test type and
        material covered, 228–229
    last-minute studying, 234
    level of learning required, 233
    physical preparation, 234

pre-test, 230, 233
review plan and schedule,
   229–230
review your notes, 232
SQ3R study method, 230–232
and test anxiety, 235
pre-test, 230, 233
preview reading material, 198
prewriting strategies, 168, 169–171
primary sources, 125
prioritize, 36–37
prioritizing, 42
problem solving, 106–107
procrastination, 45–47
Procrastination (Burka and Yuen),
   45
proofreading, 179
purpose, 172, 213
   see also define your purpose

Q
questions
   answering, 90
   asking, 90, 95, 101, 104
   clarifying questions, 196
   headings to form questions, 136
   journalists' questions, 170–171
   mark up test questions, 239
   for reading comprehension, 123
   "sit" with a question, 100
   SQ3R study method, 136
   test questions. *See* test questions
   "what if" questions, 99
quid pro quo harassment, 279
quotation, 176

R
Rahe, R.H., 48, 49
rape, 280
reaction stage, 193
reading
   active approach, 124–125
   active reading, 136
   for analytical evaluation, 127
   comprehension, 122–123
   define your purpose, 126–128
   difficult reading material,
      124–125
   digestible segments, 139
   finding the main idea, 139–140,
      141
   for general ideas, 126
   internal distractions, 126
   and learning disabilities,
      128–130
   location, 125
   math texts, 128
   media literacy, 144
   other sources, 122

for pleasure, 128
positive thinking, 123
for practical application, 127
preview reading material, 198
responding critically, 143–144
scanning, 130
science texts, 128
setting the stage for reading,
   124–133
skimming, 130
specific facts or examples, 126
speed of, 130
SQ3R study method, 133–142
step-by-step approach, 122
summary, 142
time for, 125–126
for understanding, 126
vocabulary expansion, 131–133
recalling, 213–216
receiving feedback, 271
recite, 141, 214
reference area, 158
reference materials, 125
regular breaks, 44–45
regular planning, 42
rehearse, 214
relationships. *See* personal
   relationships
relaxation, 236
repetition, 141
research
   Internet research, 164–168
   library research, 158–164
   planning stage, 171
   preliminary researching, 170
respect, 33
responding critically, 143–144
responsibility, 13–14, 33
review, 142
review of notes, 202
review plan and schedule, 229–230
revising, 177–179
revising your notes, 202–204
rhymes, 218–219
risk taking, 100–101
roots, 131–132
rushing to judgment, 194–195

S
sabiduría, 79
Sanskrit, 219
scanning, 130, 134
schedules, 40–42, 229–230
scheduling techniques, 42–43
science texts, 128
search engines, 165
search strategy
   ask the librarian, 163–164
   books on your subject, 162

general reference works,
   161–162
Internet research, 165–166
library catalogue, 162
periodical indexes, 162–163
self-activators, 302–304
self-awareness, 75
self-esteem, 12, 33
sensation stage, 192
sensory memory, 211
separation of ideas, 92
*The Seven Habits of Highly
   Effective People* (Covey), 304
sex, decisions about, 299–301
sexual harassment, 279
sexuality, 299
sexually transmitted infections
   (STIs), 299–302
shift your perspective, 98–99
short-term goals, 36
short-term memory, 211
shutting out the message, 194
sine qua non, 251
skimming, 130, 134
sleep, 214, 293–294
smoking, 296–297
Social Readjustment Scale, 48, 102
Soloway, Eliot, 166
songs, 218–219
source notes, 171, 175
specialized indexes, 163
specific facts or examples, 126
SQ3R study method
   described, 133–134
   identification of test type and
      material covered, 228–229
   question, 136
   reading, 136–141
   recite, 141
   review, 142
   review for tests, 230–232
   scanning, 134
   skimming, 134
   surveying, 134–135
statement of fact, 93
statement of opinion, 93
step-by-step approach, 122
stereotypes, 263–264
Sternberg, Robert J., 6, 88, 100, 101
strength training, 293
stress, 48
stress management, 48–49
stress score, 49
study group
   benefits of, 145–148
   formation of, 146
   leaders, 147
   note taking, 204–205
   participants, 146–147

strategies for, 145–148, 147–148
successful intelligence in, 7–8
study partners. *See* study group
study techniques, 73
subject directories, 165
subjective questions, 241
substances
    addiction, 298–299
    alcohol, 296
    drugs, 297
    tobacco, 296–297
success
    celebrating success, 18
    and higher learning, 16–20
    and successful intelligence, 8–9
successful intelligence
    see also successfully intelligent
      thinking
    achievement of goals, 89
    actions, focus on, 7–8
    career goal, 8
    changing world, 18–20
    components of, 7
    and goal achievement, 6–9
    problem solving, 106
    self-activators, 302–304
    in a study group, 7–8
    and success, 8–9
Successful Intelligence (Sternberg), 7
successfully intelligent thinking
    see also analytical thinking;
      creative thinking; practical
      thinking; successful intelligence
    asking and answering questions,
      90
    balance, 89, 109, 111
    building your ability to think,
      90–91
    illustration of, 88–89
    knowing your purpose, 90
    sex, decisions about, 299–301
    substances, decisions about,
      296–299
suffixes, 131
summarizing your notes, 204
summary, 142
support for ideas, 93
support groups, 299
survey, 134–135

T
taking action, 13
tape recorder, 215
teaching someone else, 215–216
teaching styles, 73
teamwork, 75, 145
Techno Trends (Burns), 16
test anxiety
    defined, 235

positive attitude, 235–236
thorough preparation, 235
use life experiences, 236
test mistakes, 249–250
test questions
    essay questions, 245, 246–248
    fill-in-the-blank questions, 244
    matching questions, 243–244
    multiple-choice questions,
      241–243
    objective questions, 240
    subjective questions, 241
    true/false questions, 243
test strategies
    academic integrity, 240
    easy to hard, 239
    general strategies, 238–240
    intelligent guessing, 239–240
    key facts, 238
    machine-scored tests, 239
    mark up the questions, 239
    overview, 238
    read test directions, 238–239
    watch your time, 239
test taking
    learning from your mistakes,
      249–250
    preparation. *See* preparation for
      tests
    questions. *See* test questions
    strategies. *See* test strategies
    test anxiety, 235–236
themes, 92
thesis statement, 172
thinker-dominant communicators,
    269
Thoreau, Henry David, 123
3M, 97
time management
    calendars, 42–43
    daily and weekly tasks, 43
    down time, 44
    flexibility, 47
    identification of time-related
      needs and preferences, 39
    personal time profile, 39
    planners, 40
    prioritizing, 42
    procrastination, 45–47
    regular breaks, 44–45
    regular planning, 42
    schedules, 40–42
    scheduling techniques, 42–43
    tasks and activities supporting
      your goals, 41–42
    time traps, 44
    to-do lists, 43, 45
    tracking events and
      commitments, 40–41

time-related needs and preferences,
    39
time traps, 44
Timm, Paul, 40
to-do lists, 43, 45
tobacco, 296–297
topic sentence, 140, 179
topics
    narrow your topic, 159–160
    paragraph topics, 140
true causes, 92
true/false questions, 243
trust, 33

U
underlining, 138

V
values
    academic integrity, 32–33
    and cultural diversity, 33–34
    defined, 30
    and educational experience,
      31–32
    ethical values, 32–33
    evaluation of, 31
    identification of, 31
    importance of, 30
valuing diversity, 16–17, 262
Velcro, 98
verbal cues, 195, 196, 200
violence in relationships, 279
visual images and associations, 180
visualization, 180, 209
vocabulary building, 123, 131–133
volunteering opportunities, 76

W
web address, 165
websites, 165
weekly tasks, 43
"what if" questions, 99
word parts, 131
words in context, 131–132
wordy phrases, 179
working outline, 173
writing as reciting, 214
writing from memory, 141
writing process
    described, 168
    drafting, 173–177
    editing, 179–181
    planning, 168–173
    revising, 177–179
    sample final version, 182
writing purpose, 172

Y
Yahoo!, 165
yearbooks, 162
yearly calendars, 42–43
Yoshigahara, Nob, 90
Yuen, Lenora M., 45

Z
Zull, James, 211